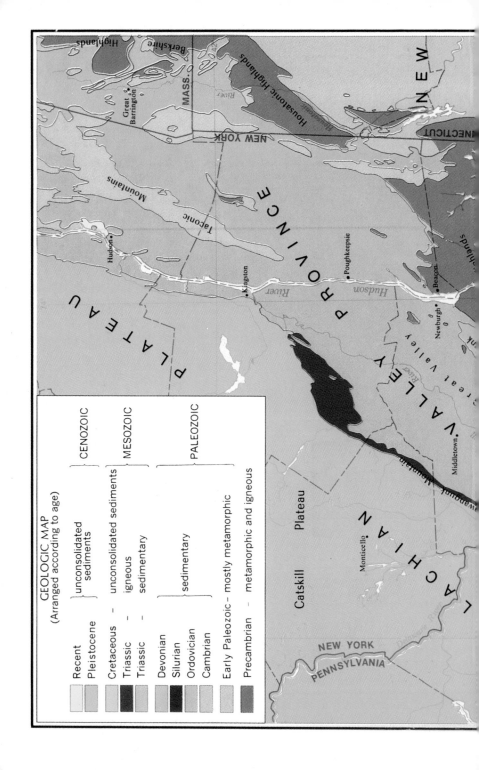

GEOLOGIC MAP
(Arranged according to age)

Recent	unconsolidated sediments
Pleistocene	

CENOZOIC

Cretaceous	— unconsolidated sediments
Triassic	— igneous
Triassic	— sedimentary

MESOZOIC

Devonian	
Silurian	sedimentary
Ordovician	
Cambrian	

PALEOZOIC

Early Paleozoic – mostly metamorphic

Precambrian – metamorphic and igneous

NEW YORK

PENNSYLVANIA

Catskill   Plateau

Monticello

APPALACHIAN

Shawangunk Mountain

Great Valley

VALLEY PROVINCE

Middletown

Newburgh

Wallkill River

Beacon

Highlands

Hudson River

Kingston

Poughkeepsie

PLATEAU

Hudson

Taconic Mountains

Great Barrington

Housatonic Highlands

Housatonic River

Berkshire Highlands

MASS.

NEW YORK

CONNECTICUT

NEW

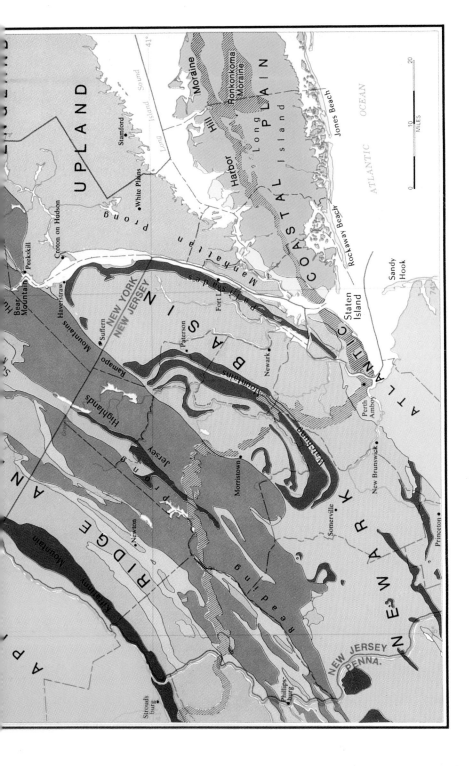

NEW YORK WALK BOOK

SEVENTH EDITION

NEW YORK
WALK BOOK

A COMPANION TO THE NEW JERSEY WALK BOOK

Illustrations by
Robert L. Dickinson and Jack Fagan

NEW YORK–NEW JERSEY TRAIL CONFERENCE
2001

PUBLISHED BY
NEW YORK-NEW JERSEY TRAIL CONFERENCE
156 RAMAPO VALLEY ROAD
MAHWAH, NEW JERSEY 07430

First edition published in 1923.

Library of Congress Cataloging-in-Publication Data

New York walk book / illustrations by Robert L. Dickinson and Jack Fagan.— 7ᵗʰ ed.
   p. cm.
   "A companion to the New Jersey walk book."
   Includes bibliographical references and index.
   ISBN 1-880775-30-1 (pbk.)
      1. Hiking—New York Metropolitan Area—Guidebooks. 2. Trails—New York
Metropolitan Area—Guidebooks. 3. New York Metropolitan Area—Guidebooks. I. New
York-New Jersey Trail Conference

   GV 199.42.N652 N486 2001
   917.4704'44—dc21
                2001051184

Illustrations by Robert L. Dickinson and Jack Fagan
Cover design by Nora Porter
Cover photo: View of the Hudson River from Storm King Mountain, by Nick Zungoli
Book design, layout, and typesetting by Nora Porter

Although the editor and publisher have attempted to make the information as accurate as possible, they accept no responsibility for any loss, injury, or inconvenience sustained by any person using this book.

CONTENTS

MAPS

GEOLOGIC MAP *(frontis)*

TRAIL MAPS
(back of book)

PREFACE

When the first edition of the *New York Walk Book* appeared in 1923, it was designed to enable "the busy city dweller [to] make the best use of the precious hours—all too few—when he escapes the thralldom of office, shop, and factory." In those days, few "city dweller[s]" had cars, so the "main walking regions [were] plotted in conjunction with the railroad lines."

The intervening 78 years have brought many changes. Most hikers now live in the suburbs and are not dependent on public transportation. Scores of guidebooks to hiking trails abound, with specialized guides available for many of the hiking regions in the New York metropolitan area.

Yet the demand for the *New York Walk Book* remains strong, and the book still fulfills an important need. Together with its companion volume, the *New Jersey Walk Book*, it continues to be the only comprehensive guide to the trails in the area. Beginning and experienced hikers alike will find much useful information in the book, considered by many to be the "hiker's bible."

The marvels of modern technology—including desktop publishing—have made it possible for the New York-New Jersey Trail Conference to produce a new edition of the *New York Walk Book* a mere three years after the previous edition was published. This seventh edition of the *Walk Book* builds upon the masterful work of Jane Daniels, editor of the sixth edition. The basic arrangement of the material is largely unchanged, and many of the trail descriptions from the sixth edition are retained in the present book.

Yet this latest edition incorporates many new features and changes. First and foremost are the contributions of Jack Fagan, a retired professor of geology and outstanding illustrator. For this edition, Jack has sketched many world-class illustrations of scenes encountered by hikers who make their way along the trails described in this *Walk Book*. Along with these new sketches, we have retained many historical sketches by Robert L. Dickinson, a member of the triumvirate which produced the first edition of the *Walk Book* in 1923. Fagan's sketches give the book a refreshing, updated appearance, while those by Dickinson preserve the historical ambiance which is very much a part of the *Walk Book*.

Jack Fagan has also contributed his expertise in geology by entirely rewriting chapter 4 of the book, "Geology," as well as those portions of other chapters that deal with this subject. In each case, the new text is accompanied with detailed illustrations which graphically demonstrate the various geological features or events described in the text. The combination of Jack's geological expertise and artistic talent has produced a chapter that can readily be understood even by those with no prior knowledge of the subject.

For this edition, a number of chapters have been substantially rewritten. Dan Case has written a completely new trails section for chapter 12, "The Catskills," which provides significantly expanded coverage of this magnificent hiking area. Chapter 17, given the title "The Palisades" for the sixth edition, has been rewritten and its scope broadened, through the efforts of Arlene Sandner, George Zoebelein, and John Jurasek. Now entitled "Rockland County," it includes additional parks and trails in this popular hiking area. Chapter 18, formerly entitled "The Greenwood Lake Area," is now called "Sterling Forest." Material on trails in New Jersey (which is included in the *New Jersey Walk Book*) has been dropped, and descriptions of new trails in Sterling Forest State Park have been added, based on the fieldwork of John J. Moran and Ruth Rosenthal.

The "Long Distance Trails" chapter (chapter 19) has also undergone a major revision. We felt that it was more useful to the reader to present—where possible—descriptions of the major hiking trails in the chapter of the book corresponding to the location where these trails are actually situated. As a result, the "Long Distance Trails" chapter has been reduced in size, but descriptions of the Appalachian Trail and Long Path in areas such as Bear Mountain-Harriman State Parks, Rockland County, and the Shawangunks are now included in the chapters covering these areas.

Although this edition of the *New York Walk Book*, unlike the first edition in 1923, is not organized based on the proximity of the trails to rail lines, information on public transportation to trailheads is included in the trail descriptions. A new feature for this edition is an index entry "Public Transportation" that indicates which trails can be accessed by those without cars.

Every chapter in the book has been updated for this edition. Thanks are due to Neil Woodworth and John Myers, who provided information needed to update chapter 1, "Trails and Trails Development." Chapter 2, "Suggestions for Hikers," has been enhanced by the careful editing of Wanda Davenport. Eric Kiviat has updated chapter 3, "Mountain Ecology." As for chapter 5, "New York City," Ruth Rosenthal and Demitris P. Haldeos provided revised descriptions of trails in Manhattan and The Bronx, Victor Gabay rewrote the pages on the Brooklyn-Queens Greenway, and Ken and Nancy Clair contributed their expertise to improve the material on trails in the Staten Island Greenbelt. Chapter 6, "Long Island," was updated thanks to the efforts of Tom Casey. John J. Moran made valuable contributions towards the updating of chapter 7, "Westchester County."

Jane and Walt Daniels, John and Karen Magerlein, Christian Lenz Cesar, and Daniel Eagan contributed to the extensive changes made in chapter 8, "Fahnestock State Park," and chapter 9, "East Hudson Highlands," in light of the significant alterations to the trail systems in these areas that have taken place since the publication of the previous edition. Ruth Rosenthal made helpful suggestions concerning chapter 10, "Dutchess County," while Ben Frankel reviewed and corrected chapter 11, "The Southern Taconics." Chapter 13, "The Shawangunks," has been updated and reorganized thanks to the efforts of Malcolm Spector and Linda Lawson Fagan. John Jurasek and John Blenninger, along with Pete Heckler, contributed information needed to update chapter 14, "Schunemunk Mountain," and chapter 15, "Storm King and Black Rock Forest." Pete Heckler also helped to update chapter 16, "Bear Mountain-Harriman State Parks." Chapter 19, "Long Distance Trails," benefited from the expertise of Eric Meyer, Bob Moss, and Mike Willsey in their respective areas. Much valuable information was also provided by officials of federal, state, county and local parks and Trail Conference supervisors and maintainers, too numerous to mention individually.

The selection of "Further Reading" was updated and expanded thanks to the efforts of Loren Mendelsohn, Chief of the Science/Engineering Library of the City College of New York. John Jurasek contributed towards the revision of the maps, with cartography by Robert L. Murray. Geraldine Ryan assisted with the proofreading.

Last but not least, this book could not have been produced without the dedicated efforts of Nora Porter, who not only so aptly fit the illustrations into the text, but also designed a completely new cover for this edition. She was always available when needed for advice, and contributed her expertise in the area of design and layout to make this such a beautiful book.

Daniel D. Chazin
Editor
New York Walk Book, 7th edition

'Send your road is clear before you when the old
Spring-fret comes o'er you
And the Red Gods call for you

Kipling: Feet of the Young Men

THE LOOK-OFF

(from the first edition, 1923)

oil that was ever *Indian* seems to never lose all of that impress. On the Island of Islands, borne down at one end by the world's biggest burden of steel and stone and pressure of haste and material gain, the primitive sweep of its further free tip, with the forest trees on the stately ledges, still holds the red man's cave, the beached canoe, the air of the Great Spirit. The magic of the moccasin still makes good medicine. Fortunate we are that in civilization lurks the antidote to civilization— that strain in the blood of us, all of us, of cave man and tree man, nomad and seaman, chopper and digger, fisher and trailer, crying out to this call of the earth, to this tug of free foot, up-and-over, to this clamor for out-and-beyond. Happy are we, in our day, harking back to this call, to be part of an ozone revival that fits the growth of our desire, to see the beginning of a break-away into everybody's out-of-doors, and the happy find of a wide, fair wilderness.

The order and fashion of the revival were somewhat in this wise. Our seniors remember the days of swift expansion, when the sole concern was the building site. "Blast the scenery," said the seventies and proceeded to do it. Railroads and roads and money returns from quarries and lumber had full right of way. Into our towns one came through ugly suburbs into uglier urbs. And then, when hope was least, a messenger of the new-old freedom appeared. The bicycle swung us, a generation now gray-haired, round a wide radius of country roads and gave back to us the calves and the leg gear of our patroon saint, Father Knickerbocker, and with the legs two eyes for environs. When the time came for supplanting tandem tires by a rubber quartette, and a touch of the toe leapt past all two legs could do, the motor radius that swept a circle almost infinitely wide gave a new concept of the country. Still attention was focussed on the roadway, and the new driver saw even less over wheel than over handlebar. Next golf arose, and the well-to-do strolled upon greenswards, ever watching a ball. Then scout training arrived to set the young generation on its feet and to teach it to see what it saw and to care for itself in the open. With it came nature study to fill the woods and fields with life and growth. (Our Old-World citizens brought their outing habits with them.) Last of all the war gave us brief glimpses of the happiness of simple living and to marching multitudes of indoor men the sense of hardy well-being. And now the fashion for walking is upon us—walking, with its leisure to observe the detail of beauty; walking, organized and planned, imparting impetus to safeguard and preserve the best of the countryside; walking, the single simple exercise, at once democratic, open-air, wide-eyed, year-round.

It is amusing to watch New York, which is hardly in other ways hesitant, waken by degrees to the idea that as a center for exercise on foot she may claim variety and advantage and adventure surpassed by few cities. You shall choose your walk along the sweep of the beaches of the Atlantic, or the deep hill bays of Long Island, or the rocky coves of Connecticut; over ridges showing fair silhouettes of the citadels and cathedral of commerce—or where beavers build; on the looped, mile-long bridges that span an estuary—or across a canal lock; above precipices overhanging a mighty river and through noble community forests between lonely peaks and little lakes—or just in lovely common country, rolling and wooded, meadowed and elm-dotted, interlaced with chuckling brooks. To and from these multitudinous footways and camp sites transportation is provided with an expedition and diversity possible only to a large city. And last of all the chance at all this will be under the variegated stimulus of our particular climate and around the only great capital that is within easy reach of the second color wonder of the world—Indian summer in steep-hill country.

Truly with the "Englysche Bybels" that antedate King James', we may say:
Blessed of the LORDE is *this* land,
    for the sweetnesse of heven, and of the scee vnderliende;
    for the sprynges;
    for the precious thinges off the Sonne;
    for the sweetnesse of the toppes of the oold mounteynes,
      and for the daynties of the hillis that last foreuer.

TRAILS AND TRAIL DEVELOPMENT

rails were the first paths in America. The routes of the early Native Americans[1] led from villages and campsites to hunting and fishing grounds, often following streams and crossing mountain ranges through the notches and divides of the rugged terrain. The white settlers adopted these routes for hunting, trading, and military expeditions. But unlike the footpaths of Europe, these American paths were marked by ax blazes on trees. Because these early paths often followed the easiest grades, they were natural routes for the highways and railroads to come.

Early Trails and the Search for Open Space

By the early part of the twentieth century, few of the original Native Americans' paths remained. With the advent of railroads, rural areas became more accessible for the city dweller, and people with leisure time sought out the woods and streams for recreation. However, farmers found these fun-seekers to be a nuisance, and so they often posted their property against trespassing. In response, "clubs" of wealthy businessmen from the cities purchased lakes, ponds, and natural areas, and then closed them off to public use.

Barred from access to open space, those who sought exercise and a chance to enjoy nature followed rural roads. Up to about 1900, these roads provided pleasant walking, to be shared with only an occasional slow-moving

[1]The term "Native American" is used throughout this book when a specific nation is not known.

3

horse-drawn vehicle. In the first decade of the twentieth century, with the invasion of the automobile, highway surfaces were improved to meet the demands of auto traffic. Secondary routes were asphalted to extend state and county road systems. Walkers began searching for safer, more pleasurable routes. With the state park system making publicly owned land more available, walkers retreated to long-abandoned paths and eighteenth century woods roads, which offered delightful strolls through second-growth forest. However, because these routes were originally meant to take people someplace, they often missed the scenic areas. So hiking clubs and individuals began to build their own trails over routes that the Native Americans and settlers would never have thought of using. These routes were selected because they offered a vista, a stroll through a stand of silver beech, or access to a place that had previously been inaccessible or unknown. Deer paths often proved useful because they followed natural terrain and were frequently the easiest routes up a mountain or across a valley.

The New York-New Jersey Trail Conference

As trails began to spread throughout the Hudson Highlands and the Wyanokies, it became evident that planned trail systems would be necessary if hiking areas were to be properly utilized and protected. In 1920, Major William A. Welch, general manager of the Palisades Interstate Park, called together representatives of hiking organizations in New York. Their goal was to plan a network of marked trails that would make the Bear Mountain-Harriman State Parks more accessible to the public. The meeting resulted in an informal federation known as the Palisades Interstate Park Trail Conference. Raymond Torrey, Will Monroe, Meade Dobson, Frank Place, J. Ashton Allis and their friends planned, cut, and marked what are now the major park trails. The first one to be completed was the 20-mile Ramapo-Dunderberg Trail from Jones Point on the Hudson River to Tuxedo. In 1923, the first section of the Appalachian Trail to be finished was constructed in Bear Mountain Park. That same year, the organization changed its name to the New York-New Jersey Trail Conference, uniting under one banner a number of hiking organizations throughout the metropolitan area.

R. L. DICKINSON

From its founding, the Trail Conference has been an organization of volunteers. In 2001, this not-for-profit federation of over 85 hiking and outdoors clubs and nearly 9,500 individuals maintained a network of over 1,300 miles of marked trails from the Connecticut border to the Delaware Water Gap. With few exceptions, the trails are for foot traffic only. The Trail Conference's veritable corps of trained volunteers has been both repairing eroded and overused trails and building new trails to standards designed to prevent deteriorating conditions. In 1999, 1,512 volunteers and 65 clubs devoted over 30,000 hours to trail maintenance. But in spite of the Conference's massive efforts, it is estimated that only 2 to 3 percent of the hiking public knows who takes care of the trails.

The Trail Conference also serves as a unified voice for trail concerns and land protection in New York and New Jersey. While not always recognized as an environmental organization, the Trail Conference has, in fact, over many years, been involved in saving open space. When an issue affects trails, the volunteers and staff of the Trail Conference bring their concerns to the attention of organizations that are geared financially and legally to pursue the task. In other instances, the Trail Conference forms a coalition with its affiliated hiking clubs, governmental and law enforcement agencies, other nonprofit groups, and interested citizens to resolve an issue. Partners on various projects have included the Adirondack Mountain Club, Catskill Center, Highlands Coalition, Mohonk Preserve, National Park Service (NPS), New Jersey Department of Environmental Protection (Division of Parks and Forestry), New York-New Jersey Highlands Regional Study, New York Office of Parks, Recreation and Historic Preservation, New York Department of Environmental Conservation, Open Space Institute, Palisades Interstate Park Commission, Scenic Hudson, United States Forest Service (USFS), and the Sterling Forest Coalition. The Trail Conference's advocacy work also includes generating position papers and conducting public education activities.

Since its founding, Trail Conference volunteers and its member clubs have worked to extend hiking opportunities to the public and to build trails opening new areas. Although much of the land upon which they have built trails is publicly owned, about 25 percent is not. Hikers have enjoyed some areas only through the kindness of landowners on whose property the trails traversed. Unfortunately, the acquisition of public land progressed slowly. As the population grew, public access to some trails was limited when commercial developers and landowners closed trails due to occasional abuses.

Open Space Preservation

In the 1960s, federal, state, and county governments began acquiring land for public use. About the same time, but on a much smaller scale, The Nature Conservancy, the Audubon Society, and numerous local land trusts and conservancies began preserving open space. These acquisitions increased opportunities for outdoor recreation.

Preservation of open space in New York is a result of Environmental Quality Bond Acts, budget line items, and private donations. The 1960 and 1972 bond acts added Highland Lakes, Goose Pond Mountain, the Old Croton Aqueduct, the Rockefeller Preserve, Storm King, and Hook Mountain to the state park system and purchased additional acres for Bear Mountain, Rockland Lake, Fahnestock, and Taconic parks. The 1986 bond act set aside $250 million to acquire, protect, and improve state forest preserves, environmentally sensitive areas, municipal and urban cultural parks, and historic sites. Additions to the Catskill Forest Preserve were a result of both the 1972 and 1986 bond acts.

Although the voters defeated another proposed bond act in 1990, the New York state legislature in 1993 established the Environmental Protection Fund, which provides a dedicated stream of revenue for environmental projects, including a land acquisition fund. Now fully funded at $150 million per year, the Environmental Protection Fund contributes over $30 million annually towards the acquisition of open space lands identified as priorities in the Statewide Open Space Plan. The Clean Water/Clean Air Bond Act of 1996 provided an additional $150 million, over the following five years, to purchase lands to be preserved as open space.

Since 1994, the State of New York has acquired about 300,000 acres for preservation as state parks and wilderness areas. For example, in 1996, the state acquired the 3,800-acre Hubbard parcel to expand Clarence Fahnestock Memorial State Park. The state has also acquired the summits of Plateau, Bearpen, and Vly mountains in the Catskills, leaving only two of the Catskill high peaks (Doubletop and Graham) in private ownership. Just south of the Catskills, the state has agreed to purchase the 5,000-acre Lundy Estate in Ulster County, which will provide a protected woodland trail for the Long Path between Minnewaska State Park and the Catskill Forest Preserve. In 2001, the state announced the purchase of 2,100 acres on Schunemunk Mountain, which will be incorporated into a new state park. Some of these transactions have been facilitated by the efforts of the Open Space Institute, which purchases the properties from their owners and then conveys the properties to the state as

JACK FAGAN

funds become available.

The Adirondack Mountain Club (ADK) and the New York-New Jersey Trail Conference have formed a partnership to lobby for additional purchases of open space lands by the State of New York and increased funding to maintain hiking trails and parklands. In 2001, the ADK and the Trail Conference are advocating a replacement source for the 1996 bond act funds, which were appropriated for a five-year period only.

Minnewaska

Just before the stunning Storm King victory over Con Edison in 1980 (see chapter 15, "Storm King"), the Trail Conference helped organize yet another massive grass-roots effort, this time to preserve the Shawangunk Ridge. The fight to save Minnewaska, as it became known, was to prevent the Marriott Corporation from constructing a hotel, condominium complex, and championship golf course. In the process, many miles of trails would be destroyed and

Lake Minnewaska would be polluted (see chapter 13, "The Shawangunks").

In 1980, the Marriott Corporation submitted a draft of its environmental impact statement. Testimony at public hearings pointed out the recreational value of the area and questioned the adequacy of the proposed water supply. The New York State Department of Environmental Conservation gave conditional approval to the environmental impact statement. However, DEC was taken to court, with the case eventually reaching the New York Court of Appeals. By 1985, the Marriott Corporation, exhausted by seven lawsuits, and having spent over a million dollars without ever having broken ground, gave up on their plan. Environmental groups pushed for permanent protection, and the property was absorbed into Minnewaska State Park Preserve.

Sterling Forest

The fight to save Minnewaska was barely over when the next threat reared its ugly head—the proposed development of Sterling Forest. This 20,000-acre parcel connects New York's Harriman Park with the New Jersey Highlands.

As early as 1930, Raymond Torrey recognized the importance of preserving Sterling Forest, with its spectacular views and its accessibility for urban residents in search of nature and open space. His vision was not to be fulfilled in his lifetime. When the Harriman family offered the land to New York State as a park in the 1940s, the state declined the acquisition. At that time, state officials believed that the land had too many wetlands, that there were insufficient funds for management, and that New York had sufficient parklands for the future. Instead, in 1947, City Investing Company purchased the property, and immediately announced plans for development. Fortunately, the several small communities that sprang up in the valley did not impinge on the forests, which stayed intact.

By 1980, Sterling Forest had become the largest single tract of undeveloped forested private land remaining in the New York metropolitan area and had been sold several times. In the late 1980s, the Sterling Forest Corporation, owner of the property, proposed a massive development, with homes for 35,000 residents and 8,000,000 square feet of office space.

Spearheaded by the efforts of JoAnn Dolan, former Executive Director of the Trail Conference, and her husband Paul, an executive with ABC News, the Trail Conference and the Appalachian Mountain Club co-founded the Sterling Forest Coalition in 1988. Strengthening the resolve to protect the forest, a Public-Private Partnership to Save Sterling Forest was formed, pooling the skills and resources within the environmental community. Over 30 groups—including the Palisades Interstate Park Commission, New York-New Jersey Trail Conference, Passaic River Coalition, Environmental Defense Fund, Adirondack Mountain Club, The Nature Conservancy, Regional Plan Association, Scenic Hudson, Appalachian Mountain Club, Sierra Club, Appalachian Trail Conference and other regional/national organizations—participated in the most coordinated effort that had ever been made to protect land in this region.

In 1990, Passaic County—with the help of the New Jersey Green Acres program—took the first bold step and paid $9.2 million to condemn the entire 2,100-acre New Jersey section of Sterling Forest. In 1994, New Jersey Governor Christine Whitman signed a bill authorizing $10 million to purchase Sterling Forest land in New York, but only if New York also funded the purchase. Subsequently, New York Governor George Pataki matched New Jersey's support with $16 million, and Congress appropriated $17.5 million. The Open Space Institute and Scenic Hudson each contributed $2.5 million from the Lila Acheson and DeWitt Wallace Fund for the Hudson Highlands, and the Victoria Foundation contributed $1 million. Smaller donations from the private sector, including gifts from school children, totaled $500,000. The sale was assured when the Doris Duke Charitable Foundation donated the remaining $5 million in December 1997 to create the Doris Duke Wildlife Preserve, for which the Trail Conference currently holds the easement. Much of the private funding was sought by the negotiating land trust leaders of the Trust for Public Land and the Open Space Institute.

Finally, in February 1998, the Palisades Interstate Park Commission (PIPC) purchased approximately 15,280 acres of Sterling Forest for $55 million, forming the nucleus of Sterling Forest State Park. In December 2000, an additional 2,000 acres were acquired from Sterling Forest Corporation, expanding Sterling Forest State Park to over 17,000 acres.

Trail Development

Interest in trail development is more than a local issue. A nationwide project, Trails for All Americans, seeks to have trail opportunities within 15 minutes of most Americans' homes or places of work. In 1988, the President's Commission on Americans Outdoors called for the creation of a vast network of hiking and jogging trails, bikeways, and bridle paths. The commission envisioned a nationwide system of trails that would tie this country together with threads of green, linking communities and providing access to the natural world.

The New York metropolitan area already has an extensive hiking trail system in place. A perusal of the tables of contents of earlier editions of the *New York Walk Book* attests to the long-term availability of trails in this area. What was not always evident was the need for linkages between areas, although two major linkages have existed for years. The Long Path begins on the New Jersey Palisades and extends for over 300 miles northward past the Catskills toward the Adirondacks, linking Harriman with smaller parks and the Catskills. On its way from Georgia to Maine, the Appalachian Trail links the Kittatinnies, the Jersey Highlands, Harriman-Bear Mountain, the East Hudson Highlands, Fahnestock, and the South Taconics.

Many counties, cities, and towns are connecting their parks with greenways. Existing linkages include the Patriots' Path in New Jersey and the Paumanok Path on Long Island. More linkages are possible as the Highlands Trail wends its way between the Delaware and Hudson Rivers.

Assistance in Developing Trails

The expertise gained in the 1980s when the Appalachian Trail was moved onto protected woodlands helped fuel interest in other trail projects. Although Trail Conference volunteers work with park officials to build new trails, trails connecting protected open space need another type of assistance. The National Park Service Rivers and Trails Assistance Program (later renamed the NPS Rivers, Trails and Conservation Assistance Program) funded portions of the project to extend the Long Path north to the Adirondacks. The Trail Conference's volunteer corps grew to meet the challenge of building 100 miles of trail, and the Trail Conference began building relationships with local residents, municipalities, and private landowners. The 28-mile Shawangunk Ridge Trail also forged similar relationships on a smaller scale.

Another multi-partner trail project—the Highlands Trail—highlights the natural beauty of the New Jersey and the New York Highlands region. Begun in 1992 and funded through grants from the NPS Rivers, Trails and Conservation Assistance Program, this trail will run for about 160 miles along the Highlands Ridge from the Delaware River to the Hudson River. When complete, the Highlands Trail will be a greenway in New York and New Jersey linking the publicly owned open spaces. The threat of development in some areas along the route has spurred the project forward. By the fall of 2001, 120 miles of trail were built and open to the public.

Permanent Protection for Trail Corridors

In 2001, the Trail Conference is implementing a program to permanently protect trail corridors for the Long Path, Highlands Trail, and Shawangunk Ridge Trail. The Trail Conference's long-term goal is to assemble various parcels to create these linear corridors and then transfer them to public ownership. In 1998, pursuant to this plan, the Trail Conference acquired five parcels, totaling 400 acres, needed to protect five miles of the Long Path on the Ginseng Ridge, north of the Catskills. New York State Governor George Pataki announced the purchase of this trail corridor by the state in 2001.

The 28-mile Shawangunk Ridge Trail, which connects Minnewaska State Park Preserve in New York with High Point State Park in New Jersey, has been threatened by several proposals for commercial development on the top of the ridge. Together with other non-profit organizations and the New York State Department of Environmental Conservation, the Trail Conference is actively working to close the remaining gaps at Roosa Gap, in the Basha Kill area, and north of High Point State Park.

Threats to Trails and Trail Lands

Even with increased interest in protecting open space and providing more trails, threats that were never before envisioned now endanger both trails and trail lands. Interaction with other special interest or non-traditional user groups has become critical to solving problems.

Fiscal Threats

By the end of the 1980s, increased demands for reduced taxes resulted in massive cuts in state budgets. Moneys were no longer available for land purchases, and funds for park management or maintenance were severely curtailed. As a result, not-for-profit organizations have formed partnerships with the state to ensure open space protection and management. For example, since its origin in 1920, the Trail Conference has supplied volunteer trail maintainers. With the budget cuts, state partners have come to rely on these maintainers even more. In New York, Scenic Hudson Land Trust and the Open Space Institute own land, that by agreement, the state will manage until it has funds to purchase it. Fishkill Ridge Conservation Area and Hubbard-Perkins Conservation Area are two examples of land managed in this way. These close relationships allow each partner to specialize in what its staff and volunteers do best and to stretch ever-shrinking budgets.

Children's camps have also suffered from the recession. They require open space, but the cost of upkeep is sometimes too great for a not-for-profit organization to justify holding on to the property. In 1994, the Open Space Institute succeeded in protecting Clear Lake, a Boy Scout property adjacent to Fahnestock State Park. A portion of the property is open to the public for hiking.

Physical Threats

Without proper education, well-meaning outdoor enthusiasts can love a particular trail or scenic place to death. For example, on a holiday weekend in 1994, a nature sanctuary was overrun with visitors because a newspaper article recommended the place. Even when an area can tolerate many visitors, it cannot accommodate the six-pack of beer and the bonfire that some folks consider a necessary part of their outdoor experience.

Non-hiking user groups instinctively use the vast trail network that exists in the New York-New Jersey region, often not realizing that hikers maintain the trails for other hikers. Bicycles, horses, and motorized vehicles cause damage because the soil and trail design are not suited for anything other than foot traffic. Education and signage are important to ensure that correct users are on the trail and to prevent user conflicts.

The illegal use of motorized and other vehicles on park lands destroys trails that volunteers have labored hard to build. Users of all-terrain vehicles (ATVs) often run through sensitive areas, destroying vegetation and damaging the trails by causing siltation, creating potholes, and widening the narrow path that has been built to respect and fit into the natural environment. Their noise further degrades the outdoor experience by destroying the natural tranquility that hikers seek.

Public Education

As part of its effort to promote public interest in hiking and to educate people about available resources and the safe, proper use of the trail system, the Trail Conference publishes maps and guidebooks. The maps cover trails in the Catskills, Bear Mountain-Harriman State Parks, Sterling Forest State Park, North Jersey, West Hudson, East Hudson, Shawangunks, South Taconics, Hudson Palisades, and the Kittatinnies. Besides the *New York Walk Book* and its companion volume the *New Jersey Walk Book*, the Trail Conference's publications include *Circuit Hikes in Northern New Jersey, Day Walker, Guide to the Long Path, Harriman Trails: A Guide and History, Health Hints for*

Hikers, Hiking Long Island, Iron Mine Trails, Scenes and Walks in the Northern Shawangunks, and others. These books complement the *Walk Books,* providing more detailed information.

To join the New York-New Jersey Trail Conference, order publications, or receive more information, contact the New York-New Jersey Trail Conference, 156 Ramapo Valley Road, Mahwah, NJ 07430; (201) 512-9348; visit the Conference's web site, www.nynjtc.org; or send e-mail to info@nynjtc.org.

SUGGESTIONS FOR HIKERS

f you can walk, you can hike; age is no obstacle. Sometimes, you don't even have to be able to walk to enjoy a trail, as a few trails are now accessible to the handicapped. Whatever your goals, the suggestions presented here should provide enough information to help you start hiking.

A good way to become familiar with hiking trails is to meet and learn from experienced hikers, something easily accomplished by hiking with a club, an organized group, or friends who hike regularly. Hiking clubs abound in the New York area. For a list of them, send your request, with a self-addressed, stamped envelope, to the New York-New Jersey Trail Conference, 156 Ramapo Valley Road, Mahwah, NJ 07430.

Whether you hike with a club or with friends, you will need a knowledge of the area in which you plan to hike if you want to have a safe and enjoyable outing. Trail maps, guidebooks, park offices, and experienced hikers can give you valuable information. Guidebooks and trail maps are available for purchase from the New York-New Jersey Trail Conference. Most camping and outdoors stores, as well as many bookstores, carry trail maps and guides. Trail maps for state, county, and local parks are sometimes available at park entrances, but often lack important details.

Planning Your Hike

Planning a hike is easy if you hike with a club. Most hiking clubs publish a regular schedule of hikes. Read the description in the club literature or talk to a member, and pick a hike that suits your abilities and interests. If you cannot or prefer not to hike with a club, and you are a beginning hiker, go with several friends. Choose your route from the trails described in this book or in the books listed in "Further Reading," and bring a trail map along.

Level of Hiking Difficulty
Be realistic about your physical condition and any limitations you might have; neither you nor your fellow hikers will enjoy the outing if you are frequently stopping to catch your breath. Once on the trail, start slowly and pace yourself. If you are in doubt, consult with your doctor before going on a hike.

On smooth, level ground, your pace may be two to three miles an hour. It takes longer to pick your way over a rocky path or to hike uphill. You should allow at least 30 minutes per mile, not including rest stops. Measure all the ascents and add five minutes for every 100 feet of elevation gain.

Types of Hikes
The simplest type of hike is *out and back*, which starts at a trailhead, follows the trail (or a network of trails), and returns by the same route. Often, more than one trail begins at a trailhead, so it is possible to go out on one trail and return on another trail, forming a *loop hike*.

Safety and Comfort

You can do many things to make sure that your hike proceeds without incident. Begin by making sure that your maps and guidebooks are up to date and your equipment is in good condition.

Hiking Alone
Hiking alone is generally discouraged, especially for those who have not had any trail experience. A group of at least four hikers is advisable, because in case of injury, one person can stay with the injured hiker while two people go for help. Whether you are hiking alone or with someone else, always let someone know where you will be hiking and when you plan to return.

First Aid
For a one-day hike, carry Band-Aids®, an antiseptic for cuts and scratches, moleskin for blisters, and tweezers to remove splinters and ticks. Put the moleskin on irritated spots before a blister forms. Other useful items are an Ace®

bandage with clips, gauze pads, antibiotic ointment, adhesive tape, and safety pins. Carry these items, plus a pencil and paper, in a lightweight metal box or waterproof case, in your pack.

Learn to recognize the symptoms of hypothermia and heat stroke, which often sneak up on their victims and can be fatal. Hypothermia occurs when the body loses more heat than it can generate, and the body temperature drops. The symptoms of hypothermia include shivering, difficulty using hands, stumbling, losing articles of clothing, speech deficiency, blurred thinking, and amnesia. In heat stroke, the body temperature rises to over 105 degrees Fahrenheit, and the pulse rate can soar to over 160, possibly followed by convulsions and vomiting. For more details on hypothermia, heat stroke, and other medical emergencies on the trail, refer to books listed in "Further Reading."

Waste Disposal and Sanitation
Carry toilet paper in a plastic bag. If no toilet facilities are available, bury waste six inches deep, at least 200 feet away from any stream or lake, and at least 50 feet from the trail.

Hunting Season
Many area parks have a hunting season in the late fall. Park offices can give you hunting schedules, and the *Trail Walker*, published by the New York-New Jersey Trail Conference, prints a hunting schedule in its September/October issue. If you want to hike during hunting season, it is best to hike in areas where hunting is prohibited. Be sure to wear some item of blaze orange if you hike in areas where hunting is permitted.

Inclement Weather
Inclement weather can be any weather from severe cold to excessive heat, with or without rain or snow, and with or without a thunderstorm—which is dangerous primarily because of lightning. If you are on an exposed ledge or on a mountain peak during a thunderstorm, go to lower, covered ground quickly. If you are on the trail, avoid taking shelter under a lone tree, which may attract lightning.

Wet weather is dangerous to hikers even during the summer, because it can cause hypothermia in the event of exposure. The best way to avoid hypothermia is by carrying the proper clothing in your pack: waterproof rain gear (including a jacket or parka with a hood and rain pants), a wool or pile sweater or shirt, and a polypropylene undergarment for warmth.

Winter Hiking

Hiking in winter requires special equipment, such as crampons and snowshoes, to enable you to safely traverse the snow and ice you are likely to encounter. The first time you try a winter hike, make sure you are properly equipped, and go with an experienced group of four or more.

Wild Fruits and Mushrooms

Do not eat any wild plants without positively identifying them. Learn to recognize the common edible berries by hiking with someone who has experience, and by reading some of the publications listed under "Further Reading."

Poison Ivy

Poison ivy grows aggressively in all kinds of conditions. In the woods, it either acts as a ground cover or becomes a climbing vine. It is identified by a group of

three green, asymmetrical leaves, which include a short-stemmed middle leaf; often, one edge of a poison ivy leaf is smooth and curved, while the other edge might have one or more serrations. It may bear white or green berries. Avoid contact with all parts of the plant, including the bare vines.

Contact with poison ivy causes a rash which appears from 12 to 48 hours after exposure. The rash is accompanied by intense itching. Neither your own nor someone else's rash can transmit poison ivy's toxic oil; only exposure to the oil itself will. Over-the-counter medications help control the itching.

Figure 2-1. Poison ivy

If you suspect you have come in contact with poison ivy, wash the affected areas as soon as possible with strong soap or laundry detergent.

Insects

Insect repellent, long sleeves, long pants tucked into your socks, and a hat are the best guards against insects. While DEET (*diethyl M toulamide*) is an effective insect repellent, it can be toxic, especially to infants and children, so it should be used sparingly (30 percent DEET maximum) and only when absolutely necessary.

Ticks are a problem in the New York area—especially deer ticks, which carry Lyme disease. Deer ticks are no bigger than a pin-head, making them difficult to spot. But the prevalence of ticks should not deter you from hiking as long as you take the proper precautions. Wear long sleeves, and tuck long pants into socks. As soon as you return home, examine your body thoroughly for ticks, especially in the groin area and armpits. If you are bitten by a tick, take care to remove it slowly with tweezers, so that its mouth part does not remain embedded in the skin.

If you suspect that you have Lyme disease, contact your doctor. Lyme disease symptoms include flu-like symptoms, joint and muscle pain, fatigue, or a bulls-eye rash. Lyme disease can be treated with antibiotics, but if not treated, it can become a disabling chronic condition.

Some people are strongly allergic to bee or wasp stings. If you have had a strong reaction in the past, ask your doctor for instructions.

Snakes

The region's two poisonous snakes, the eastern timber rattlesnake and the copperhead, are rarely encountered and are not found on Long Island. When confronted, these snakes will generally attempt to escape rather than attack.

A rattlesnake is recognized by the rattle on its tail. Its markings are not uniform, varying in coloration from yellow or tan to nearly black. When suddenly disturbed, a rattlesnake will rattle.

The copperhead is pale brown with reddish blotches on its body and a coppery tinge on its head. It is slow-moving and quiet, which increases the chance of an unexpected encounter.

When hiking during the snake season (spring to late fall), be alert, particularly when climbing rock ledges and over logs. Look before placing your hand on an overhead ledge for support. If you are bitten, do not panic; note the size and distinguishing marks of the snake. Wrap the bite tightly with a bandage, but not so tightly that you cut off circulation. Proceed at a moderate pace and, once out of the woods, promptly seek medical assistance.

Rabies

In the New York metro area since 1990, rabies has become endemic to wild animals, particularly skunks and raccoons. Do not attempt to feed any wild animal. Stay well clear of any animal acting strangely or a nocturnal animal that is out prowling around in broad daylight. Do not touch any dead animals, as you can contract rabies from a dead animal. Rabies is fatal if not treated promptly. If bitten by any animal, leave the trail immediately and seek medical assistance.

Bears

While brown bears (grizzlies) are not found in New York's hiking areas, their smaller relative—black bears—are becoming more common in many parts of the region. They are more dangerous to your food than to you, and hence are more of a problem for backpackers than for day-hikers. Do not make any attempt to feed them. If you are lucky enough to see one, do not approach the bear. Instead, make lots of noise and move slowly but deliberately in the opposite direction.

Equipment

If you are a new hiker, try using your existing gear and equipment as much as possible until you see what other hikers use, hear their opinion, and decide what will suit you best. You might also wish to rent or borrow equipment to help you better determine what you should buy.

Necessary equipment for a day hike includes adequate footwear, clothing, a hat, rain gear, a first-aid kit, insect repellent (in season), food (or at least a snack), and at least two quarts of water. Some hikers find that a hiking stick gives them added stability. You will also need a pack to carry your gear comfortably.

Footwear

A good pair of boots is of vital importance for hiking. At a minimum, hiking boots should provide water resistance, ankle support, and a non-slip sole. For protection against blisters, wear a pair of heavy socks (such as wool) over light liner socks that can wick away moisture. Make sure your boots fit properly; your feet should have enough room, but they should not slide forward in the boot, which can bruise the toes, nor should they have too much heel lift. Remember that if boots are uncomfortable in the store, they will be even more uncomfortable on the trail.

Make sure to break in your boots before wearing them for a full day of hiking. Wear them for short intervals at home and then on a few short hikes, making sure they are completely comfortable before you wear them on a longer hike.

Clothing

What you wear depends, of course, on the weather and the time of year. In summer, you can wear a tee-shirt and shorts, or you may prefer to wear a lightweight pair of pants and a long-sleeved shirt to protect yourself against insects, sun, or scratches from vegetation. A hat with a brim provides protection from the sun.

Be prepared for wet weather, whatever the season. Wool and some synthetics such as polypropylene provide warmth when wet. Cotton is a poor choice because it retains moisture and takes hours to dry once it becomes wet. Down is also a poor choice, as it also loses its ability to insulate when wet. If there is any chance of rain or very strong winds, you will want a highly water-resistant, wind-resistant parka.

In cold weather, layering is especially important. Wear your hiking clothes in several thin (rather than fewer heavy) layers. Begin with a light polypropylene garment next to your skin, and add a long-sleeved wool or synthetic shirt and/or sweater, depending on the conditions in which you will be hiking. Colder weather may warrant wool pants or long underwear. Your outer garment should be a waterproof and windproof parka. A head covering (preferably, a wool cap) is essential in cold weather, since you lose most of your body heat through your head. Other clothing to take in cold weather are wool or synthetic gloves or mittens (mittens retain heat better) and spare dry socks in a waterproof plastic bag.

As soon as you feel yourself beginning to perspire, remove a layer (or layers, if needed) of clothing. Put the layer(s) back on when you stop to rest.

Safety Gear

When hiking with a group, share the weight, as not everyone needs everything. Everyone should have a first-aid kit, flashlight, map, and compass. Additional safety items might include cigarette lighter, pocket knife, personal medications, safety pins, duct tape (wrapped around your water bottle), and a space blanket—an emergency blanket made from aluminized Mylar film, available in camping and outdoor stores.

Food

Hiking is not the time to skip breakfast or scrimp on lunch. A good lunch might include one or two sandwiches, chips or pretzels, an apple or orange, and a candy bar. Many people fare better snacking continually through the day, rather than having one large meal. Fresh and dried fruit, raw vegetables, trail mix, granola bars, nuts, chocolate, and hard candy are all good snacks. Small children, in particular, often run out of energy while hiking and need frequent snacks.

Water

The importance of taking sufficient water on a hike cannot be overemphasized. Most people need at least two quarts of water, more in hot weather or on a very long hike. Do not wait until you are thirsty to drink. To prevent dehydration, make sure you take frequent drinks of water as you hike.

For day hikes, fill a plastic bottle with tap water from home. A Nalgene® bottle (available from camping supply stores) is a good choice, but an empty soda bottle will also suffice. Unless you purify the water by means of tablets or a filter, do not drink from springs, streams, or ponds, as they may be polluted with *Giardia* or coliform bacteria. Do not depend upon finding a reliable water supply at shelters or along the trails.

Pack (Knapsack)

A pack should be large enough to carry your extra garments, lunch, water bottles, safety gear, and insect repellent comfortably. A pack that is jammed tight will not be comfortable to carry, and will feel heavier than it actually is.

On the Trail

Hiking is just like walking—you put one foot in front of the other. Your speed will vary as the terrain varies. In rocky areas, be careful about your foot placement. Do not trust a rock or a log to remain still when you put your weight on it, particularly going downhill. A log can easily roll, and lichen or moss on rocks can be deceptively slippery. Hiking downhill is harder on your knees because of the additional weight dropped on the joint.

Stop and rest periodically. At lunchtime, take off your boots and air out your feet if it is not too cold. Stop at trail junctions if you are traveling in a group and let everyone catch up before proceeding.

Blazes and Cairns

Members of the New York-New Jersey Trail Conference volunteer to be responsible for marking and maintaining over 1,300 miles of trails in the New York metropolitan area. The trails are marked with either painted blazes or plastic or metal tags.

These blazes communicate various messages. Two blazes, with one painted higher than the other, indicate a change in direction; the top blaze indicates the direction of the turn. Three blazes painted as the three points of a triangle indicate a trail's end or beginning. Each trail is blazed in its own individual color or shape to distinguish it from other trails that it crosses. The trail descriptions in this book indicate the color or shape of each trail's blaze. Where a paint blaze is not practical (for example, above treeline), watch instead for a pile of stones—called a *cairn*—purposely placed to lead you to the next step on the trail.

Unless the route of the trail is very clearly defined, you should normally be able to see the next blaze in front of you.

Lost—You or the Trail?
If you can't find a blaze in front of you, turn around and see if you can spot one going the other way. If you can, use its placement and direction to try and find the next blaze in front of you. If you can't, you should stop, look around, then go back to the last blaze or cairn that you saw. If no blaze or cairn is in sight, look at the ground for a trace of the path. If no trail is visible, stop and relax. Think about where you have been. Look at your map. Do not wander. Three of

Figure 2-2. Cairn

anything—a shout, whistle, or flash of light—is a call for help. If you are with a group or have recently seen other hikers, signal every few minutes while you wait for your absence to be noted, and for someone to come to your aid.

While waiting for help, begin planning what you will do next. With your map, choose the most direct route out to the nearest road or known trail, based on your best estimation of where you are. Note where north is on the map and correct your bearing for magnetic declination—generally about 12 degrees west of true north in the New York region. Use your compass to follow the route that you select. In most places, following any stream downhill is a good route. If darkness falls, stay put and keep warm with those extra garments in your pack and possibly with a fire, *but note the following precautions:* build the fire in front of a rock, because its heat will be increased by reflection, having first made sure that you have cleared the ground down to mineral soil. Be careful not to let the fire spread.

Taking Care of the Trails and Woodlands

Hiker Etiquette

Do not pick flowers or collect rocks or artifacts—leave them there for other hikers to enjoy. Hike quietly! Use existing trails, and try to stay in the middle of the path. Do not shortcut switchbacks. Not everyone likes dogs, so if you hike with them, keep them under control on a leash. If your dog defecates on or near the trail, bury the waste farther away or pack it out. When hiking with a group, walk single-file except on wide woods roads. If you encounter a wet or muddy spot, walk through it, getting your boots wet, rather than widening the trail at the edges.

Litter

The conscientious hiker's motto is "Leave nothing but footprints." Whatever you carry into the woods, you can carry it out. Help keep the trails the way you would like to find them by picking up litter left by inconsiderate trail users.

Smoking

Leave your cigarettes home when you go hiking, but if you must smoke, do it only when you stop for a break—never when you are moving along the trail. Carry a plastic bag or small metal container to carry out used matches and cigarette butts, and always make sure they are completely out.

Multi-Use Trails

Some trails mentioned in this book are multi-use trails, which means they may also be open to other users, such as cyclists, horseback riders, in-line skaters, and, in season, cross-country skiers or snowshoers. People in wheelchairs, even motorized ones, are considered to be on foot. No other type of motorized vehicle, however, should be on a trail. If you encounter an ATV on the trail, take down the license number and report it to the park police.

On trails used by horseback riders, cyclists, and pedestrians, the common practice is for bicycles to yield to pedestrians, and both bicycles and pedestrians to yield to horses. On ski trails, hikers should stay out of the ski tracks.

Fires

On day hikes, you should have no need for a fire at all. The only good reason for building a fire is for warmth in the event you become lost and cold and find yourself in emergency bivouac conditions.

Trail Problems
Report trail problems, such as permanent wet spots, missing blazes, and trees blocking the trail, to the New York-New Jersey Trail Conference. Their volunteers maintain most of the trails in the area, and the Trail Conference knows who maintains the remainder of the trails. If you hike often, obtain a supply of trail report cards from the Trail Conference, which you can use to keep a record of trail problems. The sooner you report problems, the sooner they will be fixed.

Do not be a phantom maintainer—that is, do not do the maintainer's work of clearing and blazing the trail. The assigned maintainer will not mind if you pick up small amounts of litter or throw an occasional small branch off the trail, but for more serious problems, be sure to contact the Trail Conference. If you want to maintain a trail, become a Trail Conference member, and let them know of your interest in trail work. A volunteer will assign you to maintain a trail or have a trail crew contact you. Trail crews are made up of Trail Conference members who go out regularly to repair trails in a specific area. By maintaining trails with other hikers, you will learn the correct trail maintenance skills.

Private Property
Hiking trails are not always on public land. They sometimes cross private land, with the owner's permission. When hiking on private property, stay on the trail, leave no litter, and build no fires, so that the landowner will continue to allow the public access.

Park Closings
When the woods are dangerously dry from lack of rain, parks and public areas may be closed to hikers. The New York-New Jersey Trail Conference urges complete cooperation with the public authorities who make these decisions. When the parklands are closed, stay out of the woods, and request others to do likewise.

Overnight Backpacking Trips
Some parks permit overnight backpacking. However, before you go, check with the park concerning their regulations. Adhere to the group size restrictions. Many areas restrict group sizes to ten or fewer, a good rule even if there is no official restriction. If your group is larger, consider staying at two or more distinct campsites in order to lessen the impact on the environment.

THREE

MOUNTAIN ECOLOGY *

nly a few substantive natural history publications cover the mountains in the greater New York region where much of the hiking is done. Vegetation and fauna are shaped by hard rock and shallow soils on hills, ledges, and mountains. In most of the *New York Walk Book* region, these crest environments are widespread at elevations of about 800 to more than 2,000 feet. Elevation *per se* is not responsible for distinctive crest vegetation. Due to the sun's heat, some exposed rocky crest habitats are warmer, at least seasonally, than *coves* (sheltered lower areas). Crest vegetation also occurs at low elevations, even at sea level along the Hudson River, where rocky knobs and bluffs have thin soil exposed to the weather.

Vegetation is part of the scenery, stabilizes the soil against erosion, provides habitat, and makes up the base of the food chain. Crest vegetation is influenced by various factors. Shallow soils and bare rock exposed to extremes of weather have little space for roots, hold little water, and are prone to drought. As a result, they generally have low nutrient levels, and may be unstable. Rapid changes in temperature and moisture, high winds that desiccate and physically stress plants, and wind-driven ice crystals in winter that abrade plants all add to the harsh growing conditions. Soil drought and exposure to lightning strikes make crests fire-prone. Charred wood is rarely far away in these mountains. People are attracted to picturesque, rocky overlook areas, where untended fires

This chapter was written by Erik Kiviat, Executive Director of Hudsonia, Annandale, New York.

and discarded cigarettes add to the fire risk. Hikers who trample vegetation by wandering off trails, and browsing deer attracted to sunny, south-facing slopes in cold weather, add to the difficult conditions. Trees, if present at all, grow slowly, do not reach large size, and are often damaged. Crest vegetation may include old-growth forests that lack large trees. Lower-growing plants may be less affected by harsh weather and poor soil, and are able to root successfully in crevices or soil pockets.

Crests of the Hudson Highlands, Shawangunks, Taconics, Stissing Mountain, Westchester Hills, Palisades, and many other areas commonly have stunted forests or savannas characterized by red oak and chestnut oak. Co-occurring trees may include red maple, pignut hickory, white oak, gray birch, pin cherry, black cherry, shadbush, red cedar, white pine, pitch pine, and—if enough moisture is available—hemlock. Sprouts and occasionally larger trees of American chestnut are generally scattered in the forest but may be absent from the rockiest habitats. The size and, in places, the density of trees generally increases on deeper soils, in areas sheltered from the weather, and at lower elevations. Also, other trees become common, such as black birch, hop-hornbeam, or sugar maple.

Pitch pine dominates large areas of the environmentally extreme crests of the Shawangunks. There, tree size decreases toward the summit of Ice Caves Mountain, where vast areas of dwarf pitch pine "plains" appear as dense thickets only 3–6 feet high. Elsewhere in the Shawangunks, tupelo and sassafras may be prominent on level crest areas that apparently collect moisture.

Figure 3-1. Mountain laurel

Between the well-spaced trees, or in bald patches where there are few or no trees, many other plants may thrive. Among the shrubs are scrub oak, mountain laurel, low blueberries, huckleberry, chokeberry, bush-honeysuckle, and occasionally bearberry. Where conditions are less severe, mountain laurel can form dense thickets, crowding out other plants, and creating formidable barriers to walkers leaving established trails. In addition, mostly in the more southern

JACK FAGAN

Figure 3-2. Reindeer lichen

areas, there may be downy arrowwood, black-haw, and New Jersey tea. Little bluestem and a few other grasses are often present, and they may form picturesque meadows. Prickly-pear cactus thrives here and there on warm, dry rocks. Among the many typical herbaceous plants are goat's-rue, orange-grass, pink corydalis, sand-rush, and stiff-leaf aster. The most exposed areas may have three-toothed cinquefoil, Greenland sandwort, or other species rare in this region. Level ledges occasionally are deeply carpeted with reindeer lichens, and vertical rock faces frequently have large rock tripe lichens. Lush growths of lichens indicate that the local air quality is relatively good and that hikers and climbers have not been trampling on the fragile ground off the trail.

Most of the more rugged hiking areas have schist, gneiss, granite, quartz conglomerate bedrock, or quartzite that has given rise to acidic soils. The common crest plants are tolerant of this acidity. Large areas of the Shawangunks and Schunemunk Mountain, and the quartzite ledges occurring locally at Stissing Mountain in Dutchess County, are good examples of very hard rock and acidic soils. Yet, other areas have plants indicative of neutral or even alkaline soils, including many spots in the Hudson Highlands, portions of the Shawangunks, and pockets in the Taconics. It is not clear what factors have mollified acidity of the soil, but some plausible suggestions are local glacial deposits containing limestone or other limy rocks from nearby valleys, calcium-bearing bedrock such as amphibolite or calc-silicate, or ash from vegetation fires. Calcareous (limy) shales are responsible in parts of the Shawangunks. Whatever the reasons, the typical flora of acidic crests may be punctuated by species associated with limy soils, such as basswood, bladdernut, round-leaf dogwood, and harebell.

Talus slopes, comprising piles of more-or-less loose rock below cliffs and ledges, are extensive in the Palisades, Shawangunks, portions of the Hudson Highlands, and at Stissing, but are more localized elsewhere. The sunnier, drier areas of talus support many of the plants found on dry, sunny crests. Moister, shadier habitats may have hemlock and a variety of other plants. The cool, moist crevices beneath talus blocks are secure refuge for many animals. Talus slopes are often unstable, and the individual blocks are subject to movement and thus may be dangerous to climb.

The Catskills are a special case. Their near-level strata of softer sandstones and shales create flat summits that above about 3,500 feet may have moist, organic soils and red spruce-balsam fir forests. Some of the spruce-fir stands are old growth. Plant communities resembling the crest vegetation described above are most noticeable on ledges or around the exposed edges of the summits. In places, one can see conifers flagged into a one-sided growth pattern by high winds, and *krummholz* (dwarf woods) spreading out at the base where deep snow shields the low branches from ice crystal abrasion.

Some areas have been disturbed historically by hard rock mining (in the early 1900s, for example). Notable examples are on the east face of Hook Mountain in the New York Palisades, Little Stissing Mountain, and at the southwest end of Breakneck Ridge (Hudson Highlands). Along with the typical crest plants, introduced and native weedy species flourish, among them tree-of-heaven, black locust, empress tree, wineberry, Morrow or Tartarian honeysuckle, garlic mustard, and common ragweed. The same invasions have occurred at some locations of serious trail erosion or off-road vehicle damage.

Extensive wetlands are rare at higher elevations. Yet depressions on level bedrock, pockets between ledges, or wet stream margins often support small wet meadows, bogs, or intermittent pools. These wet areas may have highbush blueberry, sweet pepperbush, red maple, sphagnum moss, and other plants tolerant of acidic, wet soils. Dwarf ginseng and other unusual wildflowers may occur in these habitats.

Wildlife may be sparse on crests, but some interesting species are associated with these habitats. Hawks, eagles, and vultures migrate along the Appalachian ridges in late summer and fall, and under some weather conditions fly close to the ridgetops. Migration is pronounced along the Shawangunks, and ledges just south of US 44/NY 55 provide an excellent vantage point. Breakneck Ridge and the Storm King complex are also good places to watch hawks. The peregrine falcon formerly nested on ledges along the Hudson River and in the Shawangunks, but disappeared due to DDT poisoning and human disturbance. Since the 1990s, however, breeding pairs have become installed on bridges, buildings, and two natural ledge sites. The breeding population of the common raven is slowly increasing in our region; their low-pitched, croaking calls may be heard in many mountainous areas. Eastern bluebirds commonly nest in cavities in dead or damaged trees in the balder crest habitats.

JACK FAGAN

Figure 3-3. Pitch pine

Two species of lizards occur in the mountains. The eastern fence lizard has a restricted distribution on sunny crests near the river, but the five-lined skink is widely distributed in the region and more common in the Ramapos and the Hudson Highlands west of the river. Crests and their often-associated talus slopes are frequently inhabited by snakes. The remaining winter denning and spring basking locales of the threatened timber rattlesnake are often associated with ledge-and-talus habitats that have a warm, sunny exposure. Northern copperhead dens are commonly in talus as well, as are the black racer and black rat snake. Eastern box turtles also use crest habitats in the southwestern portions of the region. The slimy salamander may be found in pockets of moist soil among rocks. Woodland pools, where not too acidic (for example, on Breakneck Ridge, Stissing Mountain, and shale terrains in the northern Shawangunks), may support breeding congregations of spotted salamander, wood frog, and sometimes marbled salamander.

Porcupines are fond of crevices in talus and beneath ledges. The long-tailed shrew occurs in talus in the Shawangunks, and the northern water shrew may be seen along mountain streams in the Catskills. The eastern woodrat, nearly gone from the region, builds stick nests in rock crevices. Following reintroduction, the fisher occurs in the Catskills and the northern Shawangunks. It is not unusual to find tracks or scat of bobcat in the Catskills and the Taconic Mountains.

There has been little study of invertebrates in the mountains. A rare butterfly, the falcate orange-tip, frequents ledges west of the Hudson River, where there are abundant rock cresses, food for the caterpillars. Another rare butterfly, the pipevine swallowtail, has been rediscovered on the New Jersey Palisades.

Dry rocky habitats may bear a surprising resemblance to dry sandy habitats, such as those that hikers see at the New Jersey Pine Barrens, the Jersey Shore, and the Long Island shores. Pitch pine, scrub oak, blueberries, little bluestem, bluebird, box turtle, and other species that have adapted to dry soil are prominent in both rocky and sandy landscapes. Inland sand barrens are quite acidic, whereas seaside habitats may be salty. Sandy areas support many burrowing animals not found in rocky terrains.

Some rare animals and plants occur mostly or only in rugged environments that have harsh conditions and are difficult for human beings to reach. For those species that can tolerate the harsh weather, poor soil, sparse vegetation, and relatively frequent fires, mountainous landscapes can provide refuges from biological competition, predation, and human disturbance. This appears true for animals that den in rock crevices or nest on remote ledges, as well as for plants that survive on nearly bare, weatherbeaten rocks but not in the shade of forests or tall shrubs.

The biological refuge function of mountains, as well as the sensitivity of mountain soils to trampling and erosion, forces us to consider the carrying capacity of mountain landscapes for recreational use. Hikers in fragile areas can lessen the human impact on nature by staying on the trails and being careful not to trample vegetation and soils unnecessarily. They should avoid disturbing wildlife, especially bird nests, and resist the temptation to collect plants or animals.

Hikers can cultivate interest in nature, using field guides and regional books. Many local organizations sponsor nature-study field trips open to the public. Rare or unusual observations may be reported to Hudsonia, Bard College Field Station, Annandale, NY 12504; (845) 758-7053; www.hudsonia.org.

FOUR

GEOLOGY

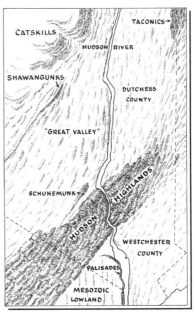

ost walkers pay little attention
to the rocks they encounter along the trail unless they seem unusual or constitute a barrier, such as a cliff face or a
difficult bouldery slope to be sur-
mounted. But many rocks have interesting stories to tell—of how and when
they were formed—which can add to
the enjoyment of a day out on the trail.
The geology of southern New York
state can be particularly rewarding to
the hiker because of the great variety
of rock types that may be found within
100 miles of New York City.

Looking at a satellite image of our
region is a good way to get an over-
view of the various features of our landscape that are a result of the underlying geologic formations. Figure 4-1
shows the principal elements of the topography—the ups and downs—of
southern New York. Note the contrast
between the relief of the Hudson Highlands and that of the regions just to

Figure 4-1. Simplified topography

33

their north and south. Observe the differences in height of the ridges in the Highlands and those of the nearby areas of gentler relief. These ridges were formed by the folding, tilting, or fracturing of the various layers of the underlying bedrock, and the varying appearance of the different ridges reflects the various types of bedrock and their resistance to erosion, as well as the degree to which the layers of rock have been tilted or otherwise disturbed.

Except in the Catskills and on Long Island, almost all of the bedrock of our region is made up of layers that are no longer flat-lying. The weathering and partial erosion of these tilted layers have produced the linear relief of roughly parallel high-and-low topographic elements. The difference in the heights of these layers reflects the different resistance to erosion of the various rock layers and their mineral content (Figure 4-2).

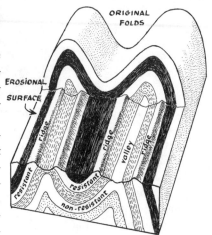

Figure 4-2. Erosion of folded strata produces outcrop bands: a topography of more or less parallel ridges.

Broadly speaking, the entire region (except for the Catskills) is part of the Appalachian Fold Belt, an elongate zone of the earth's crust extending from Alabama to Newfoundland. Long ago, this region underwent compression, mountain-building, and various periods of general uplift. The overall term for such events is *orogeny*. Geologists now believe that the orogenies of the Appalachian Belt were the result of the slow interaction of separate sections or *plates* of the earth's crust. The outer surface of our planet appears to be composed of more than a dozen of these crustal plates. Over billions of years, these plates have slowly migrated across the earth's surface in various directions, driven by forces operating from the zone below the crust known as the *mantle*. At various times, plates have gradually moved apart, slowly collided, or slid past one another. The collision of plates appears to have caused the orogenies that resulted in the formation of mountain chains, while the *drifting apart* of plates has allowed the development of ocean basins.

The early North American plate seems to have collided three separate times with crustal plates now located across the Atlantic. These collisions caused three periods of orogenic folding during the Paleozoic Era, known as the Taconian, the Acadian, and the Alleghenian. They are noted in Figure 4-3, which shows the standard subdivisions of geologic time. The time values assigned to these subdivisions are based on the study of fossils and the analysis of radioactive minerals found in rocks.

Some layered rocks found in northern New Jersey and in Rockland County, New York—within the Appalachian Belt—are not folded. These rocks were formed in the Mesozoic Era, after the last Paleozoic orogeny had taken place, and they actually overlie an older

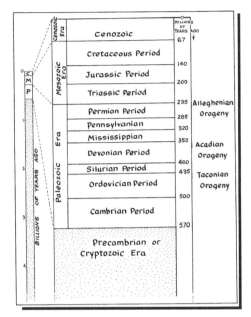

Figure 4-3. Geologic time scale

folded terrain. The Catskills are also composed of unfolded, nearly flat-lying rock layers, but these mountains are just outside of the Appalachian Belt, far enough from the margin of the North American plate not to have undergone the orogeny caused by the collisions of continental plates. As we shall see, the Catskills represent a great piling up of sediments derived from the erosion of mountainous uplifts that formed within the nearby Appalachian Belt.

The oldest rocks found on the surface of the earth are over four billion years old. They are called Precambrian, which simply means that they were formed before the Cambrian Period. In most of the United States (including New York), the surface rocks are usually from the Paleozoic, Mesozoic, or Cenozoic eras. However, this upper stratum is always underlain by a "basement" of Precambrian rock (see Figure 4-4).

In some areas of New York, younger rocks are absent or have been eroded away, so that the Precambrian rocks are exposed at the surface. In southern New York, the most extensive area of Precambrian outcrop is the Hudson Highlands (including the Ramapos) (see Figures 4-1 and 4-4). Long strips of

Precambrian surface rocks are also found in Westchester County and on Stissing Mountain in Dutchess County. These Precambrian outcroppings are between one and 1.3 billion years old.

The Hudson Highlands may be thought of as an upraised block of Precambrian basement rock. Part of this uplift must have taken place along the great Ramapo Fault that runs northeast-southwest along a line drawn between Suffern and Peekskill. This fault line marks the dramatic contrast between the high rampart of the ancient upraised Highlands rocks to the northwest, and the Mesozoic lowland of slightly-dipping sandstone and shale to the southeast (see Figure 4-1 and 4-4).

Named after the great river that cuts through them, the Hudson Highlands are a northeast-trending mass of ridges on both sides of the

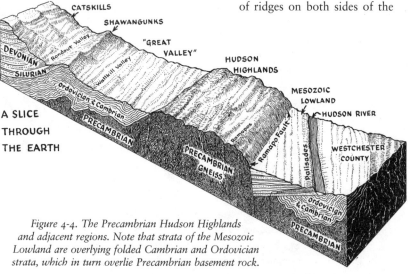

Figure 4-4. The Precambrian Hudson Highlands and adjacent regions. Note that strata of the Mesozoic Lowland are overlying folded Cambrian and Ordovician strata, which in turn overlie Precambrian basement rock.

river, most of which rise to 1,200 or 1,300 feet above sea level. Their rugged topography makes the Highlands an ideal location for hiking trails. Indeed, many familiar regions described in this book are part of the Hudson Highlands. These areas include Bear Mountain-Harriman State Parks, Storm King and Black Rock Forest, the East Hudson Highlands, and Fahnestock State Park.

The bedrock of the Hudson Highlands consists largely of relatively hard and weather-resistant minerals which are highly resistant to erosion. As a result, these rocks—despite their age—attain higher elevations than adjacent younger rocks which have been eroded away. Today, the Highlands present the hiker with a scenic landscape of glacially-smoothed mountaintops and valleys with sparkling lakes. The dominant rock type is granite gneiss—a coarsely-layered rock, characterized by light bands of feldspar and quartz alternating with darker bands of biotite mica and hornblende. Almost all of the ridges of the Highlands have gneiss outcrops, usually with conspicuous, steeply-dipping mineral bands. It is the northeast-southwest orientation of this

Figure 4-5. Precambrian gneiss: Black Rock Forest

gneissic banding—easily seen on summits in Harriman Park and Black Rock Forest (Figure 4-5)—that accounts for the direction of most Highlands ridges. These granite gneisses (as well as other metamorphic Highlands rocks) were originally formed, under conditions of extreme heat and pressure, miles below the surface of the earth. Subsequently, they were exposed by a combination of uplift and erosion.

Several varieties of gneiss may be found in the Hudson Highlands, including the Storm King Gneiss, a metamorphosed granite which is particularly resistant to erosion. This type of gneiss forms the summits of Bear Mountain, Dunderberg, and Storm King. Other types of rocks are also occasionally found in the Highlands. One example is marble, a rather soluble rock, which forms narrow bands, rarely conspicuous and typically hidden beneath stream valleys.

Another mineral found in the Highlands is magnetite, an oxide of iron, which occurs in thin layers or veins. The presence of magnetite gave rise to the iron-mining industry, important during Colonial times and in the nineteenth century. Ore from the Highlands was processed in a number of furnaces located in and around present-day Harriman Park. Obtaining fuel for these furnaces required the cutting of vast expanses of woodland.

Stretching south along the east side of the Hudson River, from the Hudson Highlands to New York City, lies a folded metamorphic terrain made up of several different formations. Each of these formations was once buried several thousand feet below the surface of the earth. Now exposed by erosion, they are found in elongate outcrop bands that trend approximately north-northeast.

Most of the bedrock of Manhattan consists of the durable early-Paleozoic Manhattan Schist, which provides the firm foundation needed to support the city's skyscrapers. Steeply dipping layers of contorted, mica-rich schist may be found in the low hills and ridges of Manhattan's Central, Inwood Hill, and Fort Tryon parks.

To the north, from the Bronx through Westchester County, schist exposures alternate with valleys underlain by marble and ridges capped by Fordham or Yonkers Gneiss (Figure 4-6). These gneiss formations are Precambrian in age, with radioactive dates up to 1.1 billion years. In most places, the schist-marble-gneiss bedrock of Westchester County expresses itself in a gentle, rolling landscape, typical of the county's parks and preserves. Here and there, bedrock outcrops—especially of the gneisses—form bold ridges or knobs, though never much higher than 800 feet above sea level.

Figure 4-6. Typical specimen of the Fordham Gneiss—a Precambrian-aged formation of Westchester County.

Northwest of the Hudson Highlands lies a broad expanse of Paleozoic rock outcrops, generally lower in elevation than the Highlands. The region is sometimes called the Great Valley—in contrast to the Highlands and the still-higher Shawangunks and Catskills further northwest (see Figure 4-1). The Great Valley extends northeast and northward on both sides of the Hudson River. Despite its low elevation, this expanse is part of the Appalachian Fold Belt and has experienced several episodes of folding. Because most of the strata of the Great Valley (formed in the Cambrian and Ordovician eras) are composed of relatively weak shales and limestones, most of the folds have long ago been worn down to elevations of only a few hundred feet above sea level (see Figure 4-2).

Most of Dutchess County lies within this Great Valley. Some of the hiking areas in this county feature low elongate hills or ridges, which represent slightly

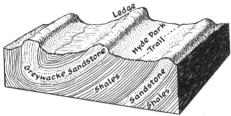

Figure 4-7. Ordovician strata, folded and eroded, now outcropping in Dutchess County just east of the Hudson River.

more resistant beds of graywacke sandstones interbedded with otherwise easily eroded shales of the Ordovician era. These hills are characteristic of the riverside parklands near Hyde Park (Figure 4-7).

Twenty-five miles north-west of the Hudson Highlands, across the worn-down Great Valley, rises a long, narrow mountain range—the Shawangunks. Approaching the range from the southeast, the elevations of the Great Valley increase by several hundred feet to form the lower slopes of the Shawangunks. The bedrock of these slopes consists of Ordovician shale which is much folded and occasionally contains marine fossils. But the ridges and cliffs of these mountains are formed of a white, extremely durable quartz pebble conglomerate of the Silurian era (Figure 4-8). The highest elevations in the Shawangunks are over 2,000 feet above sea level.

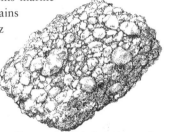

Figure 4-8. Typical specimen of Silurian Shawangunk Conglomerate.

This hard conglomerate bedrock—composed almost entirely of quartz—has formed spectacular cliffs throughout the Shawangunk Mountains. These cliffs, with near-vertical cracks and step-like layers, are world-famous for rock climbing. Climbers call this region "the Gunks." The Shawangunks are part of the Appalachian Fold Belt.

Followed further west, the beds of conglomerate dip down into the Rondout Valley, which is eroded onto the Silurian-Devonian limestones and shales that were folded along with the conglomerates during the Acadian Orogeny. The Rondout Valley is the westernmost extent of the Appalachian Fold Belt in New York. The Catskills, which adjoin the Rondout Valley, are part of an unfolded section of the earth's crust known as the Allegheny Plateau.

The Catskills are the highest mountains in southern New York. Its bedrock, which is thousands of feet thick, is composed of alternating layers of Devonian sandstones and shales as well as some conglomerate beds, usually consisting of pebbles of various compositions, set in a reddish matrix (Figure 4-9). Nearly flat-lying, these rock layers are the remains of an enormous compound delta formed at the foot of an ancient mountain chain that rose well to the east of the present-day Catskills (in what is now New England) during the Acadian Orogeny. Elevated by a series of uplifts, the delta became a plateau.

Erosion over the course of millions of years has gradually altered the plateau. Streams have cut the deep valleys or "cloves" so typical of the Catskills, leaving areas of steep-sided "mountains" between them. This erosion has removed the portion of the plateau that once reached across the

Figure 4-9. Typical specimen of Devonian conglomerate of the Catskill Mountains.

Great Valley, resulting in the impressive Escarpment—familiar to hikers—that marks the easternmost boundary of the Catskills. Figure 4-10 shows the relationship of these mountains to the adjacent Appalachian Fold Belt, while Figure 12-1 suggests the stages of millions of years of erosion that carved a mountainous region from a plateau.

Schunemunk Mountain lies just to the northwest of the Hudson Highlands. Seen from space, this eight-mile-long mountain resembles ridges in the Highlands, having approximately the same northeast trend. However, Schunemunk is made not of Precambrian rocks (such as the gneiss of the nearby Highlands), but of sandstone and conglomerate rocks from the Devonian era.

Most of the strata encountered by the hiker ascending the trails of Schunemunk are gray sandstones—part of a 2,000-foot-thick formation. But near the summit, a remarkable change takes place. Capping the high crests of the ridge is the Schunemunk Conglomerate. Sometimes called "puddingstone," this conglomerate contains many well-rounded pebbles of white quartz and pinkish sandstone in a reddish-purple matrix (Figure 4-11). The largest pebbles

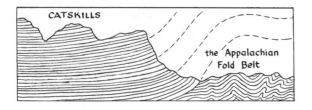

Figure 4-10. Relationship of the Catskill Mountains to the adjacent Appalachian Fold Belt.

are seven or eight inches in diameter, but most are only an inch or two across. Schunemunk Conglomerate greatly resembles the conglomerates found high in the Catskills (for example, at Sunset Rock on the Escarpment Trail and atop Slide Mountain), and both formations are of similar geologic age (see Figure 14-2).

Much of Schunemunk is a geologic syncline that now rises as a double-ridged mountain. This folded structure reflects the last of the plate collisions to produce orogenic folding in eastern North America—the collision between the plate we now know as Africa and the North American continent, which took place toward the end of the Paleozoic era. Subsequently, this interaction was reversed: the two plates began to move apart, and an intervening oceanic crust began

Figure 4-11. Typical specimen of the Devonian Schunemunk Conglomerate.

to form and widen. This tensional movement (or rifting) also caused a number of great breaks to develop roughly parallel to our coastline. These became the major faults that are found along the eastern United States, from Virginia to Massachusetts. Strips of crust adjacent to these faults began to subside about 200 million years ago, forming basins (or rift valleys) similar to those forming today in East Africa. In our region, the Ramapo Fault is the northwestern boundary of an ancient rift valley, labeled Mesozoic Lowland in Figure 4-4.

Beginning late in the Triassic period, much sediment was deposited in this broad valley. Under pressure, these sediments were transformed into shales and reddish-brown sandstones (the latter is the stone used to construct the familiar brownstone houses of Manhattan). Both crustal subsidence east of the Ramapo Fault and sedimentation continued into the Jurassic period. They were followed by an intrusion of magma that hardened into igneous rock, forming the rock outcropping across the Hudson River from New York City known as the Palisades.

The Palisades of the Hudson River were given their name by reason of their resemblance to the vertical log walls that protected early settlements in the area. The cliffs extend for over 35 miles, from Jersey City, New Jersey to Haverstraw, New York. At Haverstraw, the Palisades ridge curves inland, and it disappears just before reaching the Ramapo Fault—the boundary between the Precambrian Highlands and the Mesozoic Lowland (Figure 4-4).

The Palisades ridge along the Hudson is the edge of a *sill*, a layer of molten material that forced its way between the layers of shale and sandstone that comprise the Mesozoic Lowland (Figure 4-12). These strata, as well as the intrusive sill, all tilt downward toward the west. The Palisades are made up of a rock called diabase, of essentially the same composition as volcanic basalt, but with a coarser texture that reflects slower cooling underground. This very durable rock stands out as a prominent ridge above the adjacent, more easily eroded sedimentary layers of the Mesozoic Lowland (Figure 4-1).

Wherever we hike in our area, whether the bedrock is Mesozoic (as in the Palisades), Paleozoic (as in the Catskills, Schunemunk, or the Shawangunks), or Precambrian (as in the Hudson Highlands), it is more than likely that we will find evidence of a much more recent geologic phenomenon—the glaciers of the Ice Age. During the last two million years, great ice sheets (similar to those of modern Antarctica) spread southward from northern Canada into the United States (Figure 4-13). There were at least four distinct periods of ice advance, each advance being separated by hundreds of thousands of years from the others. Between the periods, the ice sheets melted away. Each sheet left a deposit of debris—a *terminal moraine*—marking its maximum advance. The last of these major ice advances, known as the Wisconsin Glaciation, produced most of the glacial features still visible in the New York landscape.

The glaciers that passed over our region during the Ice Age were, on average, over 1,000 feet thick, covering almost every part of our landscape when they were at their maximum thickness. With embedded rock debris, the glacial ice acted as a massive grindstone, eroding hills and valleys alike. The overall effect was the smoothing of the bedrock surfaces. Where large rock fragments (carried from upglacier) were

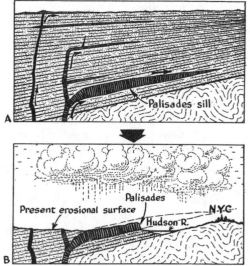

Figure 4-12. Two stages in the development of the Palisades. A: Intrusion of the Palisades sill into sedimentary strata during the Jurassic period. B: Present remnant after long-term erosion.

dragged over the bedrock, deep grooves, striations (scratches), and chattermarks were produced (Figure 4-14). Where only fine rock fragments scoured the bedrock, a gleaming polish often resulted. Glacially-smoothed bedrock is quite common in the Hudson Highlands and throughout New York state, and especially well-preserved striations, polish, and chattermarks may be found in the Shawangunks.

Bedrock knobs overridden by ice typically develop an asymmetrical profile. Smoothed by abrasion on the side from which the glacier advanced, they are steepened on the opposite or leeward site by a process of "plucking," which involves ice freezing into cracks and pulling out rock fragments. Such outcrops are called *roches moutonées*. Several good examples of these "sheep-shaped" outcrops may be seen atop Schunemunk

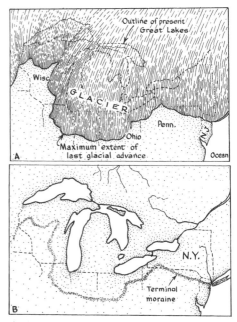

Figure 4-13. A: Maximum extent of Ice Age glaciers in Eastern United States. B: Terminal moraine after melting away of the glaciers.

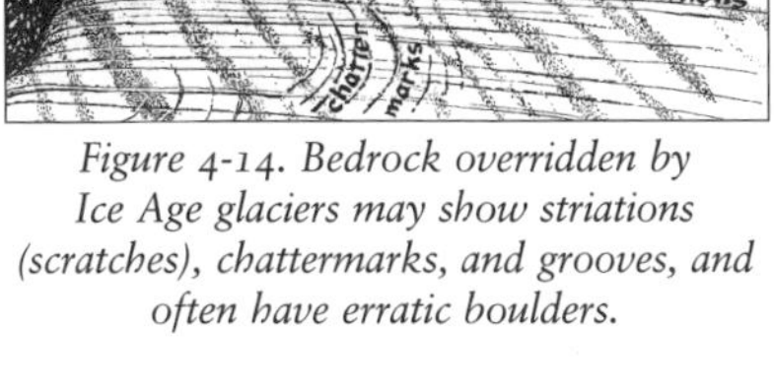

Mountain, and there are many other examples in the Hudson Highlands.

Perhaps the most widespread evidence of the great Ice Age glaciers are the "erratics"—boulders transported by ice and laid down as the ice melted away approximately 10,000 years ago. Erratics, which are most easily recognized when formed of a rock type very different from the bedrock on which they rest, may be found almost everywhere in New York state.

Figure 4-14. Bedrock overridden by Ice Age glaciers may show striations (scratches), chattermarks, and grooves, and often have erratic boulders.

Many glacial erratics have worn edges or were rounded during ice transport (Figure 15-3).

Stream valleys were often modified and deepened by the advancing ice sheets if they were oriented in approximately the same direction as the glacial movement. The Finger Lakes of upstate New York are good examples. Another example from our region is the valley of the Hudson River, which was deepened and steepened by glacial ice where the valley cuts southeastward through the Highlands. Although this glacial effect may be observed from Bear Mountain southward, the most dramatic example is the narrow passage between Storm King and Breakneck Ridge. Here, a true *fjord* has been created, the bedrock having been carved out by the glacier to nearly 1,000 feet below sea level (Figure 4-15).

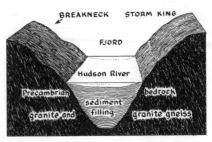

Figure 4-15. The Hudson River gorge or fjord.

Erosion also resulted from the action of glacial meltwaters. Swirling pebbles activated by the rushing water created glacial potholes, which are circular cavities cut into bedrock when meltwaters rushed through openings or crevasses near the edge of a waning glacier. Although similar in origin to potholes cut into the bedrock of river channels, glacial potholes are not confined to river valleys, but occur even high up on hillsides. A good example is the pothole cut into gneiss along the Ramapo-Dunderberg Trail, just north of the "Times Square" trail junction in Harriman State Park. Other examples are found in Inwood Hill Park in Manhattan, where several glacial potholes were cut into the Manhattan Schist.

As we have seen, a great variety of rocks may be found in southern New York, and each represents an ancient environment. The Precambrian gneisses of the Highlands formed deep below ground, as did the once-molten Jurassic diabase of the Palisades. The cliffs of the Shawangunks consist of rock layers formed in shallow Silurian seas, whereas those of the Catskills were deposited along the banks of Devonian rivers. Elsewhere in southern New York, hikers encounter rocks representing still other ancient environments and geologic ages, but *every* outcrop has some story to tell of its past.

NEW YORK CITY

Solitude and open space are in short supply within the New York City limits, but a number of places in the city still offer a respite from the bustle of the metropolis. Most of these walks are rewarding for their biological, geological, or historical significance as well as for the tranquility they offer to the city dweller. Walkers can visit valuable wetlands, stroll along rivers, or explore sites of Revolutionary War skirmishes.

More than 26,000 acres of city parkland—13 percent of New York's land area—lie in the city's five boroughs. The city is in the process of connecting many of its parks with urban greenways that eventually will total some 350 miles of "walker-friendly" trails along the coasts, overland on reclaimed transit rights-of-way, and on long-forgotten paths that have been restored.

For more information on New York City parks, contact the City of New York, Parks and Recreation, The Arsenal, Central Park, New York, NY 10021; (212) 360-8111; www.nyc.gov/parks.

THE BRONX

Named for Jonas Bronck, the Bronx is a borough of contrasts. It is densely populated yet boasts the first and third largest city parks—Pelham Bay and Van Cortlandt. The prosperous section of Riverdale is a striking contrast to burned-out buildings and high-rise public housing projects. Highways crisscross the borough, making it easy for a traveler to pass through, yet there are many places to stop and visit. Choices range from Van Cortlandt's urban forests to Orchard Beach Promenade. Walkers can find solitude if they know where to look.

Bronx Park

Bronx Park is really three parks in one—the New York Botanical Gardens, the Bronx Zoo International Wildlife Conservation Park, and Bronx Park East. The first two charge admission, but they offer lots of walking opportunities, with flora and fauna to see. Bronx Park East runs parallel to the Bronx River Parkway on the east side. It has a paved path, is accessible from numerous side streets, and is free.

R. L. DICKINSON

The Hemlock Gorge and Dam, Bronx Park   *1922*

Figure 5-1. Bronx Park

To reach the New York Botanical Gardens, take the number 4 or the D train to the Bedford Park Station and walk east to Southern Boulevard. The Gardens are also accessible via the Metro-North Harlem Line (Botanical Gardens station) and the Bx9, Bx12, Bx19, and Bx22 buses.

To reach the Bronx Zoo, take the number 2 train to the Pelham Parkway Station, walk two blocks west to Boston Road, turn left on Boston Road, and then turn right into the park; or take the Liberty Lines Express BxM11 bus.

For more information, contact the New York Botanical Gardens, 200th Street and Kazimiroff Boulevard, Bronx, NY 10458; (718) 817-8700; www.nybg.org; or the Bronx Zoo, 2300 Southern Boulevard, Bronx, NY 10460; (718) 367-1010; www.wcs.org.

Pelham Bay Park

Encompassing over 2,700 acres, Pelham Bay Park, the largest of New York City's parks, is a natural mosaic of forest, meadow, and salt marsh. Hunter Island, Twin Island, Orchard Beach, Thomas Pell Wildlife Sanctuary, numerous unmarked trails, and several short marked hiking trails are of interest to hikers. The park's recreational facilities include Orchard Beach, two golf courses, ball fields, and a running track. Orchard Beach is man-made, created in the 1930s when Robert Moses (then New York City's Parks Commissioner) filled in Pelham Bay, connecting Hunter Island to the Bronx, and brought in enough sand to create the mile-long, crescent-shaped beach.

Hunter Island is the wooded area north of Orchard Beach. It is of interest for its great trees and jutting rocks, as well as its tide pools, salt marshes, and glacial boulders. A rock of significance to the Native Americans, "Mishow," located near a cove at the northern end of the Orchard Beach boardwalk, is now almost buried by fill. "Gray Mare," an unusually formed erratic, lies off the northwestern tip of the former island. In additional to waterfowl, the park harbors great horned, long-eared, and saw-whet owls.

The Thomas Pell Wildlife Sanctuary encompasses the natural areas along the Hutchinson River and south of the park's golf courses. The tract includes woodland, salt marsh, and a tidal estuary.

To reach Pelham Bay Park by public transportation, take the number 6 train to the last stop, Pelham Bay Park. From the subway station, the Bx29 bus goes to City Island Road, the first stop over the Pelham Bridge. An 0.3-mile feeder trail to the Siwanoy Trail begins directly across from the bus stop. In the summer, the Bx5 and Bx12 buses continue from the subway station to Orchard Beach. The park is also accessible via a multi-use pedestrian and bike path that starts at the intersection of Boston Post Road and Bronx Park East and runs east along Pelham Parkway.

To reach the park by car, take either the Hutchinson River Parkway or the New England Thruway (I-95) to the City Island/Orchard Beach exit, and follow signs to the Bartow traffic circle. For the Pelham/Split Rock Golf Courses parking lot, proceed north on Shore Road for about a quarter of a mile to the golf course (on the left). For Orchard Beach (parking fee charged in season), proceed east from the traffic circle.

For more information, contact the Van Cortlandt and Pelham Bay Parks Administrator's Office, One Bronx River Parkway, Bronx, NY 10462; (718) 430-1890; www.nyc.gov/parks.

Kazimiroff Nature Trail   *Length: 1.3 miles, 1.0 mile Blazes: blue, red*
This trail is named in memory of Dr. Theodore Kazimiroff, a noted amateur naturalist, archeologist, and historian, and a friend of Pelham Bay Park. He

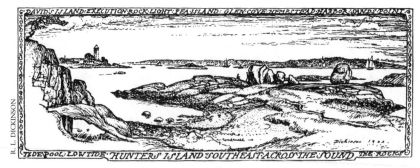

Figure 5-2. Pelham Bay Park

and other Bronx environmentalists prevented the I-95 construction from obliterating Split Rock, a glacial erratic with historic significance. Although unsuccessful in their attempts to block the Pelham Bay landfill in the center of the park, they were able to stop its expansion to other nearby marshes.

Beginning at the northern end of the Orchard Beach parking lot, the Kazimiroff Nature Trail circles Hunter Island on two partially overlapping red- and blue-blazed loops, with the blue trail the longer loop. Well-trodden side trails take hikers to "Gray Mare" and the rocky shoreline of Twin Island.

Siwanoy Trail

The trail has three sections—the Central Woodland section, which leads south to Orchard Beach, the Bartow-Pell Mansion section, which proceeds east and north to the mansion, and the Hutchinson Marsh section, which heads to the southwest. All three trail sections begin from the southern end of the Pelham/ Split Rock Golf Courses parking lot.

Central Woodland Section   *Length: 1.6 miles Blaze: yellow*

To reach this section of the Siwanoy Trail, walk across Shore Road to the trailhead. Take the right fork and proceed southward. In about 0.3 mile, the feeder trail from the bus stop on City Island Road comes in from the right. The Siwanoy Trail bears left, passing a golf driving range on the right. A short side trail leads to Glovers Rock, named for Colonel John Glover, who in October 1776 led 750 soldiers from Massachusetts in the Battle of Pells Point. They succeeded in holding off the British troops, under the command of General William Howe, long enough for George Washington to lead his Continental

Army from Manhattan north to White Plains. The trail crosses Park Drive, curves around a large meadow on the left, and soon reaches Orchard Beach, where it ends.

Bartow-Pell Mansion Section *Length: 1.0 mile Blaze: yellow*
To reach this section of this trail, walk across Shore Road and take the left fork at the trailhead. This trail route proceeds east along the shore of a lagoon (a remnant of the original Pelham Bay) used for boating and kayaking. Since the trail passes through a phragmites wetland, it may be muddy in places, especially after a rain. At 0.3 mile, the trail divides into two branches, which eventually rejoin. Hikers should stay to the right (the return route is via the other branch), soon passing a small pond on the left. Once part of the lagoon, this pond was formed when its outlet was blocked by fill. This is a good place to spot a variety of birds, particularly during migration periods. The trail ends at a rocky high point, with a view over the lagoon and Long Island Sound.

On the return trip, hikers should take the right fork and continue along the other branch of the trail, which leads past the Bartow-Pell Mansion, with its gardens and the Pell family burial plot. Built in the Federal style in 1836, the mansion was the home of the Pell family. It is now a designated historic landmark, and a small admission fee is charged when the museum is open (primarily on weekend afternoons). For more information, call (718) 885-1461.

Hutchinson Marsh Section *Length: 1.5 miles Blaze: yellow*
This section of the trail begins at the southwest corner of the golf course parking lot. After following a bridle path for some distance, the trail splits off to the right. It continues through the woods and then turns right onto the access road leading to the Hutchinson River Parkway. Soon the trail reaches the beginning of a loop. Follow the left fork, which proceeds through the Hutchinson Marsh and under a bridge. Shortly after the bridge, a side trail on the right leads through a phragmites marsh to a small island, with views over the Hutchinson River. The Siwanoy Trail continues to a junction with the Split Rock Trail, and it ends at the beginning of the loop.

Split Rock Trail *Length: 1.7 miles Blaze: none*
The Split Rock Trail leaves from the Hutchinson Marsh section of the Siwanoy Trail and proceeds north, paralleling the Goose Creek Marsh along the Hutchinson River Parkway, west of the Split Rock Golf Course. It ends at Split

Figure 5-3. Van Cortlandt Park: The Croton Aqueduct

Rock, at the southeast corner of the intersection of the New England Thruway and the Hutchinson River Parkway. Unfortunately, Split Rock is located in the middle of the interchange, making access to it difficult and dangerous. The parkway runs between the trail and the park's westernmost marshes, and there is no access from the trail to the Thomas Pell Wildlife Sanctuary.

Van Cortlandt Park

The first known inhabitants of the land that now makes up Van Cortlandt Park were the Wiechquaeskeck band of the Lenapes. One of their settlements stood on what is today called the Parade Ground. In 1639, they sold much of what is now the park to the Dutch West India Company. The Van Cortlandt family owned the property from 1699 until 1888, when the City of New York purchased it. Today, three major highways cut across the park, making access from section to section difficult. An ecology center, historic house, and recreation areas are in the southern part of the park. Of most interest to hikers are the three large tracts of woodland in the northern end of the park.

The park's Northwest Forest is between Broadway and the Henry Hudson Parkway. Three interconnecting trails have loops and informal paths which provide park users with a variety of hiking choices. The 1.4-mile Cass Gallagher Nature Trail is part of a multi-use paved trail system. Along the western part of the Northwest Forest, a bridle path follows the Yonkers Branch of the Putnam Division of the New York Central Railroad. Between 1888 and 1943, this short commuter route ran from High Bridge in the Bronx to Getty Square in Yonkers. The 1.3-mile Cross Country Trail is part of two cross-country running courses, of three and six miles, respectively, that extend south and circle the Parade Ground. Hikers can reach the trails from Mosholu Parkway near the stables and from the Parade Ground via Vault Hill.

A second tract of woodland in the park's northern end, known as Croton Woods, is wedged between the Henry Hudson Parkway, Mosholu Parkway, and Major Deegan Expressway. Two trails—Old Putnam and Old Croton Aqueduct—run the length of the Croton Woods. The former is an abandoned rail line—the Putnam Division of the New York Central, which ran between High Bridge in the Bronx and Brewster in Putnam County. The railroad ceased passenger operations along this line in 1958, but it carried occasional freight until 1981. The 1.5-mile portion in the park serves as a wildlife corridor as it passes through wetlands and divides the Van Cortlandt Golf Course. Portions of the 1.2-mile John Kieran Nature Trail, which begins and ends near the Van Cortlandt Golf House, follow the Old Putnam Trail. The 1.1-mile Old Croton Aqueduct Trail also runs through the center of Croton Woods. This trail follows a short section of the 41-mile-long aqueduct that brought water from the Croton Dam in Westchester County to New York City. Built about 1840 as the city's first extensive water supply, it was largely replaced by the New Croton Aqueduct in 1890, but it remained in service until 1955. An informal path connects the Old Croton Aqueduct Trail with the Old Putnam Trail at the north end of the golf course, permitting hikers to make a loop. Access to the trails is from the Van Cortlandt Golf House and Yonkers.

Finally, the Northeast Forest is between the Major Deegan Expressway and Van Cortlandt Park East. Two major unnamed trails cross the area. One parallels the Major Deegan Expressway; the other runs east-west toward the Croton Woods. A network of informal trails criss-crosses the forest, but they are overgrown and hard to follow. Access to the area is through the service road from Van Cortlandt Park East, from Yonkers, and via the trails from Croton Woods.

The 1.7-mile John Muir Nature Trail crosses the park from west to east, connecting the three woodland tracts in the northern area of the park. It begins at the pedestrian bridge over the Henry Hudson Parkway, a short distance east of the stables, and runs east to the intersection of East 233rd Street and Van Cortlandt Park East.

Buses along the west side—the Bx9, Westchester Beeline 1, 2, and 3, and the Manhattan Express Bus BxM3—provide access to the Northwest Forest. The Bx16, Bx34, Westchester Beeline 4, 20, and 21, and the Manhattan Express Bus BxM4B provide service to the east side of the park and the Northeast Forest. The 242nd Street station of the number 1 and 9 trains is at the southwest corner of the park, while the Jerome Avenue station of the number 4 train provides access to the southeastern corner.

For more information, contact the Van Cortlandt Park Administrator's Office, One Bronx River Parkway, Bronx, NY 10462; (718) 430-1890; www.nyc.gov/parks.

BROOKLYN

First settled in 1636, Bruekelen, as it was then known, was a stronghold of religious freedom. As a result, it welcomed diverse groups, reflected now as a melting pot of contrasting customs in its multi-ethnic neighborhoods. Brooklyn is also a borough of churches and synagogues, with every block boasting another one. Walkers can develop routes reflecting various themes. A walk over the Brooklyn Bridge to Manhattan can be a daily commuter route or a recreational stroll. Esplanades in Brooklyn include the Brooklyn Heights and Shore Road promenades, the Coney Island Boardwalk, and the Manhattan Beach Esplanade. A portion of the Brooklyn-Queens Greenway is described in the Queens section.

Prospect Park

Frederick Law Olmstead and Calvert Vaux designed Prospect Park in the late 1860s. Its 526 acres are divided into Long Meadow, a woodland section, and a lake. The 100-acre forested area lies across a *terminal moraine* (an accumulation of earth and stones carried and finally deposited by a glacier). Its southern sector is dominated by tulip trees. To the north, a steep valley and stream with a series of glacial knobs and kettles have oak, sycamore, and Norway maples. The roads inside the park are closed to vehicular traffic on weekends. Unmarked trails meander around the grounds. To reach the park, take the number 2 or 3 train to Grand Army Plaza or Prospect Park.

MANHATTAN

This ultimate urban area offers something different to walkers—"theme hikes" by which routes can be charted according to architecture, churches and synagogues, or the city's many and varied neighborhoods. The pedestrian walkways on the George Washington, Brooklyn, and Henry Hudson bridges offer unique views, while Battery Park and the East River Esplanade bring the walker close to a river. Urban parks, while they do not offer the same solitude as their rural counterparts, nevertheless provide a respite from the hustle of city life. It is possible, with surprisingly little road walking, to circumnavigate Manhattan on foot, always near the water, or to walk on auto-free paths from Greenwich Village to the South Street Seaport.

Riverside Park

Seven miles long, Riverside Park is the longest urban waterfront park in the United States. Frederick Law Olmstead and Calvert Vaux—the great architects of Central Park and close to eighty other parks—designed the park from West 72nd Street to approximately 125th Street, but it is not the Riverside Park of today. At that time, the waterfront was too valuable to be included as parkland and was best used for a railroad and shipping docks. Robert Moses, in the late 1930s, used landfill from the Eighth Avenue subway to create the present park, which extends north to Fort Washington Park under the George Washington Bridge.

The park's trail system comprises three north–south

Figure 5-4. Riverside Park

walkways: one along the river, the sidewalk along Riverside Drive, and the third winding between the first two, with frequent connections. Each path is at a different elevation in this terraced park and thus offers its own unique perspective on the nature of the park. In 2001, the paved riverfront path is not continuous, although dirt paths fill the gaps.

Highlights of a walk through Riverside Park include the 79th Street boat basin and arcaded rotunda; the Soldiers and Sailors Monument, a classically designed Civil War memorial at the Riverside Drive level at 89th Street; the community gardens at the intermediate level at 90th Street; and Riverside Church and President Ulysses S. Grant's Tomb at about 120th Street.

Above 123rd Street, it is necessary to walk a short distance alongside a highway entrance. The reward is a look at the iron arched understructure of the Riverside Drive viaduct that links the original Riverside Park with its newer segment above 135th Street. At 137th Street and again at 144th Street, walkers can enter Riverbank State Park, built on the roof of a sewage treatment plant.

The park is readily accessible via public transportation. The M5 bus travels along Riverside Drive from 72nd to 135th Street; the M11 runs from there to Riverbank State Park and connects with the Bx19 bus. The Bx6 bus provides access from 155th to 161st streets. Access from the number 1 and 9 trains is by walking west from the subway stations.

Fort Tryon and Inwood Hill Parks

These two parks, located at the northern tip of Manhattan, have an extensive network of paths (mostly paved) that wind over and around rock outcrops and along the Hudson and Harlem rivers. Readily accessible by public transportation, the parks are popular with local residents, but they are also worth a visit by people living elsewhere.

The 200-acre Inwood Hill Park is situated at the junction of the Hudson and Harlem rivers in the northwest corner of Manhattan Island. Extending from Dyckman Street to the Spuyten Duyvil, it features the last natural forest and salt marsh in Manhattan. For the early Native Americans, the area offered shelter from the icy winds that made Manhattan's rocky ridge inhospitable, a good freshwater spring, and level planting fields. Fish, especially shad, were in ample supply, and the surrounding forests provided bear, deer, and beaver. The park is perhaps best known for several rock shelters used by the Native Americans, who called their village "Shorakapok." Large quantities of oyster shells

Figure 5-5. *Rock shelters at Inwood Hill Park*

and many artifacts were found in and near these rock shelters. The artifacts are now archived at the National Museum of the American Indian, One Bowling Green, New York, NY 10004; (212) 514-3700.

To reach the rock shelters, enter the park at Isham Avenue (one block north of 207th Street). Proceed west and then north along paved paths which run directly along the base of the hill, with fenced-in ballfields and open grassy fields to your right. At the end of the grassy fields, you will come to a rock monument at a junction of paved paths. A plaque on the rock commemorates Peter Minuit's "purchase" of Manhattan from the Native Americans in 1626, which supposedly took place at this location. Turn left (south) here and proceed for about 200 feet along the paved path. Just past a campfire circle, a path leaves to the right and goes uphill to the rock shelters.

From here, walkers can continue north on the paved path, which leads to the Harlem River. Across the river are the tracks of the Metro-North Hudson Line, with a deep rock cut to the east. To the west, the swing bridge of Amtrak's line to Penn Station crosses the river at the Spuyten Duyvil. The path continues under the Henry Hudson Bridge and curves south, running between the Henry Hudson Drive on the left and the railroad tracks on the right. (Just before reaching the bridge, a crumbling paved path goes off to the left and leads up to the highest point in the park. It continues southward, providing an alternative route for those who may want a more challenging hike.)

Soon the paved path curves to the right and crosses the Amtrak line on a pedestrian footbridge which leads to the riverfront section of the park. Continue ahead, past a ballfield, and turn left on the path that runs along the Hudson River. Across the river is the Englewood Boat Basin of the New Jersey Section of the Palisades Interstate Park, with the buildings of St. Peter's College to the south along the cliffs. Continue south along the river to Dyckman Street, where the park ends.

Fort Tryon Park is best known for The Cloisters, a branch of the Metropolitan Museum of Art, with its extensive collection of medieval art. The landscaped Heather Garden, with a large variety of flowers, is at the southern end of the park, just north of the entrance from Fort Washington Avenue.

To reach these parks, take the A train to the 190th or 200th Street (Dyckman Street) stations for Fort Tryon Park, or to the 200th or 207th Street stations for Inwood Hill Park. At the 190th Street Station, take the elevator up to Fort Washington Avenue; the park entrance is just to the right. From the 200th and 207th Street stations, walk west to the park entrances.

QUEENS

The largest in land area of the five boroughs, Queens is mostly a residential area of erstwhile small towns. Residents, when asked where they live, will reply with a local neighborhood name, such as Whitestone or Bayside. The rolling kettle-moraine topography that existed in the 1920s has long since given way to development. The kettle hole ponds are wholly or partially filled in. Yet, walkers can find places to go in the network of parks and greenways.

Alley Pond Park

Located in eastern Queens amid some of the busiest highways in New York, Alley Pond Park contains fresh and salt water marshes, oak uplands, and *glacial kettles* (ponds). One kettle, Oakland Lake, is stocked with black bass. Among the species that survive in the park are muskrat, flying squirrel, opossum, and raccoon. Migratory waterfowl frequent the wetlands. North of Northern Boulevard, a paved pedestrian path along the Cross Island Parkway provides a pleasant three-mile walk along Little Neck Bay to Fort Totten. About halfway, an overpass leads to Crocheron Park, which features a small pond just off the parkway.

Near the Winchester Boulevard parking lot at the south end of the park is a pedestrian path that is a remnant of the original Vanderbilt Motor Parkway. Located on Northern Boulevard just east of the Cross Island Parkway intersection, the Alley Pond Environmental Center maintains trails and conducts educational programs.

Alley Pond Park is accessible by car from Northern Boulevard and via the Q12, Q30, and Q75 buses. For more information, including a guide to trails, contact the Alley Pond Environmental Center, 228-06 Northern Boulevard, Douglaston, NY 11363; (718) 229-4000; www.alleypond.com.

Brooklyn/Queens Greenway

In 2001, the Brooklyn/Queens Greenway extends a distance of 21 miles from Highland Park on the Brooklyn/Queens border to Fort Totten in Queens. It is designed as a multi-use trail for both hikers and bicyclists and is marked by green signs along the route. The ten-mile section described below extends from Flushing Meadow Park through Kissena Corridor Park, Kissena Park, Cunningham Park, and Alley Pond Park.

The route begins at the Willets Point station of the Flushing Line (number 7 train) on the Flushing Meadow Park road. It bears left at the end of the boardwalk and continues past the pitch-and-putt golf course. It then proceeds over the Flushing River, turns left under the Van Wyck Expressway at the first crossroad, and crosses a pedestrian bridge which leads to the Queens Botanical Garden. The route continues on the path straight ahead, which leads to Main Street. Here, the walker should turn right and then turn left onto 56th Street, passing fenced-in boccie courts on the corner. Just past the end of the courts, there is an opening in the fence. Turn left here onto a dirt path (diverging from the official greenway route, marked with the green signs), then immediately turn right and continue along a clearly defined path that runs along the fence to the right.

The route that this path follows, the Kissena Corridor Park, is actually the right-of-way of the former Central Railroad of Long Island, constructed about 1870 from Flushing to Babylon via Floral Park, and abandoned in 1879. Hardly any trace of this original use can be seen over a century later, but the fortuitous circumstance of the railroad following this route has resulted in its preservation as an open space corridor through this now heavily-populated area.

Follow the dirt path along the fence line until you reach a playground. At the far end of the playground, the path turns sharply left. Then, in another 100 feet, turn right on another dirt path which continues behind a row of houses to a paved path just before the stands for a soccer field. The path bears left, then turns right and follows the fence along the soccer field to Rose Avenue.

Now rejoining the official route designated with greenway markers, the walker should cross Rose Avenue and enter Kissena Park, following the paved path to the right which runs along the right side of Kissena Lake. At the end of the park, the marked route crosses 164th Street and continues ahead along Underhill Avenue, where there is a wide grassy strip to the right. Where the road bends to the left, the greenway markers lead to the right, following a paved trail through a grassy corridor. The corridor soon becomes a narrow strip of parkland running between Peck Avenue on the south and Underhill Avenue on the north. Much of the corridor here is occupied by playgrounds and ballfields, so walkers must follow the sidewalks or adjacent grassy strips.

The greenway markers lead up to a pedestrian bridge over the Long Island Expressway. After crossing the highway, the route bears left and then continues ahead through an open area, with a row of trees and a playground on the right. When it reaches Francis Lewis Boulevard, the walker should turn sharply right, away from the boulevard, and follow a macadam path back to 199th Street. To the left is a roadway leading into the woods. This is the western end of the Vanderbilt Motor Parkway, a private limited-access road used from 1903 to 1938. The greenway route follows the former parkway to an open grassy area. At its far end, it crosses a footbridge over Francis Lewis Boulevard and goes into the woods. Continuing on a path, it heads to the ballfields and a tunnel under the Clearview Expressway. Follow the path to the right, crossing a bridge, and continue along the old motor parkway.

The greenway route continues along the Vanderbilt Motor Parkway for almost two miles—the longest unbroken stretch of the old highway that still exists—and goes under the Grand Central Parkway and into Alley Pond Park. The road ends at Winchester Boulevard, where a ramp dead-ends at the site of a proposed bridge over the boulevard. Walkers can take the Q46 bus back to the Kew Gardens station for the E or F trains.

For those who wish to continue their hike, the greenway route continues north under the Grand Central Parkway and into the main portion of Alley Pond Park. However, as of spring 2001, this portion of the route has not yet been marked. While it is possible to follow existing paths through the park to Northern Boulevard and the Alley Pond Park Environmental Center, the maze of unmarked paths can be confusing to those who are not well acquainted with the park.

Jamaica Bay Wildlife Refuge

Part of the Gateway National Recreation Area, created in 1972, the Jamaica Bay Wildlife Refuge dates to 1953, when the New York City Parks Department set aside 9,155 of the bay's 14,000 acres and impounded ponds on either side of Cross Bay Boulevard. The 1.8-mile-long West Pond Trail, which loops around the 45-acre West Pond, begins at the visitor center, where walkers must obtain a free permit. Near the start of this trail, the short Terrapin Trail (closed during the summer nesting season) branches off and winds along the coastline and into a managed grassland. At its other end, the West Pond Trail merges with the Upland Trail, where markers describe the early stages of a mixed deciduous forest that includes stands of hollies, pines, and birches.

Across from the visitor center, on the east side of Cross Bay Boulevard, are the 115-acre East Pond, the smaller Big John's Pond, and a developing woodland, all of which may be reached by short trails. In the summer, when the water level of East Pond is lowered (to expose mudflats which provide feeding and resting sites for migratory birds), it is possible to walk along the entire perimeter of the pond. Waterproof boots and insect repellent are essential.

Many thousands of birds are attracted to the sanctuary, partly because of its prime location on the Atlantic Flyway and partly because the management's skillful clearing and planting make food and cover available. Visitors marvel at the chance to spot some of the more than 300 species that have been seen here, within the shadow of J.F. Kennedy International Airport. The breeding birds include great egret, snowy egret, glossy ibis, barn owl, and osprey.

By car, the visitor center may be reached by taking the Belt Parkway to Exit 17 and continuing south on Cross Bay Boulevard for three miles. To reach the park via public transportation, take the A train to the Broad Channel station, walk west to Cross Bay Boulevard, and walk north for half a mile. By bicycle, access is via the Shore Parkway Bicycle Path from Brooklyn. For more information, contact the Jamaica Bay Wildlife Refuge, c/o Gateway National Recreation Area, HQ Building #69, Floyd Bennett Field, Brooklyn, NY 11234; (718) 318-4340; www.nps.gov/gate.

STATEN ISLAND

Long the forgotten borough of New York City, Staten Island was discovered in 1524 by Giovanni de Verrazano. Henry Hudson visited it in 1609 and named it *Staaten Eylandt* in honor of the States General of the Netherlands. Staten Is-

Figure 5-6. Manhattan and Brooklyn seen from Staten Island

land was inhabited by many Native American tribes—Hackensacks lived on the north shore, Raritans on the south, and Tappans on the east. The nearby Fresh Kills—the only river to begin and end within the city limits—was used extensively as a canoe route to link these tribes with others living in Long Island, Manhattan, and New Jersey.

Staten Island (Richmond County) developed rapidly after the Verrazano-Narrows Bridge—which provided Staten Island with its first direct road connection to the rest of the city—opened in 1964. In the wake of this development, the New York State Department of Transportation proposed to construct two new limited-access roads, the Richmond and Willowbrook parkways. These roads were routed through parkland in the center of the borough which became known as the "greenbelt." Local residents were outraged at this plan, which would have destroyed the peace and quiet of the last major open space on Staten Island, and several citizens' groups were formed to oppose it. Between 1971 and 1979, the New York City Department of Parks worked with one of these groups, Conservation and the Outdoors, to establish 28 miles of trails on four footpaths. Finally, in 1984, 2,500 acres in the middle of the island—including Willowbrook Park, LaTourette Park, and High Rock Park—were formally designated the Staten Island Greenbelt, and the proposal to construct the parkways was abandoned.

Staten Island is accessible from the other boroughs via the Staten Island Ferry that leaves from the South Ferry Terminal at the southern tip of Manhattan. This ferry terminal is adjacent to the South Ferry and Whitehall Street subway stations, which are served by the 1, 4, 5, 9, and R trains, and it can also be reached via the M1, M6, and M15 buses. Many bus routes begin from the

St. George ferry terminal at the northeast corner of Staten Island, and several trailheads are adjacent to bus stops.

For more information, contact the Greenbelt Conservancy, 200 Nevada Avenue, Staten Island, NY 10306; (718) 667-2165; www.nyc.gov/parks.

Blue Trail   *Length: 13.4 miles Blaze: blue*
The Blue Trail extends from Forest Avenue on the north side of Clove Lakes Park to Brielle Avenue. It traverses scenic and mostly hilly terrain, primarily on parkland.

To reach the Forest Avenue trailhead, take the S48 bus from the ferry terminal to Forest Avenue and Clove Road. The largest tulip tree in the New York City park system is at this intersection. Fifty yards past the corner, the path begins on the left, just past a stream. It runs about a mile through Clove Lakes Park, in an old glacial valley that was dammed to create four lakes and several waterfalls. After an uphill stretch on paved paths, the trail continues through an oak-beech climax forest until it exits the park at the intersection of Victory Boulevard and Little Clove Road. Walkers who want to skip Clove Lakes Park may take bus S62 or S66 from the ferry terminal up Victory Boulevard to Slosson Avenue and walk back three blocks to Little Clove Road to pick up the trail. Here, the trail route is interrupted by the Staten Island Expressway. To get to the other side, walkers should follow the blue blazes through a gate in the fence and cross the expressway on a pedestrian overpass.

On the opposite side, the trail enters Deer Park Woods, part of the Staten Island Greenbelt, and turns right on a wide path. To the left, the Blue Extension Trail (blue X on white) leads in about 0.7 mile to Staten Island Boulevard, providing alternate access to the Blue Trail. The Blue Trail now ascends Todt Hill (410 feet). The greenish Precambrian bedrock outcrops here, as it does in the first nine miles of the trail. The trail offers the hiker a climb through a forest of birch, beech, oak, and sweetgum.

The trail bears west and then south, descending a steep bank into a never-dry kettle, one of a dozen or so such ponds in the area left behind by the retreating Wisconsin glacier. It then diagonally crosses the intersection of Todt Hill Road and Ocean Terrace. Soon, the Yellow Trail joins from the left, with both trails running jointly for several stretches in the next mile or so. The joint trails follow a path behind backyards of homes before turning into the woods behind a former seminary, now part of the Greenbelt's preserved lands. Two orange-blazed trails lead left to Priory Pond.

Figure 5-7. High Rock Park

The Blue and Yellow trails next pass the Kaufmann Campground and the Richmond County Country Club (RCCC) golf course. This golf course, purchased by New York State with Environmental Quality Bond Act funds, is on a long-term lease to the RCCC. On the left side of the trail, at the high point of the golf course, is a sitting area called The Overlook, with clear views out toward Raritan Bay, the Atlantic Highlands, and Sandy Hook. Several ponds in different stages of succession (the gradual replacement of open water with plants, then bushes, and finally trees) appear in this section, up to and including High Rock Park. The trail runs for half a mile along the glacial Richmond Escarpment, with views east to the Atlantic Ocean. Beyond the golf course lie the Moravian Cemetery and the private Vanderbilt Cemetery—the burial place of Commodore Cornelius Vanderbilt and family. The trail next enters High Rock Park, which is frequented by migrating birds and is the home of many plants. The park also offers short nature trails, a visitor center, and restrooms.

Near its midpoint, the trail crosses Rockland Avenue, where there are two options for concluding the hike: two blocks to the left, a bus stop across Richmond Road offers either the S57 to the New Dorp station of the Staten Island Railway, or the S74 bus, which goes back to the ferry terminal.

The Blue Trail continues ahead on Eleanor Street for a short distance, then turns left into the woods, as the White Trail joins from the right. Both trails cross Nugent Street and then turn right onto St. George Road, a quiet residential street. The White Trail soon leaves to the left, while the Blue Trail continues for about a mile along St. George Road until the street makes a sharp left turn at an overgrown field. In a few yards, the Red Trail joins, and both trails turn right and enter the field. (The S74 bus stop at St. Patrick's Place in Richmondtown may be reached by following the Red Trail ahead and down the hill.)

The joint Red and Blue trails turn right again and ascend a hill, emerging at the top onto a parking area for the adjacent LaTourette Golf Course, with the LaTourette House directly ahead. This historic brick building, which serves as a clubhouse for the golf course, was formerly the home of the LaTourette family, whose farms occupied the lands over which the golf course now extends. Here, the Red Trail leaves to the right, while the Blue Trail turns left and follows the guardrail along the service road to Richmond Hill Road. It crosses the road (caution should be exercised here, as this is a heavily trafficked road, with limited visibility) and immediately turns left. (It is anticipated that a pedestrian overpass will be built to eliminate this dangerous road crossing, with construction scheduled to begin in the summer of 2001.) The Blue Trail continues along a grassy strip, with a driving range to the right and woods to the left.

Just beyond a putting green, it re-enters the woods and begins to descend. The trail follows the edge of the hillside, with views of Richmond Creek—a habitat for many kinds of waterfowl—below. It passes Hessian Spring, which has provided water since colonial days, and crosses Burial Hill. On weekends, the sound of radio-controlled model airplanes may be heard to the left.

The Blue Trail turns back to the golf course at the fourth tee. At the third

Figure 5-8. LaTourette House

tee, the Yellow Trail joins, and both trails proceed in an northeasterly direction, parallel to Forest Hill Road. The trails cross Richmond Hill Road and continue along Forest Hill Road to Travis Avenue. Here, there is a stop for the S61 and S91 buses, which go to the St. George ferry terminal. After re-entering the woods, the Yellow Trail leaves to the right. The Blue Trail continues over Heyerdahl Hill, where it is briefly joined by the White Trail. At the bottom of the hill, the Red Trail touches briefly, and then the Blue Trail turns left and crosses Rockland Avenue, where there is a break in the concrete divider for hikers.

The trail crosses an open field, descends through a stand of sweetgum, crosses Manor Creek, and ascends parallel to a deep ravine known as Blood Root Valley, after the white-petalled flower found there. The ravine also contains maidenhair fern, sweet cicely, and other plants common farther south but rare here. The trail then follows the fence of the Seaview Hospital much of the way to the trailhead on Brielle Avenue and the S54 bus stop. (To reach the ferry terminal, hikers should transfer to the S62 or S66 bus at Victory Boulevard.)

Yellow Trail
Length: 7.5 miles Blaze: yellow
The Yellow Trail is the oldest trail on Staten Island, dating from 1930, but only three miles of the original route remain, the rest having been rerouted around encroaching developments. From the ferry terminal, take bus S74 or S76 to the Spring Street stop on Richmond Road. Buses back to the ferry terminal also stop at Doctors' Hospital on Targee Street, a block away from and parallel to Richmond Road, where the trail begins.

The trail ascends Spring Street and proceeds for nearly half a mile along quiet residential streets. It then enters deep woods, passing Reed's Basket Willow Swamp, originally a glacial pond, 200 yards to the right on an unmarked trail. The woodlands harbor many species of trees, shrubs, vines, and ferns.

Past the swamp, the trail begins to climb Todt Hill. After a short, steep climb and two blocks along Merrick Avenue, it crosses Todt Hill Road and follows the pipeline right-of-way briefly. It turns left at the end of the right-of-way and joins the Blue Trail. (These two trails run jointly for several stretches before reaching High Rock Park.) After running along the backs of several houses, it turns left into the woods behind a building which was formerly a seminary. In sight of the Kaufmann Campground, it goes left and then right along the Richmond Escarpment, passing Hourglass and Pumphouse ponds and the Moravian Cemetery.

Entering High Rock Park, the Yellow Trail parallels the Moravian Cemetery fence on the left and then turns right, passing the successional Loosestrife Swamp Pond. A park road to the left leads to the park visitor center and restrooms. After crossing two wooden bridges, the Yellow Trail splits into two branches.

The right branch of the trail crosses Manor Road and then proceeds around the base of an artificial hill known locally as "Moses Mountain." Named after Robert Moses, who championed the building of many expressways and bridges in New York City, this "mountain" was created from rock excavated during the construction of the Staten Island Expressway. The rocks were placed here temporarily, with the intention that they would be used to help build the planned complex interchange of Richmond Parkway, Willowbrook Parkway, and Rockland Avenue—which would have been located right in the heart of the Staten Island Greenbelt. Due to strenuous opposition from local residents, this interchange has never been built, and it is unlikely to be constructed in the future. The artificial "mountain"—also known as Hawk Hill—offers 360° views of the Greenbelt. The left branch of the trail continues along a branch of Richmond Creek and rejoins the right branch at the intersection of Manor Road and Rockland Avenue.

The Yellow Trail now crosses Rockland Avenue at a bus stop and runs along Meisner Avenue for 100 feet before bearing right and entering the woods of the Bucks Hollow section of the Greenbelt. Soon, the White Trail joins and, in another 0.2 mile, the Red Trail also joins. All three trails run together for a short distance. The Red and Yellow trails then bear left, leaving the White Trail, and both trails continue for 0.2 mile to a junction. Here, the "tail" of the Red Trail turns left towards the LaTourette Golf Course clubhouse and Richmondtown, while the Yellow Trail, together with the loop of the Red Trail, proceeds ahead through a wet area, crossing two bridges. The Red Trail then leaves to the right. The Yellow Trail continues ahead and soon joins the Blue Trail. Both trails turn left and head towards Forest Hill Road. At Travis Avenue, where the trails begin to run along the golf course, there is a stop for the S61 and S91 buses, which go to the St. George ferry terminal.

The combined Yellow and Blue trails parallel Forest Hill Road at the edge of the golf course, soon crossing Richmond Hill Road. They continue along Forest Hill Road and then follow an old dirt road which leads to the third tee of the golf course. Here, the Blue Trail continues ahead, while the Yellow Trail turns right into the woods and skirts a wet area to the left where swamp cabbage grows alongside a stream. The Yellow Trail reaches Forest Hill Road behind a garage for buses of the New York City Transit Authority. It crosses Forest Hill Road and continues along the road (following yellow markers on the telephone poles) to the trailhead at Richmond Avenue, where the S44 bus leads back to ferry terminal.

Red Trail   *Length: 4.2 miles Blaze: red*

Inaugurated in 1970, the Red Trail is a "lollipop"-shaped loop trail, which begins and ends at the Richmondtown Restoration at St. Patrick's Place and Richmond Road, which may be reached by the S74 bus from the ferry terminal.

Richmondtown was once called Cocklestown because of the mounds of shells left by the original inhabitants. It became the county seat in 1730 and remained so for two centuries until it was eclipsed by the development of St. George on the northeast corner of Staten Island (where the ferry terminal is located) and lapsed into obscurity. In the 1960s, the Staten Island Historical Society undertook its restoration. Visitors can see many restored and sometimes transplanted houses reflecting 300 years of American history.

From the trailhead, the Red Trail climbs a small hill. It joins the Blue Trail where it turns left into an overgrown field. Both trails bear right and ascend another hill, emerging at the top onto a parking area for the adjacent LaTourette Golf Course, with the LaTourette House—the historic brick building which serves as a clubhouse—directly ahead. The clubhouse, which has a restaurant and restrooms, is open year round. Here, the Blue Trail leaves to the left, while the Red Trail continues through the parking area, crosses Edinboro Road at a stop sign, and turns right. It re-enters the woods and follows the blazes along the edge of the golf course, crossing a bridge over the outlet of a seasonal pond and passing through a small meadow (which offers excellent bird watching opportunities). The Red Trail then descends into Bucks Hollow, a beech-and-oak woodland, with areas of birch and sumac, where it joins the Yellow Trail. This intersection is the end of the "tail" of the loop of the Red Trail; the loop itself begins here, and one can go either left or right.

Following the loop to the right, the Red Trail begins to run jointly with the Yellow Trail. In another 0.2 mile, the White Trail also joins. All three trails continue jointly for 500 feet. The Yellow and White trails then bear right, while the Red Trail turns left and begins to parallel Rockland Avenue. After the Blue Trail touches briefly, the Red Trail turns left and gradually ascends

Heyerdahl Hill (238 feet). At the top of the hill, a short orange-blazed trail leads left to the homesite of the Heyerdahl family. Built in the first half of the nineteenth century, the home adjoined a vineyard (which lasted until Prohibition in the early twentieth century). Today, all that remains is the foundation of the house and its front steps. (The orange-blazed trail continues beyond the Heyerdahl homesite and ends at the White Trail.)

After the White Trail joins briefly, the Red Trail proceeds downhill and through a wet area. It then gradually ascends to a junction with the Yellow Trail. Here, the Red Trail turns left and begins to run jointly with the Yellow Trail, crossing two bridges and finally reaching the intersection where the loop begins. To return to the trailhead on Richmond Road, turn right and follow the red blazes to the golf course clubhouse, then bear left through the parking area and continue down the hill.

White Trail
Length: 4.2 miles Blaze: white

The White Trail begins at the intersection of Morani Street and Victory Boulevard, a stop for the S62 and S92 buses from the St. George ferry terminal. It proceeds south through Willowbrook Park, passing softball fields on the left and Willowbrook Pond on the right. At 0.3 mile, it passes the Carousel for All Children and then goes through a large stand of tulip trees blown down during a severe storm in 1999. It passes an archery field on the left at 0.8 mile, turns right, and crosses several bridges. There is an old stone chimney by the third bridge at 1.3 miles. After traversing a wet area, with the College of Staten Island on the left, it goes along a rather narrow strip of land (the route acquired for the de-mapped Willowbrook Parkway) between a baseball field and a residential area.

At 2.1 miles, the White Trail crosses Forest Hill Road and borders the Great Swamp to the left. It then crosses Rockland Avenue and ascends Heyerdahl Hill. Near the top of the hill, at 2.6 miles, it briefly turns left onto the route of the Blue Trail. The White Trail soon turns right, leaving the Blue Trail, and descends to Bucks Hollow. A short orange-blazed trail which departs to the left at 3.1 miles leads to the foundation of the Heyerdahl family's home and continues to the Red Trail.

After passing a swamp on the right, the combined Red and Yellow trails join from the right, and all three trails run concurrently for a short distance. The Red Trail then departs to the left, and the White and Yellow trails continue ahead, cross a bridge, and reach Meisner Avenue at 3.6 miles. The S54 and S74 buses stop here. The Yellow Trail now turns left and heads to "Moses Mountain," while the White Trail crosses Meisner Avenue and passes through Egbertville Ravine, with a stream on the left. It crosses the stream, climbs a small rise, and descends to cross Eleanor Street, where the Blue Trail joins. Both trails cross Nugent Street and then, at 4.0 miles, they turn right onto St. George Road, a quiet residential street.

In a short distance, just past Nadine Street, the White Trail turns left and proceeds to the intersection of Richmond Road and Reidel Avenue—a stop for the S54 and S74 buses—where the trail presently ends. There are plans to extend the trail south to Great Kills Park along the corridor acquired for the demapped Willowbrook Parkway.

Great Kills Park

Located on Raritan Bay and part of the Gateway National Recreation Area, Great Kills Park offers fishing, boating, sports, swimming (in summer), and walks led by park rangers. Nature trails lead out to Crooke's Point and its ocean dunes.

In 1860, John J. Crooke purchased the peninsula now known as Crooke's Point and built a cabin there. The United States purchased the land in 1919 for an Army post. In 1929, New York City purchased the Point, and Great Kills Park opened to the public in 1949 as a New York City park. In 1974, the city deeded Great Kills Park, along with Miller Field and two off-shore islands, to the U.S. Department of the Interior, National Park Service, for inclusion in the Gateway National Recreation Area.

The climate at Crooke's Point is desert-like, with little fresh water. Beach grasses grow in the dunes away from the salt spray. The plants are fragile, and the Park Service limits access to the dunes to preserve the natural balance, requesting that hikers stay on marked trails. Plants in the area include goldenrod, bayberry, beach grass, prickly pear, milkweed, reed grass, and mullein. Along the seashore are clam and mussel shells, horseshoe crabs, blueclaw crabs, green crabs, and lady crabs. Great Kills Park is a stopping place for Monarch butterflies on their annual migration to and from Mexico. The peak time to see the butterflies is mid-September. During the day they cluster near goldenrod, Joe pyeweed, or boneset, while at night they are on the lee side of the pine trees.

For access to the park, take the S78 bus from the St. George ferry terminal along Hylan Boulevard, or the S79 bus from the 86th Street subway station in

Brooklyn's Bay Ridge. Get off at the Buffalo Street stop on either bus route and follow the paved path into the park. For more information, contact Great Kills Park, c/o Gateway National Recreation Area, 210 New York Avenue, Staten Island, NY 10305; (718) 987-6790; www.nps.gov/gate.

Clay Pit Ponds State Park Preserve

Undeveloped ponds, bogs, sandy barrens, nature woodlands, and spring-fed streams make up the 260-acre Clay Pit Ponds State Park Preserve. The moraine deposited by the retreating Wisconsin glacier stabilized the geological deposit of cretaceous sands and clay. These deposits are still visible in the park in a wide range of colors and thicknesses. It is likely that the Native Americans used these clays for their cookware. In the nineteenth and early twentieth centuries, extensive commercial clay mining was undertaken for brickworks and architectural terra cotta. As a result, the soil was depleted, and the small pockets and larger pits filled in with water to form ponds. The result is a soft underfooting of colorful sands with an occasional outcrop of smooth white kaolin.

The park has hiking and equestrian trails; however, the equestrian trails are closed to hikers.

To reach the preserve from the St. George ferry terminal, take the S74 bus to Sharrotts Road. Cross Arthur Kill Road and walk on Sharrotts Road for 0.25 mile to Carlin Street. Turn left on Carlin Street to Nielsen Avenue and the park's administration building. Guided and self-guided tours are available. For more information, contact Clay Pit Ponds State Park Preserve, 83 Nielsen Avenue, Staten Island, NY 10309; (718) 967-1976; www.nysparks.com.

SIX

LONG ISLAND

uch development and increasing traffic have choked Long Island during the second half of the twentieth century and yet, paradoxically, it is a far more exciting place to hike today than it was in earlier times. Visitors can walk the barrier beaches of Fire Island National Seashore, make north–south traverses on two National Recreational Trails, and enjoy a number of individual preserves dotting what Walt Whitman called "fish-shape Paumanok." The passage in 1993 of the Long Isalnd Pine Barrens Protection Act aided in the preservation of a core of 52,000 acres in the Pine Barrens of Suffolk County, second only to New Jersey's in size, and the Pine Barrens Trail traverses the core on a nearly 50-mile route. Ambitious plans call for extending the trail about another 80 miles to Montauk Point. As of 2001, about 45 miles of this route, from the Southampton-East Hampton town line to Montauk, have been blazed.

Geology

In most of the parks and other hiking areas of New York state, rounded ridges and broad expanses of bare bedrock are the result of many thousands of years of erosion by glaciers as they advanced southward from Canada. But what happened to the various-sized pieces of rock and soil that were plucked from Canadian and upstate bedrock by the overriding ice? Much of this debris was ultimately carried to the Atlantic Ocean, resulting in the creation of Long Island—essentially, a 120-mile-long repository of rock and soil brought from the

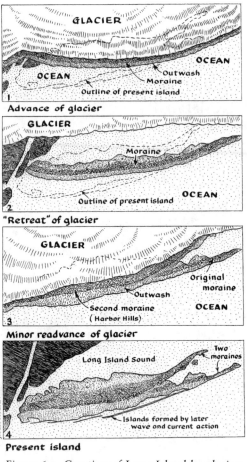

Advance of glacier

"Retreat" of glacier

Minor readvance of glacier

Present island

JACK FAGAN

Figure 6-1. Creation of Long Island by glaciers

north by glaciers.

Prior to the appearance of the Ice Age glaciers, there was probably a "proto-Long Island," consisting of a narrow outcropping of Cretaceous strata. With the advance of the mass of ice, this island—together with its shallow submarine extension to the southeast—became the site of deposition of end-glacier debris. By chance, the last advance of the ice ended at this Cretaceous outcropping. For thousands of years, an enormous number of boulders of all sizes were carried from the north and came to rest on what is now Long Island. Then, thousands of years of melting released vast amounts of finer debris— sand and silt—which spread as a broad outwash plain that slopes gently seaward from a height of about 200 feet in the middle of the island to sea level at the south shore. North of this plain are the terminal moraines—the piles of boulders and debris which stretch the length of the island. The Ronkonkoma Moraine—a band of low hills running from Lake Success, on the Queens-Nassau border, to Montauk Point—represents an early location of the end of the Wisconsin glacier. As shown in Figure 6-1, it was partially obliterated by a later advance of the ice which proceeded at a slightly different angle. The Harbor Hill Moraine, which resulted from the later ice advance, crosses the Ronkonkoma Moraine near Roslyn and proceeds eastward to Orient Point, on the north fork of the island.

The glaciers also left in their wake a number of kettle holes. These depressions—found throughout Long Island, from Queens to Montauk Point—were formed in moraine or outwash during the melting (or "recession") of the glacial margin. Blocks of ice that became separated from the main glacier as it melted away were partially or completely buried by glacial debris. When the ice blocks finally melted, a depression (or "kettle") remained. If a depression extended to below the water table, it filled with water and became a pond.

The outwash plain of Long Island once extended beyond the present shoreline. As the glacial ice melted away and the terminus of the glacier "retreated" northward, the sea level rose until it flooded most of the southern part of the outwash plain. Since the stabilization of the sea level about 6,000 years ago, ocean waves and currents have been reworking the sands of the outwash plain, creating long, narrow barrier islands along the southern shoreline. Examples of these barrier islands are Jones Beach and Fire Island.

Hiking Opportunities

Lacking high peaks and unbroken wilderness, Long Island yields its treasures more subtly to the observant walker. There is delight in finding deer or fox just minutes from a suburban tract, or in walking some of the same paths once used by Native Americans and colonial settlers. Birders, botanists, and biologists can revel in the richness of the island's species. Photographers can work in the same pure, unique daylight that has attracted generations of artists to Long Island's East End. Geologists can marvel at the abundant evidence of the last Ice Age.

The great bird migrations in spring and fall make the wetlands a feast for the eye. In May, the spring flowers brighten morainal woodlands; in June, orchids brighten the bogs; in late summer, the cranberries, blueberries, and bayberries ripen; in October, the deciduous forests present their colorful valedictory to warm, lazy days. Leaf-fall may linger into mid-November, and then begin perhaps the most satisfying times for hikers. Salmon-hued sunsets glow behind traceries of bare branches, the moorlands of the South Fork offer rugged solitude, and snow dusts the woods. Most winter days on Long Island are temperate enough for the average hiker, who can cap a day of reddened cheeks and sharpened appetite with a visit to any of the many restaurants convenient to parks and trails. There one can reflect on the essence of hiking Long Island:

enjoying the contrast of finding exquisite, undeveloped places nestled amid populous suburbs.

Knowing when to walk on Long Island is as important as knowing where. Hikers will enjoy best the months resort operators call the "off-season." From late May to mid-September, it is wise to walk early in the morning and finish by noon, especially in the warm interior. Because of the presence of deer ticks, hikers should avoid bushwhacking and check themselves periodically.

Most of the long distance trails on Long Island have been built and are maintained by the Long Island Greenbelt Trail Conference. Detailed trail maps are available for a modest fee. For a map or membership information, contact the Long Island Greenbelt Trail Conference, 23 Deer Path Road, Central Islip, NY 11722; (631) 360-0753; www.hike-li.com/ligtc.

LONG ISLAND GREENBELT TRAIL

The Long Island Greenbelt Trail, the oldest in a system developed by the Long Island Greenbelt Trail Conference, was officially established in 1978 through the cooperative efforts of the Long Island Greenbelt Trail Conference, the New York State Office of Parks, Recreation, and Historic Preservation, Suffolk County, and the towns of Islip and Smithtown. In 1982, the U.S. Department of the Interior granted National Recreational Trail status to the Long Island Greenbelt Trail. Stretching almost 32 miles from Heckscher State Park on Great South Bay to Sunken Meadow State Park on Long Island Sound, the path encompasses the drainages of the Connetquot and Nissequogue rivers, which virtually bisect the island. Along the way, one finds bay beaches, pine barrens, deciduous forests, and tidal marshes. Parts of the trail follow old Native American paths and farm-to-market roads. The trail shelters populations of deer, fox, raccoon, opossum, egret, kingfisher, and many other species.

Hiking the Long Island Greenbelt Trail is like walking in an hourglass. Large tracts of relatively undeveloped land are linked by narrow corridors within sight of suburbia; as of 2001, short sections of roadwalking remain, though most may eventually be eliminated. Though hikers seeking stretches of rugged wilderness may not find this generally flat trail to their liking, it does offer intriguing beauty and variety. Much in the fashion of Japanese gardens set in bustling urban areas, the Greenbelt's sharp contrast with its surroundings makes it memorable.

Long Island Greenbelt Trail   *Length: 31.8 miles Blaze: white*

Beginning at the east end of Parking Field 8 in Heckscher State Park, with views of Great South Bay and Fire Island, the trail follows the shoreline east and north. At 1.0 mile, it turns inland into an area noteworthy for its transition from marshland to oak and pine woods. At 1.4 miles, a blue-blazed side trail diverges right 0.3 mile to an alternative parking area at the West Marina at Timber Point County Park. At 1.8 miles, the main trail passes through a state-operated campground, open in the summer season only. Deer, fox, osprey, and pheasant inhabit Heckscher's 1,657 acres, whose picnic facilities and beaches make it a good place to end a summer hike. The trail continues north through a wooded corridor along the Heckscher Spur of the Southern State Parkway to Montauk Highway. Here, hikers can detour a few hundred yards east to the entrance of Bayard Cutting Arboretum, a 690-acre preserve notable for its conifers, spring flowers, and paths along the Connetquot River. The arboretum, closed on Mondays, contains several miles of well-marked nature walks. The Greenbelt itself continues north, crosses Union Boulevard at 3.9 miles, and enters woods east of Connetquot Avenue. The Great River station of the Long Island Rail Road, 0.1 mile north of Union Boulevard on Connetquot Avenue, provides free parking and handy trail access.

The trail crosses the tracks on a highway bridge and immediately passes through a small meadow on state-owned land that was once the Lorillard Estate, complete with two race tracks and a large circular barn, and later Westbrook Farms, a dairy. No trace remains of either. West Brook, dammed into an ice pond in the late 1800s, harbors migratory waterfowl and is a popular spot for local fishing enthusiasts. The trail crosses the dam at the south end and follows the east side of the pond to a pedestrian underpass of Sunrise Highway (NY 27) at 5.2 miles.

At this point, the trail enters Connetquot River State Park Preserve, one of the crown jewels of the Greenbelt system. Hikers can obtain a free annual permit for this preserve by writing to Connetquot River State Park Preserve, Box 505, Oakdale, NY 11769, or calling (631) 581-1005. The preserve is closed on Mondays. Formerly the Southside Sportsmen's Club of Long Island, a haunt of the wealthy and powerful, this lightly-used area of 3,473 acres is a classic pine barrens system, featuring a light canopy of pitch pine and several varieties of oak and an understory of blueberry, huckleberry, sweet fern, and other plants adapted to the desert-like, sandy outwash soil. The Connetquot River flows gently through the center of the park, affording opportunities to observe ospreys,

JACK FAGAN

Figure 6-2. The old grist mill,
Connetquot River State Park Preserve

herons, egrets, kingfishers, and a host of other species.

Near the entrance is a grist mill from the early 1700s and the large Sportsmen's Club, parts of which were built in the early 1800s; a mile north, a trout hatchery built over a century ago is still in operation. The entire section between Sunrise and Veterans Memorial highways offers a sense of solitude, in stark contrast with the busy suburbs beyond. The park's 50-mile network of trails and fire roads makes possible a variety of loop walks that take in both sides of the river and last the better part of a day.

Crossing Veterans Memorial Highway (NY 454) at 9.1 miles, the trail follows a short fire road, re-enters woods, and descends to a low-lying area known locally as Dismal Swamp. Frequent brush fires in this area may obscure the path for short distances. At 11.5 miles, an underpass of the Long Island Rail Road signals the boundary between Connetquot River State Park Preserve and Lakeland County Park to the north, where Honeysuckle Pond marks the source of the Connetquot River. A network of handicapped-accessible boardwalks allows hikers a close view of the fresh-water wetlands north of the pond.

The trail exits Lakeland County Park at Johnson Avenue, turns right, and crosses the road into a wooded corridor leading to the south service road of the Long Island Expressway (I-495). It then continues east on the service road for 0.25 mile, to an underpass at Terry Road. A short distance north of the Long Island Expressway, at 11.3 miles, the trail turns west along a Long Island Lighting Company power-line right-of-way, then diverges north through bracken fern-carpeted woodland to begin an ascent of the Ronkonkoma Moraine. The sandy soil of the flat south shore yields to coarser gravels, and north of the Long Island Motor Parkway the trail reaches an elevation of 180 feet, with a view over Long Island's North Shore. Here, oaks, maples, and hickories begin to predominate.

The trail descends the moraine through Hidden Pond Park, clinging for a time to a golf course fence, entering a grove of mixed hardwoods, then re-emerging along the fence before crossing Town Line Road, which dates from 1789, when the towns of Islip and Smithtown solved a discrepancy in competing surveys by building a road along the disputed 16-foot strip. North of Town Line Road at 14.9 miles lies McKinley Marsh, the red maple-lined source of the Nissequogue River. A visit to this area in mid-October is worthwhile for the foliage show. The trail then skirts a condominium complex, reaching NY 347 at 15.8 miles; at busy times of day, hikers can cross at a light 0.2 mile to the left, where a large farm stand is a refreshing summer stop. The route continues north through dense woods and wetlands to NY 111 at 17.6 miles. A shopping center to the north just below NY 25 provides a handy parking place.

Across NY 111, the trail swings south and west around Miller Pond, another historic ice pond, and then emerges onto Maple Avenue. Here, hikers cross and turn west for 0.7 mile of quiet roadwalking on Wildwood Lane and Juniper Avenue to Brooksite Town Park. Undeveloped land south of the road marks the course of the Nissequogue River through dense wetlands.

At 19.1 miles, the trail crosses Brooksite Drive and enters Blydenburgh County Park. With its 120-acre, L-shaped Stump Pond, early-1700s grist mill, miller's house, and quiet woods, this former estate provides a refuge amid one of Suffolk County's busiest areas. From this entrance, the 3.9-mile, blue-blazed Stump Pond Trail to the left reaches a primitive campsite intended for Greenbelt users at 0.8 mile, then continues around Stump Pond. The Stump Pond Trail stays within Blydenburgh County Park except for 0.3 mile of quiet roadwalking on the west side before rejoining the Long Island Greenbelt Trail; using both paths, hikers can circumnavigate the pond on a loop of 5.3 miles. (A short boardwalk scheduled for construction in late 2001 will eliminate the roadwalk.) The side trail affords many views of the pond with its diverse waterfowl and small Atlantic white cedar swamp near the south end. The Long Island Greenbelt Trail hugs the north side of Stump Pond, ascending at 20.5 miles to a viewpoint at the 1821 Blydenburgh-Weld House, the headquarters of the Long Island Greenbelt Trail Conference. The house is open to visitors on Saturdays.

A staircase brings the trail back to the pond at the mill complex. Beyond the dam, the blue blazes of the loop trail appear straight ahead; the main trail makes a right turn to a locked gate leading to adjacent Caleb Smith State Park Preserve. Like Connetquot, this limited-access preserve is closed on Mondays and requires a free annual permit. Write to Caleb Smith State Park Preserve, Smithtown, NY 11787, or call (631) 265-1054. When using the trail, phone

Figure 6-3. Blydenburgh County Park

ahead for the combination lock numbers for two gates here and one farther north at Sweetbriar Farm.

The trail moves away from the river into rolling wooded uplands formed by the Harbor Hill Moraine. A short, steep descent leads to a lovely stream crossing where hundreds of marsh marigolds bloom in late April. The trail ascends to a second locked gate at 21.1 miles and a crossing of busy NY 25, which bisects Caleb Smith State Park Preserve. A short roadwalk east leads to a pedestrian entrance; the hike then continues through forested terrain to Willow Pond, an arm of the river, and the park headquarters building, which houses a small nature museum. Inside this former rod-and-gun club is an impressive carving of Wyandanch, a Native American *sachem* (chief).

The trail undulates through morainal woods and crosses Peacepunk Creek as it heads northeast toward Smithtown. From a pedestrian entrance on Meadow Road, the route turns right and proceeds one-half block to a railroad underpass. On the other side, at 23.4 miles, stands a statue of a bull, commemorating Richard Smith's purchase from the Native Americans of as much land as he could encircle with his bull in one day—a ride apparently based more in legend than fact. The path crosses NY 25A and enters gently rolling woodland laced with several small streams. Parts of this area may be swampy in springtime, but boardwalks make them easy to negotiate. Here the hiker will find tulip trees, an occasional remnant chestnut, skunk cabbage, and marsh marigolds. The trail leaves the woods on an easement between two houses; just to the right at 24.5 miles is a cul-de-sac on Summerset Drive, an excellent spot for parking and car-shuttling.

The last of the three locked gates is at the end of the cul-de-sac; beyond it lies the Environmental Center of Smithtown-Setauket, also known as Sweetbriar Farm, an outdoor educational facility and wildlife rehabilitation center. Beyond, the trail is forced onto Landing Avenue and Landing Meadow Road for 1.8 miles of roadwalking, much of which may be eliminated by pending easements. The trail then follows a park road through Smithtown Landing Country Club down to the banks of the Nissequogue River. From here, the trail follows the river north through undeveloped Arthur Kunz County Park to Riviera Drive, which parallels the shore. Just before reaching the river, the trail passes through a stand of beeches, with an understory dotted with jack-in-the-pulpit and sarsaparilla. At high tide, it is possible to avoid virtually all of the roadwalk on Riviera Drive and spend considerable time exploring the water's edge. The views here are always a pleasure, though the spring and fall during the waterfowl migrations may be the most spectacular times.

The trail turns right onto St. Johnland Road for 100 yards, long enough to pass pretty Harrison Pond Park, and just south of the circa-1700 Obadiah Smith House (open on Sundays), before turning back to the shore. The blazes lead through the grounds of Kings Park Psychiatric Center, emerging upon an elevated view of the river—one of the finest vistas on Long Island—at 29.4 miles. In April 2000, approximately 150 acres of the hospital's riverfront property were dedicated as Nissequoque River State Park, with parking and restrooms available at the St. Johnland Road entrance to the park. The trail then descends to the shore and Old Dock Road Park before reaching the final hilly section in Sunken Meadow State Park. Hikers should stay on the trail to avoid eroding the tall bluffs, which offer views across Long Island Sound to Connecticut. At low tide, it is possible to follow the shore below the bluffs for an easier route or as part of a loop from Sunken Meadow. The popular state park has ample parking and picnic areas. Its beaches and breezy bluffs along the Sound are a refreshing place to end a summer hike, but for hiking it shines in the off-season.

The Long Island Greenbelt Trail is better suited for day hikes than for backpacking. However, ambitious walkers may wish to attempt a two-day traverse of the trail by making use of the campsite on the Stump Pond Trail in Blydenburgh County Park.

City residents who want to leave their cars at home can take the Long Island Rail Road to either end of the trail at the Smithtown station, 0.5 mile east of the trail, or at the Great River station, one block west of the trail. The S40, S45, S54, and S60 buses all cross the route.

Nassau-Suffolk Greenbelt Trail   *Length: 19.5 miles Blaze: white*
Previous editions of the *New York Walk Book* contained descriptions of walks in eastern Nassau County, now a densely populated area. Surprisingly, a narrow belt of open land still exists from Cold Spring Harbor south to Massapequa, and it is possible to walk most of this route today without resorting to roads. It includes picturesque ponds, moraine ridges, open fields, and a long watershed. The Nassau-Suffolk Greenbelt Trail, completed in 1986 and granted National Recreational Trail status in 1992, preserves this corridor. While this trail does not offer anything remotely resembling a wilderness experience, its incredibly diverse flora and fauna make up for the lack of isolation. Also, its northern end provides a surprising challenge to hikers expecting an easy stroll on flat Long Island.

From south to north, the trail first passes through the Massapequa Preserve, which straddles Massapequa Creek and contains a tiny remnant of the western reaches of the Long Island pine barrens. Over 175 species of birds have been spotted in this stop along the Atlantic Flyway. From Ocean Avenue and Merrick Road in Massapequa, blazes appear along the shore of Caroon's Lake. A footbridge leads away from the lake and into mixed woods, including the remnant pines. The trail reaches Sunrise Highway (NY 27) at 1.0 mile. The route proceeds east half a block to a traffic light crossing, then under the Long Island Rail Road overpass to a view of Massapequa Reservoir. The blazes continue along the west side, then head north through low-lying red maple and oak woodlands past two smaller ponds. At 3.3 miles, the path reaches a short, east–west fire road; to the east is a convenient parking access at the end of Walker Street; to the west, the trail quickly turns north again to crossings of Linden Street and the Southern State Parkway.

The Nassau-Suffolk Greenbelt Trail follows a narrow corridor along Bethpage State Parkway. Despite the presence of the road on one side and a paved bike path on the other, this section offers pleasant walking through diverse woods. Hikers should be careful, however, to avoid the thick poison ivy on the sides of the trail. At 4.9 miles, Boundary Avenue crosses above the route. At 6.6 miles, the route goes three-quarters of the way around the Bethpage Park traffic circle, then into the woods adjacent to the park's five golf courses before emerging into a relatively open area on the west side of the park. From here, a five-block walk west on Powell Avenue leads to the Bethpage Long Island Rail Road station.

At 7.5 miles, the trail veers left into rolling woodland, where lady's slippers appear in May. From here north, hikers should take care to avoid speeding mountain bikes, which use parallel and crossing paths. In order to avoid conflicts and limit trail erosion, the Greenbelt Trail Conference has been working with cycling groups to construct parallel paths between Bethpage State Park and Stillwell Woods to the north. At 8.7 miles, the trail crosses Hay Path Road.

North of Bethpage State Park, the Nassau-Suffolk Greenbelt Trail follows the right-of-way of a never-built northern extension of the Bethpage Parkway. The Plainview section of the trail traverses a narrow corridor, which includes large tracts of overgrown fields, recalling a time when the treeless Hempstead Plains stretched from here to Queens Village, and a more recent era when Nassau County was the breadbasket of New York City.

North of Washington Avenue at 10.8 miles, expressway service road construction has forced a 600-foot roadwalk under the Long Island Expressway and then a left turn to resume the trek northward through white pines, hemlocks, and oaks on the first slopes of the Ronkonkoma Moraine. From Washington Avenue, a blue-blazed side trail, the Parkway-Tower Loop, meanders 2.4 miles through rolling Manetto Hills Park to the east before rejoining the Nassau-Suffolk Greenbelt Trail below Northern State Parkway. Yet another side trail, blazed with red dots, extends eastward from the Parkway-Tower Loop to form a connection with the Walt Whitman Trail, described below.

At 12.3 miles, the Nassau-Suffolk Greenbelt Trail rises to Sunnyside Boulevard to cross the parkway. On a clear day, look westward from here for a surprising view of the Empire State Building. The woods north of here reach elevations of 300 feet before descending to a crossing of Woodbury Road and a level walk to Jericho Turnpike at 13.8 miles, where a trailside parking area is a popular spot from which to start or end a walk.

North of Jericho Turnpike, the trail is marked by signs of former inhabitants: an occasional rotting fencepost, a stand of spruces probably planted near a long-disappeared farmhouse, and broken china occasionally yielded up by frost-heaved soil. A quaint, one-lane underpass of the Long Island Rail Road at 15.1 miles brings hikers into Stillwell Woods, a Nassau County preserve characterized by scrub-oak forest and flat, open fields at the south end and peaceful morainal hills to the north. Red-tailed hawks often catch thermals here in warm weather. Some of the paths here are badly eroded, ironically opening habitat for the uncommon trailing arbutus.

At 16.7 miles, the trail crosses Stillwell Lane and descends gradually on an old railroad bed built in the 1840s, a remnant of the never-completed Hicksville and Cold Spring Branch Railroad. Large black birches, rare in this area, appear along this delightful section. A right turn leads to a footbridge and bench, a pleasant rest stop just west of NY 108.

The final 2.2 miles of the trail offer hikers the most strenuous workout available on Long Island. Elevations vary from sea level to over 200 feet in a rapid series of steep morainal hills. Large tulip poplars, white pines, white oaks, and hickories create a beautiful canopy, while thick stands of mountain laurel light up the woods in late May and early June. At 18.2 miles, a yellow side trail ascends 0.2 mile to Uplands Farm, headquarters of the Long Island Chapter of The Nature Conservancy, which allows hikers to park in its lot. North of Lawrence Hill Road, the main trail ascends Long Island's largest clay lens on a series of switchbacks, passes through more mountain laurel, and descends to the trailhead at NY 25A. The last section passes through Cold Spring Harbor State Park, established in July 2000. On the opposite side of the road is the free-flowing spring for which the historic whaling village of Cold Spring Harbor is named. Across the harbor lies world-renowned Cold Spring Harbor Laboratories. The trail ends two blocks from the shops, restaurants, and galleries of the village.

Walt Whitman Trail   *Length: 5.6 miles Blaze: white*
Walt Whitman himself doubtlessly walked some of the paths that now bear his name. The Walt Whitman Trail begins at the poet's birthplace in West Hills, an historic site that draws visitors from around the world, and it ends at the Parkway-Tower Loop of the Nassau-Suffolk Greenbelt Trail. Thus, the Walt Whitman Trail gives hikers access to a system of nearly 40 miles of trails.

From the birthplace, on Old Walt Whitman Road just west of NY 110, the trail is reached by walking up West Hills and Reservoir roads 0.6 mile to West Hills County Park. A double blaze indicates a turn to the right to enter the woods. The loop takes a sidehill route around a pretty glen, descends more gradually to a kettle hole, then winds around to the top of Jayne's Hill at 1.5 miles, the highest spot on Long Island at 400 feet above sea level. There is a view to the southwest, followed by a descent through rolling woodlands to a picnic area and parking lot at Sweet Hollow Road. Continuing south, the trail skirts the lot and recreational fields and leads to the junction of Sweet Hollow and Gwynne roads. It heads west on Gwynne Road, which quickly becomes unpaved, and continues in the woods along Northern State Parkway to Round Swamp Road at 4.8 miles. A brief roadwalk south on Round Swamp Road leads to a right turn, which takes the trail through a very narrow corridor to the Parkway-Tower Loop and the many options afforded by the Nassau-Suffolk Greenbelt Trail.

Walt Whitman Loop *Length: 4.2 miles Blazes: blue or white*
The Walt Whitman Loop, one of the most popular Greenbelt Trail walks, remains within the boundaries of West Hills County Park and includes a view all the way to the Atlantic Ocean from the top of Jayne's Hill. The walk features hills covered in oaks, maples, and hickories mixed with groves of beech and dotted with mountain laurel and trailing arbutus.

The best way to experience this trail is to park at the West Hills Picnic Area lot on Sweet Hollow Road, a short distance west of NY 110. Immediately behind the lot, blue blazes head counterclockwise. The trail makes a twisting ascent roughly eastward, then turns north on a section also used by horses. When the foliage is down, there are several views to the east across Broad Hollow to the Half Hollow Hills. At 1.6 miles, the trail crosses Reservoir Road. At this point, the white blazes of the Walt Whitman Trail supplant the blue blazes of the loop. Continue on the Walt Whitman Trail as described above to complete the loop at Sweet Hollow Road.

Other West Hills County Park Trails

A number of marked and unmarked trails crisscross this relatively unspoiled area, making a variety of loops possible. For instance, at the junction of Sweet Hollow and Gwynne roads, hikers can follow blue blazes south under the Northern State Parkway and immediately turn right into lovely woods with varying terrain. At 0.8 mile, the trail ascends to a junction with a yellow-blazed trail. The blue blazes lead hikers along the south side of a loop, with several viewpoints, and ultimately to a trailhead at Mt. Misery Road. The yellow trail yields a gentler walk, which, in another 0.6 mile, reaches the blue trail, completing a loop.

For more information, contact West Hills County Park at (631) 854-4423, or the Suffolk County Department of Parks, Recreation and Conservation, P. O. Box 144, West Sayville, NY 11796; (631) 854-4949; www.co.suffolk.ny.us/exec/parks.

THE PINE BARRENS

From the towns of Smithtown and Islip east to Hampton Bays, a distance of nearly 50 miles, lies the region of the pitch pine. Once encompassing over a quarter of a million acres, the pine barrens were decimated by development in the last half of the twentieth century. The 1993 Long Island Pine Barrens Protection Act protects a core of 52,000 acres and allows compatible growth in another 48,000. Beneath the sandy soil of the region (the glacial outwash of the Ronkonkoma Moraine) lies a huge aquifer of pure water, rising to the surface occasionally in isolated bogs. From what remains of these barrens are born the Carmans and Peconic rivers, the latter in a chain of pristine coastal-plain ponds. In the more remote sections, the gnarled pines stretch unbroken for miles. Walt Whitman described this area in *Specimen Days:* "wide central tracts of pine and scrub-oak . . . monotonous and sterile. But many a good day or half day did I have, wandering through those solitary cross-roads, inhaling the peculiar and wild aroma." The aroma comes from the pitch pines and an understory of scrub oak, blueberry, huckleberry, bearberry, wintergreen, and sweet fern—all rich in resins that promote burning. In this fire-adapted ecosystem, much of the biomass of the native plants resides underground, allowing brush fires to sweep the area and drive out competing species. This process has never been more apparent in modern times than in the brush fires that charred almost 9,000 acres in Rocky Point and Westhampton in the summer of 1995. Yet, even those vast blazes pale when compared to the 1838 fire that swept from Saint James to the Shinnecock Canal.

Deer, foxes, flying squirrels, grouse, and pheasants frequent the area. Rare lichens, insectivorous plants, and such endangered creatures as the tiger salamander greet the observant walker. Modern-day hikers who sample the barrens will find them neither monotonous nor sterile, and they still have a chance at finding solitude. Caution should be observed, however, as brush fires may alter trail routes or result in the creation of additional fire roads, which may confuse travelers in the region.

Pine Barrens Trail   *Length: 46.6 miles Blaze: white*
Officially opened by the Long Island Greenbelt Trail Conference in June 1994, the Pine Barrens Trail bisects the core area of the barrens, giving hikers the opportunity to explore the largest tracts of undeveloped land left on Long Island. The route is completely blazed from Rocky Point to the Shinnecock Canal, but likely land acquisitions and already-planned reroutes make the exact mileage subject to change. Hikers planning to traverse the three tracts managed by the New York State Department of Environmental Conservation (DEC)—Rocky Point, Navy Co-op, and Sarnoff—should obtain a free permit, good for three years, from the DEC, Building 40, State University of New York (SUNY) at Stony Brook, Stony Brook, NY 11790.

The trail begins in Rocky Point at the entrance to the DEC's Rocky Point Preserve, on the south side of NY 25A, west of Rocky Point Road. Used as a base for transatlantic broadcasting towers for decades, this 5,100-acre tract was acquired from RCA by New York State in 1978. The initial section of trail bears blue DEC markers as well as white Pine Barrens Trail blazes. The trail passes through a morainal section of hardwoods and bisects a glacial kettle hole before leveling off and swinging southeast through classic dry, upland pine barrens. A network of paths, jeep trails, and firebreaks traverses the area. Among the ground-cover plants are yellow cinquefoil, violet, hay-scented fern, and bearberry.

The trail crosses Rocky Point Road (County 21) at 3.5 miles; a yellow-blazed side trail a short distance before the road leads south 0.2 mile to a convenient parking area. On the east side of the road, hikers will notice concrete pads and blocks, anchor points for the towers of RCA's "Radio Central," scattered in the woods. At 5.2 miles, the blue DEC blazes end; red blazes head north to complete a loop of 9.9 miles back to the entrance on NY 25A. The white blazes of the Pine Barrens Trail turn south, reaching Whiskey Road and another parking area at 5.4 miles. In the vicinity of this crossing, hikers will see evidence of the 1995 fires.

Within half a mile, the Pine Barrens Trail leaves Rocky Point Preserve and enters Suffolk County's Pine Trail Preserve, a narrow corridor once slated for an extension of County 111. Here the wooded character of the trail remains, but the sense of isolation diminishes somewhat; houses occasionally are visible through the trees, and the path crosses four local roads before reaching Will-iam Floyd Parkway at 7.7 miles and a parking area on NY 25 at 8.6 miles. The Pine Barrens Trail continues south and east before opening up into Robert Cushman Murphy County Park, home of the headwaters of the Peconic River.

At 10.1 miles, the Pine Barrens Trail reaches an intersection with the Brookhaven Spur Trail (yellow), which extends north 5.3 miles through Robert Cushman Murphy County and Brookhaven State parks to a trailhead behind the parking lot of Shoreham-Wading River High School on NY 25A, in Shoreham. Similar in character to the RCA tract, Brookhaven Park was origi-nally the northern section of the U.S. Army's Camp Upton, and more recently of the Brookhaven National Laboratory. Its 2,590 acres include several small ponds but generally retain the characteristics of dry upland pine barrens.

Eastward, the land dries out briefly in an area once burned by a hot crown fire. In midsummer, the rising trill of the prairie warbler accompanies hikers. The Pine Barrens Trail crosses a footbridge between Sandy and Grassy ponds at 10.6 miles. These and the others in the chain of headwaters ponds offer view-points and are rich in plant and animal life. Insectivorous pitcher plants, sun-dew, and bladderworts line the ponds; also present are cranberries, orchids, and swamp azalea. Snapping and painted turtles abound, as do a great variety of birds. Hikers should stay away from the immediate shoreline of the ponds to prevent damage to the rare and delicate plants.

The trail crosses Schultz Road at 11.9 miles and emerges from a wetland section just south of the junction of Wading River Manor and River roads at 13.3 miles. From here eastward, hikers can expect to find reroutes in the cen-tral sections of the trail as the state and county acquire more land in the area. Currently, the trail crosses the Long Island Rail Road tracks at Mill Road. About 0.2 mile east of the tracks, an 0.7-mile yellow-blazed side trail goes off to the right and leads to the Pine Barrens Trails Information Center in Manorville, with maps, exhibits, and restrooms. Staffed by volunteers from the Long Island Greenbelt Trail Conference, the center is open during summer months and on weekends in the spring and fall. For further information, call (631) 369-9768.

East of Mill Road, the Pine Barrens Trail goes through the woods and uses short stretches of nearly deserted roads to reach an overpass of the Long Island Expressway at Halsey Manor Road. South of the overpass, the trail enters the Manorville Hills and heads eastward, parallel to and near the Long Island Ex-pressway. Nearly completed acquisitions here will make possible a more desir-able route through spectacular morainal hills with several viewpoints. The east end of this 9–10-mile tract is owned by the U.S. Navy and managed by the DEC. Crisscrossed with old boundary and fire roads, the Manorville Hills nevertheless offer a sense of remoteness unexpected on modern Long Island.

After crossing County 51 and reaching Speonk-Riverhead Road, the trail runs just north of Suffolk County Community College's Riverhead Campus, where parking is available. It then traverses a hilly, winding, relatively unspoiled 7.5-mile section of pine barrens under the jurisdiction of the county and, in the David Sarnoff Preserve, the DEC. Numerous viewpoints grace the trail, including one of Wildwood Lake and another all the way to Flanders Bay and the North Fork. The path is generally narrow, with dense stands of scrub oak and pitch pine everywhere. Side trails and fire roads make possible all-day explorations. At County 104, the trail makes a 1.7-mile swing north, east, and south, then returns to County 104 for a mile of roadwalking to Pleasure Drive. As there is much acquisition activity in this area, a reroute to eliminate the roadwalk is likely.

From the south end of Pleasure Drive, the trail follows a well-established route through gently rolling, quiet barrens for 7.5 miles to Sears-Bellows County Park. It follows a power line briefly before swinging northeast to Maple Swamp, a delightful stop in summer and a colorful one in autumn. About 3.3 miles from Pleasure Drive, the trail reaches a yellow-blazed side path that extends north 0.25 mile to NY 24 at Birch Creek, a good parking area. The Pine Barrens Trail descends to Owl Pond, another good place to view wildlife or to cool off tired feet. The path winds eastward, first through the driest part of the section, then past a series of pine barrens ponds, hugging the south side of the largest, Sears Pond. Near Division Pond, the trail branches, with a spur heading east to the main entrance of Sears-Bellows Park; the main trail turns north, proceeding another 0.3 mile to a crossing of NY 24.

The trail continues north to the fringes of the vast Hubbard Marshes, where the pine barrens touch tidelands, then meanders eastward past Penny Pond and through the Town of Southampton's Red Creek Park. Parts of this section are double-blazed, the yellow marks representing circular (loop) trails of the Southampton Trails Preservation Society in Red Creek. The last off-road section of the Pine Barrens Trail ends at Red Creek Road. As of 2001, the last 2.5 miles to the Shinnecock Canal were on pleasant roads, but reroutes along Peconic Bay are possible. For information on trail reroutes and conditions, contact the Long Island Greenbelt Trail Conference, 23 Deer Path Road, Central Islip, NY 11722; (631) 360-0753; www.hike-li.com/ligtc.

Dwarf Pine Plains

The Dwarf Pine Plains is a globally rare area of fully grown pines standing from three to six feet tall, products of infertile soil and frequent brush fires. It plays host to the rare buck moth, which emerges from the parched earth to mate in great numbers in mid-October. The following 2.4-mile walk is flat and easily accessible. From Exit 63 of Sunrise Highway (NY 27), a wide dirt parking area is located just south of the interchange on County 31. An unmarked trail runs south, parallel to the highway, until it reaches a commercial building in 0.25 mile and turns back to the northwest. The trail runs almost to Sunrise Highway (NY 27) and crosses a wide, sandy spot colonized by *hudsonia* and pine barrens heather. On the far side, a trail heads west and then south to an east–west road once paved with coal slag, traces of which remain. This area was used as a practice bombing range during World War II. To the south and west, evidence of the extremely hot crown fire that blackened the Dwarf Pine Plains in 1995 is visible. The route continues east back to County 31, then north along the road and the original parallel trail back to the parking area.

Quogue Wildlife Refuge

The Quogue Wildlife Refuge, operated by the DEC, is on the north side of South Old Country Road, 1.4 miles east of its intersection with Montauk Highway. A nature exhibit, including live animals, greets visitors at the entrance. Just beyond lie Old Ice Pond and North Pond, good sites for birding. The sanctuary is rarely crowded, and relatively few visitors venture into the quiet pine woods north of the ponds. A walk to the north end and back covers about three miles, depending on the exact route, and takes the visitor from wetlands through pine barrens to dwarf pines. Trails are unblazed, but a map board at the entrance and several signposts make them easy to follow. With vacant land on one side and little-used Suffolk County Airport on the other, the narrow preserve seems much larger than it actually is. For more information, contact Quogue Wildlife Refuge, P.O. Box 492, Quoque, NY 11959; (631) 653-4771; www.dec.state.ny.us/website/reg1/quogue.html.

PAUMANOK PATH

The most ambitious trails project ever undertaken on Long Island is the Paumanok Path, an umbrella term for a trail linking existing and future trails that bear discrete names. The Paumanok Path is a collaborative effort of the Long Island Greenbelt Trail Conference, Southampton Trails Preservation Society, East Hampton Trails Preservation Society, and the Group for the South Fork. When it is completed, the "Appalachian Trail of Long Island" will extend from Rocky Point eastward to Montauk Point, a distance of almost 100 miles.

The Pine Barrens Trail, described above, makes up the western half of the path. East of the Shinnecock Canal, much work remains to be done in the Town of Southampton, where the path will likely follow power-line or railroad rights-of-way until it passes the heavily developed sections of Southampton. It will then swing northeast into woods above Bridgehampton and connect with the Long Pond Greenbelt, a preserved corridor running from Bridgehampton to Sag Harbor. Beyond the town line in East Hampton, the picture is more complete, as existing county and state holdings such as Hither Hills State Park, the Lee Koppelman County Preserve, and state and county parks at Montauk make a route more feasible. The goal of the cooperating groups is to have the entire trail open by 2005. Some representative hikes in the Town of East Hampton are described below.

Northwest Path   *Length 6.5 miles Blaze: yellow triangles*
The woods behind the Village of East Hampton feature glacial erratics, stands of native white pine, kettle holes, and rolling terrain. This section runs from NY 114 and unpaved Edwards Hole Road northeast to the 608-acre Cedar Point County Park, and it ends at a landing on Northwest Harbor at Alewive Brook Road, where hikers will find a view of Cedar Point Light.

George Sid Miller Trail   *Length: 2.0 miles Blaze: white or horse's head on white*
A key link in the Paumanok Path, this short stretch includes rolling uplands with small, steep hills near salt-water Fresh Pond. From Fresh Pond Road, 0.1 mile east of Cross Highway, it extends to Springs-Amagansett Road, also known as the Old Stone Highway.

Stephen Talkhouse Path   *Length: 4.0 miles Blaze: white*
Named for a fabled ruler of the Montaukett, this section takes in the wonderful dune lands of 1,800-acre Hither Hills State Park, one of the most spectacular places on Long Island. It will, when completed, connect directly to the Koppelman Preserve to the east and to Montauk beyond. Blazes appear about

0.2 mile north of NY 27 on Napeague Harbor Road, which intersects the state highway just west of the state park.

To the east lies an amazing world of shifting sands, the so-called Walking Dunes. Here the oak forest is slowly being buried; the tops of 50-foot trees rise from the sand like young saplings. The trail runs eastward through dunes, ancient hollies, and heather. When finished, the Stephen Talkhouse Path will encompass over eight miles, ending near the Town of East Hampton Recycling Center. In addition to the white blazes of the Paumanok Path, this section will feature orange T markings.

Napeague State Park

Napeague State Park is a vital link in the Paumanok Path. Once the site of the Gilbert P. Smith fish-rendering factory at Promised Land, this 1,362-acre tract of several separate parcels was transferred to the State of New York in 1978 by The Nature Conservancy. An undeveloped park, it is largely a level area, a fragile one of salt marsh, cranberry bogs, low dunes, pitch pine woods, and a few ponds (the largest of which is called the Pond of Pines, or Napeague Pond). It includes most of the peninsula west of Napeague Harbor and runs from the tip of Hicks Island to the ocean, fronting the sea with nearly three miles of undeveloped beach. On that side, little more than a mile of motels and other buildings separates it from Hither Hills State Park. The northern section is composed primarily of dunes, pines, and salt marsh; the central, of salt marsh and cranberry bogs; the southern, of extensive primary dunes and beach vegetation, including *hudsonia*, reindeer moss, and varieties of mushrooms and orchids.

The Paumanok Path skirts the marshes by clinging to the bay beaches north of the Long Island Rail Road tracks. To the east, it connects with the Stephen Talkhouse Path as it ascends the Ronkonkoma Moraine. For more information about Napeague State Park, contact Hither Hills State Park, 50 South Fairview Avenue, Montauk, NY 11954; (631) 668-2554 or (631) 668-3781; www.nysparks.com.

Montauk Point

With the 724-acre Montauk Point State Park contiguous to the 1,059-acre Theodore Roosevelt County Park, much of the land east of Lake Montauk is protected. It is a country of lonely, rolling moors, some forested, reaching el-

Montauk Light
and the two forms
of cliff

R. L. DICKINSON

Figure 6-4. Montauk Point: the lighthouse

evations of 100 feet or more. Cattle once grazed this range, but now it is renowned for its bird life. Sea ducks and many offshore species such as gannets, kittiwakes, dovekies, and razor-billed auks are found at Long Island's easternmost point. Harbor seal visit in winter, and deer and fox are abundant.

Atop the cliff of Turtle Hill stands the octagonal sandstone tower of the Montauk Point Light Station, commissioned by George Washington in 1795. At that time, the edge of the bluff lay some 300 feet to the east; the unrelenting sea has eroded the cliff to within a few feet of the Light.

Head west on foot from the lighthouse. Two miles along the shore of Block Island Sound lies the beautiful, land-locked Oyster Pond, its east bank lined with a thick holly forest. To the northwest stands Shagwong Point, with a view of the entire Montauk headland. From here, a dirt road leads 0.4 mile southwest to Big Reed Pond, the easternmost body of fresh water on Long Island, designated a National Natural Landmark.

For more information on Montauk Point State Park, contact the park at

The South Shore of Long Island : dunes, Beech grass : arbor : dories : drift wood fire wave markings : Beech pools : wreck : coal Barges : sunshine.

R. L. DICKINSON

Figure 6-5. South shore of Long Island

50 South Fairview Avenue, Montauk, NY 11954; (631) 668-3245 or (631) 668-3781; www.nysparks.com. For more information on Theodore Roosevelt County Park, contact the park at (631) 852-7878, or the Suffolk County Department of Parks, Recreation and Conservation, P.O. Box 144, West Sayville, NY 11796; (631) 854-4949; www.co.suffolk.ny.us/exec/parks.

ATLANTIC BARRIER BEACHES

The barrier islands along the South Shore of Long Island are justly famed as some of the finest bathing beaches in the world. Consequently, they are often filled to overflowing on hot summer days. In the off-season, however, they become excellent territory for walks of almost unlimited length and surpassing beauty. Any walk along the ocean in the nearly 100-mile stretch from Atlantic Beach to Montauk will be a rewarding experience; the walks noted below may offer the best combinations of accessibility and attractiveness. The beaches are administered by a variety of federal, state, county, and town governmental entities.

Until 1931, Great South Beach stretched from Fire Island Inlet eastward for more than 55 miles without a break to Southampton. A storm in March of that year breached the dunes opposite Center Moriches and carved Moriches Inlet, through which the ocean now pours swiftly and dangerously. Similarly, the great hurricane of 1938 opened the inlet to Shinnecock Bay.

When Congress created the Fire Island National Seashore in 1964, the boundaries of the national seashore ran from the community of Kismet for 26 miles to Moriches Inlet. The Fire Island Lighthouse Station was added later. Seventeen beach communities occupy parts of the island, but several magnificent sections of untouched beach remain.

Access by car is limited to Robert Moses State Park on the western end and Smith Point County Park on the eastern end. Both are toll facilities during the summer season. Ferries operate from May to November from Bay Shore, Sayville (to Sailors Haven Visitor Center), and Patchogue (to Watch Hill Visitor Center). Everywhere along the barrier islands, the primary dunes offer the only coastal protection against violent storms. They have taken years to form, are extremely fragile, and can be destroyed by careless tramping—so hikers should not climb the dunes or cross them except at designated spots.

Short Beach

At the west end of 2,400-acre Jones Beach State Park, there is a winter walk 0.5 mile from the West End parking field to the jetty at Short Beach. A two-mile boardwalk parallels the waterfront. Snowy owls, short-eared owls, and snow buntings frequent the dunes, and large flocks of brant geese come to the inlet. To reach the park, take the Meadowbrook State Parkway to Jones Beach State Park, and drive to the West End parking

Figure 6-6. *Shells on Jones Beach*

field. Near West End, an old bathhouse has been converted into the Theodore Roosevelt Nature Center, with displays of shore life and occasional programs. For more information, contact Jones Beach State Park, Wantagh, NY 11793; (516) 785-1600; www.nysparks.com.

John F. Kennedy Memorial Bird Sanctuary

In 1959, this former hunting preserve became the first area in the state to be placed under the protection of the Long Island Wetlands Act. Managed jointly by the Town of Oyster Bay and the New York State Department of Environmental Conservation, its 500 acres contain several miles of trails through one of the finest sanctuaries on the Atlantic coast. Walkers can see a large, brackish pond, maritime forest, salt marsh, and dunes. The sanctuary is accessible from

Ocean State Parkway. Parking is available in the small field just east of the wooden lookout tower. A free permit can be obtained from the Town of Oyster Bay Department of Parks and Recreation, 977 Hicksville Road, Massapequa, NY 11758; (516) 797-4110.

Cedar Beach

Operated by the Town of Babylon, this 1.2-mile beach is open to all in the off-season, and affords beach-walking toward Gilgo Beach or Captree State Park. It is accessible from the eastern end of the Ocean State Parkway. For more information, contact Town of Babylon, Department of Parks and Recreation, 151 South Phelps Lane, North Babylon, NY 11703; (631) 893-2100.

Robert Moses State Park

Serving as the western gateway to Fire Island, this park offers visual proof of the power of the littoral drift—the inexorable scouring of the barrier beaches by ocean currents that carry the sand westward. To the east of Robert Moses Causeway lies the Fire Island Lighthouse Station, part of the Fire Island National Seashore. The lighthouse was built in 1858 on what was then the tip of the island; since that time, the island has grown almost five miles westward to Democrat Point. The lighthouse is a good destination for an out-and-back walk of 2.5 miles from Field 2. Access to it is via the Robert Moses Causeway, which has a toll during the summer and on weekends and holidays during the off-season. For more information, contact Robert Moses State Park, P.O. Box 247, Babylon, NY 11702; (631) 669-0449; www.nysparks.com.

Fire Island Lighthouse

Accessible from Robert Moses State Park Field 5, this 200-acre area contains a freshwater pond and diverse plant communities. The 168-foot-high lighthouse is open for tours on a limited basis. A short distance west on the boardwalk nature trail, the crumbling base of the original 1825 lighthouse is visible. For more information or to sign up for a tower tour, contact the Fire Island Lighthouse Preservation Society, 4640 Captree Island, Captree Island, NY 11702; (631) 661-4876.

Sailors Haven Visitors Center

A ferry from Sayville provides access to Sailors Haven Visitor Center. A 1.5-mile-long, handicapped-accessible boardwalk loop trail leads west to Sunken

Forest, so called because of its location down behind the dunes. Holly, sassafras, tupelo, and shadbush envelop the walker in a cool, dark environment. For more information, contact the Fire Island National Seashore, 120 Laurel Street, Patchogue, NY 11772; (631) 289-4810; www.nps.gov/fiis.

Watch Hill to Smith Point

Accessible via the ferry from Patchogue, Watch Hill features a boardwalk nature trail looping through several ecosystems, including an expansive salt marsh and a small maritime forest on secondary dunes.

Figure 6-7. Fire Island Dunes

In 1980, the seven miles from Watch Hill to Smith Point earned designation as a wilderness area, the only federal one in New York State. It is accessible either by taking the ferry from Patchogue to Watch Hill and walking east, or by driving to Smith Point and walking west. It attains a primitive, wild beauty that will leave an indelible impression on any visitor. Here lie thick groves of pitch pine, with deer, fox, and rabbit everywhere, though hikers are more likely to hear the animals in the dense undergrowth than to see them. The shifting dunes rise hauntingly to an elevation of 40 feet or more. In the swale behind the primary dunes, the abundant plant life includes salt spray rose, bayberry, beach plum, and poison ivy.

West of the Fire Island Wilderness Visitor Center at Smith Point is a mile-long, handicapped-accessible boardwalk trail. This self-guided route is a good introduction to Fire Island's cross section of ecosystems. Smith Point features an expanse of swale or desert-like area behind the primary dunes.

Near Old Inlet, about two miles west of Smith Point, the first transatlantic steamship, *S.S. Savannah*, sank on November 5, 1821. The Life Saving Service built Halfway Huts in this area, which served as shelters for shipwreck victims, and contained oil lamps and stores of dried beans. For modern hikers, the only overnight refuge is a limited primitive camping area near Old Inlet. A permit is required. For more information, contact the Fire Island National Seashore, 120 Laurel Street, Patchogue, NY 11772; (631) 289-4810; www.nps.gov/fiis.

Smith Point County Park (Smith Point to Moriches Inlet)

Heading east from the Fire Island Wilderness Visitor Center, walkers can trek 4.2 miles along undeveloped beaches to the raging maw of Moriches Inlet. Harbor seal frequent the area in winter. In cold weather, a brisk walk east along any of these beaches can turn into a chilling experience when it comes time to turn back to the west in the face of the prevailing winds, so dress accordingly. For more information, contact Smith Point County Park, William Floyd Parkway, Shirley, NY 11967; (631) 852-1313; www.co.suffolk.ny.us/exec/parks.

Elizabeth A. Morton National Wildlife Refuge

This long sandspit on Jessup Neck, west of Sag Harbor on Peconic Bay, remains relatively undiscovered despite its beauty and variety. Due east from the parking area off Noyack Road, hidden in the woods, is a wood duck pond. The trail itself goes north through cedar woods, then drops to a pristine beach facing westward. Side trails on the east side lead through the undergrowth to rich marshlands complete with short boardwalks over some of the wetter areas. Farther north lies a forested bluff, which eventually drops down to a sand bar jutting into the currents of Noyack and Little Peconic bays. There is no main trail. Once past the initial short section of woods, visitors can opt for walking either beach or bluff, or take one way out and the other back. This peninsula is very narrow, and the route becomes apparent upon reaching the beach. Total distance from the parking area to the tip is 2.0 miles; side trips can—and should—stretch a visit into an all-day affair. For more information, contact the U.S. Fish and Wildlife Service, P.O. Box 21, Shirley, NY 11967; (631) 725-2270, or (631) 286-0485.

OTHER PARKS AND PRESERVES

Long Island is rich in parklands varying greatly in size and character, ranging from converted private estates or narrow parks along streams to larger wooded preserves. Some are crowded, some are quiet; all offer worthwhile day walks.

Belmont Lake State Park

Easily accessible from Exit 38 of the Southern State Parkway, this 459-acre state park has paths on both sides of the lake, extending north to a feeder brook. In the other direction, a pedestrian underpass of the parkway leads to a 2.5-mile trail paralleling the narrow Carlls River, a good example of a Long Island stream system. For more information, contact Belmont Lake State Park, P.O. Box 247, Babylon, NY 11702; (631) 667-5055; www.nysparks.com.

Caumsett State Park

The former Marshall Field estate at Lloyd Neck in the Town of Huntington is located on a beautiful peninsula. It contains 1,500 acres of woodland, meadows, rocky shoreline, salt marsh, and former farm and garden areas. A number of permanent buildings on the property are used for environmental education programs and other activities. There are paved and unpaved roads as well as some narrow foot trails. A freshwater pond 1.5 miles from the gatehouse can be viewed from a hill in the northeastern section of the park, with the expanse of Long Island Sound in the background. The northwestern section projects two miles into a marshy, sandy, open site from which a boardwalk directs the visitor to the tip, known as Lloyd Point.

From Main Street in Huntington, West Neck Road (four blocks west of NY 110) heads north to the park entrance. There is an entrance fee for cars from Memorial Day through Labor Day. Maps are available at the gate. For more information, contact Caumsett State Park, Lloyd Harbor Road, Huntington, NY 11743; (631) 423-1770; www.nysparks.com.

Charles T. Church Nature Sanctuary

A private preserve operated by North Shore Wildlife Sanctuary, this lovely parcel in Mill Neck is a combination of wetlands and a forest of oak, maple, and beech. A parking lot, complete with map and information board, is located on Frost Mill Road, just south of the Mill Neck Long Island Rail Road station. Hikers can wander around in the sanctuary and the woods to the south of Shu Swamp Road. The North Shore Wildlife Sanctuary also maintains two other close-by mature upland forests— Coffin Woods and Pennoyer Woods. For more

R. L. DICKINSON

Figure 6-8. Peconic Bay near Orient Beach State Park

information, contact North Shore Wildlife Sanctuary, P.O. Box 214, Mill Neck, NY 11765.

Gardiner County Park

Originally owned by the Gardiner family, Suffolk County's first non-Native American landowners, and later part of Sagtikos Manor estate, it contains a transition zone between inland woods and bayside salt marshes within its 231 acres. The entrance is on Montauk Highway (NY 27A) in West Bay Shore, a half-mile east of Robert Moses Causeway. For more information, contact Gardiner County Park at (631) 854-0935, or the Suffolk County Department of Parks, Recreation and Conservation, P.O. Box 144, West Sayville, NY 11796; (631) 854-4949; www.co.suffolk.ny.us/exec/parks.

Garvies Point Preserve

This preserve consists of 62 acres of glacial moraine covered by forests, thickets, and meadows and about five miles of trails. Small animals and over 140 species of birds have been spotted here. High cliffs along the shore of Hempstead

Harbor exhibit such erosional features as alluvial fans, talus slopes, and slumping caused by ancient clays oozing from the beach. Signs from the Glen Cove By-pass direct visitors to the preserve, which includes a museum of Long Island geology and Native American archeology. For more information, contact Garvies Point Preserve, Barry Drive, Glen Cove, NY 11542; (516) 571-8010.

Muttontown Preserve

With a visitor center and 20 miles of trails (including both hiking-only and multi-use trails), this 550-acre tract of uplands is one of the more beautiful open areas left in populous Nassau County. The entrance is at the south end of Muttontown Lane, one block west of the intersection of NY 106 and NY 25A. For more information, contact Muttontown Preserve, Muttontown Lane, East Norwich, NY 11732; (516) 571-8500.

Orient Beach Parks

Almost at the tip of the North Fork lies 363-acre Orient Beach State Park. A 4.6-mile loop walk begins at the parking lot and heads west to Long Beach Point and back. At all times of the year, the Orient area is an outstanding birding area and a favorite place for beachcombers. In spring, the prickly-pear cactus and beach plum bloom; in summer, there are roseate terns and por-poises; in fall, tremendous numbers of migrating monarch butterflies hang from the cedars; in winter, there are sea birds and snowy owls.

For a shorter but equally enjoyable walk, hikers can park near the end of NY 25 in the small lot for Orient Point County Park. Additional parking is available at the New London ferry ramp across the road. Unmarked but clear trails lead north through open meadows to Long Island Sound, and then head east along the beach to the Point, which offers a view of Plum Island and Plum Gut Light. The round trip is approximately 1.7 miles.

For more information, contact Orient Beach State Park, Box 117, Orient, NY 11957; (631) 323-2440; www.nysparks.com.

Southaven County Park

The first and one of the largest parks opened by Suffolk County, Southaven protects the Carmans River. Hikers wandering north from the picnic areas and other developed facilities will find rewarding, wild country along a major Long Island stream. It is possible to walk for miles in the area between Sunrise Highway (NY 27) and the Long Island Expressway (I-495) far to the north. The park entrance is on the north side of Sunrise Highway, between the Yaphank Avenue and William Floyd Parkway exits. Farther south along the east bank of the Carmans River, west of William Floyd Parkway, is the Wertheim National Wildlife Refuge, a large area of pines and marshland at the end of Great South Bay. To the east in Mastic Beach is the William Floyd Homestead, with more woodland and marsh, as well as peat bogs, fronting Moriches Bay. For more information, contact Southaven County Park at (631) 854-1414, or the Suffolk County Department of Parks, Recreation and Conservation, P.O. Box 144, West Sayville, NY 11796; (631) 854-4951; www.co.suffolk.ny.us/exec/parks.

Tackapausha Preserve

Operated by Nassau County, this extremely narrow preserve in Seaford protects the Seaford Creek watershed. Though walkers are rarely out of sight of neighboring houses, the preserve is worthwhile for its wet-woods walks and spring wildflowers. A nature museum is situated at the south end of the property, on Washington Avenue at Merrick Road. For more information, contact Tackapausha Preserve, Washington Avenue, Seaford, NY 11783; (516) 571-7443.

Wildwood State Park

For walkers, this park offers access to the North Shore beaches, with spectacular high bluffs overlooking Long Island Sound. These beaches are much different in character from those along the Atlantic. Since wave action is much less intense, the beaches are not as well developed. Pebbles and boulders from many of the rock formations—sedimentary, igneous, and metamorphic—as far north as the Berkshires of Massachusetts and the Green Mountains of Vermont were carried hundreds of miles in the continental glacier and deposited on this shore. From Wildwood to Orient Point, the beach is the resting place of large boulders from the gneisses, granites, and schists of eastern Connecticut and central Massachusetts. For more information, contact Wildwood State Park, P.O. Box 518, Wading River, NY 11792; (631) 929-4314; www.nysparks.com.

SEVEN

WESTCHESTER COUNTY

ewly established parkways in Westchester were praised in the 1934 edition of the *Walk Book* for setting "a new standard in highway construction" and providing "adequate highways in beautiful surroundings with paths for the walker, as well as seats, gardens, and occasional camping spots with fireplaces." This concept of leisurely auto routes wedded to idyllic walkways has long since succumbed to the pace of modern traffic and the sprawl of residential and corporate complexes. Yet the hiker will find that today's wider and straighter parkways still lead to as extensive a collection of parks and preserves as can be found anywhere this close to New York City. From smaller parks in the urbanized southern part of the county to more rugged ridges in the less populous highlands to the north, there remain quiet open spaces rich in geological and historical interest.

The hiker has many opportunities to explore the varied history of the region. The Old Croton Aqueduct, for example, passes near estates that mark major periods of the county's history. The restored manor houses of Frederick Philipse, who traded with the Native Americans at Tarrytown, and of the Van Cortlandts of Croton-on-Hudson recall the age of the Dutch patroons. Sunnyside, Washington Irving's cozy retreat at Irvington, overlooks the Hudson, as does Jay Gould's Lyndhurst. A large portion of the John D. Rockefeller estate just north of Tarrytown is open to the public as a park preserve.

Westchester County has an extensive park system that includes many of the hiking areas described in this chapter as well as numerous smaller parks. Information on Westchester County parks, preserves, and historical sites may be obtained from the Westchester County Department of Parks, Recreation

R. L. DICKINSON

The Rook

Typical Westchester: rolling country: Nyack & Hook Mountain

Figure 7-1. Westchester landscape looking toward the Hudson and Hook Mountain

and Conservation, 25 Moore Avenue, Mt. Kisco, NY 10549; (914) 864-PARK; www.westchestergov.com/parks. County residents may purchase a park pass, which is required for admission to a few parks (as noted in the descriptions below) and which provides discounts on some user and parking fees. Other hiking opportunities are found in New York State parks and in preserves owned by conservation and educational institutions.

BLUE MOUNTAIN RESERVATION

The 1,583-acre Blue Mountain Reservation south of Peekskill includes 12 miles of trails. Mountain biking is a popular activity at the reservation, and bicycles are permitted on most of the trails. A special feature of the reservation is the Blue Mountain Trail Lodge, which provides dormitory accommodations and kitchen and dining facilities for groups of up to 30 people. Reservations must be made in advance by calling (914) 737-2194.

To reach the reservation, take US 9 to the Welcher Avenue exit in Peekskill, and follow Welcher Avenue east for half a mile to the reservation entrance. A parking fee is charged in the summer. Detailed trail maps, showing the numbers on the wooden posts at trail junctions, are available at the entrance booth. Due to the complex trail network in the park, an up-to-date trail map is essential. The trails may not be well blazed, and it is recommended that hikers place primary reliance on the numbered wooden posts rather than on the colored trail blazes. For more information, contact the Westchester County Department of Parks, Recreation and Conservation, 25 Moore Avenue, Mt. Kisco, NY 10549; (914) 864-PARK; www.westchestergov.com/parks.

Several trails can be combined to make an attractive loop hike of about five miles which goes over the two principal summits, Blue Mountain and Mount Spitzenberg, with their panoramic views of the Hudson River and the mountains to the south and west.

The hike starts at the entrance to the long parking lot beyond the lodge. Proceed south on the Yellow Trail, which bears left at a fork (post #1) and loops into the woods, briefly approaching the paved road opposite the lodge. It then heads northeast, following a stream. At the next trail junction (post #38), follow the Yellow Trail as it turns left to cross the stream on a wide wooden bridge. On the other side of the bridge (post #37), turn right onto the Red Trail, which continues up the valley, recrossing the stream on another bridge (post #36). At the following trail junction (post #31), turn sharply right (south) onto the Blue Trail, which climbs the northern slopes of Blue Mountain. Near the top (at post #30), an unmarked trail leads left, over rock outcrops, to a broad viewpoint, with the Hudson River, Bear and Dunderberg mountains, and Indian Point to the west, and Anthony's Nose to the north. Just before the viewpoint, another unmarked trail to the right leads past an abandoned stone shelter to the summit of Blue Mountain (665 feet). There are no views from the wooded summit.

After visiting the viewpoint and the summit, return to the Blue Trail and turn left (south). At a gas pipeline (post #26), the Briarcliff-Peekskill Trailway (green) joins from the right. Turn left here and cross unpaved Montrose Station Road, now following both blue and green blazes. Continue south, climbing steadily. At the next trail junction (post #21), turn left, following the green blazes of the Briarcliff-Peekskill Trailway, then (at post #22) turn right onto an unmarked trail which heads uphill to the summit of Mount Spitzenberg. Just before the summit, the trail passes another abandoned stone shelter. There are clear views from the summit over the Tappan Zee to the southwest and the hills of Harriman State Park to the west.

Retrace your steps to the green-blazed trail and turn left. At the junction with the Blue Trail (post #21), turn left, following the blue blazes, then turn right at the next junction (post #20), eventually recrossing Montrose Station Road and the gas pipeline. The trail descends to a pond, where it skirts its southern and western shores and crosses its outlet (turn left at post #12 and right at post #13). A short distance beyond the pond, a junction is reached with the Briarcliff-Peekskill Trailway (post #5). Turn left here and follow the green blazes back to the parking lot.

BRIARCLIFF-PEEKSKILL TRAILWAY

Acquired in the 1920s for a proposed parkway extending what is now NY 9A from Briarcliff to Peekskill, this land became a trailway in 1977 and is blazed with leaf-green diamonds. The trail is owned and maintained by the Westchester County Department of Parks, Recreation and Conservation. Most access points to the trail are marked with brown Westchester County Park signs. Parking is minimal except at Teatown Lake Reservation, Croton Gorge, and Blue Mountain Reservation parks, through which the trail runs. The trail offers generally level, easy walking, although occasional blowdowns and wet areas may be encountered. Attractions include the massive Croton Dam and Hudson River views in Blue Mountain Reservation, as the trail weaves its 13-mile path through Westchester County. Trail maps are available from the Westchester County Department of Parks, Recreation and Conservation, 25 Moore Avenue, Mt. Kisco, NY 10549; (914) 864-PARK; www.westchestergov.com/parks.

The southern trailhead is on Ryder Road in Ossining just east of the NY 9A overpass. The trail crosses Grace Lane, NY 134, and then Spring Valley Road at 2.9 miles. It continues along the west side of Teatown Lake, crosses Blinn Road at 5.1 miles, and follows Croton Dam Road for half a mile. Just before reaching the dam, the blazed trail turns left onto a gravel road, from which it soon turns right. The northern trailhead of the Old Croton Aqueduct Trail is about 100 yards farther along the gravel road. The Briarcliff-Peekskill Trailway descends to cross through Croton Gorge Park, crosses the Croton River below the dam, and ascends to regain Croton Dam Road on the other side of the dam.

The trail is less used and harder to follow north of Croton Gorge Park. It goes north to the intersection of Mount Airy Road East and NY 129 at 6.6 miles. Continuing along, with several short sections on paved roads, the trail crosses Furnace Dock Road at 8.7 miles. Parts of the trail between this point and Watch Hill Road at 10.0 miles were often under water, but the Parks Department built a wooden walkway to alleviate the problem. The northern trailhead of the Briarcliff-Peekskill Trailway is at Lounsbury Pond in the Blue Mountain Reservation at 12.9 miles.

BRONX RIVER RESERVATION

A bicycle and walking trail follows the Bronx River and the Bronx River Parkway in two sections from Bronxville to Scarsdale and from Hartsdale to the Kensico Dam in Valhalla. It is paved asphalt with a few short sections of packed dirt. It is accessible from several stations along the Metro-North Harlem Line. Parking is available at the Kensico Dam and, for a fee, at railroad stations. Trail maps are available from the Westchester County Department of Parks, Recreation and Conservation, 25 Moore Avenue, Mt. Kisco, NY 10549; (914) 864-PARK; www.westchestergov.com/parks.

Hikers should be aware that this is a popular bicycle route. On summer Sundays from 10 A.M. to 2 P.M., the Bronx River Parkway from Scarsdale Road

Figure 7-2. Along the Bronx River in Westchester

to the County Center is closed to automobile traffic and opened to bicycles, diverting some bicycle traffic off of the trail.

The southern section of the trail begins at the intersection of Palmer Avenue and Paxton Avenue just west of the Bronxville railroad station. The trail goes north, passing the Crestwood railroad station at 2.1 miles and continuing to Harney Road in Scarsdale at 3.6 miles. Here the southern section ends. The northern section is reached by going east on Harney Road and north on Scarsdale Avenue for 0.7 mile, then east on Crane Road and north on Fox Meadow Road for two miles.

The northern section starts behind Hitchcock Presbyterian Church on Greenacres Avenue just west of Walworth Avenue in Hartsdale. After reaching the White Plains railroad station at 2.0 miles, the trail follows Bronx Street north for several blocks. The trail reaches the North White Plains railroad station at 3.3 miles, where it crosses the river on the Fisher Lane bridge at the north end of the parking lot. The trail continues north and ends at the Kensico Dam at 4.7 miles.

BUTLER MEMORIAL SANCTUARY

The Arthur W. Butler Memorial Sanctuary is probably better known by birders than hikers, though a number of trails crisscross its forested lands. Mrs. Arthur W. Butler donated 225 acres of the 363-acre tract to The Nature Conservancy in 1954, in memory of her husband.

Open year-round, the sanctuary is located southeast of Mount Kisco and can be reached from NY 172. About 0.3 mile west of the interchange with I-684, Chestnut Ridge Road goes south from NY 172. In 1.2 miles, a side road to the right leads to a bridge that crosses over I-684. This unnamed side road quickly dead-ends; cars can be parked along the west side of the road. From the south, visitors can reach the sanctuary by taking Exit 4 of I-684 and following the above directions. For more information, contact the Eastern New York Chapter of The Nature Conservancy, 19 North Moger Avenue, Mt. Kisco, NY 10549; (914) 244-3271; www.nature.org.

A short distance along the main trail (red) from the parking area is a kiosk with a large wooden map. It explains the types of forest that make up the sanctuary. Trail maps are sometimes available near a register box. The hike described below is about 3.5 miles and covers most of the sanctuary. It is easy walking, with elevations varying from about 500 to 750 feet.

Starting from the kiosk, the route follows the red-blazed trail to the west. This trail soon intersects a blue-blazed trail. From here, hikers may either stay on the red trail ahead or follow the blue trail to the right. Together, these trails make a figure-8 toward the north. The red trail climbs more gently as it contours two hills, while the blue trail immediately climbs the first of the two hills and stays close to the steep eastern slopes. A brief descent brings the blue trail to a valley where it intersects the red trail. After a white-blazed trail begins on the left, the blue trail climbs the second hill. Soon after passing between rock cliffs, the blue trail terminates where it meets the red trail to close the figure-8.

Hikers who want to explore the north end of the sanctuary can turn left and continue on the red trail. After passing a white-blazed trail, the route begins a gentle descent to the west into a valley that feeds into Howlands Lake (which is not accessible through the sanctuary) to the north. At the valley floor, a yellow-blazed trail begins on the left just before the red trail ends at the sanctuary boundary.

The north-end route turns left (south) to follow the yellow trail, which passes under rock cliffs, after which an alternate trail blazed orange branches to the right. The two trails rejoin in 0.2 mile. The trail then climbs more steeply and descends into a narrow valley where, to the left, a white-blazed trail goes by a tussock sedge meadow and rejoins the yellow trail.

The yellow trail descends steeply to the floor of a secluded valley and climbs the other side on a few short switchbacks. It intersects the blue trail, which can be followed left (north) to rejoin the red trail. A more interesting route, however, is to continue on the yellow trail as it climbs one of the higher hills of the sanctuary to a viewpoint called the Robert J. Hammerschlag Hawk Watch. At the height of land, for the benefit of birders, wooden bleachers have been built facing east. From the only unobstructed viewpoint in the sanctuary, birders can observe, in autumn, northern harriers, ospreys, turkey vultures, bald and golden eagles, various kinds of hawks, American kestrels, merlins, and peregrine falcons on their migration south. Notwithstanding the annoying rumble of I-684, the bleachers are a place to sit and relax.

From Hawk Watch, the most direct route back to the kiosk is along an orange-blazed trail that follows the cliff edge north along a protective wire fence. The dead-end road that gives access to the sanctuary is soon visible ahead.

CRANBERRY LAKE PRESERVE

Cranberry Lake Preserve, bordered by the Kensico watershed and private property, lies across NY 22 from Kensico Dam, which was constructed from stone quarried east of the lake. The principal geographic feature of the 135-acre preserve is a ten-acre lake surrounded by bogs and wetlands. The land also rises to rocky outcroppings and wooded hillsides, with a woodland trail, a lake trail, and a self-guided nature trail. There are seven miles of trails in all. A trail map is available at the nature center, which also has rest rooms and exhibits. Picnicking is allowed near the nature center only. The nature center is open Wednesday through Sunday; for more information, contact the Westchester County Department of Parks, Recreation and Conservation, 25 Moore Avenue, Mt. Kisco, NY 10549; (914) 864-PARK; www.westchestergov.com/parks, or call the nature center at (914) 428-1005.

The park is reached by following NY 22 north past Kensico Dam, turning right on Old Orchard Street, and then turning right into the preserve. Visitors wishing to travel by train should take the Metro-North Harlem Line to Valhalla, walk across Kensico Dam or across the plaza area to NY 22, and go 0.8 mile north to the preserve; alternatively, visitors can take the train to North White Plains, follow the bicycle path through the Bronx River Reservation to the dam, and continue to the preserve.

KITCHAWAN PRESERVE

Kitchawan Preserve is a 200-acre Westchester County park that surrounds the main building and 12 acres of the research station formerly owned by the Brooklyn Botanic Garden and now operated by the Kenneth S. Warren Institute, which conducts medical research. The park contains about six miles of trails which traverse abandoned fields that have reverted to woodlands. Access to the park is from NY 134, approximately one mile west of NY 100 or one mile east of the Taconic State Parkway. Parking is available for five to ten cars. Hiking in this area is generally easy, though sometimes muddy, and trails may be poorly blazed and difficult to follow.

The terrain includes a mature hemlock forest, fields and meadows where the old demonstration gardens used to be, and a hardwood forest that borders the Croton Reservoir. The Little Brook Nature Trail and its connecting Red

Oak Trail are easy for families with younger children. These are reached by turning left down a small dirt road from the parking area. The North County Trailway also goes through the preserve.

For more information, contact the Westchester County Department of Parks, Recreation and Conservation, 25 Moore Avenue, Mt. Kisco, NY 10549; (914) 864-PARK; www.westchestergov.com/parks.

EUGENE AND AGNES MEYER NATURE PRESERVE

From the rocky west shore of Byram Lake, three miles north of Armonk, rise the steep, wooded hills of the Eugene and Agnes Meyer Nature Preserve. Once the home of Eugene Meyer, editor and publisher of *The Washington Post* in the 1940s and 1950s, this woodland and open-fields tract of 247 acres has been owned and managed by The Nature Conservancy since 1973.

There are two trailheads for the preserve. The Sarles Street entrance is reached by taking Exit 4 off I-684 and going west on NY 172 toward Mt. Kisco. A left (south) turn onto Sarles Street leads in 2.7 miles to its intersection with Bretton Ridge Road; the trailhead, with parking for two cars, is directly across from this intersection. In addition to a woodland trail, unmarked but mowed trails wind just over a mile through open fields and along stone walls. A walk on a hot, muggy July day is a feast of sight and sound. Butterflies, dragonflies, and grasshoppers move among the grasses and wildflowers, their constant humming enhanced with the birds' songs.

To reach the Oregon Road entrance, take Exit 3 off I-684, follow NY 22 north for half a mile, turn left onto Cox Avenue for 0.2 mile, then fork right onto Byram Lake Road. Half a mile from the intersection, turn left on Oregon Road and go 0.2 mile to the preserve. There is room here for one or two cars. A short distance from the road is a shelter containing trail maps. Hikers have a choice here of three parallel trails heading north through the preserve: the Cliff Trail (blue) that overlooks Byram Lake, the Ridge Trail (red), and the Ravine Trail (orange). All three emerge from the woods in approximately 1.2 miles at the private drive past Seven Springs Center, formerly the Meyer home.

For more information, contact the Eastern New York Chapter of The Nature Conservancy, 19 North Moger Avenue, Mt. Kisco, NY 10549; (914) 244-3271; www.nature.org.

MIANUS RIVER GORGE

Maintained since 1953 by the Mianus Gorge Preserve, the 700-acre preserve extends approximately 2.5 miles along the gorge of the Mianus River in the Westchester County towns of Bedford, North Castle, and Pound Ridge. This preserve was the first one established by The Nature Conservancy, which manages preserves throughout the United States and in other parts of the world. A foot trail with several side loops runs south along the west bank of the gorge from the visitors' entrance to the upper end of a reservoir.

After about a mile, the hiker reaches the heart of the preserve, the Hemlock Cathedral—20 acres of hillside covered with virgin eastern hemlocks, some of which are giants dating back to the 1680s. The V-shaped gorge is rugged and spectacular, dropping sharply 200 feet below the trail. Along the path, the roar of water can be heard. Mineral outcrops occur, and over five hundred species of flora and fauna have been catalogued. A round trip on the main trail requires two hours, but additional time can and should be devoted to the exploration of the various side trails, such as the one that leads to an abandoned mica and quartz mine. Detailed trail maps are available at the entrance.

From Exit 34 of the Merritt Parkway, go north 7.7 miles on Long Ridge Road (CT 104) to Millers Mill Road. Turn left here for 0.1 mile over the bridge to Mianus River Road and then left again for 0.7 mile to the entrance. From the Bedford area, take Pound Ridge Road and Stamford Road (Long Ridge Road) to Millers Mill Road on the right. Cross the river and turn down Mianus River Road 0.1 mile to the entrance.

The preserve has limited hours and is closed in the winter. The rules prohibiting picnicking, dogs, and mountain bikes are strictly enforced. For more information, contact the Mianus Gorge Preserve, Mianus River Road, Bedford, NY 10506; (914) 234-3455; www.nature.org.

NORTH COUNTY TRAILWAY

The Putnam Division of the New York Central Railroad ran for 54 miles from the Bronx to Brewster between 1881 and 1958, when it ceased passenger operations. It carried occasional freight until 1982. During the 1990s, most of the Putnam Division railbed from Eastview to Baldwin Place was paved to become a 22-mile bicycle and walking path called the North County Trailway. Trail maps are available from the Westchester County Department of Parks, Recreation and Conservation, 25 Moore Avenue, Mt. Kisco, NY 10549; (914) 864-PARK; www.westchestergov.com/parks. The trailway is accessible by public transportation via Westchester County Beeline buses to Yorktown and Millwood. It is primarily a bicycle route, so hikers should be alert for passing cyclists.

In Tarrytown (in what was Tarrytown Heights), from the intersection of Neperan Road and Sunnyside Avenue, the trail runs behind the Tarrytown Reservoir, reaching the Eastview exit of the Saw Mill River Parkway at 1.2 miles. Parking is available at both ends of this segment. Crossing Old Saw Mill River Road, the path continues north on a section of the railroad constructed in the 1930s to bypass the estate of John D. Rockefeller. At 4.2 miles, the trail is interrupted for 0.6 mile, but begins again at NY 117 where there is parking and a tunnel for the trailway under NY 117. It is anticipated that the missing segment will be completed by the spring of 2002.

The trail continues north to the Briarcliff Manor station (now a public library) at 6.5 miles. The Tudor-revival style station was built in 1909 by home furnishings magnate Walter Law. The old station was loaded on a railroad car and deposited in Millwood to be used as its station, where it still stands. The trail follows NY 100 (on the road shoulder for 1.4 miles), passes the Millwood station at 9.9 miles, where there is parking, and crosses NY 120. At 12.0 miles, the trail crosses NY 134 just west of its intersection with NY 100. Cars may be parked on the road shoulder at the trail crossing. The entrance to the Kitchawan Preserve is a short distance farther west along NY 134.

The trail briefly passes through the Kitchawan Preserve, after which it crosses a massive truss bridge over the Croton Reservoir and reaches NY 118, where parking is available. The trail turns west and then north, paralleling NY 118. At 17.0 miles, it reaches Underhill Avenue at the south end of Railroad Park in Yorktown Heights, where parking is available. The trail continues north, crossing US 202 near Quaker Church Road at 18.0 miles and Granite Springs Road at 19.6 miles. After crossing Mahopac Avenue, where parking is available, the trail ends at 22.6 miles at the Westchester-Putnam county line, just east of its intersection with US 6 in Baldwin Place.

OLD CROTON AQUEDUCT

From 1842 to 1955, the Old Croton Aqueduct, a National Historic Landmark, supplied New York City with water. Following the damming of the Croton

River, water flowed through the aqueduct to above-ground reservoirs in Central Park and on the present site of the New York Public Library on Fifth Avenue. The northernmost section was reopened in 1988 to furnish water to the Village of Ossining. Although interrupted in places by major highways and urban congestion, the 26-mile surface of the aqueduct provides level, pleasant walks with views of the Hudson River and the Palisades.

Along its journey through eleven river communities, the trail offers an opportunity to combine walking with other interests. In Irvington, it passes through the grounds of Lyndhurst and near Sunnyside, and in Tarrytown, it passes near Philipsburg Manor and the 300-year-old Old Dutch Church. There is a small museum with excellent exhibits relating to the construction of the aqueduct adjacent to the Double Arch at Broadway in Ossining. For the naturalist, trail neighbors include Lenoir Nature Preserve on the Yonkers-Hastings border and the Rockefeller State Park Preserve in Sleepy Hollow.

R. L. DICKINSON

Vents (stone towers constructed to keep the water fresh) are located at roughly one-mile intervals. Larger stone buildings, located in Ossining, above the Pocantico River, and in north Yonkers, are waste weirs, which allowed workers to maintain the aqueduct. Access to the "tube" itself can be arranged for groups by contacting the park manager in Dobbs Ferry. The trail, except north of Ossining, is convenient to buses along US 9 and is also served by the Hudson Line of Metro-North. There are signs at key intersections where walkers must take to the local streets.

For additional information, contact Old Croton Aqueduct State Historic Park, 15 Walnut Street, Dobbs Ferry, NY 10522; (914) 693-5259; www.nysparks.com/hist.

Figure 7-3. Old Croton Aqueduct: Dobbs Ferry vicinity

Yonkers—Tarrytown

Length: 9.2 miles Blaze: yellow
From the Greystone railroad station in Yonkers, a walk uphill and across Warburton Avenue to Odell Avenue leads to the aqueduct. Continuing north, in less than half a mile, a short trail heads east to a gate in the fence surrounding the Lenoir Nature Preserve. A similar distance farther north, an old quarry on the east side was served by a railway running from the river under the aqueduct. After passing the original Overseer's House and the State Historic Park maintenance barns and office in Dobbs Ferry at 4.2 miles, the trail continues through the grounds of Mercy College and past Nevis, a colonnaded home built by Alexander Hamilton's son. It passes the

Figure 7-4. *Sleepy Hollow, near the Aqueduct*

Victorian Stiner-Ross octagonal house and eventually enters the grounds of Lyndhurst. Leaving Lyndhurst, the trail goes north along Broadway, crosses the New York State Thruway, and turns right for 100 yards on White Plains Road before returning to the aqueduct again on the left at 8.3 miles. From the second road crossing, the Tarrytown railroad station is reached by following US 9 north (the aqueduct runs underneath the sidewalk) and turning left down Franklin Street.

Tarrytown—Scarborough

Length: 5.0 miles Blaze: yellow
From the Tarrytown railroad station, this hike begins on Main Street, going east, turns left on North Broadway, and quickly turns right on Hamilton Place, joining the trail on the left in 100 yards. At 1.0 mile, where the route is blocked by a breezeway at Sleepy Hollow High School, hikers can go around the east side of the buildings, and shortly after that they will enter Rockefeller State Park Preserve. After crossing 90 feet above the Pocantico River and passing a waste weir (a square stone building), a wide trail leads off to the east and into the preserve. The route follows US 9 for a short distance and then detours to

the east, paralleling NY 117. It makes a sharp left turn, crosses a bridge over NY 117, and turns left again. Soon it bears right, rejoining the historic aqueduct route, and continues ahead to the next vent at 3.0 miles. It then bears left (the narrow trail straight ahead is for equestrians) and crosses over US 9 on a bridge constructed in 1998. This location is known as Archville, after the stone-arch bridge over the highway that was removed in the 1920s because the width of the arch was insufficient to accommodate the increasing volume of traffic. Commemorative markers on the west side of the bridge provide additional historical information. In another 100 yards, a carriage road to the left leads down into Rockwood Hall, part of the Rockefeller State Park Preserve, which offers magnificent views of the Hudson River. The aqueduct route then curves to the north, crosses Country Club Lane, and continues down a short set of steps. After passing another vent, the trail reaches US 9, where another detour is required. The marked route turns sharply left onto River Road, right on Creighton Lane, then right again on River Road, which leads down to the Scarborough railroad station.

Ossining—Croton Dam

Length: 5.5 miles Blaze: yellow

Going east uphill on Main Street from the Ossining railroad station and turning left on the red-brick-lined path just short of US 9 takes the hiker to the Double Arch, where the aqueduct crosses above Broadway. Broadway, in turn, crosses Sing Sing Kill (the aqueduct museum is in the community center below the bridge on the right), and the trail passes a waste weir at 0.7 mile, ascends some steps, and eventually passes through the grounds of the Crane House, now the Engelhard Corporation. The white stone marker on the lawn is directly above the center of the "tube." Crossing US 9, the trail leads at 2.1 miles to a small maintenance barn, turns left down the road immediately after the barn, makes the first right, and, on emerging from the underpass, rejoins the trail at the markers above and to the right, around the General Electric Management Center.

Figure 7-5. Old Croton Aqueduct Trail near Ossining

From this point, the trail sections are all in woodland, passing above the roaring waters of Croton Gorge and on to the dam. The 19-acre, DEC-owned Croton Gorge Unique Area, located between the trail and the Croton River near the midpoint of this trail segment, allows hikers to visit the river's edge.

If two cars are available, hikers will not have to retrace their steps, and the journey might include the renovated Briarcliff-Peekskill Trailway (green diamond markers), which runs east from the dam to Teatown Lake Reservation (parking lot and exhibits at 1.9 miles).

ROCKEFELLER STATE PARK PRESERVE

The Rockefeller State Park Preserve consists of 1,066 acres, which were donated to the state beginning in 1983 by the Rockefeller family, along with an endowment for the maintenance and operation of the park. The preserve encompasses rolling hills, woods, fields, streams, and a small lake. The 20 miles of wide carriage roads are ideal for strolling and cross-country skiing. Permits are available for horseback riding, but bicycles are prohibited.

The preserve represents a portion of the estate of John D. Rockefeller, which stretched from the Hudson River to the Saw Mill River some three miles north of where the Tappan Zee Bridge crosses the Hudson. Southeast of the preserve is another large portion of the estate, which is managed by the Greenrock Corporation and is also open to the public.

Access to the preserve is from NY 117 about 1.3 miles east of US 9. The Visitor Center and the main parking area are to the right. There is a parking fee. Maps are available at the Visitor Center, and are posted there and near Swan Lake to the southeast. For more information, contact the Rockefeller State Park Preserve, P.O. Box 338, Tarrytown, NY 10591; (914) 631-1470; www.nysparks.com.

For their first foray into the park, many visitors choose a stroll around Swan Lake or up the Overlook Trail. The many carriage roads are well defined, but they are so winding and interconnected that a trail map or at least a good sense of direction is needed.

The Greenrock Corporation property is generally hillier than the preserve and less densely honeycombed with trails. Like the preserve, it offers excellent carriage roads. This area is accessible from trails on the south side of the preserve. Parking is restricted along adjacent roads. The trails to the northwest side of NY 448 lead back to the preserve; those to the east lead to Buttermilk

Hill and the Pocantico Ridge near the Saw Mill River Parkway, which bounds the eastern edge of the property.

TEATOWN LAKE RESERVATION

Teatown Lake Reservation, a 730-acre nature preserve and education center north of Ossining, offers over 15 miles of marked trails, including a portion of the Briarcliff-Peekskill Trailway, which connects to the Old Croton Aqueduct Trail. From the Taconic State Parkway, take the NY 134 exit and go west 0.2 mile to Spring Valley Road. Turn right and follow the road to the entrance on the right. The reservation is a five-mile taxi ride from the Croton-Harmon or Ossining train stations. Admission and parking are free, though fees are charged for programs and Wildflower Island tours. The nature center is wheelchair-accessible, and handicapped parking is provided. A public pay telephone is available.

At Teatown, hikers will find a wide variety of natural areas to explore, including the 33-acre Teatown Lake, a scenic gorge, hardwood swamps, mixed forests, meadows, and hemlock and laurel groves. The 1.6-mile Hidden Valley circuit is a particularly rewarding hike. The Lakeside Trail features a 600-foot boardwalk over the lake and access to a bird observation blind. Trail maps are available at the Nature Center.

Teatown's Nature Center features numerous natural history and live animal exhibits and a nature gift shop. Outdoor exhibits include a working maple sugar house and live birds of prey. Weekend and after-school educational and outdoor programs for children and families are also offered, as well as children's birthday parties. Tours of Teatown's two-acre Wildflower Island are available from April to September; advance reservations are recommended.

For more information, contact Teatown Lake Reservation, 1600 Spring Valley Road, Ossining, NY 10562; (914) 762-2912; www.teatown.org.

WARD POUND RIDGE RESERVATION

The largest of Westchester's parks, the Ward Pound Ridge Reservation occupies 4,315 acres in the northeastern part of the county. Over 35 miles of hiking trails wind through hilly terrain, offering a mix of second-growth hardwood forest, hemlock and laurel, bold rock outcroppings, steep ravines, wetlands,

WARD POUND RIDGE west to BEAR MOUNTAIN

R. L. DICKINSON

Figure 7-6. Ward Pound Ridge Reservation

and open meadows. The low stone walls that crisscross the forest floor remind the visitor of the more than thirty farms that once existed within the park's boundaries. These farms were purchased by Westchester County, and the park was dedicated in 1938. It is named for William Ward, former County Parks Commissioner, who was instrumental in creating the park. The "pound" in Pound Ridge refers to the enclosure or pound used by the Native Americans to capture prey.

The entrance to the park is off NY 121 at the bridge over the Cross River, about 100 yards south of NY 35. A basic map showing hiking trails may be obtained at the park entrance; a more detailed map is available at the nature museum. For more information, including parking fees and use of park facilities, contact the Westchester County Department of Parks, Recreation and Conservation, 25 Moore Avenue, Mt. Kisco, NY 10549; (914) 864-PARK; www.westchestergov.com/parks, or call the park at (914) 763-3493.

Park facilities are concentrated in the northern half of the park along Boutonville Road. Most of the park's picnic areas, a nature museum, and the park office are located along this road, which parallels the course of the Cross River. The southern half of the park offers a more secluded atmosphere. It is reached most easily from the Michigan Road parking and picnic area, which also serves as the center for winter ski touring.

The trail system consists of five major loop trails and numerous minor trails. All the major trails and many minor trails are woods roads with easy grades.

The 4.7-mile white-blazed trail traverses the northernmost section of the park. Accessible from the picnic areas along Boutonville Road, the southern part of the loop offers a pleasant walk along the Cross River. The four-mile-long blue-blazed trail extends south from the Kimberly Bridge picnic area through the eastern side of the park. One side of this loop rises through open forest to the highest point in the park at 860 feet. Once occupied by a fire tower, the site is marked by an ancient hand pump. The other side of the loop follows the base of the park's rocky eastern escarpment.

From the Michigan Road picnic area, the red trail takes the hiker into the park's more remote southern area. The longest loop, at five miles, it offers access to the greatest variety of scenery, from the wetlands of Honey Hollow to open ledges along the park's southern border where the terrain plunges steeply into the Stone Hill River valley. Two shorter loops, the two-mile yellow and three-mile green trails, also originate at Michigan Road; both of these use parts of, and are enclosed within, the red-blazed trail.

Hikers on the red, yellow, and green trails should note that these trails are marked for ski touring. Ski traffic is one-way counterclockwise, so the hiker walking these trails clockwise must look backward to check trail markers.

Side trails off the red trail lead to some of the park's more interesting features. Most popular is the Leatherman's Cave, named after a homeless nomad clad in scraps of leather who, from 1858 to 1889, followed the same path through the New York and Connecticut countryside, stopping at each of his campsites every thirty-three days. A white-blazed trail leaves the western side of the red trail at a well-marked intersection. After a short distance it forks, becoming a loop of its own. The left fork leads most quickly to the cave. The trail continues over a hill above the cave, where open rocks offer a view to the west over the Cross River Reservoir.

Another side trail, this one off the east side of the red trail loop, leads to Indian Rock Shelter, also called Spy Rock. A sign marks the intersection on the red trail. Purple blazes mark the path to the rock. Native American artifacts found under an overhang suggest that it was used as a shelter. From a small pine grove on top, there is a view of a deep ravine and the cliffs on the opposite side.

Lying to the south of the red loop, an unmarked trail leads to Dancing Rock and Bear Rock. The former is a very broad flat rock surface forming the summit of a hill, which, according to stories, was used for dancing by local settlers. It is reached by leaving the trail at three faded blue blazes on a tree, then proceeding up the slope on a faint path to the highest point in the area. Lying farther to the southwest, Bear Rock is noted for the carving—perhaps prehistoric—on the rock's west face, which looks like the head of a bear in profile.

Hikers seeking something more challenging than easy walking on woods roads will find opportunities for more strenuous exercise in the many rocky summits, cliffs, and steep ravines in the southern and southeastern sections of the park.

WESTMORELAND SANCTUARY

The 625-acre Westmoreland Sanctuary, with over nine miles of interconnecting foot trails, has open grassland, stands of hardwood and evergreen trees, a brook valley, modest rocky summits, and Bechtel Lake, named for one of the sanctuary's founders, Edwin Bechtel. The varied habitat produces an abundance of flowers and birds. Established in 1957, this private, not-for-profit sanctuary sponsors wildlife and botanical research as well as educational programs for the public. Activity schedules and trail maps are available at the museum. The paths are identified by signposts at junctions.

The Westmoreland sanctuary is reached from NY 172 southeast of Mount Kisco. About 0.3 mile west of the interchange with I-684, Chestnut Ridge Road goes south from NY 172. In 1.4 miles, this road leads to the entrance of the sanctuary on the left. Parking is available in front of the museum. From the south, the sanctuary is reached by taking Exit 4 of I-684 and following the above directions. For additional information, contact the sanctuary at 260 Chestnut Ridge Road, Bedford Corners, NY 10549; (914) 666-8448; www.westmorelandsanctuary.org.

The sanctuary is crossed by thirteen interlocking trails, most less than a mile long. Because all of the trails are blazed yellow, trail junction signposts are prominent. A half-day hike will of necessity use most of these trails. A 5.5-mile hike that visits the perimeter of the sanctuary is described below. It is easy hiking, with elevations varying from 390 to 730 feet.

Trail maps can be picked up at the trailhead kiosk, located at the end of the museum ramp that leads from the parking lot. The hike begins on the Easy Loop Trail, which descends to join the Catbird Trail on the right. This connects to the northern terminus of the Spruce Trail. Turning right (south) onto the Spruce Trail, the hike goes over one of the major hills in the sanctuary and descends toward a marshy area. At the edge of a stream, the Spruce Trail ends where the Brookside and Hemlock trails begin. The hike continues across the stream, where it joins the Hemlock Trail. After 0.4 mile, a side trail to the right leads to Coles Kettle, a remote tract of wetlands at the southern end of the sanctuary. The Coles Kettle Trail is a 1.5-mile closed loop around the wetlands and is itself quite wet in places. A 500-foot-long interpretive boardwalk is located on the southern portion of the loop.

After completing the Coles Kettle loop, the hike resumes following the Hemlock Trail toward the east. The Hemlock Trail ends at the midpoint of the Laurel Trail, and the hike follows its right branch, which passes a pretty patch of sparsely wooded grass field and soon terminates at a T junction. A right (north) turn to join the appropriately named Brookside Trail leads to a descent along the brook to a wooden bridge, beyond which the Brookside Trail ends and the Veery and Fox Run trails begin. The Veery Trail offers a direct route back toward the parking lot.

The Fox Run Trail is the gateway to the hilly northeastern corner of the sanctuary. This trail contours around the base of rocky cliffs, climbs to a col, and meets the Sentry Ridge Trail. The route makes a right (east) turn here and follows this trail for 0.2 mile to the top of a hill with steep slopes and partially obscured views toward the east. The trail turns sharply left (north) to follow the ridge and then descends to a T junction with the Lost Pond Trail. The route turns right (north) and crosses the outlet of the pond on a wooden bridge, after which the small pond comes into view.

Continuing west along the Lost Pond Trail, the route passes a side trail to the even smaller Scout Pond and then begins to climb in earnest. At a level spot, the Lost Pond Trail ends, and the Chickadee and Wood Thrush trails begin. The Chickadee Trail is a direct route down toward the parking lot, while the Wood Thrush Trail begins a steep ascent to the highest point in the sanctuary at an elevation of 730 feet. From the broad wooded summit, the Wood Thrush Trail descends to a narrow valley, follows it toward Bechtel Lake, and ends near a small wooden shelter for birders. From the lake, the Easy Loop Trail climbs through a dark forest of evergreen trees and emerges north of the museum.

OTHER WALKS IN WESTCHESTER

The following areas have more limited hiking opportunities than those described above. Nevertheless, they provide a variety of interesting shorter hikes, as well as opportunities to visit a variety of habitats.

Betsy Sluder Nature Preserve

Located west of the village of Armonk and east of Whippoorwill Road, this preserve is managed by the Town of North Castle. It consists of approximately 70 acres of a ridge typical of those found in north-central Westchester. Outcroppings of schist in a beech-maple forest give it a special attractiveness. Access is from Old Route 22, 0.25 mile south of its intersection with Main Street (NY 128). For more information, contact the Town of North Castle, Recreation and Parks Department, 85 Cox Avenue, Armonk, NY 10504; (914) 273-3325; www.northcastleny.com/recreation.

Graham Hills Park

This 431-acre county park in Mount Pleasant has about five miles of trails which can be combined to form a loop hike. Although these trails are primarily designed for mountain biking, they are also open to hikers. Access to the park is from NY 117 just east of NY 9A. For more information, or to obtain a trail map, contact the Westchester County Department of Parks, Recreation and Conservation, 25 Moore Avenue, Mt. Kisco, NY 10549; (914) 864-PARK; www.westchestergov.com/parks.

Marshlands Conservancy

This 169-acre county-owned sanctuary offers walks of one or two hours on trails that wind through woods, brush, and open fields sloping to salt-marsh areas and tidewater land overlooking Milton Harbor on Long Island Sound. In spring, waterfowl nest along the quiet shore, and herons may be seen high in the trees. John Jay, the first chief justice of the Supreme Court of the United States, is buried nearby in a private plot. The Marshlands Conservancy is located on US 1, the Boston Post Road, a mile southeast of the Harrison station on the Metro-North Railroad's New Haven Line. For more information, or to obtain the conservancy's schedule of guided walks, lectures, and study sessions, contact the Westchester County Department of Parks, Recreation and

Conservation, 25 Moore Avenue, Mt. Kisco, NY 10549; (914) 864-PARK; www.westchestergov.com/parks, or call the conservancy at (914) 835-4466.

Mountain Lakes Park

This 1,000-acre camping area, situated in North Salem, contains several ponds and the beginnings of Crook Brook. From I-684, take Exit 6 (Katonah/Cross River), go east on NY 35 to NY 121 in Cross River, follow NY 121 north to Grants Corner, make a right onto Hawley Road, and go two miles to the entrance. A trail map is available at the office near the entrance. For more information, contact Mountain Lakes Park, Hawley Road, North Salem, NY 10560; (914) 669-5793.

Muscoot Farm

This 777-acre interpretive farm, owned by the Westchester County Department of Parks, Recreation and Conservation, offers several miles of easy trails through fields and woodlands. A trail map is available at the Visitors Center. The park facilities and programs depict farm life of the 1920s. Muscoot Farm is located in Somers on NY 100, about 1.5 miles south of NY 35. For more information, contact Muscoot Farm, Route 100, Katonah, NY 10536; (914) 232-7118; www.westchestergov.com/parks.

Saxon Woods Park

Stretching for 2.5 miles through Scarsdale and Mamaroneck along the Mamaroneck River, this county park offers birding in the spring, as well as an interpretive board describing the well-marked trails. Year-round parking is possible at the Saxon Woods Swimming Pool, on the west side of Mamaroneck Avenue just north of the Hutchinson River Parkway. Walk under the parkway, and follow the trail to the picnic parking area (open only from May through October with a parking fee). A park pass is required. For more information, contact the Westchester County Department of Parks, Recreation and Conservation, 25 Moore Avenue, Mt. Kisco, NY 10549; (914) 864-PARK; www.westchestergov.com/parks, or call the park at (914) 995-4480.

Sprain Ridge Park

Grassy Sprain Reservoir, which supplies water to the City of Yonkers, is bounded on the west, beyond the Sprain Brook Parkway, by a ridge and an area of woods about half a mile wide and three miles long. The 278-acre county park is heavily wooded, with paths and trails throughout. It may be entered at the north end, on Jackson Avenue, about half a mile west of the Sprain Brook Parkway. A park pass is required. For more information, contact Sprain Ridge Park, 149 Jackson Avenue, Hastings-on-Hudson, NY 10706; (914) 478-2300; www.westchestergov.com/parks.

Figure 7-7. *Sprain Ridge Park: the reservoir*

Turkey Mountain Nature Preserve

The 124-acre Turkey Mountain Nature Preserve is managed by the Town of Yorktown Department of Parks and Recreation. The entrance is on the west side of NY 118, 0.9 mile north of NY 129 or 1.7 miles south of Underhill Avenue in Yorktown Heights, the latter more convenient for those coming from the Taconic State Parkway. In either case, look for the sign for Peter Pratt's Inn across from the intersection. For more information, contact the Town of Yorktown, Department of Parks and Recreation, 176 Granite Springs Road, Yorktown Heights, NY 10598; (914) 245-4650.

Two trails lead to the summit of Turkey Mountain, one blazed white and the other blazed blue. Together they form a loop hike about two miles long. Going up the blue trail and coming down the white trail is preferable. The blue trail goes north from the parking lot; in a short distance, a wooden map shows the trail system. The blue trail is level for a while, climbs gently, and then rises steeply to the eastern spur of Turkey Mountain, a climb of nearly 370 feet. At 1.4 miles, the trail reaches the broad rocky summit (831 feet), which affords a view of the Croton watershed. To the south, just above the curving northbound lanes of the Taconic State Parkway, is the Manhattan skyline. To the west, one end of the Croton Reservoir and the Hudson River just beyond it are visible. To the northwest, the tower on Bear Mountain stands out clearly against the horizon. And to the north, a portion of the Hudson Highlands is recognizable.

The white trail descends from the summit to the southeast. A short distance below the summit, the trail passes by a minor viewpoint to the east. From this viewpoint, the trail descends steeply and levels off to cross the marshy lowlands of the preserve, reaching the parking lot half a mile from the summit.

Several short trails, each no longer than 0.5 mile, are clustered in the southeast corner of the preserve. These trails can be combined with the blue and white trails to make shorter loop hikes through the relatively flat old farmlands at the base of the mountain.

EIGHT

FAHNESTOCK STATE PARK

estled in the wooded hills of northern Putnam County on the east side of the Hudson Highlands lie Clarence Fahnestock Memorial State Park and the Hubbard-Perkins Conservation Area. The original core of the park consists of lands acquired by Major Clarence Fahnestock, who began purchasing abandoned farmsteads around 1900. In 1915, he bought the property of the Pennsylvania and Reading Coal and Iron Company, which had discontinued its iron mining operations in the area forty years earlier. Fahnestock, a Manhattan physician, created a gentleman's farm and shooting preserve, but did not enjoy it for long. He died in France in 1918, leaving his property to his brother, Dr. Ernest Fahnestock. In 1929, Ernest Fahnestock donated 2,400 acres of this property to the State of New York for a park in memory of his brother and 105 acres which would be flooded by the construction of Canopus Lake. By purchase and gift, the park has grown to its present size of 6,732 acres. Fahnestock State Park is administered by the Taconic Region of the New York State Office of Parks, Recreation, and Historic Preservation.

In addition, the state manages the adjacent Hubbard-Perkins Conservation Area. In 1991, the Open Space Institute purchased more than 3,700 acres and then, in 1995, added more than 700 acres from the Perkins estate. Some 2,000 acres of the first purchase were from the estate of Helen F. Hubbard, the sister of Clarence and Ernest Fahnestock. The state purchased the Hubbard portion of the conservation area in 1996 and intends to acquire the Perkins property when funds are available.

The terrain in the park, which is generally not rugged, is dominated by a series of ridges that tend to run from southwest to northeast. One of these ridges culminates in Shenandoah Mountain on the Appalachian Trail just north of the park. The overall elevation in the park is higher than in neighboring districts; thus, snow may remain in the park until the end of March, long after it has disappeared from adjacent areas. Between the ridges lie several lakes and ponds. Just northwest of NY 301 is Canopus Lake, with Pelton Pond opposite it. Stillwater Pond is west of the Taconic State Parkway, and there are several small ponds

Figure 8-1. Canopus Lake

elsewhere, which in summer mirror Queen Anne's lace and flowering water lilies. Canopus Creek flows through a beautiful ravine.

The park contains a few old hemlock groves, threatened by the woolly adelgid, and large areas of second-growth hardwood forest. Swamps and thick undergrowth of laurel make many sections difficult to penetrate, except where there are trails. Deer are numerous in the park, and a wide variety of birds, including ruffed grouse and wild turkeys, are frequently seen.

The park, which cannot be reached by public transportation, is accessible from NY 301 between the Taconic State Parkway and US 9. Within a mile west of the parkway are a public beach on Canopus Lake, a picnic area at Pelton Pond, and a campground. The park office is located across the road from the picnic area. Free parking is available on NY 301, at several locations near Canopus Lake, at the intersection of Dennytown and Sunk Mine roads, and on the east side of Dennytown Road near an old stone building 1.2 miles south of NY 301. Sunk Mine Road, an unmaintained, unpaved road, has several turnouts where one or two cars may be parked to give access to trails. For more information, contact Fahnestock State Park, RD 13, Route 301, Carmel, NY 10512; (845) 225-7207.

History

The Fahnestock area was once known for its thriving iron industry. The Sunk mines to the southwest and the Canada mines near Canopus Lake are part of the Reading Prong, a formation stretching from Pennsylvania to the Berkshires, rich in magnetite, an iron ore. Beginning soon after the American Revolution, these mines were exploited under various owners. At first, the ore was smelted and used locally. Later, it was hauled to the foundry, the furnaces, and the docks in Cold Spring. The West Point Foundry in Cold Spring was best known for its manufacture of the Parrott gun. Robert Parker Parrott, the foundry operator, developed the rifled cannon, which played an important role in the Civil War. Unfortunately, there was never an economical way to transport the ore from these hills to wider markets. Only in boom times could the mines compete. They closed down in 1876 in the midst of a depression, and even Thomas A. Edison's attempt to reopen them in 1890 was a failure. An exhibit at the Nature Center in the Fahnestock campground gives more information about the local iron industry.

Visitors to the park have to imagine this land cleared for farm and pasture, with settlements containing houses, schools, and stores. The schoolhouse foundation in Dennytown (along Dennytown Road near Indian Brook Road) and the Methodist chapel ruins in Odletown (near the junction of Sunk Mine Road and Bell Hollow Road), as well as old stone walls, root cellars, wells, and foundations, attest to a long-gone community life. Miners, charcoal-makers, teamsters, farmers, and their families lived in tiny houses and in boarding houses throughout this part of Fahnestock Park. Dennytown, where the Denny family began iron mining soon after the American Revolution ended, is now a ghost town. So, too, is Odletown, where only a large dam reminds us of the three bloomery forges by Canopus Creek that made bar iron in the early nineteenth century, using ore from the Sunk mines, charcoal from the nearby forest, and the abundant water power from the creek to operate bellows and triphammers.

Old woods roads, often lined with stone fences, are found throughout the park, their contours depressed by the weight of countless heavily loaded wagons. Most roads led to the Hudson at Fishkill or Peekskill. Some connected with the Old Albany Post Road, which was authorized in 1703 to carry the royal mail and in 1785 as a stage line from King's Bridge in the Bronx to the ferry at Albany. Built during the reign of Queen Anne and originally known as one of the Queen's Roads, it has since been mostly obliterated by US 9, though several sections remain unspoiled. One such section, going east from US 9 about a mile south of NY 301, is preserved much as it was in the eighteenth century and is listed in the National Register of Historic Places. Another section is in the Hubbard property, purchased by the Open Space Institute.

In 1815, a toll road was constructed from Connecticut to Cold Spring to carry goods, especially iron ore and farm produce, to the Hudson River. Much of the Philipstown (or Cold Spring) Turnpike was obliterated by NY 301, but parts of the original route may be sighted in the park south of the more modern highway.

Canopus Lake, whose waters cover several openings of the Canada iron mines, was created when the Civilian Conservation Corps (CCC) dammed Canopus Creek during the Depression in the 1930s. "Canopus" was the name of an important leader of the Wappingers, one of whose settlements was in a downstream valley of this creek. The CCC also created Stillwater Pond, enlarged Pelton Pond, and constructed picnic and camping facilities and bridle trails in the park. Hidden Lake and John Allen Pond were created about the same time on land that was still owned by the Fahnestock family.

Trails in Fahnestock and Hubbard-Perkins

There are approximately 50 miles of marked hiking trails in Fahnestock State Park and the Hubbard-Perkins Conservation Area. In addition to the marked hiking trails, many woods roads run through the park. Trails for horses and mountain bikes, some of which are marked, run along many of these woods roads. For example, a horse and mountain-bike trail beginning at the campground and running south past the west side of Stillwater Pond provides foot access to the Clear Lake Scout Reservation. The trail, which begins on a woods road near the end of the campground access road, is blazed white for about the first mile.

Fahnestock's rolling terrain provides opportunities for cross-country skiing along the woods roads when the snow cover is suitable. Another skiing route is Sunk Mine Road, which is not maintained.

Appalachian Trail
This major long distance trail traverses Fahnestock State Park and can be com-

bined with other trails to make a variety of loop hikes. Since most hikers will want to begin their hike at NY 301, where ample parking is available, the Appalachian Trail (AT) route through the park will be described in two sections—north and south of NY 301.

North of NY 301   *Length: 3.0 miles Blaze: white*
From NY 301, the AT ascends a ridge and turns right, paralleling Canopus Lake to the west, with some views of the lake through the trees. The hike is particularly nice at the end of June, when the mountain laurel is in bloom. It passes the eastern end of the Fahnestock Trail (blue), which leaves to the left at 0.6 mile. At 2.3 miles, after a short, steep climb, the AT reaches a beautiful viewpoint over the lake. Just beyond, a short side trail leads to a viewpoint to the west. From here, the hiker should return to the viewpoint over the lake, where a path leads steeply downhill to the beach at the northern end of the lake. A road leads south from the beach to NY 301. To return to your car, turn right and follow NY 301 for about 1.5 miles.

South of NY 301   *Length: 4.8 miles Blaze: white*
From NY 301, the AT follows the route of an old mine railway through the ravine of Canopus Creek, crossing a low-lying area on a curved stone causeway. At 0.7 mile, the AT bears left, with the Old Mine Railroad Trail (yellow) continuing ahead on the old railway bed. The Three Lakes Trail (blue) is crossed at 0.9 mile. To the left, this trail leads 1.3 miles back to NY 301. The AT now descends steeply, goes over a knoll, and passes through a level area that was once a swamp. After going along a hemlock-lined ridge, the AT descends a short, steep cliff and crosses a bridge over a stream.

At 2.1 miles, the AT reaches Sunk Mine Road. It briefly turns right and follows the road, then turns left into the woods. (The

Figure 8-2. Curved stone causeway along the route of the old mine railway

Three Lakes Trail, which can be used as a return route to make a 5.5-mile circular hike, is 0.6 mile further along Sunk Mine Road.) The AT goes over a ridge, with several views, then descends and goes along a swamp. The Catfish Loop (red) leaves to the left at 3.4 miles. At 3.6 miles, the Three Lakes Trail joins from the right, and both trails cross Dennytown Road, where parking is available. (Returning on the Three Lakes Trail from here will provide a 7.4-mile circular hike.) On the opposite side of the road, the Three Lakes Trail leaves to the right, while the AT continues ahead, reaching the Catfish Loop at 4.8 miles. To the left, the Catfish Loop leads back to the AT, just north of Dennytown Road, in 1.1 miles. To the right, it leads 2.5 miles to the southern end of the Three Lakes Trail, which can be followed for another 1.1 miles to Dennytown Road. A 12.2-mile loop hike can be made by combining the AT, the Catfish Loop, and the Three Lakes Trail.

Cabot Trail
Length: 1.0 mile Blaze: white

The Cabot Trail begins on the Charcoal Burners Trail (red) 0.6 mile north of NY 301, branches off to the west, and descends along a woods road, passing through open woods. At 0.4 mile it turns left. Straight ahead is private property; please do not enter the posted area. At 0.5 mile, the trail crosses a stream. A short unmarked side trail to Jordan Pond has a bench with a view over the lake. The Cabot Trail crosses a second stream and gradually ascends until, at 1.0 mile, it reaches a clearing and ends at the Perkins Trail (yellow).

Candlewood Hill Trail
Length: 2.1 miles Blaze: red

This trail begins where the Appalachian Trail (white) crosses Sunk Mine Road. There are several turnoffs near the trailhead where one or two cars may be parked.

The Candlewood Hill Trail begins with easy walking on an unpaved, fairly level section of Sunk Mine Road. The trail crosses Canopus Creek, passes the end of Bell Hollow Road on the right at 0.7 mile, and turns right into the woods at 1.2 miles. After a moderate ascent of Candlewood Hill, it reaches open rocks and ascends more

Figure 8-3. Sunk Mine Road

steeply to the open summit at 1.4 miles, with views in all directions. Continuing south over rocks, the trail turns right onto a woods road at 1.8 miles. At 2.0 miles, the trail turns left at a break in a rock wall and descends to Bell Hollow Road, where it ends.

To return to the starting point, hikers can turn right on Bell Hollow Road, follow it 0.7 mile to Sunk Mine Road, and go left 0.7 mile back along the Candlewood Hill Trail to the Appalachian Trail crossing. The section of Bell Hollow Road north of the end of the trail is a woods road and is not suitable for cars.

Catfish Loop   *Length: 3.6 miles Blaze: red*

Beginning on the Appalachian Trail (white) just east of Dennytown Road, the Catfish Loop follows a sinuous path that takes it across the Appalachian Trail, up to a lookout with a view of the Hudson Highlands, and finally back to the southern end of the Three Lakes Trail (blue). The trailhead can be reached by walking 0.2 mile on the northbound Appalachian Trail from the parking area on Dennytown Road, 1.2 miles south of NY 301.

The Catfish Loop heads west, away from the Appalachian Trail, through woods and a barberry thicket, and at 0.2 mile it crosses Dennytown Road about 800 feet south of the parking area. It continues to the southwest through open woods, crossing several stone walls and two small brooks, and ascends to reach a register box at 0.6 mile. The trail crosses a small stream and follows along the park boundary for a short distance. It crosses the Appalachian Trail at 1.1 miles and a horse trail at 1.4 miles, then crosses a brook and passes the end of the now-closed southern section of the Three Lakes Trail on the right at 1.5 miles. The Catfish Loop then leads left, departing from a faint yellow-blazed trail, and ascends to reach rock outcroppings at 1.7 miles. From the top of a large rock formation to the right side of the trail there is a view of the Hudson Highlands, including Storm King and Crows Nest.

The trail continues on its undulating course over rocks and through thickets of mountain laurel. It descends and turns right, with a trail to the left heading toward Catfish Pond, which is outside the southern boundary of the park. Having reversed its direction via a 180° loop, the trail crosses a brook and ascends over more rocks. At 2.8 miles, it starts to follow a stone wall on the left, which is the park boundary. After leaving the stone wall, the trail crosses two unmarked trails and several stone walls before reaching a side trail to Duck Pond on the left at 3.4 miles. It finally descends and terminates at 3.6 miles at the Three Lakes Trail (blue). To return, hikers should turn left and walk for 1.1

miles on the Three Lakes Trail, which crosses Dennytown Road at the parking area.

Cedar Ridge Trail   *Length: 0.8 mile Blaze: yellow*

This trail runs through a private farm just outside Fahnestock State Park, following an easement held by the Open Space Institute. In late summer, it offers meadows filled with wildflowers and chirping crickets, along with a view of the Hudson River. Cars may be parked on Old Albany Post Road just south of its intersection with Philipse Brook Road. The trail begins fifty yards west of this intersection at a gate on the north side of Philipse Brook Road. Since this is a working farm, it is important to make sure gates are closed. After passing through the gate, the trail turns left to follow the edge of a pasture, then goes through two more gates and pastures before entering woods at 0.4 mile. It passes an old wagon at 0.6 mile and enters another pasture, then enters the woods again through another gate (beware of the electric fence here). At 0.7 mile, there is a view of the Hudson River through a small clearing. Soon afterwards, the trail ends at a rock wall.

Charcoal Burners Trail   *Length: 3.3 miles Blaze: red*

The nineteenth-century iron industry in what is now Fahnestock State Park depended upon charcoal, which was a wood product readily available from the forests. The men who felled trees to burn into charcoal were called woodchoppers or charcoal burners. The Charcoal Burners Trail recognizes those men who spent many lonely hours in the woods.

The trail serves as a connection between Fahnestock State Park and the network of trails in the Hubbard-Perkins Conservation Area. The southern terminus is at the Three Lakes Trail (blue), 0.6 mile north of Sunk Mine Road. The trail crosses the Old Mine Railroad Trail (yellow) at 0.2 mile. Working its way north, up and down over small ridges, the Charcoal Burners Trail passes through open woods and laurel groves until it reaches NY 301 at 1.1 miles. This crossing is 1.5 miles west of where the Appalachian Trail crosses NY 301. In addition to the red blazing, the trail crossing is marked by a white cross painted on a rock outcrop along the north side of the road.

After crossing the road, the Charcoal Burners Trail goes up and over rocks. It turns right at the beginning of the Perkins Trail (yellow) at 1.2 miles and ascends gradually along a woods road through laurel and blueberry bushes. It passes the beginning of the Cabot Trail (white) on the left at 1.7 miles and joins the Fahnestock Trail (blue) at 2.0 miles. Together they reach the dam at Beaver Pond at 2.2 miles, and then, at 2.3 miles, the Fahnestock Trail goes straight ahead while the Charcoal Burners Trail turns right. Rising up to the ridge, the trail offers limited views at 2.6 miles and a view to the east at 3.2 miles. The Charcoal Burners Trail ends at 3.3 miles at the terminus of the Wiccopee Trail (blue).

East Mountain Loop   *Length: 1.5 miles Blaze: red*

Starting 1.4 miles from the beginning of School Mountain Road (white) on US 9, this loop trail crosses over the top of East Mountain, with a view of Fishkill Ridge at 0.7 mile. After reaching a false summit at 0.9 mile, the East Mountain Loop begins its descent on the north slope of the mountain. It makes a sharp right turn at 1.1 miles. After going through former farm fields and passing stone foundations, the East Mountain Loop ends on School Mountain Road, 2.0 miles from US 9.

Fahnestock Trail   *Length: 7.3 miles Blaze: blue*

The Fahnestock Trail is the main east–west trail in the Hubbard-Perkins Conservation Area. Along its route to the Appalachian Trail in Fahnestock State Park, it is coaligned with three other trails. Hikers need to pay attention as, in all three cases, the Fahnestock Trail is the trail that turns off of the other trails. Parking is on US 9 just north of its intersection with NY 301 and near the Appalachian Trail crossing just west of Canopus Lake on NY 301.

To reach the western trailhead, walk 0.2 mile north along US 9 and turn right onto a paved road leading into the Hubbard-Perkins Conservation Area. The Fahnestock Trail and multi-use School Mountain Road (white) begin 0.1 mile from US 9 at a gate, where there is a signboard.

At 0.1 mile, this broad woods road crosses two steel-decked bridges in quick succession. After passing stone pillars on the left and crossing a third steel-decked bridge, the two trails separate at 0.4 mile. The Fahnestock Trail makes a sharp right turn, while School Mountain Road continues straight ahead.

As the Fahnestock Trail parallels a stream, hikers have the opportunity to gaze out over the adjacent wetlands. At 0.6 mile, the trail leaves the stream and then, at 0.9 mile, makes a sharp left turn. The ascent of Round Hill is steep to the first view to the west at 1.1 miles. The trail climbs gradually up a long ridge dotted with red cedars. Continuing to ascend, the trail crosses a flat area and ascends with steeper switchbacks until, at 2.0 miles, it reaches a view to the southwest that includes the Bear Mountain Bridge over the Hudson River. Over the next mile, the trail contours along the south slope near the top of Round Hill, with occasional views, and descends, steeply at times, with several switchbacks, to a pass where it follows a woods road over a broad low hill. After crossing a seasonally wet area and making a slightly steeper ascent, the trail reaches a westerly view of the interior of the conservation area at 3.0 miles. Continuing its ascent, the trail reaches a high point with no view and then descends gradually to join the Perkins Trail (yellow), which comes in from the left at 3.9 miles.

The two trails are coaligned along a woods road until the Fahnestock Trail turns left at 4.3 miles while the Perkins Trail (yellow) continues straight ahead. The Fahnestock Trail now runs along the side of a lake, passing a short unmarked trail to a view of the lake at 4.7 miles. The trail gradually turns right, crossing the inlet of the lake on a cement bridge at 4.9 miles. After the bridge, it gradually turns north, still on the woods road, and then, at 5.1 miles, turns right and leaves the woods road. The woods road, if followed, connects with the middle of the Wiccopee Trail (blue), but it is often covered with water in wet weather. The Fahnestock Trail reaches the bottom of a gully at 5.3 miles and then ascends through laurel groves to turn right onto a woods road at 5.5 miles.

At the next junction, private property signs are to the right. The Fahnestock Trail bears left and then almost immediately turns right. Take care in this area, as there are unmarked woods roads entering and leaving from the left. As the Fahnestock Trail gradually goes uphill, it passes through wet spots and by a sea of ferns. At 6.0 miles, the Charcoal Burners Trail (red) comes in from the left, and together they pass the dam at Beaver Pond at 6.1 miles. The Fahnestock Trail turns left at 6.3 miles, while the Charcoal Burners Trail continues straight ahead.

After leaving the Charcoal Burners Trail, the Fahnestock Trail descends for about 100 yards, joins a woods road, and then crosses two streams. It then joins another woods road, which it follows to a high point at 6.8 miles. The Fahnestock Trail passes through uneven but moderately open country and descends a short slope. At 7.3 miles, it ends at the Appalachian Trail (white), 0.6 mile north of NY 301, where parking is available.

Old Mine Railroad Trail   Length: 2.2 miles Blaze: yellow

The Old Mine Railroad Trail is of historical interest and also gives access to some unusual and beautiful areas in the park. During the Civil War, a narrow-gauge railroad was built from the Sunk mines to Dump Hill, located where

Figure 8-4. Along the Old Mine Railroad Trail

Dennytown Road meets NY 301. In 1874, another branch was built to the Canada mines. Mule-drawn rail cars carried the ore to Dump Hill, where it was dumped and shoveled into horse-drawn wagons for the final five-mile trip to Cold Spring. This laborious method of hauling was antiquated the day the mine railroad was built, and the local mines could not compete with ore shipped from the Midwest by steam-powered trains. As a result, the mines closed in 1876. Much of this mine railbed was opened as a hiking trail in 1994.

The Old Mine Railroad Trail runs from the Appalachian Trail (white) south of NY 301 along the west side of Hidden Lake and then down to the point where the railbed disappears under the west side of John Allen Pond. A connection is provided out to Sunk Mine Road. The trail offers level walking, as railbeds avoid or eliminate the small ups and downs that are a normal part of the terrain. It also affords an unusual opportunity to hike through a marsh without getting wet feet, taking advantage of two causeways that were built up to carry the railbed.

Parking is along NY 301 near the Appalachian Trail crossing or on a small peninsula jutting into Canopus Lake. The mine railbed is evident almost immediately when hiking south along the Appalachian Trail from the road. Hikers will notice the extensive rock work that was done to bridge several low areas. After 0.7 mile, the Appalachian Trail crosses a small stream and veers left off the railbed. The Old Mine Railroad Trail begins here, following the railbed straight ahead. It passes through dense laurel growth and, at 0.3 mile, crosses the inlet stream to Hidden Lake. After the trail crosses a causeway, it begins to run along the northwest shore of the lake. The trail goes over a second causeway and through the woods, picking up a woods road at 0.6 mile. This road was built in the 1930s and appears to follow the approximate route of the railroad. The Charcoal Burners Trail (red) crosses at 1.1 miles. At 1.5 miles, just before the woods road reaches the park boundary, the trail turns sharply left off the road, passing through laurel to cross the inlet stream to John Allen Pond and reach a point of land at 1.8 miles, where the railbed disappears under the pond.

The trail continues to the right over rocks and soon joins a woods road which leads out to Sunk Mine Road, 0.3 mile east of Dennytown Road, where the Old Mine Railroad Trail ends. The Three Lakes Trail (blue) is 120 yards east (left) along Sunk Mine Road.

Pelton Pond Nature Trail   *Length: 1.5 miles Blaze: yellow*
This easy trail offers a pleasant stroll around Pelton Pond. Parking is available on the south side of NY 301, 0.6 mile west of the Taconic State Parkway. From the sign near the west end of the Pelton Pond parking lot, a short path leads uphill to the trail, which circles the pond. Following the trail to the right, hikers pass through a picnic area and cross the dam at the southwest end of the pond. After a short distance, a woods road goes off to the right, heading toward the campground and a horse trail beyond. Farther on, a red-blazed trail goes uphill to the right to the Nature Center, which is open during the summer. The trail continues around the northeast end of the pond and back to the starting point.

Perkins Trail   *Length: 4.0 miles Blaze: yellow*
Named for the former owners, the Perkins family, this trail starts from the Charcoal Burners Trail (red) less than 100 yards north of NY 301, where the Charcoal Burners Trail takes a sharp right just after crossing an intermittent stream. Heading west over several small ridges, the trail makes a steep descent at 0.3 mile into a field filled with fir trees. The southern terminus of the Cabot Trail (white) is to the right. The Perkins Trail immediately turns left, following the edge of the field, turns right, and heads straight to a gate in the fence. After passing through the gate (please close after using), the trail follows a farm road to reach Glynwood Road, a dirt road on private property, at 0.5 mile. The trail turns left along the road for 200 feet and then turns right through a farm gate (please close). Over the next tenth of a mile, the trail crosses a farm field, parallel to and south of a stone wall. The continuous views to the north over working farm fields and the chance to travel through a different ecosystem make this portion of the trail an unusual opportunity. In the summer, the sun glaring down does not detract from a seemingly endless array of insects, flowers, grasses, and birds.

At the end of the field, the trail goes through another gate at 0.7 mile and makes a 45° right turn to cross a rocky field. After going through yet another gate into a third field, the Perkins Trail turns right, follows the fence, and crosses the field on a farm road. The trail descends on the farm road, winding its way through several small fields to enter the woods at 1.2 miles. After passing a high point, it reaches a rocky outcropping with a view to the west and north, before beginning its descent along the ridge.

At the end of the ridge at 1.9 miles, the Perkins Trail makes a sharp right turn, continues its descent, and reaches the eastern bank of Clove Creek at 2.0 miles. The trail bears right and begins to parallel the creek. At 2.6 miles, the trail crosses Glynwood Road, goes up the hill to a telephone line, and turns right. It reaches a T junction at 3.0 miles and makes a left onto a woods road. In 150 feet, the Fahnestock Trail (blue) comes in from the right.

The trails run jointly until, at 3.5 miles, the Fahnestock Trail continues straight ahead to ascend a ridge, while the Perkins Trail turns right and descends. After crossing a series of stone walls, the trail makes a sharp left off a former logging road at 3.8 miles. The Perkins Trail descends along the south bank of a cascading stream, ending at 4.0 miles at School Mountain Road near a bridge. The northern end of East Mountain Loop (red) is on the left side of School Mountain Road on the other side of the bridge.

School Mountain Road *Length: 4.1 miles Blaze: white*

School Mountain Road, a multi-use trail, is the main artery into the conservation area. In winter, even light snow cover offers cross-country skiing opportunities. To reach the trailhead from the parking area just north of the intersection of US 9 and NY 301, walk 0.2 mile north along US 9 and turn right onto the road leading into the Hubbard-Perkins Conservation Area. School Mountain Road and the Fahnestock Trail (blue) begin 0.1 mile from US 9, at a gate where there is a signboard.

At 0.1 mile, this woods road crosses two steel-decked bridges in quick succession. The first bridge is over Clove Creek. Just before a third bridge, there are stone pillars on a woods road to the left which leads to the site of the former Hubbard mansion. On the other side of that bridge, at 0.4 mile, the Fahnestock Trail (blue) leaves to the right. At 1.4 miles, the East Mountain Loop (red) begins at the left to traverse East Mountain. School Mountain Road continues its steady ascent and reaches the terminus of the Perkins Trail (yellow) on the right at 1.9 miles at a bridge. The northern end of the East Mountain Loop is on the other side of that bridge. School Mountain Road continues to climb and reaches a Y junction at 2.1 miles, with the trail taking the less distinct left fork. Still climbing, the road reaches a height of land where the Wiccopee Trail (blue) begins to the right at 3.6 miles. Now descending, the road reaches its northern terminus at East Mountain Road at 4.1 miles, where there is parking for several cars.

Three Lakes Trail

Length: 4.8 miles Blaze: blue

The Three Lakes Trail starts from NY 301 near Canopus Lake and travels generally southwest through the park. Various segments of the trail are accessible from NY 301, Sunk Mine Road, and Dennytown Road. Several circular

hikes are possible by combining sections of the Three Lakes Trail with sections of the Appalachian Trail. The northern portion of the trail gets fairly heavy use; the section south of Dennytown Road is quiet and very pretty.

To begin at NY 301, cars should be parked at either parking area at Canopus Lake. A walk west on the remnants of the Philipstown Turnpike just

Figure 8-5. Rock bridge across Canopus Creek

south of NY 301 leads, in approximately 250 feet, to the trailhead on the left. The trail follows a woods road to pass old mine pits and then a swamp on the right. Turning right off the woods road at 0.7 mile, the trail bears southwest. Straight ahead on the woods road is the Green Trail to Clear Lake Scout Reservation. The Three Lakes Trail now descends gradually and soon begins to parallel Canopus Creek. After crossing the creek on a rock bridge, it bears sharply right, passes a swamp on the right, and ascends moderately to the Appalachian Trail crossing at 1.3 miles.

The Three Lakes Trail goes over some gentle rises before descending to the southern end of Hidden Lake. An unmarked woods road at 1.8 miles leads right and reaches the lakeshore in a short distance, then crosses the outlet of the lake (difficult to cross at times of high water) to intersect the Old Mine Railroad Trail (yellow) 0.1 mile from the Three Lakes Trail.

The Three Lakes Trail continues over fairly level terrain through mountain laurel. After passing the southern terminus of the Charcoal Burners Trail (red) at 2.1 miles, the Three Lakes Trail descends slightly to reach a section of railbed from the mine railroad coming from Sunk Mine to the left. Just before reaching the railbed, the foundations of several buildings from John Allen's homestead can be seen along the trail. The trail goes right along the railbed, but after a short distance it leaves to the left. The reason is visible to the right, where hikers will see impressive stone abutments, but the bridge they supported is long gone. The trail continues to the shore of John Allen Pond, follows the lakeshore, goes over a narrow concrete dam, and crosses the brook below the lake spillway. The trail then ascends, reaching Sunk Mine Road at 2.7 miles. To the left, Sunk Mine Road leads to the Appalachian Trail in about 0.6 mile.

The Three Lakes Trail turns right on Sunk Mine Road for 0.2 mile and reenters woods on the left. The trail follows a woods road and then turns left and climbs more steeply, passing the remnants of Denny Mine off the trail to the left. After a steep descent over rocks, the trail passes a swamp on the left, swings right, and reaches Dennytown Road, with a large grassy parking area on the east side, 3.7 miles from the start. The two stone buildings at the north end of the field were built during the 1920s or 1930s by an amateur stonemason. The one that might be mistaken for a chapel reportedly served as a chicken coop. There is water available at a pump.

Joining the Appalachian Trail briefly to cross Dennytown Road, the Three Lakes Trail enters woods to the west. After about 100 feet, the Appalachian Trail goes off to the left. The Three Lakes Trail crosses a stone wall and passes a group camping area on the right. The trail ascends moderately through open woods, then levels off and crosses a woods road at 4.1 miles. It passes through a large patch of blueberries to reach a trail register at 4.3 miles. A yellow-blazed trail, which comes in from the Taconic Outdoor Education Center on the right and later goes off to the right, should not be followed, since this area is closed to hikers. The Three Lakes Trail descends through mountain laurel, crosses a stream, and reaches the western end of the Catfish Loop (red) on the right at 4.8 miles. As of summer 2001, the trail is closed beyond this point to protect a wildlife habitat. The Catfish Loop, together with the Appalachian Trail, can be used as an alternate return route.

Wiccopee Trail *Length: 1.9 miles Blaze: blue*

This interior trail provides a northern link between the Charcoal Burners Trail (red) and School Mountain Road (white). Starting from the northern terminus of the Charcoal Burners Trail, the Wiccopee Trail heads north as it descends the ridge through open oak and blueberries. Turning west and then north again, the trail continues to descend, now through a sparse laurel grove, and reaches a woods road at 0.8 mile, where it turns left. It follows the woods road for 0.2 mile and then leaves to the right. The Wiccopee Trail winds its way gradually uphill, bypassing wet areas and laurel groves. At 1.9 miles, it reaches School Mountain Road (white), where it ends. Parking for several cars is available on East Mountain Road 0.5 mile to the right.

OTHER AREAS IN PUTNAM COUNTY

There are additional open spaces in Putnam County that provide a range of hiking opportunities. These areas are worthy of exploration, although they are not nearly as large as the great state parks such as Harriman and Fahnestock, and generally lack marked trails and detailed hiking maps. Opportunities range from bushwhacking and hiking in DEC multiple-use areas to a simple stroll along a cascading brook. For more information on the DEC multiple-use areas, contact the Stony Kill DEC Forestry Office, 79 Farmstead Lane, Wappingers Falls, NY 12590; (845) 831-8780 x309, for the brochure, *Putnam County Multiple-Use Areas.*

Clear Lake Scout Reservation

Protruding into the southeastern section of Fahnestock State Park is the Clear Lake Scout Reservation, a camp owned by the Westchester-Putnam Council of the Boy Scouts of America. The scouts obtained the property from a noted authority on glaciers, Dr. William B. Osgood Field, Jr., who had purchased it from the estate of Dr. Ernest Fahnestock in 1935. In 1994, the Open Space Institute acquired permanent conservation easements to preserve the 1,400-acre tract. The Open Space Institute's action prevented the threatened sale and development of the reservation.

Under the terms of the easement, the northern and western parts of the reservation are open to the public for hiking, but hikers must stay away from the area used by the scouts near Clear Lake. Pertinent intersections are clearly marked with signs which read: STOP NO PUBLIC ACCESS. The area is not open to pets or bicycles. Bushwhacking is also prohibited. Most of the major intersections have maps of the area posted on large signs. Hiking in the Clear Lake Scout Reservation is particularly nice in the leaf-off season, when the views are more open. Many of the trails are well suited to cross-country skiing.

Hikers can gain access to the reservation by walking south from NY 301 on the Three Lakes Trail (blue) or east from Sunk Mine Road near Candlewood Hill. Warning: Sunk Mine Road is a rough, unmaintained road and is not plowed during the winter. A third access route is via the multi-use trail on the east, which may be reached from NY 301 near Pelton Pond.

Blue Trail   *Length: 2.6 miles Blaze: blue*
The Blue Trail goes east from the Candlewood Hill Trail (red) along Sunk Mine Road about 300 yards south of Bell Hollow woods road, where there is limited parking. It proceeds along a woods road for 0.2 mile, and it turns sharply left off the road just before a gate. The trail climbs steadily until it reaches the ridgetop at 0.6 mile, with a narrow view, seasonally much wider. At 1.0 mile, there is an open view of Clear Lake below. The upper end of the Purple Trail is reached at 1.5 miles. The junction with the Green Trail, which leaves the Clear Lake property almost immediately and proceeds left (north) into Fahnestock to connect with the Three Lakes Trail, is at 1.9 miles. From here, the Blue Trail follows a woods road heading south. The White Trail branches off to the left at 2.1 miles, and the lower end of the Purple Trail is on the right at 2.4 miles. Shortly after crossing a stream, the part of the Blue Trail which is open to the public ends at the junction with the Blue-White Trail at 2.6 miles. The Blue Trail actually forms a complete loop, with part of it in the area open only to scouts staying at Clear Lake Scout Reservation.

Blue-White Trail   *Length: 0.3 mile Blaze: blue/white*
The Blue-White Trail connects the Blue and the White trails. It is a woods road whose eastern end was a street of Odletown.

Green Trail   *Length: 0.3 mile Blaze: green*
The Green Trail connects Fahnestock State Park with Clear Lake Scout Reservation. It begins where the Three Lakes Trail turns right off the woods road, 0.7 mile from NY 301, and continues along the woods road, ending 0.3 mile later at the Blue Trail.

Purple Trail *Length: 0.2 mile Blaze: purple*
The Purple Trail is a shortcut across the northern end of the Blue Trail, providing a loop back to the top of the ridge. From the lower end, it is a gentle climb
for the first 300 yards and then climbs steeply with switchbacks to the top of
the ridge in the next 100 yards.

White Trail *Length: 1.4 miles Blaze: white*
From the junction with the Blue Trail, the White Trail climbs, steeply at times,
to Bushy Ridge, where it turns gently to the right along the ridge. At 0.6 mile,
there are limited views to the west as the trail follows a stone wall for more
than 100 yards. At the end of the stone wall, the trail starts winding down the
ridge to end at Odletown at 1.4 miles. Many stone walls and foundations from
the settlement of Odletown may be seen here. If one follows "Main Street" to
the left between double stone walls, one reaches the multi-use trail in 0.2 mile.
To the left, the multi-use trail leads to Stillwater Pond and eventually to NY
301 near Pelton Pond.

Walter G. Merritt Recreation Area
Nestled against the Connecticut-New York line is a county park with a quiet
trail over a mile in length, much of it along a cascading brook. The park entrance is on Haviland Hollow Road, 2.4 miles east of NY 22. For more information, contact Putnam County Veterans' Memorial Park, 199 Gypsy Trail
Road, Carmel, NY 10512; (845) 225-3650.

Ninham Mountain Multiple-Use Area
The 1,023-acre Ninham Mountain Multiple-Use Area was established in 1962
on lands purchased from the Rohner farm and the Cornell estate. Bordered on
the south by a county park and on the north by private forests, it includes most
of the southern end of a long and rugged mountain mass. The focal point of the
forest is Ninham Mountain. The highest point for miles around, the mountain
was once known as Smalley's Hill after a local family. In the nineteenth century,
it was renamed in honor of Daniel Nimham, *sachem* (chief) of the Wappingers,
who once ruled all the land in Putnam and southern Dutchess counties. (The
name "Nimham" was eventually transformed into "Ninham.") After having
fought beside the British in the French and Indian wars, Nimham and his fol-
lowers returned to the Highlands to find their lands occupied by tenants of the
Philipse family. Believing that he had been defrauded of his ancestral lands by

the Philipses, Nimham appealed to the royal courts in 1765, but without success. He fought on the side of the colonists in the American Revolution. In the end, Nimham and forty of his band, deserted by a company of American soldiers, were killed in 1778 at the Battle of Indian Bridge in the northern Bronx. Surrounded by lakes and reservoirs and commanding a dramatic view of the vast lands once occupied by Nimham and his people, Ninham Mountain is a fitting memorial.

On the lower valley fields, the DEC planted red pine, Norway spruce, and European larch. A fire lookout tower was erected on the mountain, and the DEC established a field headquarters, an office, and a storehouse for forest fire control operations for Westchester, Putnam, and Dutchess counties. The area is open for hiking, cross-country skiing, mountain biking, camping, hunting, trapping, and fishing; a permit from the ranger is required for camping more than three nights, or for groups of 10 or more. For more information, contact the Stony Kill DEC Forestry Office, 79 Farmstead Lane, Wappingers Falls, NY 12590; (845) 831-8780 x309.

Ninham Mountain lies some seven miles east of Fahnestock State Park on NY 301. A shorter southern approach from the Taconic Parkway is via Peekskill Hollow Road to Kent Cliffs. Ninham Mountain is reached by turning east on NY 301 and driving about 3.5 miles to the point where NY 301 crosses West Branch Reservoir on a stone causeway. A sharp left turn onto Gypsy Trail Road (before the causeway crossing) leads to the entrance to the field headquarters, two miles beyond on the right. Parking areas have a specified limit on cars to regulate the number of hunters using the forest in season. Another parking area is located off the dirt road running northwest from Gypsy Trail Road to the fire tower. During hunting season (approximately September to February), these limits must be observed. The rules are: do not block roads, do not park on the road, do not drive off the road, and confine rambles to state land.

Three well-defined trails or woods roads, all of which run north–south, penetrate portions of the forest. These woods, save for an occasional wetland or pocket of dense laurel and greenbrier, are generally open terrain. With a compass, it is possible to fashion a loop of three or four miles.

One recommended hike is to descend east from the field headquarters via a wide woods road to a beautiful pond created by a small dam across Pine Pond's south inlet. In autumn, the massed effect of steepled golden larches rising to the eastern hill line is a magnificent sight. Near the dam, a narrow trail leads back to the east end of the headquarters' road. From here, the trail leads south through the red pine plantation to another forest of larches, with views of Ninham Mountain and the valley and hills to the north.

After reaching the county park boundary, the route turns west through the pines and descends, crossing Gypsy Trail Road, into the deep wooded gully of Pine Pond Brook, with its towering tulip trees. Hikers can cross the brook in several places on boulders or fallen trees to follow the clearly marked forest boundary around the south end of an extensive marsh. Here begins the steep climb up the easternmost ridge of Ninham Mountain, a route that keeps always to the west, with the blazed boundary in sight. Beyond the crest are several attractive hollows among low hills. Approximately half a mile from the brook, the forest boundary turns sharply southeast, but hikers should continue northwest to west to skirt a marsh and the thickest laurel. At the top of the next hill, the route comes out on the well-defined north–south woods road that descends the south spur of the mountain. Turning north, the route follows old stone walls, passes patches of farmland long returned to woods, and comes out at the locked gate on the gravel road to the tower, where there is parking for about six cars. In another 0.7 mile, the highest point on Ninham Mountain (1,270 feet) is reached, with an 80-foot steel fire tower, which is closed to the public. The view from this point is mostly obscured by trees.

Going down, a traverse southeast through an open young hardwood forest offers a pleasant alternative to the gravel road. A compass bearing of 135° carries the hiker over a lower rocky summit out onto the gravel road at a parking spot for three or four cars. Larches edge this lovely field. From this point, hikers may walk out on the gravel road, which leads to the paved highway and, to the right, the field headquarters. Alternatively, a short trail begins here and leads south to a brook, which may be followed east to its confluence with Pine Pond Brook. The latter is best crossed by turning north and coming out at the bridge on Gypsy Trail Road a short distance beyond. Just up the hill on the left from Pine Pond Brook is an abandoned mine, which was worked in the 1840s by the Hudson River Mining Company in the hope of finding silver, and sporadically as an arsenic mine until 1907. By either route, the distance from the small parking area to the headquarters is less than a mile.

NINE

EAST HUDSON HIGHLANDS

o other part of the Hudson Valley can match the scenic grandeur of the river's gorge through the Highlands. From Dunderberg north around Anthony's Nose to Storm King and Breakneck, the Hudson is narrow and winding, flanked by hills of a thousand feet or more. Many of the region's most spectacular and popular hikes are found here. Anthony's Nose offers a panoramic view over the Bear Mountain Bridge and the vast expanse of Bear Mountain-Harriman State Parks, while along the rocky spine of Breakneck Ridge, the vistas improve with every step upward.

History

The history of the Highlands is rich and colorful. The naming of Anthony's Nose, the southern gate to the Highlands, is the subject of much conjecture and folklore. On early maps it was called St. Anthony's Nose. Various Dutch Anthonies are also said to have lent it their names, while Washington Irving tells his own tale about the mountain in *A History of New York from the Beginning of the World to the End of the Dutch Dynasty*. About all that can be said for certain is that it was named long before the days of General Anthony Wayne and the American Revolution.

During the Revolution, control of the narrow river passage under Anthony's Nose was critical to Washington's army. Both shores were heavily fortified, lest the British cut off New England from the rest of the rebelling colonies. In 1777,

Figure 9-1. Bear Mountain-Harriman Park panorama from Anthony's Nose

a great iron chain was laid across the river from the foot of Anthony's Nose to Fort Montgomery. The remains of the fort are still visible on a knob overlooking the river, and just to the south across Popolopen Creek, one wall of Fort Clinton stands below the Trailside Museum at the western end of the Bear Mountain Bridge.

These log and stone ramparts were the scene of a brave defense by Orange County militia on October 4, 1777, against an assault by British troops under Sir John Vaughan. The British finally took the posts and, with the aid of ships, broke the chain. They failed to take advantage of their success, however, and retreated downriver after hearing of the American victory at Saratoga. A second, heavier iron chain laid in 1778 from West Point to Constitution Island, where the river is narrowest, was never breached. Constitution Island, once known as Martelaer's Rock, was fortified in 1775 and renamed in honor of the unwritten British constitution that the Americans claimed to be defending. The island, which has been owned since 1908 by the U.S. Military Academy, may be reached only by special launch from West Point.

Midway between the locations of the two chains, at the foot of Sugarloaf Hill, is the site of the Beverly Robinson House, where the most notorious act of treachery in American history took place. Benedict Arnold, commander at West Point, used that house as his headquarters. On September 25, 1780, while at breakfast, he received word of the capture of Major John André, his liaison with the British. Arnold fled immediately, ordering his boatman to row him downriver to the safety of the British ship *Vulture*, anchored near Croton Point. Shortly after his departure, George Washington, Alexander Hamilton, and LaFayette arrived at the house, expecting to meet Arnold. Upon reading the

BEAR MOUNTAIN — LONG MT. — TURKEY MT. — TORNE — CROWN RANGE

BROOKS LAKE

BEAR MT. INN — HESSIAN LAKE — FORT CLINTON — POPOLOPEN CREEK — FORT MONTGOMERY

From Photo by N.Y. Howell

R. L. DICKINSON

dispatch describing the detainment of one "John Anderson" at Tarrytown, then the subsequent confession of Major André regarding his true identity, Washington realized Arnold's treason. Hamilton, sent to intercept Arnold, returned instead with Arnold's letter of explanation to Washington. The next day André was brought to the house under guard.

On the east end of the ridge of Anthony's Nose are the extensive dumps of the old Manitou Copper Mine. This mine was originally opened about 1767 for iron by Peter Hasenclever, but it was not successful because the ore, smelted in one of his furnaces at Cortlandt south of Peekskill, proved too sulfurous. During the Civil War, the Hudson River Copper Company attempted to mine copper there. When they found iron sulfide instead of copper, they switched their name to the Highland Chemical Company and produced sulfur. The chemical plant, which closed in 1913, was at the foot of the mountain in the hamlet of Manitou.

From Anthony's Nose, one looks down on the Bear Mountain Bridge, the first road bridge over the Hudson constructed south of Albany and the longest suspension bridge in the world at the time it was built. Substantially funded by the Harriman family, who owned an estate on the west side of the river and had donated land there for a state park, the bridge was completed in 1929 for $5 million as a privately owned toll bridge. High tolls (80 cents for car and driver plus 10 cents per passenger in each direction) deterred customers, and the bridge lost money. In 1940, the state purchased the bridge for $2.3 million.

The sentinels of the northern gate of the Highlands are Breakneck on the east and Storm King on the west. This area was the scene of one of the most extraordinary engineering feats of the day when the Catskill Aqueduct was tunneled under the river at this point. Most of the time between groundbreaking in 1907 and the opening of the reservoir floodgates in 1912 was taken up by geologic boring of the river bed to find bedrock. Glacial action and erosion had filled in the gorge nearly 800 feet above bedrock. Nearly as impressive an engineering triumph was the construction of the Storm King Highway across the sheer rock wall on the face of Storm King. The highway, completed in 1922, can be seen from Breakneck.

To the northeast is Beacon Mountain, named for the beacon fires kept there by American militia during the Revolution. From 1902 to 1975, the Mount Beacon Incline Railway climbed the northwest face from the City of Beacon to a casino on the mountaintop. A monument on the summit of North Beacon Mountain erected by the Daughters of the American Revolution was badly damaged by lightning but was reconstructed in 1928.

HUDSON HIGHLANDS STATE PARK

The first efforts to preserve the scenic beauty of the Storm King–Breakneck section of the Hudson River valley were made by the Hudson River Conservation Society, which worked to persuade landowners to donate property to the State of New York or to include restrictive clauses in their deeds regarding quarrying, mining, and other land uses detrimental to the area's natural beauty. In 1938, the Society succeeded in having 177 acres on the northwest face of Breakneck Ridge deeded to the New York State Conservation Department as gifts of Rosalie Loew Whitney and the Thomas Nelson estate. In 1939, this same group made an appeal to save Anthony's Nose and create a memorial to Raymond Torrey. The donations purchased 200 acres in Putnam County just north of Anthony's Nose, which eventually became part of the Hudson Highlands State Park.

In 1965, as large corporate purchases began to threaten the Highlands with industrial development, the State Council of Parks began planning a program of scenic preservation, which was referred to the temporary Hudson River Valley Study Committee. By citing the Highlands as a high-priority project in its recommendations to the newly formed Hudson River Valley Commission in 1966, and bolstered by continuing enthusiasm for the Highlands among conservation groups, the State Council of Parks and its supporters succeeded in saving Little Stony Point from proposed industrial development in 1967.

In the same year, Jackson Hole Preserve, Inc., a conservation foundation supported primarily by the Rockefeller family, presented a deed of trust to New

Figure 9-2. The Hudson River Gorge: Storm King and Breakneck Ridge

York State for acquisition within the Highlands. Within a year, more than 2,500 acres—including Sugarloaf Mountain, Bull Hill (Mount Taurus), Pollepel Island, the south and west faces of Breakneck Ridge, and several riverfront properties—were acquired. These areas form the major part of the northern section of the present Hudson Highlands State Park.

North of the park and the Beacon watershed property lies the 923 acres of the Fishkill Ridge Conservation Area, which is owned by Scenic Hudson Land Trust, Inc., and managed as an extension of the park. The land was purchased in 1992 and 1993 with the assistance of the Lila Acheson and DeWitt Wallace Fund for the Hudson Highlands.

A separate 1,033-acre section of the Hudson Highlands State Park known as the Osborn Preserve lies south of Garrison. The acquisition of this section began when William Henry Osborn II, past president of the Hudson River Conservation Society, donated the Sugarloaf Hill area to the State of New York in 1974. In 1981 and 1982, the National Park Service purchased two additional tracts on the top of Canada Hill for the Appalachian Trail reroute and corridor protection. Just north of the preserve lies the Castle Rock Unique Area, managed by the Department of Environmental Conservation. This area surrounds a privately owned picturesque and romantic castle (closed to the public), which was built in the 1880s as a summer home for the first William H. Osborn, president of the Illinois Central Railroad and grandfather of William Henry Osborn II.

Altogether, Hudson Highlands State Park comprises approximately 3,800 acres. The Taconic Region of the Office of Parks, Recreation, and Historic

Preservation administers the park. The park office is located in Clarence Fahnestock State Park, on NY 301 about a mile west of the Taconic State Parkway. For more information, contact Hudson Highlands State Park, RD 13, Route 301, Carmel, NY 10512; (845) 225-7207; www.nysparks.com.

Trails in the Northern Highlands

The region north of NY 301 includes the highest peaks in the area and offers the most strenuous and scenic hiking. Fishkill Ridge to the north, North and South Beacon mountains, Sugarloaf Mountain, Breakneck Ridge, and Bull Hill (Mount Taurus) are favorite destinations. While most of the trails are within Hudson Highlands State Park and the Fishkill Ridge Conservation Area, others cross lands owned by the City of Beacon and by private landowners. It is important for hikers to stay on marked trails in these areas so that trail access is not endangered.

The trails are accessible from a number of entry points. Access from the south is available at Secor Street in the Village of Nelsonville and at several points along NY 9D north of the Village of Cold Spring. Local streets near the City of Beacon provide access to trails in the north, while the eastern trailhead of the Wilkinson Memorial Trail can be reached from US 9. More detailed information is provided in the trail descriptions below.

Those traveling by train may use the Cold Spring station for access to the Cornish, Nelsonville, and Washburn trails or the Beacon station for access to the Fishkill Ridge Trail. On weekends, certain Metro-North trains stop at the Breakneck Ridge station, which provides convenient access to the Wilkinson Memorial and Breakneck Ridge trails. For more information, contact Metro-North at (212) 532-4900 or from outside New York City at (800) 638-7646, or visit their web site, www.mta.nyc.ny.us/mnr.

Breakneck Ridge Trail   *Length: 4.6 miles Blaze: white*
The most rugged and scenic of the park trails, the Breakneck Ridge Trail follows an open ridge from the Hudson River to the top of South Beacon Mountain, with major drops into valleys along its route. Because of its steep terrain and sweeping vistas, it has become a very popular trail, and on beautiful days, many hikers choose to follow this trail at least as far as the first viewpoint. As a result, there has been serious erosion in the first 0.2 mile. Hikers are requested to stay on the switchbacks and permit the eroded slopes to recover. The

Figure 9-3. Breakneck Ridge and Bull Hill from the south

steep climb up the ridge is dangerous in slippery weather or in high winds. The southern end of the Breakneck Ridge Trail is just north of the tunnel on NY 9D, 2.1 miles north of Cold Spring, where Breakneck Point juts into the Hudson River. There is a small parking area on the west side of the road at the trailhead as well as ample parking a few hundred yards farther north along the road.

The Breakneck Ridge Trail begins its ascent on the river side of the highway and gradually turns onto Breakneck Point, with views up and down the Hudson River. Curving inland, the trail begins its arduous ascent as it crosses over the tunnel. The first few hundred feet of elevation are gained quickly, this being one of the steepest trail sections in the East Hudson Highlands. The trail avoids one long rocky wall by contouring to the left and then goes between large rocks to reach the first of many panoramic viewpoints. Perched high above the Hudson, this first view is breathtaking, and the viewpoint is an ideal place to rest from the most demanding part of the hike.

Looking back toward the ridge, it is clear that the climb is far from over. The trail now settles into a pattern of descending moderately after reaching a viewpoint, and then climbing steeply to the next viewpoint. In a few places, the trail briefly traverses sloping rock slabs near the edge of the south-facing cliffs. Hikers may need to use their hands in order to negotiate some of these rocks. In two places, an easier alternate route is marked with X blazes. At 0.7 mile—the low point of the second major dip, just before a steep uphill section—the Undercliff Trail (yellow) leaves to the right.

At the upper reaches of the ridge, the views are broader, though less dramatic. The trail continues its ups and downs through terrain that gradually becomes more wooded. At 1.5 miles, the Breakneck Bypass Trail (red on white) begins on the left. A huge boulder on the left of the trail with a triple blaze indicates this easily missed trail junction. Continuing ahead, another 360° view is soon reached at one of the ridge's highest points.

At 1.7 miles, the Notch Trail (blue) joins from the right. Halfway up to the next knob, a short side trail on the right leads to a view down into the valley between Bull Hill and Breakneck Ridge. After reaching the highest point along the ridge at 2.2 miles, the trail begins to descend. At 3.0 miles, the joint Breakneck Ridge/Notch Trail joins a woods road and soon comes to a fork where the Notch Trail leaves to the left, connecting in 0.1 mile with the Wilkinson Memorial Trail. The Breakneck Ridge Trail bears right, crosses the outlet of a marshy area on the left, then veers left and uphill, leaving the woods road. Sunset Point, at 3.3 miles, offers a view across the Hudson River, but the view is not as broad as the vistas along Breakneck Ridge.

From Sunset Point, the trail descends gently at first and then more steeply toward Squirrel Hollow Brook. Just after crossing the brook, at 3.8 miles, the Wilkinson Memorial Trail (yellow) comes in from the left on a woods road. The Wilkinson and Breakneck Ridge trails climb together until, at 3.9 miles, the Breakneck Ridge Trail diverges left and uphill into the woods. This easily missed left turn is usually marked by a small cairn. After a steep climb via the Devil's Ladder, the trail reaches a viewpoint and continues to the fire tower on South Beacon Mountain, which it reaches at 4.4 miles.

South Beacon Mountain, the highest point in Hudson Highlands State Park, towers over the surrounding terrain and offers a commanding view of urban, rural, and mountain scenery. Beacon lies below, and Newburgh is across Newburgh Bay in the Hudson River. In the middle ground are the farms and fields of Dutchess and Orange counties, with interspersed woodlots; beyond them, across the Wallkill Valley, are the long, level-topped line of the Shawangunk Mountains; and, on the far horizon, the sharper outlines of the Catskills. From the top of South Beacon Mountain, to the right of the tower, the trail descends. It ends, at 4.6 miles, at a woods road that can be followed to the right to rejoin the Wilkinson Memorial Trail (yellow).

Because of its steepness, the Breakneck Ridge Trail takes about three and a

Figure 9-4. Atop Breakneck Ridge

half hours to hike in good weather. A popular and shorter circular hike is to climb via the Breakneck Ridge Trail to the Undercliff Trail (yellow), turn right on the Brook Trail (red) back to NY 9D, and then walk back 0.4 mile through the tunnel to the starting point. A slightly longer hike is to take the Breakneck Bypass Trail and follow the Wilkinson Memorial Trail (yellow) west back to NY 9D, 0.3 mile north of the starting point. Another possible circular hike is to come down the ridge via the Notch Trail to the south and follow the Brook Trail back to NY 9D, 0.4 mile south of the starting point. Energetic hikers wishing a long day hike should consider walking the entire length of the Breakneck Ridge Trail and returning via the Wilkinson Memorial Trail, a demanding but rewarding trek.

Breakneck Bypass Trail   *Length: 0.8 mile Blaze: red on white*
The Breakneck Bypass Trail provides access to Breakneck Ridge, but avoids the difficult rocks at the southern end of the Breakneck Ridge Trail. It begins just over half a mile from the southern end of the Wilkinson Memorial Trail, con-

necting it to the Breakneck Ridge Trail. At 0.3 mile, there is a close view of Sugarloaf Mountain. At 0.5 mile, the trail follows a gullied woods road. After reaching a viewpoint at 0.8 mile, the bypass descends from a rock onto the Breakneck Ridge Trail (white), 1.5 miles from its southern end.

Brook Trail   *Length: 0.9 mile Blaze: red*
The Brook Trail follows Breakneck Brook in the valley between Bull Hill (Mount Taurus) and Breakneck Ridge along the numerous old roads that crisscross the valley.

The Brook Trail begins immediately south of where Breakneck Brook crosses under NY 9D, 1.7 miles north of Cold Spring. Limited parking is available at the trailhead, with room for a few more cars a bit north or a few tenths of a mile south. The trail follows a paved surface and quickly ascends to a woods road. After a few switchbacks to rise above the brook, the trail turns left on a hard-surfaced road lined with several dilapidated houses and foundations. A short distance before this road veers left and crosses the brook over a small dam, the trail splits off to the right, going up a short flight of steps and staying on the same side of the valley. A moderate climb within view of the stream brings the trail to another dam. The trail goes right on the woods road coming from the dam, and at 0.5 mile intersects the Catskill Aqueduct, recognized as a road-like clearing through the forest. The trail soon passes the northern terminus of the Cornish Trail (blue), which follows the road through the former Cornish estate (also known as Dairy Road because of the dairy farm that existed in the valley). The Cornish Trail can be followed back to NY 9D, 0.7 mile south of the trailhead. The Brook Trail continues on the heavily eroded road. At 0.7 mile, the Undercliff Trail (yellow) joins from the left and soon leaves to the right. After crossing the brook on a wooden bridge, the Brook Trail ends at the Notch Trail (blue), which may be followed straight ahead (north) to Breakneck Ridge or right (east) to Bull Hill (Mount Taurus).

Cornish Trail   *Length: 1.0 mile Blaze: blue*
The Cornish Trail connects the Washburn Trail with the Brook Trail, making it possible for hikers to complete a circuit hike around Bull Hill. The trail is named after the Cornish estate, owned by Edward G. Cornish, chairman of the board of the National Lead Company, who lived here in the 1920s. His mansion, which was destroyed by fire in 1956, and the other major buildings were built by James W. Eaton using rocks from Breakneck Ridge.

The Cornish Trail begins at the Washburn Trail (white), just north of its trailhead opposite the parking area on NY 9D at the entrance to Little Stony Point. It parallels NY 9D for 0.2 mile until it reaches a cement road of the Cornish estate. The trail follows the road, climbing steadily, with views through the trees down to NY 9D and over the Hudson River, and passing below the massive rock face of Bull Hill. At 0.5 mile, the stone ruins of the Cornish mansion are visible below to the left. The concrete paving ends at 0.9 mile, and the trail soon passes a large cement-and-rock cistern on the left. After crossing a cleared strip marking the route of the Catskill Aqueduct, the Cornish Trail ends at the Brook Trail (red).

Crossover Trail   *Length: 0.3 mile Blaze: blue*
This trail connects the Fishkill Ridge Trail (white) at Dozer Junction with the Wilkinson Memorial Trail (yellow). From Dozer Junction, the trail proceeds west on a woods road. Just past some metal debris (but before a major wash-out), it turns left and descends into the gap between Lambs Hill and the Scofield Ridge. At a low point, the Crossover Trail turns left at a T junction, ascends slightly, and bears left at a fork. It ends at the Wilkinson Memorial Trail.

Fishkill Ridge Trail   *Length: 4.9 miles Blaze: white*
Fishkill Ridge is the northernmost of the Fishkill mountains, extending for three miles between the Breakneck-Scofield Ridge and I-84. The abrupt drop at the north edge of the ridge from about 1,400 feet to sea level at the Hudson marks the great fault that bounds the Highlands on the north. The Fishkill Ridge Trail runs from the City of Beacon to the top of the ridge, where it makes a loop with many views.

Access to the western end of the trail is from East Main Street in Beacon. Hikers can follow this road uphill for about 0.2 mile past the intersection with Howland Street, where a narrow road branches off to the right past private homes until it reaches a metal water tank of the Beacon water supply system. The parking situation is unclear. There is space for a couple of cars on the shady shoulder of the road just before the gate that leads to the water tank. More appropriate may be curb parking on one of the streets near East Main Street. Local police suggest parking at the foot of the old incline railway near the point at which NY 9D makes a sharp left turn as it enters the city, though that adds a walk of several city blocks to the hike. From the Beacon railroad station, hikers should walk up Ferry Street and continue on Main Street for a total of about 1.5 miles. Alternatively, the trail may be reached from a parking area at the end of Sunnyside Road in Beacon Hills, a residential community. From here, the Overlook Trail goes up to the Fishkill Ridge Trail.

From Beacon, the trail begins along the continuation of the road that passes in front of the water tank. Following the south side of scenic Dry Brook, the trail ascends steadily, reaching a waterfall at 0.7 mile. It then turns north and climbs steeply to Reservoir Road (a dirt road), passing through a hemlock grove. To the left, Reservoir Road is an easier return route to Beacon; it is recommended in snowy or icy conditions, as the trail descent to the falls can be hazardous.

The trail turns left onto Reservoir Road, but almost immediately leaves it and crosses a woods road. Heading north, the trail ascends, gently at first, then steeply, to a ledge at 1.1 miles, with views of the Hudson Valley. Here, the Overlook Trail (red) begins to the left. The Fishkill Ridge Trail now heads east, passes over a series of knobs, and at 1.5 miles reaches the summit of Lambs Hill (1,500 feet), with further panoramic views.

Descending gradually to the south, the trail intersects an eroded woods road at 1.9 miles. This intersection is known as Dozer Junction in honor of the abandoned bulldozer that rests nearby. To the right, the Crossover Trail (blue) leads 0.3 mile along woods roads to the Wilkinson Memorial Trail, providing a convenient route for hikers heading south along Scofield Ridge. The Fishkill Ridge Trail continues northeast along the ridge, with viewpoints both north and south. Near the north end of the ridge at 3.2 miles, it reaches the no-longer-bald summit of Bald Hill, the highest point on the ridge, marked by two USGS markers.

From the summit, the trail continues northeast until a switchback to the right brings it down from the ridge crest into the woods. After a gentle descent, the trail turns sharply right to join a rough woods road heading south. The vegetation is lush and varied along these east-facing slopes. The Fishkill Ridge Trail ends at 4.9 miles, where it meets the Wilkinson Memorial Trail (yellow).

The Wilkinson Memorial Trail, which proceeds straight ahead past Hells Hollow, leads back toward the starting point. When the Wilkinson Memorial Trail turns off to the left, the return route continues on the woods road straight downhill, passing the southwest end of the Crossover Trail, which leads back to Dozer Junction. After about half a mile, the woods road reaches the Fishkill Ridge Trail at its intersection with Reservoir Road. From here, either the trail going left or Reservoir Road straight ahead may be taken back to the trailhead.

Lone Star Trail   *Length: 1.0 mile Blaze: blue*
The Open Space Institute purchased the Lone Star property in 1993, protecting more than 500 acres in the East Hudson Highlands. It provides alternate access to Bull Hill, starting about 200 feet higher than the Washburn Trail. There is no public transportation to the trailhead. The parking area is on Fishkill Road, 0.4 mile from its intersection with NY 301 in Nelsonville.

The Lone Star Trail is a woods road that works its way gradually uphill. At 0.3 mile, the trail passes the terminus of the Split Rock Trail (red), which heads off to the left. The Lone Star Trail continues to climb gradually, reaching a steeper pitch at 0.7 mile, and then shortly returns to the former grade. At 0.8 mile, the trail goes through a small laurel grove and passes onto state property. At 1.0 mile, the Lone Star Trail ends at the Nelsonville Trail (green).

Nelsonville Trail   *Length: 2.6 miles Blaze: green*
Following a portion of the route of the former Three Notch Trail up Bull Hill, the Nelsonville Trail begins in the hamlet of Nelsonville, which has worked with the Trail Conference to reopen this historic trail route. The trail is blazed with unique green markers which feature the logo of a bull.

The trailhead, on Secor Street in Nelsonville, is readily accessible by public transportation. Take the Metro-North Hudson Line to the Cold Spring station, and walk up Main Street, which becomes NY 301 after crossing NY 9D (Morris Avenue/Chestnut Street). Turn left at the village hall on Pearl Street, and walk one block north to Secor Street. The trailhead is just to the east, past the Masonic Lodge, where parking is available for those arriving by car. Vehicles may also be parked on Gatehouse Road, which intersects the trail 0.6 mile from its start.

Soon after it enters the woods, the Nelsonville Trail crosses two streams. At 0.3 mile, it turns right onto a wide, eroded woods road, the route of the Undercliff Trail (yellow). At 0.6 mile, the Nelsonville Trail crosses paved Gatehouse Road, where there is an information kiosk and parking is available, and begins its ascent of Bull Hill. The Catskill Aqueduct is crossed at 0.7 mile, marked by a large stone edifice on the left. This structure is not a pumping station, as some have presumed, but rather one end of an inverted syphon that carries the water down to and under NY 301 and then up to the next ridge.

The Nelsonville Trail now begins to climb more steeply. At 1.2 miles, it passes gate posts which mark the boundary of Hudson Highlands State Park and almost immediately reaches the terminus of the Split Rock Trail (red), which leaves to the right. After several turns in the road, the Lone Star Trail (blue) begins to the right. The Nelsonville Trail continues to climb until it ends at 2.6 miles at a junction with the Washburn Trail (white) and the Notch Trail (blue).

Notch Trail   *Length: 5.8 miles Blaze: blue*

The Notch Trail begins at the northern end of the Washburn Trail and crosses through notches in the shoulders of Bull Hill, Breakneck Ridge, and Sunset Point. Formerly called the Three Notch Trail, the trail was renamed the Notch Trail in the late 1970s, when several sections were closed by the landowners or rerouted. One section of the original trail, which goes south along the eastern side of Bull Hill, has since been reopened and is now known as the Nelsonville Trail.

Except for the climb up Breakneck Ridge and the walk along the ridge line, the Notch Trail is almost entirely on woods roads. Because a significant portion of the trail is outside Hudson Highlands State Park, hikers may encounter noisy motorized vehicles, which have caused severe damage, especially near Gordons Brook.

The northern end of the trail is on NY 9D, four miles north of Cold Spring. There is parking for a few cars in pullouts near the trailhead. Its southern terminus is at the junction of the Washburn Trail (white) and the Nelsonville Trail (green). The Notch Trail is actually a continuation of the Washburn Trail, proceeding north from the summit of Bull Hill.

Beginning at the southern trailhead, the Notch Trail continues the steep downhill of the Washburn Trail, then veers left (west) and descends less steeply, following woods roads for part of the way. At 1.0 mile, it passes stone foundations. Crossing first a tributary of Breakneck Brook and then the brook itself on a wooden bridge, the Notch Trail reaches the end of the Brook Trail (red) at 1.1 miles. At this junction, the Notch Trail turns sharply right, passes the ruins of a dairy farm once operated by the Cornish family, and skirts the northwest side of a pond. Near the end of the pond, the trail turns left, leaving the road. It now climbs steeply to the crest of Breakneck Ridge, with views in several directions.

At 1.7 miles, the Breakneck Ridge Trail (white) joins the Notch Trail from the left in the saddle of the notch, and both trails continue along the ridge, with many views. Halfway up the next knob, a short side trail on the right leads to a view down into the valley between Bull Hill and Breakneck Ridge. After reaching the highest point along the ridge at 2.2 miles, the trail begins to descend. At 3.0 miles, the joint Breakneck Ridge/Notch Trail joins a woods road and soon comes to a fork where the Breakneck Ridge Trail leaves to the right. The Notch Trail takes the left fork and, at 3.1 miles, joins the Wilkinson Memorial Trail (yellow), which comes in from the left.

The trails make a steady, gradual descent, curving around Sunset Point. After the trails cross Squirrel Hollow Brook on a narrow bridge at 3.7 miles, the Wilkinson Memorial Trail branches off to the right, while the Notch Trail turns left. At 3.9 miles, the Notch Trail goes right at a fork, with the left fork a woods road that descends along Squirrel Hollow Brook to the Melzingah Reservoir. The Notch Trail ascends slightly to a shallow notch and then descends to cross Gordons Brook. After a short ascent, the trail descends steadily until it ends at NY 9D at 5.8 miles. In the last mile before reaching NY 9D, the trail crosses numerous woods roads and unmarked trails. Hikers should take care to follow the blue blazes.

Overlook Trail   *Length: 1.7 miles Blaze: red*
The Overlook Trail runs along the northern end of the Fishkill Ridge, providing an alternate access to the Fishkill Ridge Trail. To reach the trailhead from 1-84, take Exit 12 (NY 52/NY 52 BUS) and continue on NY 52 BUS towards Beacon. Across from Fishkill Town Hall, turn left onto Glenham Road. Just after passing the post office on the left, turn left on Maple Street. After crossing the railroad tracks and Fishkill Creek, turn left onto Old Town Road, which parallels the creek, and then turn right onto Sunnyside Road. The trailhead parking area is at the end of the road, up a steep gravel road to the left.

The Overlook Trail begins at the Scenic Hudson kiosk. Almost immediately, it turns left on a woods road and then bears right, leaving the road, where the road curves to the left. Climbing steadily, at 0.2 mile the trail passes a large glacial erratic, a conglomerate made up of many striated rocks. At 0.6 mile, the trail cuts into the shoulder of a hill and descends steeply. After crossing a stream, the trail turns right onto a woods road and then left onto another road, steadily ascending the north side of Lambs Hill. At 1.1 miles, the trail comes out on open rocks, with views over the Hudson River, Danskammer Point, and the Newburgh-Beacon Bridge. The trail continues to ascend steeply, reaching more viewpoints, until it levels off at 1.4 miles. After passing through abandoned orchards and running along old stone walls, the trail turns left at 1.6 miles and resumes its ascent. The Overlook Trail ends at the Fishkill Ridge Trail (white) at 1.7 miles, with an expansive view just before the junction.

Split Rock Trail   *Length: 0.3 mile Blaze: red*
This short trail makes it possible to hike a loop in the Lone Star property purchased by the Open Space Institute in 1993. The Split Rock Trail begins at a massive glacial erratic 0.3 mile from the start of the Lone Star Trail (blue), and then goes gradually uphill. Although there are no views, glacial erratics litter the woods off the trail to the right after it turns out of a laurel grove at 0.2 mile. At 0.3 mile, the Split Rock Trail ends at the Nelsonville Trail (green).

Undercliff Trail   *Length: 4.0 miles Blaze: yellow*
Crossing the shoulder of Bull Hill, the Undercliff Trail provides a scenic connection between Nelsonville and Breakneck Ridge, often proceeding under or along cliffs. Its southern terminus is at a kiosk and gate by the Masonic Lodge on Secor Street in Nelsonville, where parking is available. The trail is also accessible via the Cold Spring station of the Metro-North Hudson Line (see the Nelsonville Trail description for directions from the station).

The Undercliff Trail begins by heading north along a series of woods roads. The Nelsonville Trail (green) joins from the right at 0.4 mile, and both trails run together for the next 0.2 mile. After turning left at 0.6 mile, leaving the Nelsonville Trail, the Undercliff Trail bears right at a Y junction and begins to ascend Bull Hill on switchbacks, first gently and then more steeply.

At 1.0 mile, the Undercliff Trail reaches a sweeping view to the south over the Catskill Aqueduct, the Hudson River, and Fahnestock State Park. After descending, it turns right and ascends steeply on a woods road. It crosses a wide ledge at the top of a ravine and then climbs steeply on switchbacks to reach, at 1.5 miles, a viewpoint over West Point, Cold Spring, the Hudson River, and Storm King. At 1.7 miles, the Undercliff Trail crosses the Washburn Trail (white), which leads left to NY 9D in 1.2 miles.

The Undercliff Trail now begins an undulating traverse of the western shoulder of Bull Hill. Along the way, stone outcroppings afford views to the south and over Cold Spring, nestled at the foot of the mountain. Hikers should stay on the trail to avoid damaging the low plants that keep the soil from eroding. Upon reaching the far end of the shoulder at 2.1 miles, the trail opens to a view of the ragged profile of nearby Breakneck Ridge, the brooding hulk of Storm King across the river, and the Catskills in the far distance.

From the viewpoint, the trail reverses direction and descends east into a narrow valley. It crosses a seasonal creek, proceeds north along the western flank of Bull Hill, and descends on switchbacks to reach a woods road sup-

Figure 9-5. Bridge over Breakneck Brook on the Undercliff Trail

ported by a stone wall. The trail skirts the rubble of what must have been the source of the rocks used to build the wall and descends gently until the road surface vanishes in the undergrowth. The trail turns northwest and continues through what was once a cow pasture on the Cornish estate. At 3.3 miles, it turns left onto the Brook Trail (red), which follows an eroded woods road and leads down to NY 9D in 0.7 mile.

The Undercliff Trail immediately turns right, leaving the Brook Trail. It crosses Breakneck Brook on a wooden bridge and ascends over forested, but rocky slopes. After reaching a cliff, a short traverse along its base leads to a viewpoint over the Hudson River valley. The trail descends away from the cliff over rocks with boring holes. It then turns right and ascends again, this time to pass over huge boulders that the trail crew dubbed the "Rock Jumble." It ascends more steeply via switchbacks to return to the base of the cliffs. Continuing west, the trail hugs the towering cliff wall, gains some elevation, and turns a corner to penetrate one of the many shallow notches along Breakneck Ridge. Switchbacks ease the final short but steep rise to the trail's northern terminus on the Breakneck Ridge Trail (white), 0.7 mile from its trailhead on NY 9D.

Washburn Trail   *Length: 2.3 miles Blaze: white*

Starting from river level, the Washburn Trail climbs 1,400 feet to the top of Bull Hill (Mount Taurus). The trail ends half a mile past the summit, where it links with the Notch Trail. The climb to the summit is one of the most strenuous hikes in the Highlands.

The Washburn Trail starts on NY 9D, 0.8 mile north of NY 301 in Cold Spring and 200 yards north of the intersection with Fair Street. The trailhead parking area is opposite the bridge over the railroad which leads to Little Stony Point. The trail begins by following an old road leading to a former quarry, opened in 1931 by the Hudson River Stone Corporation and abandoned in 1967. All that remain are cuts in the rocks and some discarded pipes.

At 0.4 mile, just before reaching the quarry, the trail leaves the road, veers sharply right, and follows the rim of the quarry. It soon bears right, leaving the quarry rim, and begins a steep ascent of Bull Hill, with views to the right over Cold Spring and the Hudson River. The best viewpoint is from a rock outcrop about 30 feet to the right of the trail. The trail continues ascending even more steeply, soon crossing a small rise and then passing an abandoned trail that goes off to the right. Returning hikers should be careful not to miss this right turn. Continuing north, the trail resumes its steep ascent, with ever-increasing views of the river valley to the west and south. After crossing the Undercliff Trail (yellow) at 1.2 miles and climbing some false summits, the Washburn Trail finally reaches the wooded summit at 1.8 miles. This point is marked by the end of an old carriage road that circles the summit. The trail joins the road and soon reaches an unmarked trail which goes off to the right, leading to a viewpoint to the east and south. In a short distance, the Washburn Trail reaches another viewpoint over Breakneck Valley, Breakneck Ridge, the Shawangunks, and the Catskills.

From the viewpoint, the road swings to the east face of the summit, with a second similar lookout. After a couple of descending switchbacks, the trail splits off from the carriage road at the end of a left curve. (This turn right and downhill is easily missed.) The trail descends straight into Bull Gap, crossing the carriage road twice, and ends at 2.3 miles at the beginning of the Notch Trail (blue), where the footpath crosses the same carriage road that was followed higher up. The road to the right is the Nelsonville Trail (green), which continues down to Nelsonville.

A popular circular hike is to combine the Washburn Trail, the Notch Trail, the Brook Trail, and the Cornish Trail.

Wilkinson Memorial Trail   *Length: 9.5 miles Blaze: yellow*
Named after Samuel N. Wilkinson, a tireless worker for trails, the Wilkinson Memorial Trail begins on NY 9D, 2.4 miles north of Cold Spring and 0.3 mile north of the Breakneck tunnel. There is ample parking on the west side of the road south of the trailhead. The eastern end of the trail may be reached from Old Albany Post Road (also known as Uhl Road), which goes west from US 9 about four miles north of its intersection with NY 301. Roadside parking is available just before a bridge. Do not park close to the houses at the junction beyond the bridge.

From NY 9D, the trail steadily climbs a curving woods road and then, at 0.3 mile, crosses a small brook. At 0.5 mile, the Breakneck Bypass Trail (red on white) begins on the right. Continuing ahead, the Wilkinson Memorial Trail turns left off the woods road and crosses a brook to begin a steady, steep climb up Sugarloaf Mountain. Switchbacks and stone steps help ease the ascent. At 1.0 mile, after a short, steep climb, the trail reaches the open summit, with views over Breakneck to the south, Storm King and Schunemunk to the west, and Bannerman's Castle on Pollepel Island below.

Leaving the summit, the trail turns north and, at 1.1 miles, reaches a view to the north over the Hudson River and the Newburgh-Beacon Bridge. Turning northeast, the Wilkinson Trail descends, sometimes steeply. At 1.4 miles, the trail turns right at a T junction with a woods road, and then makes an immediate left to pass through former farm fields. It crosses a stream at 1.6 miles and, at 1.7 miles, reaches Cascade Brook. Turning right, the trail heads upstream, paralleling the brook and then crossing it at 1.9 miles.

The Wilkinson Memorial Trail turns right on a woods road and then leaves it to the left. Almost immediately, it begins to climb steeply. Along the ridge, the trail passes open flat rocks at 2.2 miles. It turns to begin another climb and reaches, at 2.5 miles, an expansive view to the west and northwest. Melzingah Reservoir is visible in the foreground, with the Newburgh-Beacon Bridge and Stewart Airport in the distance.

Descending to a notch below Sunset Point, the trail turns left on a woods road at 2.9 miles and is joined by the Notch Trail (blue) coming down from Breakneck Ridge. Both trails descend steadily to Squirrel Hollow Brook and cross it on a narrow bridge. Here, at 3.5 miles, the two trails divide, with the Notch Trail descending to the left and the Wilkinson Memorial Trail ascending to the right.

The Wilkinson Memorial Trail follows Squirrel Hollow Brook upstream. The Breakneck Ridge Trail (white) merges in from the right at 3.9 miles and leaves to the left at 4.0 miles, while the Wilkinson Memorial Trail continues to follow a woods road up the valley. It leaves the woods road, crosses a brook at 4.6 miles, and begins climbing more steeply, reaching the crest of Scofield Ridge at 5.3 miles. The 360° views includes the hills of Fahnestock State Park to the southeast, the Manhattan skyline 45 miles away and bits of the Hudson River and Bull Hill to the south, Beacon to the north, and the reservoir below. As it meanders along the ridge, the trail ascends and descends, sometimes climbing over rocks, and passing a number of viewpoints. At 6.5 miles, the trail dips and then climbs out of the low point on slabs of rock. Here the trail is marked with paint blazes on rocks or with cairns.

At 7.1 miles, at the north end of the ridge, a narrow lookout enables hikers to peer over Hells Hollow. From here, the Wilkinson Memorial Trail turns northwest in preparation for its descent into the notch at the end of Scofield Ridge. At 7.3 miles, the Wilkinson Memorial Trail makes a sharp right turn. The path straight ahead leads about 300 feet to a viewpoint to the south. The trail descends steadily on a woods road, reaches the notch at 7.7 miles, and turns right onto a woods road. To the left, the Crossover Trail (blue) goes 0.3 mile to the Fishkill Ridge Trail (white) at Dozer Junction.

The trail heads to the top of Hells Hollow, where the eroded road narrows, crossing below cliffs. After reaching the end of the Fishkill Ridge Trail (white) at 8.0 miles, the Wilkinson Memorial Trail turns right and starts a long descent on switchbacks. It crosses a stream at 8.4 miles and becomes less steep. Strewn with fallen boulders, this deep valley retains a refreshing layer of cold air throughout most of the summer. The trail descends steeply and reaches the valley floor at 8.8 miles. Crossing a rock field, it goes slightly uphill and skirts a pond, reaching the dam at 9.0 miles. Ascending gently, the trail rounds the end of a ridge to reach a private driveway at 9.3 miles, where it turns right. After passing a dam, the trail again turns right when it reaches a gate on Reservoir Lane, a private road. It follows the road to Old Albany Post Road (Uhl Road), where it ends at 9.5 miles.

Trails in the Southern Highlands

The long wooded ridges of Canada Hill (840 feet) and White Rock (885 feet) and the prominent cone of Sugarloaf Hill (765 feet) rise from the eastern shore of the Hudson River north of Anthony's Nose and South Mountain Pass. Cloaked in a forest of oaks, hemlocks, and laurel, and concealing several small ponds, these hills are interlaced with a network of graded trails.

The four primary trails are the Sugarloaf Trail, the Osborn Loop, the Carriage Connector, and the Appalachian Trail. Hikes of nearly any desired length are possible by combining segments of different trails. These trails, which lie mostly within the Hudson Highlands State Park, generally provide relatively easy walking. Unmarked carriage roads extend the number of circular hikes possible even further. These wide woods roads are suitable for snowshoeing and cross-country skiing when conditions are favorable.

There are four major access points to the trail network in this area. The Sugarloaf Trail is reached from NY 9D south of NY 403. The Appalachian Trail crosses US 9 at its intersection with NY 403, with parking on a small road running between the two highways just north of the intersection. Very limited parking is available where the Appalachian Trail crosses South Mountain Pass. For those climbing Anthony's Nose on the Appalachian Trail, parking is available on the west side of NY 9D just north of the Bear Mountain Bridge.

Appalachian Trail   *Length: 5.1 miles Blaze: white*

A 5.1-mile section of the Appalachian Trail (AT) passes through Hudson Highlands State Park. At the southern end of this section, parking is available along NY 9D, just north of the Bear Mountain Bridge, where the trail leaves the paved road and begins its climb. At the northern end, parking is available along a road which connects US 9 with NY 403 just north of the intersection of these two roads. The southern end can also be reached by taking a Metro-North Hudson Line train to the Manitou station (limited service provided, primarily on weekends).

From NY 9D at the Westchester/Putnam county line, 0.2 mile north of the Bear Mountain Bridge, the AT proceeds steeply uphill. At 0.5 mile, it reaches a gravel road. To the right, this road is blazed as the Camp Smith Trail (blue) and leads in 0.6 mile to the cliffs atop Anthony's Nose, which afford views over the Bear Mountain Bridge and up and down the Hudson River. The AT turns left onto the gravel road, which it follows for a short distance, then bears left onto a footpath and soon begins to descend. After a short ascent, a blue-blazed trail leads right to the Hemlock Springs Campsite, where primitive overnight camping is permitted. The trail then rejoins the gravel road, which it follows to South Mountain Pass (a dirt road open to vehicular traffic) at 1.7 miles.

The AT turns right and follows the road for 250 feet, then turns left and reenters the woods on a footpath. It begins a steady ascent of Canada Hill, reaching, at 2.1 miles, a viewpoint to the south near the crest of the ridge. The AT continues along the ridge and, at 2.7 miles, turns right onto a carriage road. The Osborn Loop (blue), which can be combined with the AT to make a circular hike, goes left on this carriage road and rejoins the AT in 3.4 miles. The AT continues north along the carriage road and passes, at 3.2 miles, the eastern terminus of the Curry Pond Trail (yellow), which leads to the Manitoga Nature Preserve. At 4.0 miles, a blue-blazed side trail to the left leads a short distance to an expansive viewpoint over the Hudson River, with views north to West Point and south to the Bear Mountain Bridge. Soon afterwards, the AT turns sharply right, leaving the carriage road, and begins a steady descent, steeply in places. (Continuing ahead on the carriage route is the blue-blazed Osborn Loop, which ends here.) The AT turns right onto another carriage road at 4.6 miles. Here, the Carriage Connector (yellow) begins and proceeds north on this carriage road. At a corner of a fenced-in pasture, the AT turns left. It follows puncheons through the pasture and reaches the intersection of US 9 and NY 403 at 5.1 miles.

Carriage Connector   *Length: 0.9 mile Blaze: yellow*
The main purpose of the Carriage Connector is to bypass the moderately strenuous climb to White Rock. As the name implies, the trail is entirely on old carriage roads, which makes for easy walking. The trail begins where the southbound Appalachian Trail, coming from the intersection of US 9 and NY 403, leaves the valley and climbs west to White Rock. The Carriage Connector continues north along the valley bottom. At 0.5 mile, a road to the right leads in 0.8 mile to the summit of a hill with an obstructed view. At 0.6 mile, two roads intersect the Carriage Connector; the road to the right leads to NY 403, while the road ahead leads to the park boundary. The Carriage Connector turns left (west) and climbs gently to the saddle between White Rock on the left and Castle Rock on the right. The trail ends where it meets the Osborn Loop (blue). Hikers heading for Sugarloaf Hill should continue straight (west) and those heading for White Rock should turn left (south).

Curry Pond Trail   *Length: 0.6 mile Blaze: yellow*
The Curry Pond Trail connects the Appalachian Trail with the Osborn Loop, providing a convenient short cut between the two trails. It begins where the Osborn Loop turns right, leaving a woods road, and heads toward Curry Pond. At 0.1 mile, it crosses the outlet of the pond and runs close to its shore. It then begins to ascend, steeply in places, and ends at the Appalachian Trail (white), 0.5 mile from the southern end of the Osborn Loop.

North Redoubt Trail   *Length: 0.3 mile Blaze: red*
North Redoubt is the site of one of the forts built in 1776-1777 to defend the Hudson Highlands. The trailhead is on Philipse Brook Road (known locally as Snake Hill Road and officially as County 11, Bill Brown Road), 0.3 mile east of

NY 9D. The nearest parking is along NY 9D, since parking is not available at the trailhead.

The trail begins on the south side of the road directly across from the gate to the Walter Hoving home. The trail becomes apparent beyond some roadside rocks and goes left (east), paralleling the road. The climb is gentle and contours above a brook. As the trail gradually curves more and more to the right (south), it passes within sight of a private home on the left. At the edge of the property, the trail curves further right (southwest) and becomes steeper. The climb is moderated by a few switchbacks, the last leading toward the summit ridge. The footpath is faint here and disappears entirely as the height of land is reached. Even with the trail blazed, hikers are advised to identify landmarks that can be used to locate the trail on the way back. Continuing in a northerly direction through open woods, the trail leads to the summit, with a view of the Hudson River framed by the rounded bulk of Storm King and Bull Hill (Mount Taurus). Ruins of stone structures used by the Continental Army can be found near the summit.

Osborn Loop   *Length: 3.4 miles Blaze: blue*
The Osborn Loop forms most of a loop around the mid-section of the southern part of the Hudson Highlands State Park. A section of the Appalachian Trail completes the loop. The Osborn Loop can be reached from the northwest via the Sugarloaf Trail and from the south or east via the Appalachian Trail. From the west, it can be accessed via the trails of the Manitoga Nature Preserve. A contribution for parking at Manitoga is expected.

One end of the Osborn Loop is at White Rock at a junction with the Appalachian Trail. The latter provides the shortest access, in this case from the junction of US 9 and NY 403. The Osborn Loop proceeds north, first following a level route, then descending, steeply in places, to the valley that separates White Rock from Castle Rock to the north. At the bottom, at 1.1 miles, it meets the Carriage Connector (yellow) coming in from the right. The Osborn Loop turns left (west) and descends gently to the saddle between Sugarloaf Hill and Castle Rock, where it meets the Sugarloaf Trail (red), at 1.4 miles. Here, the Osborn Loop veers sharply left, now heading in a southerly direction. At 1.6 miles, the trail splits off to the left, away from the descending rough and sometimes wet woods road that circles the base of Sugarloaf Hill.

From this point, the Osborn Loop climbs gently at first and then more steeply for a short distance. The Osborn Loop turns left again at 1.9 miles,

JACK FAGAN

Figure 9-6. View from Sugarloaf Hill looking south

crossing the flank of Canada Hill and numerous streams as it descends. At 2.5 miles, the trail leaves a laurel grove and turns left onto a woods road. After a short level section, the Curry Pond Trail (yellow) leaves to the left at 2.7 miles, and soon afterwards a trail blazed with branded wooden markers leaves to the right and descends to the Manitoga Nature Preserve. The Osborn Loop now makes a steady but gentle ascent, and at 3.4 miles it ends at the Appalachian Trail (white). One can continue ahead to return to the starting point via the Appalachian Trail or turn right to head south to South Mountain Pass.

Sugarloaf Trail   *Length: 1.6 miles Blaze: red*
Though less than 800 feet high, Sugarloaf Hill is a prominent landmark in the southern Hudson Highlands because of its long summit ridge, conical southwestern shoulder, and proximity to the river. The profile of the mountain is said to resemble a sugarloaf, the solid cone shape in which sugar was imported before the days of granulated sugar.

The shortest hike to the summit begins from NY 9D, 0.5 mile south of its junction with NY 403. Southbound drivers should turn left at the DEC sign for the Castle Rock Unique Area, passing through a gate with two square pillars, one bearing the inscription "Wing & Wing." After turning onto the dirt road, bear left at the fork, pass a red barn on the right, and continue to a gravel parking area. Metro-North Railroad riders can reach the trailhead from the Garrison station by walking half a mile up to the junction of NY 403 and NY 9D and then proceeding south on NY 9D.

Hikers can reach the trail from the parking area by walking back to the fork, turning left toward the hills, and turning right at the first unpaved road. Very shortly the trail makes an abrupt turn left across an uncultivated field, climbs straight uphill to a narrow woods road at the edge of the forest, and then goes right. A wooden gazebo located here is an excellent place from which to enjoy the pastoral setting, with West Point and the Highlands in the background.

From the gazebo, the trail is level until it turns sharply left uphill on a wide dirt road. An alternative approach to the Sugarloaf Trail is to continue straight ahead on an unmarked trail that circles the base of the mountain. This 2.3-mile trail connects with the Osborn Loop (blue) on the far side of Sugarloaf Hill. Along this path, in the open field at the foot of Sugarloaf, is a marker indicating the site of the Beverly Robinson house, used as a headquarters by Benedict Arnold.

Continuing on the Sugarloaf Trail, long switchbacks lead up the shady northern slopes. A short distance beyond a small pond on the left is the broad saddle between Castle Rock and Sugarloaf Hill. At a major trail junction, two arms of the Osborn Loop (blue) lead ahead, while the Sugarloaf Trail turns right and begins the final half-mile ascent to the summit. The climb is at first moderately steep, then levels off as it continues to the southern outlook, with its view of the Hudson River, Fort Montgomery, and the distant hills of Harriman Park. One can appreciate the importance of Sugarloaf Hill during the American Revolution as a vantage point for monitoring traffic on the Hudson River. The trail ends here and hikers must double back to the trail junction at the saddle.

OTHER AREAS NEAR THE HUDSON RIVER

Within the Hudson Highlands, there are a potpourri of places to visit, ranging from walks along the river to rugged hikes and even a walk across the river on the Bear Mountain Bridge. A few hours are all that are needed to explore some locations, while others require more time. Some sites are so small or ecologically sensitive that they cannot accommodate more than a few visitors per week. Others are managed as sanctuaries, and public access for hiking is not a top priority. These last two groups are best left for people to discover on their own.

Arden Point

Arden Point juts out into the Hudson River near Garrison. Its two trails are short, easy to follow, have little elevation gain, and include several viewpoints, making them ideal for families with young children. The trails can be combined to make a 1.7-mile loop.

Arden Point is located just south of the Garrison Metro-North station, thus facilitating access by public transportation. To reach Arden Point by car, take NY 9D to the intersection of NY 403 and Lower Garrison Station Road, proceed west on Lower Garrison Station Road, and descend to the train station. Parking is free on weekends, and trains run hourly from Grand Central Terminal.

Blue Trail *Length: 0.8 mile Blaze: blue*
The Blue Trail begins at a chain between two pillars at the southeast corner of the station parking lot. It follows an abandoned road parallel to the railroad tracks, soon passing the ruins of two houses to the right and crossing Arden Brook on a log bridge. At 0.5 mile, the trail reaches a clearing on the left, and it turns right to cross a bridge over the railroad tracks. From the bridge, the Bear Mountain Bridge is visible to the south, with the mountains of Harriman State Park beyond.

After crossing the bridge, the Red Trail leaves to the left, following the old road, while the Blue Trail turns sharply right onto a narrow footpath heading into the heart of Arden Point. The trail winds through undulating wooded terrain, passing a small seasonal pond at 0.7 mile and ending at 0.8 mile at a junction with the Red Trail, which can be followed back to the bridge over the tracks.

Red Trail *Length: 0.4 mile Blaze: red*
The Red Trail begins on the west side of the bridge over the railroad tracks. It soon reaches a fork, where it bears right and climbs a small rise. A short distance beyond its crest, the Red Trail makes a sharp right turn and heads north. About 100 feet to the left is the southern tip of Arden Point, where a low rock outcropping offers broad views over the Hudson River to the west and north.

Generally staying well back from the often steep shoreline, the Red Trail proceeds through woods, with brief glimpses of the river through trees on the left. At 0.3 mile, the trail veers left towards the river and reaches the water at a rocky protrusion. Here, a rough-hewn bench offers views reaching from the Fishkill Ridge south to Highland Falls. The trail continues north, passing between two knobs, to reach the end of the Blue Trail at 0.4 mile. The Red Trail continues through a gap in a stone wall to its end at the northern tip of Arden Point, where there are open views over the Hudson River, West Point (with Bull Hill behind it), and Garrison.

Camp Smith

Views abound on this rugged trail from Anthony's Nose through the Camp Smith National Guard Training Site. The trail, opened in 1995, follows a 100-foot-wide strip, managed by Hudson Highlands State Park, through the Camp Smith property. The trail was constructed by volunteers from the New York-New Jersey Trail Conference, with assistance from a group of high school dropouts who were part of a federally funded military-style program. Parking is available along US 6/202 at the southern terminus of the trail and at its midpoint. Access to the northern terminus is via the Appalachian Trail, with parking along NY 9D just north of the Bear Mountain Bridge. This strenuous trail, which is best approached with a car shuttle, has a net elevation gain of 1,100 feet when hiked from south to north. Hikers may see military personnel engaged in tactical maneuvers, and everyone is asked to remain on the trail.

Camp Smith Trail   *Length: 3.7 miles Blaze: blue*
The Camp Smith Trail starts at the old toll house on the road up to the Bear Mountain Bridge (US 6/202), 0.7 mile north of the Camp Smith entrance. Behind the toll house, the trail turns left and parallels the road, climbing steadily. It drops steeply down through a rock field and turns left before reaching a massive cliff. At 0.3 mile, the trail crosses a breached earthen dam. Staying within sight and sound of US 6/202, it works its way gradually uphill, crossing small ridges. At 0.6 mile, it begins a serious ascent of Manitou Mountain, soon climbing very steeply on a series of rock steps. It turns left, climbs more gradually, and makes a right turn onto the top of the Knife Edge, an open rock face.

The trail drops slightly and resumes its ascent of Manitou Mountain, all the while turning west and toward the river. It passes through a gully as it approaches viewpoints on the brow of the mountain and, at 0.9 mile, turns away from the river and passes through the aftermath of the extensive 1993 fire. The trail turns left toward a rock outcropping with views, and then turns right and away from the views to begin its descent. The rock steps, switchbacks, and sidehill construction make it possible safely to descend the steep talus slope.

At 1.2 miles, the trail reaches the bottom of the slope, crosses a flat area, turns gradually left, and reaches a small rock outcropping with a view. From the viewpoint, the trail heads inland and comes to a trail junction at 1.3 miles, where a 440-foot X-blazed trail bypasses the 0.4-mile loop to a view. After the two branches rejoin at 1.6 miles, the Camp Smith Trail continues its descent, crossing intermittent brooks. At 1.9 miles, it reaches a parking area on US 6/202 at a large bend in the road 2.2 miles north of the Camp Smith entrance.

Continuing north to Anthony's Nose, the trail crosses Broccy Creek and heads uphill, paralleling the road. Turning away from US 6/202, it joins and leaves woods roads and crosses streams. It rises out of a ravine and turns right on a rock outcropping at 2.4 miles, with views down to Iona Island. Paralleling the river high over the road, the trail soon begins to climb steeply. Another rock outcropping with a view at 2.7 miles provides a rest spot before the trail turns sharply right. The remaining 0.4 mile is an unrelenting assault on Anthony's Nose. There are seasonal views along the way, with year-round views on open rock slabs and on the top. The trail dips down off the summit to join a woods road. A left turn leads to panoramic views of the Bear Mountain Bridge, Bear Mountain-Harriman State Parks, and the Hudson River. A right turn takes the hiker to the Appalachian Trail, where the Camp Smith Trail ends at 3.7 miles. NY 9D is 0.5 mile downhill to the left.

Dennings Point

This 66-acre section of the Hudson Highlands State Park is located in Beacon. Acquired by the state in 1988, the park is open to the public for walking and cross-country skiing. A 1.2-mile trail, which is a woods road, circles the heavily wooded point. The trail is near the water and has vegetation that attracts wildlife, making it a great spot to watch birds.

Though small, Dennings Point is rich in interesting vegetation, wildlife, and local history. In 1785, William Denning, a New York merchant, purchased lands in the area that were forfeited by Beverly Robinson, a Tory who had returned to England. In later years, the Denning family lived on the southern two-thirds of the point. A carpet of myrtle and flowering shrubs are evidence of landscaping long abandoned.

The northern third of the point was formerly the site of the Dennings Point Brick Works (built in 1925), a lightweight building materials factory, and the Noesting Pin Ticket Company, which made paper clips and other wire products. Clay pits and piles of rejected bricks are scattered throughout the area, and the pin ticket factory building still stands.

Dennings Point can be reached by taking NY 9D to South Avenue in Beacon, turning right onto Dennings Avenue, and following Dennings Avenue Extension over the bridge and onto the point. The trail begins 0.3 mile from the end of the road.

The trail starts on the other side of the Noesting Pin Ticket Company factory building. Just past the trailhead, at a Y junction, the trail bears left to follow the eastern shore of the point. Along the way it passes a berm, a cement block house, and a stone foundation. The trail contours some 50 feet from the shore. At 0.6 mile, it passes through a carpet of myrtle. At the end of the point, the trail turns to head north along the western shore, with views out over the river. At low tide, one can walk along the rocky beach. At 1.1 miles, the trail turns away from the river and arrives back at the pin factory 0.1 mile later.

Little Stony Point

In 1967, this former quarry and gravel shipping site was saved from industrial development. Now a public park, it is managed by the Little Stony Point Citizens Association, a volunteer group, under an agreement with the New York State Office of Parks, Recreation, and Historic Preservation. Parking is near the trailhead on the west side of NY 9D, 0.6 mile north of Cold Spring.

After crossing the railroad tracks on a bridge, an unmarked trail of 0.8 mile circles the point, while an 0.2-mile trail leads to a viewpoint out over the river from a rocky crag. The trails offer wide, open views over the Hudson toward Storm King as well as up and down the river. A sandy beach on the north side of Little Stony Point is popular during the summer.

Manitoga

In 1942, designer Russel Wright purchased property which had been damaged by logging and by quarrying rock used to build the New York Public Library. Calling his property Manitoga, which means "Place of the Great Spirit" in the Algonquin language, Wright began restoring the land. Although the landscape appears natural, it was actually carefully designed with native trees, ferns, mosses, and wildflowers as a backdrop. Opened to the public in 1975, the year before

Wright's death, Manitoga is now a nature preserve and education center.

Wright is one of the best-known designers of home furnishings. It is estimated that by the 1950s over 125 million pieces of his American Modern dinnerware were made. Examples of his work are in the Metropolitan Museum of Art and the Museum of Modern Art.

All the trails begin and end together and are laid out in the form of a ladder, with each rung crossing over a little higher on the hill. At the top, the trails connect to the Osborn Loop and Appalachian Trail on Canada Hill. The trails at Manitoga are blazed only for clockwise travel and are typically narrower than most hiking trails. The blazes are wooden disks with unique patterns burned into them.

Manitoga is on the east side of NY 9D, 2.5 miles north of the Bear Mountain Bridge and 2.0 miles south of NY 403. It is also accessible from the Manitou station on the Metro-North Hudson Line by walking through the Manitou Point Preserve (see below) and then north along NY 9D. Parking is available with a suggested contribution. For more information, contact Manitoga, P.O. Box 249, Garrison, NY 10524; (845) 424-3812; www.manitoga.org.

Deer Run Trail   *Length: 0.8 mile Blaze: wooden disc*
The Deer Run Trail is the first trail to branch off to the right from the main trail. It soon crosses a brook on a split log bridge. At Four Corners Room, it rejoins the main trail for the descent back to the trailhead.

Lost Pond Trail   *Length: 1.8 miles Blaze: wooden disc*
After the White Pine Trail splits off to the right, the main trail becomes the Lost Pond Trail, named after a small spring-fed pond. The trail starts its descent at the pond and goes through a blueberry field, Boulder Amphitheater, and a fern meadow. It rejoins the main trail at Four Corners Room for the final descent.

White Pine Trail   *Length: 1.2 miles Blaze: wooden disc*
The White Pine Trail is the second trail to the right from the main trail. It ascends steeply to a hawk's-eye view of the forest below. On the descent to Four Corners Room, it crosses a fern meadow which has New York, Interrupted, Cinnamon, Christmas, and other ferns.

Figure 9-7. The River Trail at Manitou Point Preserve

Manitou Point Preserve

Just north of the Bear Mountain Bridge, a 136-acre peninsula juts into the Hudson River. Formerly known as Mystery Point, Manitou Point Preserve offers the enduring natural beauty of the river as well as a sense of the grace of a bygone era. The natural features of the property include a mature wooded upland with numerous rock outcrops, a steep-sided ravine, a portion of Manitou Marsh, and sheer rocky bluffs along the Hudson River.

Manitou Point Preserve was formerly a portion of the estate of Edward Livingston, a descendant of Philip Livingston, a signer of the Declaration of Independence. Edward, a New York City businessman, purchased the property in 1894 as a country home for his family and to establish stables and kennels for his horses and champion Irish wolfhounds. Following the construction in 1894 of a 50-foot stone-arch bridge over the railroad tracks and a dam on Copper Mine Brook to create a reservoir, Edward hired the architect George Frederick Pelham to design a home. The brick colonial revival mansion was completed in 1897, with extensive carriage roads, a smaller residence, an ice house, a carriage house, and an ox barn added later.

Livingston's daughter, Clarice, maintained the property until she sold it in 1938. In 1984, Lee Pomeroy, a New York architect, formed the Mystery Point Associates to acquire the property. After extensive renovations, he sold the property in 1990 to Open Space Institute, Inc. and Scenic Hudson, Inc. The mansion is now the national headquarters of Outward Bound, Inc. and is not open to the public.

The property has two distinct trail systems connected by a bridge over the railroad tracks. Some of the trails are old carriage roads, while others are narrow trails. On the point, there is a loop trail through a mixed forest, a little over a mile long. One third of it is on a narrow ledge, with sheer drops into and views over the Hudson River. It may be closed in icy weather. There are also several miles of·trail that go through a primarily hemlock forest.

To reach the Manitou Point Preserve by car, take NY 9D north from the Bear Mountain Bridge and continue for 1.8 miles to the preserve entrance. Turn left, and proceed through stone pillars with a white gate to the parking lot on the left side of the entrance road. From the parking lot, walk down the road and cross the bridge over the railroad tracks to reach the trails on Manitou Point. Those who wish to use public transportation should take a Metro-North Hudson Line train to the Manitou station (limited service, primarily on weekends). From the station, proceed east on Manitou Station Road for 0.1 mile, then turn left and pass between stone pillars with a white gate onto a dirt road which runs along the southeast edge of Manitou Marsh. On the right side of the road, there are several trailheads which lead into the upland area of the preserve. To reach the trails along the river, follow the road for 0.6 mile until it ends at the entrance road which leads down into the preserve from NY 9D. Turn left on this road and cross the bridge over the railroad tracks to the trailhead.

The trails at Manitou Point can be combined with trails at Manitoga (see above) and the Appalachian Trail to make a loop hike of seven or more miles starting and ending from the Manitou station, or more ambitious hikes that end at Peekskill via the Camp Smith Trail or at Garrison via the Osborn Loop and Sugarloaf Trail.

TEN

DUTCHESS COUNTY

utchess County, one of the original counties of New York State, was formed in 1683. The name of the largest city, Poughkeepsie, is derived from the Wappingers' name for it, which is reputed to mean "reed-covered lodge by the little water place." Surprisingly enough, three centuries later, some quiet places by the water still exist in the county, and some are accessible to the public.

Much of the county is farmed, but a considerable area remains in returning forest. Stands of great trees of mixed deciduous and evergreen varieties are found in a few small areas. Several streams traverse the county, among them the Fishkill Creek, Wappingers Creek, and Ten Mile River.

Hiking Opportunities

As the mild-natured scenery suggests, most of the hiking opportunities here are not especially rugged. Nonetheless, Dutchess County is far from devoid of hiking pleasures and challenges. Lovely walks can be combined with picnics or with visits to historic mansions along the Hudson River. Hudson Highlands State Park, with trails up Breakneck Ridge and Sugarloaf, lies in the southwest corner of the county. Scenic Hudson's protection of Beacon Mountain and Fishkill Ridge ensures that hikers will be able to continue enjoying the open space adjacent to the park (see chapter 9, "East Hudson Highlands"). Brace

Mountain is in the extreme northeast part of the county (see chapter 11, "The Southern Taconics"). The Appalachian Trail traverses the county for about 28 miles from the Putnam County line to where it enters Connecticut. Peggy Turco's book, *Walks & Rambles in Dutchess and Putnam Counties*, describes other interesting hikes.

There are six New York State Department of Environmental Conservation Multiple-Use Areas in the county. Most of these areas have only a parking area and a few logging roads. Their primary use is for hunting and logging, but when hunting season is over, they provide many hiking and bushwhacking opportunities. Stissing Mountain and Taconic-Hereford are described in this chapter. For the others, obtain a pamphlet, *Multiple-Use Areas in Dutchess County*, from the DEC, Stony Kill Farm Environmental Education Center, 79 Farmstead Lane, Wappingers Falls, NY 12590; (845) 831-8780 x309.

For general information, contact the Dutchess County Tourism Promotion Agency, 3 Neptune Road, Suite M17, Poughkeepsie, NY 12601; (845) 463-4000 or (800) 445-3131; www.dutchesstourism.com. For information on public transportation, contact Metro-North at (212) 532-4900 or (800) 638-7646; www.mta.nyc.ny.us/mnr; Amtrak at (800) 872-7245; www.amtrak.com; or the Dutchess County Loop Bus System at (845) 485-4690; www.dutchessny.gov/loop.htm.

APPALACHIAN TRAIL

The Appalachian Trail (AT) passes through the southeast corner of Dutchess County. Several interesting sections of the trail are described below, and two of the hikes can be reached by public transportation. For a complete description of the AT through Dutchess County, see the *Appalachian Trail Guide to New York-New Jersey*.

Depot Hill   *Length: 2.5 miles Blaze: white*
This northbound hike starts at the intersection of Stormville Mountain Road and Grape Hollow Road near the bridge over I-84. Parking is available along Grape Hollow Road. A pleasant walk of 2.2 miles rewards the hiker with views over the surrounding hills and west over the Hudson Valley to the distant Catskills. The remaining 0.3 mile leads to the Morgan Stewart Shelter. The return hike is via the same route (5.0 miles round trip).

Cat Rocks *Length: 3.3 miles Blaze: white*
This southbound hike begins at the Appalachian Trail railroad station, which is served by several Metro-North Harlem Line trains on weekends only; for information, call Metro-North at (212) 532-4900 or (800) 638-7646, or visit their web site, www.mta.nyc.ny.us/mnr. The station is located on NY 22, 1.1 miles north of Corbin Road in Pawling. Parking is available a short distance north along NY 22.

After proceeding west across the railroad tracks, the AT traverses a wet area on puncheons, crosses the Swamp River on a wooden bridge, and begins a steady ascent of Corbin Hill, reaching the top at 1.5 miles. On the western slope, it goes through almost a mile of open fields (caution is advised, as the fences around the fields may be electrified). At 2.4 miles, the AT crosses West Dover Road at a large oak tree, thought to be the largest tree on the entire trail. The AT steeply climbs West Mountain, with a side trail to the left at 3.1 miles leading to the Telephone Pioneers Shelter. At 3.3 miles, a short side trail to the right leads to Cat Rocks, with views over farmlands to the east and south. The return hike is via the same route (6.6 miles round trip).

NY 22 to Hoyt Road (Pawling Nature Reserve) *Length: 7.0 miles Blaze: white*
This seven-mile hike includes three miles through the Pawling Nature Reserve. Parking is available at both ends of the hike. The southern end is at NY 22, 1.1 miles north of Corbin Road, at the Appalachian Trail railroad station (see description of Cat Rocks hike, above).

From NY 22, the AT proceeds east and soon crosses Hurds Corners Road (Old Route 22). The trail passes an historic water tower that formerly supplied water to the farms and homes along the road, with buildings of the former Sheffield Farms Dairy visible across the road. After crossing fields actively used for grazing and farming, the AT enters the Pawling Nature Reserve at 0.8 mile. There is a register box here, and a map of the reserve is posted (copies of the map may also be available). The AT proceeds through the reserve, intersecting the Yellow, Red, Green, and Northern Yellow trails. These trails may be combined with the AT to make loop hikes. The AT leaves the reserve at 3.6 miles, and at 4.7 miles it passes the Gate of Heaven Cemetery, on property formerly part of the Harlem Valley State Hospital. After crossing Leather Hill Road, the AT arrives at the Wiley Shelter, built in 1940. A short distance beyond the shelter, at 6.1 miles, the trail crosses paved Duell Hollow Road, where parking is available. It crosses Duell Hollow Brook on a footbridge and reaches Hoyt

Road, at the New York-Connecticut state line, at 7.0 miles. Limited parking is available here.

JAMES BAIRD STATE PARK

Located amid working farms, this 590-acre state park was donated to New York State in 1939 by James Baird, an engineer. The following year, a Civilian Conservation Corps camp was established in the park, and the golf course and clubhouse were started, to be officially opened in 1948. Other facilities were completed in 1951. In 2001, the park offers hiking, cross-country skiing, golf, tennis, picnic facilities, and a restaurant.

Four well-marked, wide trails wind through wooded areas with deciduous trees and some hemlocks. The terrain is generally a series of small ridges, with elevation changes of approximately 75 feet. Vertical slaty rock strata form the ridges and are exposed in a few locations. The trails are wide enough for two or three people to walk side-by-side or for cross-country skiing during the winter. Using the trail map that is available from the park office, hikers can combine the park's trails to make longer hikes.

The park has its own exits north and south from the Taconic State Parkway, located 1.2 miles north of the NY 55 exit. For more information, contact James Baird State Park, 122D Freedom Road, Pleasant Valley, NY 12569; (845) 452-1489; www.nysparks.com, or call the restaurant at (845) 473-0744.

BOWDOIN PARK

Located adjacent to New Hamburg, Bowdoin Park is part of the Dutchess County park system. Its 300 acres offer a hiking trail system, cross-country course, baseball and soccer fields, picnic areas, and a nature center with displays of local flora and fauna. The hilly terrain and large, open fields offer views of the Hudson River and the hills on the other side. The well-used park trails are not clearly marked. A trail map is posted at the park office. The longest trail (2.8 miles) is a loop and follows the park's perimeter.

To reach Bowdoin Park by public transportation, hikers can take a Metro-North Hudson Line train to New Hamburg, walk 0.5 mile from the station up Main Street to Sheafe Road, and continue along the road for another 0.5 mile. Automobile access is from NY 9D in the Village of Wappingers Falls or from the southbound lane of US 9, 1.5 miles south of Spackenkill Road (County 113). Bowdoin Park has ample parking. For more information, contact Bowdoin Park, 85 Sheafe Road, Wappingers Falls, NY 12590; (845) 298-4600; www.dutchessny.gov/dpw-pk.htm.

HARLEM VALLEY RAIL TRAIL

The Harlem Line of Metro-North currently extends from New York City north to Wassaic in Dutchess County. The line formerly continued north to Chatham in Columbia County, but service on the northern portion of the route was discontinued in 1972. The New York State Office of Parks, Recreation and Historic Preservation (NYS-OPRHP) purchased the 22 miles between Wassaic and Copake Falls State Park in Columbia County in 1989. It then leased to Dutchess County all but the northern four miles of the line (which are in Columbia County) for 30 years. Dutchess County is proceeding to develop the right-of-way as a multi-use trail. The County Planning Department and the state received an Intermodal Surface Transportation Efficiency Act (ISTEA) grant for the construction of the 8.2-mile segment from Mechanics Street in Amenia to US 44 in Millerton. The 4.6-mile segment from Amenia to County 58 (Coleman Station) was opened in 1996, and the remaining 3.6 miles from County 58 to Millerton were opened in 2000. Funding has been obtained for the construction of the final ten miles in Dutchess County, and work is progressing on the extension of the trail from Amenia south to the Metro-North station in Wassaic.

The completed portions of the trail are paved to a width of ten feet and are available for various types of non-motorized use (horses are not allowed). The trail is accessible to the handicapped. For more information, contact the Dutchess County Department of Public Works, 22 Market Street, Poughkeepsie, NY 12601; (845) 486-2121; www.dutchessny.gov/dpw-pk.htm; or the Harlem Valley Rail Trail Association, 51 South Center Street, P.O. Box 356, Millerton, NY 12546; (518) 789-9591; www.hvrt.org.

HYDE PARK

The Town of Hyde Park boasts a 10.4-mile trail system linking the Franklin D. Roosevelt National Historic Site, Val-Kill National Historic Site, Vanderbilt

*Figure 10-1. The Carriage House,
FDR National Historic Site*

Mansion National Historic Site, and Mills-Norrie State Park. These trails are the results of cooperative efforts of federal, state, and local governments, not-for-profit organizations, and private individuals. The north–south trail from the Roosevelt home to the Vanderbilt property and the River Trail in Mills-Norrie State Park are designated segments of the Hudson River Greenway Trail.

Roosevelt National Historic Site contains Franklin Delano Roosevelt's home, library, rose garden, grave, and a small museum. Val-Kill, built in 1925, is the former home of Eleanor Roosevelt. Housing her effects and memorabilia, it is the only National Historic Site dedicated to a First Lady. Vanderbilt National Historic Site, the former home of Frederick Vanderbilt, contains a vast collection of antique furnishings obtained in Europe. The landscaping, including a formal Italian garden restored by volunteers, and the views of and across the Hudson River are magnificent. Mills-Norrie State Park has an historic mansion, environmental center, marina, golf course, and camping area.

There are guided tours at the historic buildings, but times are different for each. Admission is charged at the home of Franklin Roosevelt and at the Vanderbilt mansion. This section of the county contains fine examples of large estates that have survived, more or less intact, from the earliest European settlement. Originally they were self-sufficient farm and property holdings comprising thousands of acres, and much of the landscaping is over 100 years old. Since the estates were in the hands of only a few families, their furnishings represent stylistic continuity. The properties were groomed and the vistas developed with a distinct style that, in the case of each family, was allowed to mature.

Aside from the link to Val-Kill, the Hyde Park Trail rolls along beside the

Hudson River, sometimes climbing the bordering ridge. Around the mansions, the trail meanders through beautiful tailored grounds. In other parts of the estates, the trail passes large specimen trees, small swampy areas, streams, rock outcrops, and wooded areas. Bard Rock, at the north end of the Vanderbilt estate, and Crum Elbow Point, at the Roosevelt home, provide direct access to the river. Three other places in Mills-Norrie also directly touch the river. The trail, in most places, runs along old carriage roads that are suitable for cross-country skiing, given favorable conditions. However, the walker needs to use caution on the portions along roads that connect the sites.

The Hyde Park Trail (green tulip-leaf emblem) is best done as a series of several short walks covering unique sections of the trail: the Vanderbilt Loop (2.4 miles), the Roosevelt home to Riverfront Park and return (5.0 miles), the Roosevelt home to Val-Kill and return (5.0 miles), and the Mills mansion to Norrie Point and return (4.0 miles). In addition, each of the mansion sites has additional trails showing other features of its grounds. At Mills-Norrie, the ten-mile trail system allows for a variety of circular hikes and includes carriage roads and horse trails. Cross-country skiing (no snowmobiling) is permitted on carriage roads and the golf course when conditions are favorable.

Figure 10-2. Trail along the Hudson in Mills-Norrie State Park

JACK FAGAN

Access to each site is directly from US 9, except Val-Kill, which is accessible from NY 9G. For additional information about the Roosevelt home, Val-Kill, or the Vanderbilt mansion, contact the National Park Service at the Roosevelt-Vanderbilt National Historic Site, 4097 Albany Post Road, Hyde Park, NY 12538; (845) 229-9115. For information about Mills-Norrie State Park, contact the park at Old Post Road, Staatsburg, NY 12580; (845) 889-4646; www.nysparks.com. For information about the Hyde Park Trail, contact the Town of Hyde Park Recreation Department at 4383 Albany Post Road,

Hyde Park, NY 12538; (845) 229-8086. Maps are usually available at the respective sites.

LOCUST GROVE

At the end of the eighteenth century, this privately owned historic site was part of a 350-acre tract, which included a farm, sawmill, store, and sloop landing, owned by Henry Livingston, Jr. The subsequent owner, John Montgomery, continued to operate it as a farm from 1830 until 1847, when part of the original property was sold to Samuel F. B. Morse, artist and inventor of the commercial electric telegraph. Morse was interested in landscaping the property, with the results still visible. In 1901, the estate was sold to William and Martha Young. He was a lawyer and merchant, heir to a family hardware fortune. She was a collector of Americana: furniture, china, and decorative art. It was their daughter, Annette, who endowed a trust to maintain Locust Grove as an historical site and wildlife sanctuary. The mansion houses the Young collections as well as Morse memorabilia and early telegraph equipment.

The 150-acre sanctuary includes gardens, walking trails, the historic mansion, and a visitor center. A guided tour, for which there is a charge, is conducted through the mansion. In addition, 3.2 miles of interconnected trails run through fields, woods, and gardens. Trail maps are available showing the trails and describing the historic features of the property. The trails have some steep pitches and offer views of the Hudson River.

Access to the property is from the southbound lane of US 9 just south of Poughkeepsie, with parking on the site. The Locust Grove mansion is open from May 1 to Thanksgiving. The gardens, grounds, and visitor center are open daily year-round. Bicycles are not permitted. For more information, contact Locust Grove, 2683 South Road (Route 9), Poughkeepsie, NY 12601-0649; (845) 454-4500; www.morsehistoricsite.org.

PAWLING NATURE RESERVE

The 1,060-acre Pawling Nature Reserve has been owned by The Nature Conservancy since 1958. Managed by a local volunteer committee, the reserve abounds with interesting plants, several of which are rare, and bird species. It is home to a large deer population, reptiles, amphibians, wild turkeys, and occasional coyotes, beavers, and bobcats. Members of a local gun club have permission to hunt during deer season. There are no public facilities in the reserve.

The generally hilly land contained in the reserve was cleared for farming prior to the Revolutionary War, and some of the stone fences built about that time still exist. Hammersly Ridge, trending north–south, is the high point at 1,053 feet above sea level and about 250 feet above the starting elevation. Vegetation is quite lush, and most of the forest is mixed, but some large hemlock stands can be found.

About a mile north of the village of Pawling or 2.5 miles north of NY 55 on NY 22 is County 68, North Quaker Hill Road. A right turn and a drive of 1.2 miles leads to Quaker Lake Road on the left. In another mile and a half, past Quaker Lake on the left, the main parking area is reached. Maps are sometimes available at this location and at a register box where the Appalachian Trail enters the reserve from the south. For more information about the Pawling Nature Reserve, contact the Eastern New York Chapter of The Nature Conservancy, 19 North Moger Avenue, Mt. Kisco, NY 10549; (914) 244-3271; www.nature.org.

Appalachian Trail
Length: 2.8 miles Blaze: white
From the south, access to the Pawling Nature Reserve property is either from a blue-blazed side trail which extends 0.4 mile from Hurds Corners Road, or via the Appalachian Trail. For a description of the Appalachian Trail through the reserve, see pp. 179-80 above.

Blue Trail
Length: 2.0 miles Blaze: blue
From the trailhead, 300 feet south of Quaker Lake, where the Red Trail also begins, the Blue Trail loops though the south end of the reserve. Along its route there are grape vines, striped maples, and dense undergrowth. Traveling through mixed hardwoods, the trail becomes a woods road. A large hemlock grove is at the junction of the Red and Blue trails. Another short trail, also blazed blue, provides access from Hurds Corners Road, on the western side of the reserve. This 0.4-mile trail extends from Hurds Corners Road (where parking is available along the side of the road) to the Appalachian Trail.

Green Trail
Length: 0.6 mile Blaze: green
The Green Trail provides access to the reserve from NY 22 on the west. To reach the trailhead from NY 22, take Hutchinson Road east one block to Deer

Ridge Road. From this intersection, the Green Trail proceeds for 250 feet along the edge of a neighboring landowner's lawn, and then meanders upward to a ridge with a view west. It passes through a young hardwood forest and occasional hemlock groves. It meets and turns south on the Appalachian Trail (white), which is joint with the Red Trail at this point, and then heads north to meet the Orange Trail loop which can be used to return to the starting point on Deer Ridge Road.

Northern Yellow Trail   *Length: 0.7 mile Blaze: yellow*
This access trail starts at a trailhead and parking area 1.4 miles north of the reserve's main entrance on Quaker Lake Road. The trail goes over a wooden bridge, through deep fern undergrowth, and past several overgrown stone walls. It rises steeply to end at the Appalachian Trail (white).

Orange Trail   *Length: 0.7 mile Blaze: orange*
The Orange Trail starts from the Green Trail soon after its beginning. Shortly, it turns south and then loops back to its starting point, passing through young hardwood forest.

Red Trail   *Length: 2.4 miles Blaze: red*
From the trailhead, which is south of Quaker Lake, the Red Trail climbs through a stand of hemlock and spruce to a junction with the Blue Trail at 0.4 mile. It continues uphill, crossing the Appalachian Trail and climbing north until it temporarily ends at another junction with the Appalachian Trail. There are views down to Quaker Lake along the way. The Red Trail picks up again 0.1 mile to the north (left) along the Appalachian Trail, where it continues for 0.7 mile back down to Quaker Lake Road, ending at the Yellow Trail trailhead.

Yellow Trail   *Length: 0.6 mile Blaze: yellow*
Access to the Yellow Trail is at the main parking area of the reserve. A registration station with maps and a sign-in book is 150 feet from the parking area. This main access trail almost immediately runs past a deep, cool, hemlock-and-fern-filled gorge through which a waterfall flows. At 0.3 mile, there is a swamp, which on spring evenings hosts many noisy frogs. The trail climbs gradually to the top of the ridge and ends just past the crest at the Appalachian Trail.

POETS' WALK ROMANTIC LANDSCAPE PARK

Writers and poets found inspiration in the rolling fields and woodlands over-looking the Hudson River. This 120-acre park, located on River Road in Red Hook, contains two miles of trails, which provide views of the Hudson River, the Kingston-Rhinecliff Bridge, and the Catskill Mountains. Rustic cedar-log benches and gazebos encourage visitors to pause for a while and enjoy the natural landscape. The surrounding 800 acres are protected by conservation easements, thus ensuring the visual integrity of the land.

To reach the park, take NY 199 to River Road, 0.5 mile east of the Kingston-Rhinecliff Bridge. Proceed north on River Road to the park entrance on the left. For more information, contact Scenic Hudson, Inc., 9 Vassar Street, Poughkeepsie, NY 12601; (845) 473-4440; www.scenichudson.org.

POUGHKEEPSIE-HIGHLAND RAILROAD BRIDGE

This 6,767-foot-long railroad bridge crosses the Hudson River 212 feet above the water and offers views up and down the river. First chartered in 1871, the bridge was completed in 1888 at a cost of $10 million. It was the only rail bridge across the Hudson River south of Albany. Used extensively until 1969, it was the gateway to southern New England. A fire in 1974 damaged the bridge, and Penn Central ceased operating over it. At that time, engineering studies evaluated the reconstruction possibilities, but nothing was done. Two years later, the bridge was included in the Conrail system, and Conrail sold it to a private investor in 1984. Ownership again changed in 1990 to another private investor without any work being done on the bridge. In 1991, the efforts of Poughkeepsie resident Bill Sepe to use the bridge for pedestrians and bicycles resulted in the formation of a not-for-profit organization, the Poughkeepsie-Highland Railroad Bridge Co., Inc., which acquired title to the bridge in 1998. People with past connections to the bridge have donated memorabilia, including the original construction blueprints complete with field notes. This material is displayed at public events and bridge celebrations.

Although guided tours were formerly offered, the walkway on the bridge is currently closed to the public. It may reopen in the future. For current information, contact Walkway over the Hudson, 65 Gifford Avenue, Poughkeepsie, NY 12601; (845) 454-9649; www.walkway.org.

REESE NATURE SANCTUARY

From the 1830s, industries and mills developed along Wappingers Creek, a major tributary of the Hudson River. As industry left the area, the surrounding land reverted to its wooded state. In 1982, Frances and Willis Reese donated 98 acres along the creek to the National Audubon Society as a wildlife and nature sanctuary, particularly for migratory birds. Now owned and managed by the Putnam Highlands Chapter, the Reese Nature Sanctuary provides an unmarked trail on a ridge rising steeply about 60 feet from Wappingers Creek. The trail rolls for about one mile through stands of large deciduous and pine trees. In 2001, there are plans to connect this trail with the Wappingers Greenway, which will extend further upstream along Wappingers Creek.

Metro-North Hudson Line trains stop at New Hamburg; from there, Reese Sanctuary is a short walk up Main Street, with access through the southwest corner of New Hamburg Park. Weekday parking is restricted to two hours.

For more information, contact Constitution Marsh Audubon Center and Sanctuary, P.O. Box 174, Cold Spring, NY 10516; (845) 265-2601.

STISSING MOUNTAIN AREA

About midway between the Hudson River and the Housatonic Highlands of Connecticut is 1,400-foot Stissing Mountain. The distinctive dome has striking escarpments at its northern end and slopes gently to join low hills to the south.

Soaring above all nearby hills, Stissing Mountain is unusual in that it is composed of Precambrian bedrock, yet lies many miles from the Hudson Highlands or any other area of Precambrian outcrop. Several possible explanations have been advanced by geologists. One possibility is that Stissing Mountain is an isolated, high "island" of Precambrian rock that has existed here for over 600 million years, never having been covered by the Paleozoic strata that now abut the mountain on all sides. Another, much more complex theory speculates that Stissing Mountain is a remnant of a mass of Precambrian crust that originated elsewhere, was overthrust onto Paleozoic rock, and was subsequently isolated by erosion.

Stissing's setting is more pastoral than rugged, with forest and pasture land about equal. Yet the mountain and its three lakes do convey a sense of wildness. The fire tower on the summit commands a 360° view that includes the Catskills to the west and the Taconics toward the northeast. In clear weather, the buildings in Albany can be seen with binoculars.

The American Museum of Natural History, at 79th Street and Central Park West in New York City, has a display highlighting Stissing Mountain and surrounding Dutchess County. The large-scale model, "Bird's Eye View of Stissing Mountain," shows how the dome, composed of Precambrian gneiss, dominates the Pine Plains lowlands, composed of limestone, shale, and slate. This countryside was once covered by glaciers, and the nearby ponds—Twin Island, Stissing, and Thompson—are the remnants of glacial kettles, formed when huge masses of debris-covered ice finally melted some 15,000 years ago.

In 1986, the Friends of Stissing Landmarks (FOSL) formed after the NYS DEC announced plans for the demolition of the 90-foot fire tower. Erected in 1934 by the Civilian Conservation Corps, the tower had been staffed

Figure 10-3. *Fire tower on Stissing Mountain*

and in service for forty years when aircraft assumed forest fire surveillance. As a local landmark, it appears on the seal of the Town of Pine Plains. Thanks to a citizen petition, the tower was saved. In 1991, The Nature Conservancy gave FOSL one acre of land, which surrounds the tower. FOSL restored the tower and re-opened it to the public in 1993. Thanks to a gift from the DEC in 1994, FOSL now owns the tower. Trails to the tower are on private land, accessible to the public courtesy of adjacent landowners.

Stissing Mountain

Three trailheads provide access to trails up Stissing Mountain. The first trailhead is on Lake Road, off either NY 199 or NY 82 near Pine Plains. Lake Road is reached by traveling one mile west of the junction of NY 199 and NY 82. After a left on Lake Road, drivers will find the parking area at 1.7 miles. Hikers can also reach Lake Road by turning at the firehouse one mile south of the intersection of NY 82 and NY 199. The parking area is 1.7 miles from the firehouse.

The trail from the Lake Road parking area is an ideal short hike, with an easygoing, rapid ascent, rewarding views, and a geologically interesting setting. The summit loop can be traversed in two hours or less; however, most hikers will want to allow more time to climb the tower and enjoy the views. From the trailhead on Lake Road, the trail climbs steeply for a short distance until it joins a woods road. The route then turns left, following the woods road up a gentle climb to a trail junction at 0.3 mile. At this point, the yellow-blazed road splits. A rocky, steep trail leads south (left), reaching the tower in 0.3 mile. The woods road continues to the southwest (right), reaching the tower in 0.6 mile. It is more enjoyable to ascend the ridge via the trail and to come down via the road. Both trails cross private property, so hikers must stay on the trails.

The second trailhead is on Mountain Road, 3.7 miles north of Stanfordville. Five miles south of Pine Plains on NY 82, turn west onto Stissing Lane, and then north at the T junction onto Mountain Road, continuing for two miles. There is parking at the cul-de-sac at the end of Mountain Road. A blue-blazed trail runs along a woods road through private property. Along its 2.8-mile route, it passes through young mixed hardwoods and occasional wetland areas. The soil in the area is thin and cannot support dense woodland. The land had been totally cleared by the mid-to-late 1800s, the wood used to provide charcoal for the iron furnaces at Dover Town and Millerton. At 0.5 mile, it intersects with the trail coming from Hicks Hill Road.

The third trail starts on Hicks Hill Road, off NY 199, four miles west of Pine Plains. The trailhead is 3.5 miles south of NY 199. A red-blazed trail, mostly an old logging road, leads through the Stissing Mountain Multiple-Use Area. The trail intersects the Ridge Trail at 2.0 miles. Turning north at the intersection onto the Ridge Trail leads to the tower in another two miles.

There are other trails in the 595-acre Stissing Mountain Multiple-Use Area, where hunting is permitted in season. For more information, contact the New York State DEC forestry office at Stony Kill Farm Environmental Education Center, 79 Farmstead Lane, Wappingers Falls, NY 12590; (845) 831-8780 x309; or Friends of Stissing Landmarks, Inc., P.O. Box 37, Pine Plains, NY 12567-0037; (518) 398-5673.

JACK FAGAN

Figure 10-4. Thompson Pond from Stissing Fire Tower

Thompson Pond

In 1959, The Nature Conservancy, the Dutchess County Bird Club, and a committee of interested citizens led by the *Register-Herald* of Pine Plains purchased and preserved all of Thompson Pond, at the east base of Stissing Mountain. This 507-acre tract is noted for its great diversity in plant and animal life. In 1973, Thompson Pond became a National Natural Landmark.

The shallow pond is a 44-acre bog-pond, with a deep peat deposit, bordered by an expanding cattail and bulrush marsh. It is more than a half-mile long and a quarter-mile wide, the most southern of the three glacial ponds. Thompson Pond, Stissing Lake, and Mud (or Twin Island) Pond are the remnants of a glacial kettle, formed when a huge mass of debris-covered glacial ice melted 15,000 years ago, at the end of the Pleistocene Epoch.

The pond, marsh, swamp, and upland forest offer a great diversity of fauna and flora. Over four hundred species of plants have been catalogued, and a vast number of birds recorded, including migratory warblers, marsh birds, and predatory species. The pond teems with fish; the land is home to over two dozen mammal species.

To reach Thompson Pond, drivers should take NY 82 to Pine Plains and turn west at the firehouse onto Lake Road. The parking area is 1.5 miles west and on the left. Cars can be left on Lake Road at the start of the trail, which begins at a small seasonal brook.

From the small parking area on Lake Road, a yellow-blazed trail runs around the pond and through the woods for about four miles. Several side trails branch off from the main trail. There is a register box with maps 300 yards from the preserve's entrance sign.

The preserve is open all year. Permitted uses include hiking, cross-country skiing, and studying for education and research. The Thompson Pond Committee oversees the property for The Nature Conservancy. For more information, contact the Eastern New York Chapter of The Nature Conservancy, 41 South Moger Avenue, Mt. Kisco, NY 10549; (914) 244-3271; www.nature.org.

STONY KILL FARM

The New York State Department of Environmental Conservation owns this 756-acre site, consisting of an operating farm with crop fields and pasture, rolling woodlands, and small ponds. There are about 8.5 miles of trails, including both woodland trails and trails around the active farm area. In the winter, these trails are open for cross-country skiing and snowshoeing. Snowshoes may be rented at the site. Hunting and pets are not permitted on the property.

In 1683, Gulian Verplanck and Francis Rombout bought 85,000 acres from the local Native Americans. The land was subdivided and generally farmed. James deLancey Verplanck built the Manor House in 1842 on 1,000 acres, including the present Stony Kill farm area. In 1942, 756 acres were given to the New York State Department of Education for public use and education. The New York State Agricultural and Technical College at Farmingdale managed the property until 1963, when it became inactive. In 1973, it entered its present phase as an environmental education center.

The wide trails have easy grades. There are interpretive markings along the 0.5-mile unblazed Woodland Trail. The Verplanck Ridge Trail (yellow) is 1.5 miles long, with a rise in elevation of only 70 feet. The Sierra Trail (white) runs through flat forest land with a marsh and pond near the trail, offering the choice of a 1.0- or 2.0-mile loop. The unmarked Muller Pond Trail is a scenic one-mile loop trail that circles the pond, while the 2.5-mile Freedom Trail is a woodland trail that passes through various forest ecosystems.

Stony Kill Farm is located on NY 9D, 4.5 miles south of Wappingers Falls village and 2.0 miles north of I-84. A prominent sign is located at the entrance on the west side of NY 9D. Parking is permitted at the Manor House, the farmstead, and the entrance to the Sierra Trail on County 36. For more information, contact the Stony Kill Farm Environmental Education Center, 79 Farmstead Lane, Wappingers Falls, NY 12590; (845) 831-8780 x300; www.dec.state.ny.us/website/education/stonykil.html.

TACONIC-HEREFORD MULTIPLE-USE AREA

This 909-acre multiple-use area has a network of trails, mostly on logging roads. Access is from a parking area just south of Tyrell Road on the Taconic State Parkway, a parking area on Tyrell Road, or a smaller parking area near the end of Pond Gut Road off NY 82.

The largest multiple-use area in Dutchess County is actively managed for timber. The easy trails and woods roads meander through dense chestnut oak and hickory forests, interspersed with younger growth full of dappled light. Frequent stone walls attest to the area's farming days. A hemlock forest, wetlands, and mixed hardwoods forest appear toward Pond Gut Road.

Hunting in season, mountain biking, and horseback riding are permitted. One woods road (orange) is open to snowmobiles when the conditions are favorable. Permits are required if camping for more three days or for ten or more people in a party. For a map, contact the New York State DEC forestry office at Stony Kill Farm Environmental Education Center, 79 Farmstead Lane, Wappingers Falls, NY 12590; (845) 831-8780 x309.

TIVOLI BAYS

The Tivoli Bays area is part of the Hudson River National Estuarine Research Reserve. The New York State Department of Environmental Conservation manages the site as a field laboratory for research and education about the Hudson River Estuary and as a wildlife management area.

In 1850, the Hudson River Railroad laid tracks on an embankment at the western edge of the bays. Two bridge openings in the North Bay and three in the South Bay allow water to enter and leave with each tidal cycle. Sediments in the bays have been accumulating at an accelerated rate since then, speeding up the evolution of the bays from deep water to wetland.

Tivoli Bays is a large freshwater tidal wetland surrounded by undeveloped

Figure 10-5. Tivoli Bays

land. The average tidal range at the bays is about four feet. The 1,700-acre reserve includes three miles of trails, in addition to woods roads. The 1.0-mile-long North Bay Trail follows the Stony Creek along waterfalls and a tidal creek through a hemlock ravine, mixed deciduous forest, and tidal swamp. The Cruger Island Causeway Trail extends for 0.4 mile, through a mature freshwater tidal swamp, up to the railroad tracks. The trail floods at high tide and is wet at low tide. The Overlook Trail goes 1.1 miles from NY 9G through rolling fields and woods to a panoramic view of the North Bay, Hudson River, and the Catskills. The Hogback Trail (0.6 mile) climbs through a hardwood forest with many varieties of wildflowers in the spring. It connects the parking area on Cruger Road with the midpoint of the Overlook Trail. Bard College also has trails here that skirt the South Bay.

Additional activities permitted at the site include canoeing and bird watching, as well as hunting, fishing, and trapping in season. Bicycling is permitted on internal roads except during winter and early spring. Swimming and motorized boats are not permitted. Public field programs are offered on weekends.

For additional information, including a brochure with a map, contact the Hudson River National Estuarine Research Reserve, Bard College Field Station, Annandale, NY 12504; (845) 758-7010; http://inlet.geol.sc.edu/HUD/home.html.

ELEVEN

THE SOUTHERN TACONICS

ast of the Harlem Valley of New York and west of the Housatonic Valley of Connecticut and Massachusetts rise the Taconics. They extend north through western Massachusetts and eastern New York into southwestern Vermont, where they reach their highest elevations. The name "Taconic" is a modern rendering of a Native American name variously spelled Taghkannock and Taghkanic.

Seemingly remote from civilization, much of the highland in the south is protected as a relatively wild area. Streams tumble down forested escarpments, cutting scenic ravines and gorges. The trail system features sweeping views over the adjacent valleys to Mount Greylock to the north, the Catskill Mountains to the west, and the Hudson Highlands to the southwest.

The forest of the southern Taconics is second or third growth, much of it having been cut in the nineteenth century to provide charcoal for the local iron industry on Mount Riga and at Copake Falls. Large dense stands of mountain laurel are a beautiful sight when in bloom in late June and early July, but, along with thickets of scrub oak found on the upper elevations, they encroach on trails and are a barrier to bushwhacking. Several attractive lakes and ponds bedeck the highland. Riga Lake and South Pond in Connecticut and Plantain Pond in Massachusetts have privately owned shorelines where private roads serve camps and cottages. Bingham Pond, highest in Connecticut at 1,894 feet, is a botanically interesting bog.

The Taconic range is north-south trending, with the steepest slopes on the eastern side of the ridge. The mountains rise from a base of 1,000 feet above sea level to well over 2,000 feet in elevation. The bedrock of the Taconics consists of early Paleozoic schists, phyllites, and other metamorphic rocks, all intricately folded and crumpled.

Most geologists believe that this complex rock mass actually originated to the east and was moved some distance to its present position during the Taconian Orogeny of about 440 million years ago. The Taconic mountain range seems to be made up of many slices of rock, now jumbled together, each having separated and slid westward from the slope of a rising Himalayan-scale range located miles away—the ancestral Taconics. The present Taconics are an erosional remnant of that once-greater

Figure 11-1. *Outcrop of typical Taconic metamorphic rock, phyllite with quartz pods*

rock mass. This tumultuous geologic history is evidenced by the rough surface of the bedrock and the many minor ups and downs caused by differential weathering of the thinly-layered, often contorted bedrock (Figure 11-1).

Mount Everett (2,602 feet) is the highest and most prominent feature in the southern Taconics. The highest point in Connecticut (2,380 feet), also in the South Taconics, is located at the Connecticut–Massachusetts line on the south slope of Mount Frissell, which rises from the tableland to a summit in Massachusetts. This is the only place in the United States where the highest point of a state is not the summit of a land feature. About a mile to the southeast is Bear Mountain (2,320 feet), the highest summit in Connecticut. The highest elevation of the western range is Brace Mountain (2,311 feet) in New York.

The trail system of the southern Taconics features two parallel trails running north–south: the 15.6-mile South Taconic Trail following the western range and escarpment, and a 16.5-mile section of the Appalachian Trail on the eastern range. Other hiking routes consist mostly of side trails ascending to the highland from the valleys on either side. This system provides for circuit hikes, some of which include stretches of unpaved road. Since the route of the Appalachian Trail through the southern Taconics lies entirely within Connecticut and Massachusetts, only the South Taconic Trail and its connecting side trails are described in this chapter. For a description of the Appalachian Trail in the southern Taconics, see the *Appalachian Trail Guide to Massachusetts-Connecticut.*

Figure 11-2. *Bashbish Falls*

The trail system's real beauty lies in its route through the many gorges of the highland. The best-known is Bashbish Gorge in Massachusetts, with its towering walls and cascading brook ending in Bashbish Falls. Native American legend has it that several people plunged to their deaths over the falls, notably a woman named Bash Bish, whose body was never found and who became the spirit of the falls. The South Taconic Trail and side trails provide access to the gorge. South of Copake Falls, on the west side of the highland in New York, the Robert Brook Trail and the Alander Brook Trail lead up deep hemlock-clad ravines to join the South Taconic Trail.

A large part of the New York section of the highland, which lies along the western range and slope, is in Taconic State Park. The park has outdoor recreation and camping facilities at its Copake Falls area south of Hillsdale and at its Rudd Pond area north of Millerton, both at the base of the highland. Cottages and cabins are also available for rent at the Copake Falls area. The season is from mid-May until Labor Day at Rudd Pond and until December at Copake Falls.

The Connecticut part of the highland is loosely called Mount Riga or the Riga plateau, named after a nineteenth-century community of ironworkers at South Pond (Forge Pond) on the highland, where a restored iron furnace can be seen. Most of this section is owned by Mount Riga, Inc., a private conservation-minded body, but the National Park Service has acquired 1,225 acres from this group as a protective corridor for the Appalachian Trail. In addition, the state owns an area of woodland on the eastern slope above MA 41, called Mount Riga State Park (undeveloped), while the Appalachian Mountain Club owns 125 acres adjacent to the Massachusetts state line.

The Massachusetts section is larger than that of New York or Connecticut and is occupied by the Town of Mount Washington, which has no post office or commercial establishments and a year-round population of less than a hundred. The hiking trails are mostly in Mount Washington State Forest, including the Mount Everett Reservation, and in the corridor for the Appalachian Trail. Overnight parking at trailheads and trailside camping is prohibited. Deer hunting is permitted in season.

Road access to the highland from New York on the west starts as NY 344, which goes east from NY 22 through the Village of Copake Falls, enters the scenic ravine of Bashbish Brook, and becomes Falls Road in Massachusetts. Climbing steeply past Bashbish Falls, it connects with West Street and East Street in Mount Washington.

For more information on the New York section, contact Taconic State Park, Box 100, Copake Falls, NY 12517; (518) 329-3993; www.nysparks.com. For more information on the Massachusetts section, contact Mount Washington State Forest, East Street, Mount Washington, MA 01258; (413) 528-0330.

SOUTH TACONIC TRAIL AND ACCESS TRAILS

The highly scenic South Taconic Trail lies mostly in Taconic State Park and Mount Washington State Forest along the western escarpment and range of the southern Taconics. The trail may be divided into two sections that together span 15.6 miles. The longer southern section starts in the Harlem Valley in New York about five miles north of Millerton and ends at NY 344 east of Copake Falls, while the northern section continues north to where NY 23 goes over a low point in the Taconic range just east of the New York–Massachusetts line.

Alander Brook Trail   *Length: 1.4 miles Blaze: blue*
Largely a woods road, the Alander Brook Trail ascends to the South Taconic Trail (white) from the Harlem Valley in New York on the west, following a deep ravine. Cars may be parked at the trailhead on Under Mountain Road, 0.8 mile east of its junction with NY 22; this junction is almost four miles south of the intersection of NY 22 and NY 344 in Copake Falls. The trailhead lies a little north of Boston Corners, famed for having been a lawless "no man's land" in the 1850s when Massachusetts was ceding the area to New York. Just beyond the trailhead, Under Mountain Road turns right and goes to Rudd Pond Road.

The Alander Brook Trail starts in the woods next to a field and heads north; in 150 yards, the Robert Brook Trail (red) goes right. The Alander Brook Trail continues north along the base of the highland, and at 0.8 mile crosses Alander Brook and turns right from the woods road. Ascending through mountain laurel, it turns right onto another woods road at 1.0 mile and climbs along the hemlock-clad ravine of Alander Brook. The trail ends at the South Taconic Trail (white), which comes from the opposite direction and turns north here, off the woods road.

A scenic loop hike is possible by turning left here on the South Taconic Trail (white) and ascending to the west summit of Alander Mountain, going right on the Alander Loop Trail (blue), left on the South Taconic Trail, and right on the Robert Brook Trail (red) to descend to the starting point.

Alander Loop Trail   *Length: 1.3 miles Blaze: blue*
This trail, which may be poorly maintained, ascends to the top of the east summit (2,250 feet) of Alander Mountain. It starts at the 5.0-mile point of the South Taconic Trail and goes uphill to the northeast. At 1.2 miles, the Alander Mountain Trail (blue) comes in from the right. Continuing uphill, the trail ends at 1.3 miles at the South Taconic Trail. Turning left on the South Taconic Trail (white) takes the hiker south back to the start of the Alander Loop Trail, for a total circuit length of 2.3 miles.

Brace Mountain Trail   *Length: 1.6 miles Blaze: none*
Providing the easiest access to scenic Brace Mountain, this unmarked woods road on the highland extends from Mount Washington Road in Connecticut northwest to the South Taconic Trail in New York. The trailhead, with space for parking, is on the west side of the road, two miles north of the dam at South

Pond, with a metal gate barring access to the trail by vehicles. The trail follows the woods road through mountain laurel and crosses Monument Brook at 0.5 mile, the low point on the trail (1,850 feet). At 1.3 miles, an overgrown trail forks right and leads to a Connecticut–New York boundary monument and beyond. In a few yards, the Brace Mountain Trail enters New York at a stream and climbs steeply west up Brace Mountain on a stony route, with the extension of the Ashley Hill Trail coming in on the right from Massachusetts. After climbing up to the crest, the trail ends at the South Taconic Trail (white), just north of Brace Mountain's peak. Turning left on the South Taconic Trail, hikers can climb 0.2 mile to the open summit of the mountain at 2,311 feet.

Cedar Brook Trail
Length: 1.0 mile Blaze: blue

This trail climbs north across NY 344 from the parking lot below Bashbish Falls at the start of the northern section of the South Taconic Trail (white). It follows a brook, which it crosses several times beginning at 0.6 mile. Some of the crossings are slippery and difficult. At 0.9 mile, the final crossing occurs, and the trail ascends steeply to its junction with the South Taconic Trail at 1.0 mile (1.3 miles on the northern section of the South Taconic Trail).

Mount Frissell Trail
Length: 2.2 miles Blaze: red

This trail on the highland in three states goes over two summits, has views, and reaches the highest point in Connecticut, as well as the tri-state boundary point. It also takes the hiker through dense mountain laurel, scrub oak, and gray birch. The trail starts from Mount Washington Road–East Street at the Connecticut–Massachusetts line (1,830 feet), where there is limited parking. The trail heads northwest in Massachusetts along a woods road, turning left at 0.2 mile onto a footpath that leads into Connecticut. It ascends Round Mountain steeply, with views from its open crest. Passing over the summit (2,296 feet) at 0.7 mile, it descends northwest into Massachusetts, reaching the

Figure 11-3. Cedar Brook

saddle between Round Mountain and Mount Frissell. The trail ascends Mount Frissell steeply, and passes its summit (2,453 feet) at 1.2 miles. The trail then descends the south slope of Mount Frissell. Just before the Massachusetts–Connecticut boundary is a view over the highland, after which the trail turns right and in 30 yards reaches the highest point in Connecticut (2,380 feet). It continues west along the state line, descending Mount Frissell with more views. On level terrain, the trail reaches the tri-state boundary point at 1.7 miles, where an 1898 granite monument bears the names of New York and Massachusetts but omits Connecticut on the southeast side. The trail continues westward in New York, crossing the extension of the Ashley Hill Trail, a woods road, and ending at the South Taconic Trail (white) by a scenic open section overlooking the Harlem Valley. Turning left on the latter trail, it is 0.3 mile to the summit of Brace Mountain.

Robert Brook Trail   *Length: 1.1 miles Blaze: red*
The Robert Brook Trail begins at the Alander Brook Trail (blue), 150 yards from its western trailhead. The Robert Brook Trail ascends eastward along the ravine of Robert Brook on the rocky route of an eighteenth-century road; it turns north to an 1898 state boundary monument and follows the Massachusetts–New York state line up to a second monument. It continues as a narrow trail in Massachusetts to the South Taconic Trail, making a total ascent of 1,050 feet.

South Taconic Trail, Southern Section   *Length: 9.4 miles Blaze: white*
The southern section of the South Taconic Trail goes from Rudd Pond Farms to NY 344. To reach the southern terminus, drive 5.5 miles north on NY 22 from the traffic light at Millerton, New York. Go right on White House Crossing Road to its end and then left on Rudd Pond Road for 0.2 mile. Turn right onto Deer Run Road, which leads into Rudd Pond Farms, a residential development, and follow the road around to the east side of the development, where there is a small parking area on the left.

From the parking area, the trail goes east along the edge of the field, enters the woods, and starts to ascend the western escarpment of the southern Taconics. A steep, rough section begins at 0.4 mile, the trail passing a high waterfall and ascending cliffs along switchbacks with open views to the west. At 0.7 mile, the trail turns left and continues north on the escarpment, with more views to the west, then climbs South Brace Mountain, with views to the south. At 1.4 miles,

JACK FAGAN

Figure 11-4. View of Riga Lake from Brace Mountain

the trail turns left at a junction, where a trail leads into private property which is closed to the public. Continuing, the South Taconic Trail reaches an open area on South Brace Mountain, which offers a view south over the Riga plateau section of the highland, featuring Riga Lake and South Pond.

Crossing the open area with the summit of South Brace Mountain (2,304 feet) to the right, the trail descends to a saddle and ascends along the open crest of Brace Mountain to its summit (2,311 feet) at 1.9 miles, marked by a large pile of stones. There are views to the east of Bear Mountain in Connecticut and to the northeast of Mount Frissell in Massachusetts.

The trail descends north on a woods road to a junction at 2.2 miles, where the Brace Mountain Trail, also a woods road, leads right 1.6 miles to Mount Washington Road in Connecticut. The Appalachian Trail on the east can be reached by side trails from this road. Continuing north 200 yards to another junction, the South Taconic Trail goes left from the woods road, while the Mount Frissell Trail (red) goes right.

Proceeding along an open crest with views, the trail enters Massachusetts. Regaining the woods road, it continues north on a route previously called the State Line Trail. At 3.0 miles, a blue-blazed side trail goes northeast to the Ashley Hill Trail, which connects with the Mount Washington State Forest Headquarters on the north and with the Mount Frissell Trail on the south. Hikers coming from the north rather than the south should take particular care to bear left at the fork that appears 50 yards south of this junction in order to stay on the South Taconic Trail. At 4.5 miles, the Robert Brook Trail (red) goes left.

The South Taconic Trail, at 5.0 miles, curves left to descend and the Alander Loop Trail (blue) forks right. Descending into New York from Massachusetts, the South Taconic Trail crosses Alander Brook, and 200 feet later meets the end of the Alander Brook Trail at 5.2 miles. Making a sharp right turn off the woods road, the South Taconic Trail climbs gradually and then ascends steeply up the southwest shoulder of Alander Mountain, reaching the open crest at 5.7 miles. The trail reenters Massachusetts at a boundary marker and goes northeast, featuring views. At 6.0 miles, it reaches the west summit of Alander Mountain (2,240 feet), where there are foundations of a former fire tower. A few yards beyond, the Alander Loop Trail (blue) leads right.

The South Taconic Trail goes northeast a few hundred feet and then swings north along the remainder of Alander's open crest, a scenic section. East is the Town of Mount Washington, with Mount Everett on the eastern escarpment the dominant feature. At 7.9 miles, the trail reaches Bashbish Mountain, the high point of the northern section of the ridge, and descends to a lookout point, with Cedar Mountain visible across Bashbish Gorge to the north. It then descends steeply to the beginning of a level stretch at 8.2 miles, where the South Taconic Trail goes to the left. (Hikers should avoid the blue-blazed trail to the right leading very steeply down to Bashbish Brook, which is not fordable most of the year, even far upstream. The only safe option for hikers who end up at the brook is the grinding walk back up the blue-blazed trail.)

At 8.4 miles, there is a short side trail to the right to a sweeping outlook. The trail soon descends steeply until it reaches a comparatively level area at 8.7 miles. There are old charcoal pits on the right side of the trail beginning at 8.8 miles. The trail reaches a point above a side stream of Bashbish Brook at 9.2 miles and then continues down to NY 344 at 9.4 miles. A campground (reservations should be made in advance) and swimming area in an old mining pit (for which there is a small admission fee) are located here. The Village of Copake Falls is located along NY 344 approximately one mile to the west.

South Taconic Trail, Northern Section   *Length: 6.2 miles Blaze: white*
The northern section of the South Taconic Trail, which goes from NY 344 to NY 23, begins across NY 344 from the entrance to the lower Bashbish parking

area, at an elevation of 725 feet. The Cedar Brook Trail (blue) also starts here, but the South Taconic Trail leaves NY 344 at a point 50 feet west of the Cedar Brook trailhead and then goes northwest into the woods, reaching an old road at 0.1 mile. The trail goes left on the road, leaves the road at 0.3 mile, and heads uphill to the right, passing through a grove of evergreens. At 0.4 mile, the trail reaches another old road, where it joins with an unnamed red-blazed trail coming in from the left. At 0.6 mile, just after the trail makes a sharp left, a white-blazed trail goes off to the right. A few feet after that, a yellow-blazed trail comes in from the left, so that the trail is now marked with white, red, and yellow blazes. At 0.9 mile, the yellow-blazed trail goes off to the left, while the South Taconic Trail continues straight ahead. The Cedar Brook Trail (blue) comes in from the right at 1.3 miles, and at 1.6 miles, the South Taconic Trail begins an ascent of almost half a mile, passing a field of ferns at 1.8 miles. At 2.0 miles, the trail becomes level at an open area with a commanding view. The red-blazed trail goes to the left and continues for 100 yards to Sunset Rock, a viewpoint to the west at an elevation of 1,788 feet, where it ends. The South Taconic Trail continues straight ahead and at 2.1 miles enters a covered arbor. At 2.3 miles, it makes a sharp left, which hikers often miss, as their inclination is to continue straight ahead on the woods road. At 2.5 miles, upon reaching North Road, the trail turns left, follows the road for about 25 yards, and then turns right into the woods again.

The South Taconic Trail soon crosses a brook near an old springhouse. It climbs Prospect Hill northeastward through dense scrub oak and mountain laurel, and at 2.9 miles reaches the summit (1,919 feet), with open views. Turning left at the Massachusetts–New York boundary monument, the trail reaches an open ledge with panoramic views north, west, and south, including the Harlem Valley and the Town of Hillsdale, New York.

The trail enters Massachusetts, descends Prospect Hill gradually, with a viewpoint at 3.2 miles, and follows a lower crest line. It reenters New York and, at 3.8 miles, reaches an open section along the edge of the escarpment, with views of the valley on the southwest. The trail continues to Mount Fray, parallels its crest, and, at 4.2 miles, turns right and climbs a short distance to the crest, with an open view. It goes north along the broad summit of Mount Fray, reaching the 1,900-foot level. Open areas in scrub growth offer distant views, including Mount Greylock on the northeast.

At 4.5 miles, the trail turns right on Ridge Run, a broad ski trail descending along the ridge line. An area with views that includes two chairlift stations is a short distance to the left. While following Ridge Run east for about a mile, the hiker must be careful to avoid being lured onto side trails. Just before the trail reaches a hut at 5.3 miles, a view of Jug End valley and ridge may be seen by climbing a few yards off the trail to the right.

At 5.5 miles, the trail turns sharply right into the woods, climbs steeply east for a short stretch, and continues 100 feet along the wooded crest, turning north at 5.6 miles and descending. Entering a driveway at 6.0 miles, the trail continues, partly along roads and partly through the woods, to NY 23, its northerly terminus. There is a parking area on the south side of NY 23, 150 yards to the left.

MOUNT WASHINGTON STATE FOREST

A trail network on the highland in Massachusetts, connecting with the South Taconic Trail, starts from the Mount Washington State Forest Headquarters on East Street in the Town of Mount Washington. The main components are the Alander Mountain Trail, which ascends to the summit of Alander Mountain, and the Ashley Hill Trail, which goes south to Connecticut. Both trails are woods roads, except for the upper part of the Alander Mountain Trail. There are two side trails, one between the two main trails and one connecting the Ashley Hill Trail with the South Taconic Trail. Attractive hemlock groves are a feature of this area.

The state forest headquarters can be reached from New York on the west by turning off NY 22 and following NY 344 through Copake Falls and its continuation (Falls Road) onto the highland in Massachusetts. At the end of Falls Road (3.8 miles from NY 22), a right turn onto West Street leads in 1.7 miles to its end at East Street, where there is a church. The headquarters is on East Street, 1.1 miles south of this junction. Hikers may park by the trailhead beyond the office. For more information, contact Mount Washington State Forest, East Street, Mount Washington, MA 01258; (413) 528-0330.

Alander Mountain Trail   *Length: 2.8 miles Blaze: blue*
For various reasons, it is not easy to keep the Alander Mountain Trail blazed for the first 0.8 mile, so hikers are advised to follow the description carefully. The trail starts at the signboards at the west end of the Mount Washington State Forest headquarters parking area, near a four-foot boulder. It goes west through a field and enters the woods at 0.1 mile. A few hundred feet later, the

hemlock cover is reminiscent of the line from Robert Frost's poem, *Stopping by Woods on a Snowy Evening*, "The woods are lovely, dark and deep." At 0.4 mile, the trail again enters a field and proceeds in a generally westerly direction to a brook at 0.5 mile. Crossing the brook, the trail continues to a fork at 0.8 mile, where it goes right; the left fork is the start of the Ashley Hill Trail (blue). The Alander Mountain Trail descends steeply and reaches its lowest elevation of 1,450 feet at a brook, which may be difficult to cross. The trail proceeds northwest, rising high above the brook, and at 1.1 miles swings west. The next 0.9 mile is easy walking over level terrain with only a few mild undulations. At 1.5 miles, a side trail climbs left to a state forest primitive camping area and goes through the camping area to the Ashley Hill Trail (blue). However, a brook 500 feet before the Ashley Hill Trail cannot be crossed safely much of the year.

After crossing a small brook at 1.8 miles, the Alander Mountain Trail reaches a confluence of two brooks at 2.0 miles. Crossing over the water at just the point where the two brooks meet, the trail proceeds straight ahead, with the upper brook on the left. After 30 feet, the trail turns left to cross the upper brook. From here on, the trail climbs ever more steeply to the top of Alander Mountain. At 2.2 miles, the woods road ends and the trail narrows at a cleared area 25 feet in diameter, from which it continues straight ahead to the west. A side trail to the north for cross-country skiers meets up with the main trail 400 feet later. At 2.3 miles, the Alander Mountain Trail becomes a bit difficult to follow for about 400 feet. It first swings left and then uphill to the right through a muddy area, becoming conspicuous again at 2.4 miles. At 2.7 miles, an old circular stone foundation ten feet in diameter can be seen 40 feet to the left of the trail. A spring comes out of the ground 100 feet up the trail to the left. On the way back, it is interesting to watch this spring gradually swell to a vigorous brook as it goes down the mountain.

A few hundred feet farther on, there is a small state forest cabin, and two hundred feet beyond that, the trail ends at the Alander Loop Trail (blue). Following the Alander Loop Trail to the right for a few hundred feet, the hiker reaches the South Taconic Trail (white) at the west summit of Alander Mountain (2,240 feet).

Alternatively, the Alander Loop Trail (blue) to the left leads in a few hundred feet to the east summit of Alander Mountain, with a view comparable to that of its twin. A little more than a mile later, the Alander Loop Trail leads to the South Taconic Trail (white) a mile south of Alander Mountain.

Ashley Hill Trail   *Length: 3.5 miles Blaze: blue*

From its start at the Alander Mountain Trail, the Ashley Hill Trail climbs south-west along the picturesque, steep ravine of Ashley Hill Brook. At 0.7 mile, a side trail from the Alander Mountain Trail and the primitive camping area comes in acutely from the right; at 1.0 mile, the unblazed Charcoal Pit Trail comes in from the left, where a charcoal pit is visible. The Ashley Hill Trail continues southward on relatively level terrain, crossing a brook at 1.1 miles and another small brook at 2.0 miles. About 100 feet after crossing the second brook, the Ashley Hill Trail makes a sharp left at a junction. The path that continues straight ahead is a side trail, which proceeds for 1.3 miles to connect with the South Taconic Trail (white). Hikers should take care, as both the Ashley Hill Trail and the side trail are marked with blue blazes. After making the left, the Ashley Hill Trail continues uphill, crosses a brook at 2.5 miles, and reaches the state line at 3.5 miles at a boundary monument. Although this is the official end of the trail, it does continue south without blazes. It connects with the Mount Frissell Trail (red) 100 feet later and in another 0.2 mile with the Brace Mountain Trail (unblazed). However, the continuation of the Ashley Hill Trail beyond the Mount Frissell Trail is not recommended, as it is difficult to follow and impassable at spots in wet weather, and ample alternate routes exist in the area.

THE CATSKILLS

North of the more familiar metropolitan hiking areas are the Catskills, whose high summits and steep climbs can provide especially rewarding hiking. The paved roads through the mountains are well populated with hotels, bed-and-breakfast establishments, and private homes, but the higher, more rugged and remote parts of these mountains are unspoiled. From the summits and other vantage points, the views are magnificent. To the east, the Hudson River valley is spread out against a backdrop of New England hills, and in all other directions lie the fir-topped peaks of the Catskills themselves, with little or no sign of human intrusion.

Thirty-five peaks and ridges in the Catskills have elevations of 3,500 feet or more, and sixteen of them do not have maintained trails to their summits. Almost a hundred peaks are over 3,000 feet high. Hundreds of miles of trails of all degrees of difficulty invite the hiker to this varied and delightful area.

Geology

The Catskill Mountains include nearly a hundred summits over 3,000 feet in elevation, but only two summits (Hunter and Slide mountains) reach 4,000 feet. The bedrock of the Catskills consists of a great pile of layered rocks that were laid down originally in the Devonian Period, approximately 375 million years ago.

Seen from a distance, the relatively similar elevations of these peaks become apparent, and it is easy to understand how this collection of mountainous heights originated as an ancient plateau that was gradually eroded into its present outline. For millions of years, many streams cut deeply into the nearly horizontal beds of the plateau, leaving steep-sided highland areas that were isolated as mountains by the downcutting action of rushing streams (Figure 12-1).

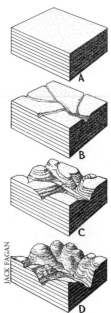

Today, the higher summits are crowned by layers of reddish conglomerate, but on most trails in the Catskills, the hiker will encounter outcrops of a grayish sandstone—the familiar, well-layered flagstone (also known as bluestone) (Figure 12-2). Fossil plant fragments are often found in the sandstone, and slopes are often underlain by reddish shales that may contain imprints of ancient tree roots. Because of the alternating rock types, the typical outcrops of bedrock in the Devonian Catskills are not as dramatic as those of the Silurian Shawangunks. The Shawangunks, although lower in elevation than the Catskills, have continuous segments of more durable quartzose conglomerate that result in dramatic, high cliffs. Catskill sandstones and conglomerates rarely form ledges or cliffs with vertical heights exceeding 20 or 30 feet. Alternating shale strata above and below the sandstone or conglomerate strata tend to form crumbly, gentle slopes.

Figure 12-1. Stages in the erosional development of the Catskills

The long escarpment that forms the eastern edge of the Catskills is an especially dramatic erosional slope *(cuesta)* that faces the Hudson River valley. The many ledges along this famous escarpment are bounded by a series of near parallel fractures, or joints, produced by the upturning of the sedimentary strata that once projected much further east (Figure 4-10).

Natural History

No area of the Catskills has typical above-timberline alpine flora, such as that found in the Taconics and the Hudson Highlands, which are lower and farther south. Above 3,000 feet, the Catskill flora is northern in association but hardly as boreal as might be expected. The heavy residual soil from the soft sandstones has encouraged the invasion of southern or lowland species. Boreal islands of subarctic plants are infrequent. Up to 3,000 feet, the vegetation is of the beech-birch-maple-hemlock zone, and above that of the northern spruce-fir. The Hudsonian or subarctic relicts are absent except for patches of three-toothed cinquefoil on the ledges of Overlook Mountain at 3,000 feet and on North Mountain east of Haines Falls.

History

The natural beauty of the Catskills is striking—the geology of the mountains, the variety of the forests, and the many wildflowers and birds. But it is also apparent that the land, now tree-covered, has been lived on and worked over. Old stone walls and the remains of a chimney or foundation here and there are evidence that someone tried to farm and perhaps raise a family. A cemetery tells a story of sickness and death in its stones. Barely distinguishable old roads climb to overgrown clearings around vanished lumber camps. Above them there is no path to the fir-clad summits, where timber is so dwarfed and inaccessible that it has never been cut, and where the ledges are covered several feet deep with a humus made by centuries of decaying fir, spruce needles, and moss.

Much has been written about Native Americans, dwarfs, and Rip Van Winkle, making the Catskills a land of mystery and fancy. The Hudson and Mohawk valleys were inhabited and well traveled by Native Americans long before Henry Hudson sailed up the river that is named after him (which he called the North River). The first European settlers were the Dutch, who built trading posts first at Albany, which they called Fort Orange, and then at Kingston, which they called Sopus. Friction soon arose between the Dutch and the local Native Americans, which led to a series of skirmishes known as the Esopus Wars (1655–63). In 1664, the British took New York, including the Catskills, from the Dutch, though fighting between the Dutch and the British continued at various points around the world for another ten years.

In 1708, Queen Anne granted a *patent*, or ownership, for about one-and-a-half million acres of what is now Delaware, Greene, Sullivan, and Ulster counties, including all of what is considered the Catskills, to a group led by Major Johannis Hardenburgh. The circumstances leading up to the granting of the Hardenburgh Patent are unknown, but it had a profound impact on the development of the area. Difficulties in surveying the land and legal battles among the descendants of the original patentees kept most settlers out of the area until well into the nineteenth century.

During the Revolutionary War, the residents of the Catskills were largely on the side of the Revolution. Despite considerable skirmishing in the Catskills between local Tories (and their Iroquois allies) and rebels, no decisive battles were fought. Nonetheless, the fighting that did occur was bloody, especially since the British offered a bounty for white scalps and prisoners.

Industry

The demand for hemlock bark, created by the tanning industry, brought large numbers of settlers to the Catskills. Tanning of hides had been carried out in the United States to a limited extent prior to the Revolution. A tannery was established in Athens, New York, in 1750, but rapid growth came after the War of 1812, when Americans were free to engage in world trade without interference from the British. Oak bark was used to tan shoe-sole leather, hemlock bark to tan leather for uppers and other uses. Because one cord (128 cubic feet) of bark was required to tan ten hides, it was more economical to ship hides to tanneries located near the woods. With their ready supply of hemlock and water, the Catskills soon became a center for the tanning industry. By 1816, there were more than seventy-five tanneries in the mountains, with others being built at a rapid pace. Palenville, Prattsville, and Edwardsville (now Hunter) are existing towns named for the proprietors of these tanneries. The name "Tannersville" recalls the whole industry. By 1825, Greene County was producing more leather than any other county in New York, with Ulster County not far behind.

The tanning industry in the Catskills reached its peak during the Civil War and declined rapidly thereafter, as the supply of hemlock was exhausted. By 1867, most tanneries had closed, although the Simpson tannery in Phoenicia operated until 1870. Some idea about the amount of bark consumed may be gained from the report that the Pratt tannery turned out more than two million hides over the course of its existence, which would have required over 200,000 cords of bark.

Cutting down these tremendous trees opened the land to sunlight and conditions more favorable to the growth of birch, maple, oak, and other hardwoods. As these took over, a new industry was born—the making of barrel hoops. This industry began about 1848 and lasted until about 1890, when machine-sawed wooden hoops and steel hoops replaced hand-hewn hoops. Another wood industry that existed for a time was the making of furniture in the *chair factories*, as they were known locally. This industry accounted for some of the large buildings, now vacant, still seen in Catskill towns.

Another Catskill industry was the quarrying of bluestone, a hard, dense, fine-grained, blue-gray sandstone. The industry thrived in the latter part of the

JACK FAGAN

Figure 12-2.
Bluestone quarry

nineteenth century, providing curbstone and flag-stone for the sidewalks of New York. The development of Portland cement provided a cheaper alternative and brought large-scale quarrying to an end. Piles of rejected stone may still be found at many places where there were workings or exploratory openings, as in Shandaken or Phoenicia. A few working quarries continue to supply bluestone for walks, patios, and veneer, but the demand is much smaller. Opus 40, near Saugerties, offers a glimpse into the bluestone industry at its Quarryman's Museum. It also has outdoor sculptures and some short hiking trails.

Evidence of farmhouses and cleared fields appears in the Catskills on land that looks impossible to farm. It took many horses to transport bark, lumber, and hides—thousands when the tanning industry was at its peak—and horses require feed. As the land was cleared of hemlock, it was plowed where possible and sown with hay on the steep slopes, with corn or oats on more level areas. Some of the better space was used for potatoes, wheat, and buckwheat for the tannery workers and their families.

After tanning ceased, some farmers attempted general farming, but the soil was poor and the conditions too difficult. All that is left now are fallen chimneys and sometimes an apple tree bearing misshapen, wormy fruit that is enjoyed only by bear and deer. The views from some of these old high-valley farms are beautiful, prompting purchase as summer vacation home sites.

Railroads came to the Catskills in 1866. Four years later, the Ulster & Delaware Railroad began service from Weehawken, New Jersey, to Phoenicia. The line was extended to Stamford, New York, in 1872, and through Stony Clove to Tannersville and the hotels in the North Lake area in 1882. Although regular passenger service has been discontinued on all lines through the Catskills, and most have been abandoned altogether, two short tourist railroads, the Delaware & Ulster Rail Ride in Arkville and the Catskill Mountain Railroad in Phoenicia, still preserve the history of Catskill railroading.

Tourism is now the major industry in the Catskills, and it has a long history. It began in 1824 when the Catskill Mountain House, built on a high ledge near North Lake, opened with ten guest rooms. Patrons were transported by stage from the steamboat docks at Catskill Landing, up through Sleepy

Hollow, to the hotel perched high above. So popular was the view from its porch that the Mountain House grew to more than 300 rooms. Among its frequent guests were Thomas Cole and other painters of the Hudson River School and President Ulysses S. Grant.

Hotel building in the Catskills reached its peak in the late 1800s. In 1878, the Overlook Mountain House was built on Overlook Mountain, then the Mount Tremper House in Phoenicia, the Grand Hotel in Highmount, and the Laurel House at Kaaterskill Falls. In 1881, the Hotel Kaaterskill was built on South Mountain. It was said to have 1,200 rooms and to be the largest moun-

Figure 12-3. Kaaterskill Falls

tain hotel in the world. None of these structures has survived. The Hotel Kaaterskill burned in 1924, and its property was acquired by the state. The state later acquired the Laurel House and the Catskill Mountain House along with their land holdings. The buildings were burned in 1963.

The Catskills have played a role in America's art and literature since the early nineteenth century. Washington Irving was not the only author to use the Catskills as a backdrop for his stories. James Fenimore Cooper's Natty Bumpo, or Leatherstockings—the hero of many of his stories—describes Kaaterskill Falls as his favorite place. William Cullen Bryant wrote a lyric poem about the falls, as did other poets. Thomas Cole and the other artists of the Hudson River School painted Catskill scenes innumerable times. Today, Woodstock continues the Catskill tradition of being an inspiration to the arts by providing a base for artists of all kinds. A walk along the sidewalks of Woodstock provides an opportunity to visit the many galleries and craft shops of the local artisans.

The writer who probably did the most to popularize the Catskills was John Burroughs, whose book, *In the Catskills*, originally published in 1910, introduced many to the beauties of Slide Mountain and the southern Catskills. By the time Burroughs's book was published, the Catskills had some level of protection for twenty-five years. They received this protection as the result of two very separate concerns: the need to protect the Erie Canal, and Ulster County's tax problems. As early as the 1860s, concerned citizens, who today would be called environmentalists, warned that the massive lumbering operations then taking place in the Adirondacks could lead to soil erosion that would silt up the Erie Canal. Since much of New York City's prosperity depended on goods shipped via the canal, they soon enlisted the support of New York City business leaders. In 1872, this alliance was able to convince the State Legislature to set up a Park Commission to study protecting the Adirondacks. While portions of the Catskills were also being denuded, this was considered to be only a local concern. A year later, the Park Commission issued a report favoring an Adirondack forest park, with no mention made of the Catskills. But opposition to the proposed park was also strong, and for over a decade no action was taken.

The Legislature may not have been able to set up a park, but it did know how to raise taxes. Traditionally, when a private landowner defaulted on his taxes, his land became the property of the municipalities. However, in 1879, the Legislature made the counties responsible for such land and the taxes on it. Ulster County soon became the owner of significant areas in the Catskills, and quickly accumulated a tax debt of $40,000.

Both of these problems came together in 1885. Pressure to protect the Adirondacks finally prevailed, and on May 15 a forest preserve was created. As the result of political maneuvering, the act creating the forest preserve also included the Catskill lands for which Ulster County owed taxes. Ulster County's debt was abolished, and in the future the state would pay taxes to the county.

While the law looked good on paper, enforcing it proved almost impossible. Lumbering continued in the Adirondacks. Protection had to be strengthened, which happened in 1894 when a new State Constitution was adopted, with Article XIV, Section 1 of the Constitution providing:

The lands of the state now owned or hereafter acquired, constituting the forest preserve as now fixed by law, shall be forever kept as wild forest lands. They shall not be leased, sold or exchanged, or be taken by any corporation, public or private, nor shall the timber thereon be sold, removed or destroyed.

This basis for the present-day protection of the Catskills has provided us with vast areas where the only human intrusion is by foot, ski, or snowshoe. Almost pure wilderness and only a few hours from our nation's largest metropolitan area, the Catskill Park covers more than 700,000 acres (1,100 square miles). About 40 percent of it is state land, falling under the "forever wild" clause of the State Constitution.

Climate

A gentle spring day in New York City may be a day of snow flurries or freezing rain in the Catskills. Temperatures are generally lower in the mountains, decreasing as altitude is gained. Snow may accumulate in November and last well into May. Weather conditions can change quickly, and one should be prepared with extra clothing and suitable equipment. Although the main roads are plowed, some side roads that have no winter residents are not cleared.

The Catskills are beautiful in the winter when covered with snow, and people who hike are likely to enjoy snowshoeing and cross-country skiing. Winter in the woods is exhilarating but exhausting. Hikers and skiers should keep this in mind, along with the fact that daylight ends sooner, when planning winter trips. Recorded weather information for Kingston can be obtained by calling (845) 331-5555.

Trails and Bushwhacking

Trails in the Catskills are marked with the New York State Department of Environmental Conservation (DEC) plastic markers nailed to trees—blue for trails that run generally north–south, red for trails running east–west, and yellow for connecting trails or trails running diagonally.

Camping is permitted on state land below 3,500 feet and at least 150 feet away from streams, water sources, and marked trails. Camping may be restricted in some areas, and designated sites may be identified to control use in popular areas. Properly built and maintained fires, using only dead and down wood, are also permitted below 3,500 feet. However, most experienced hikers find the safety and efficiency of backpacker stoves a real convenience. The topography above 3,500 feet is subject to harsher weather conditions, where plants and soil do not recover well or rapidly from camping use (and abuse).

For administrative purposes, the DEC has subdivided the Catskills into two regions. DEC Region 3 encompasses Ulster and Sullivan counties; DEC Region 4 includes Delaware and Greene counties. For more information about trails in Ulster and Sullivan counties, contact DEC Region 3, 21 South Putt Corners Road, New Paltz, NY 12561; (845) 256-3082 or (845) 256-3083. Recorded trail information may be obtained by calling (845) 256-3000 x4182. For information about trails in Delaware and Greene counties, contact DEC Region 4, Jefferson Road, Stamford, NY 12167; (607) 652-7365.

Many of the marked trails are described below. The New York-New Jersey Trail Conference publishes a set of hiking maps for Catskill trails. The backs of these maps contain a brief summary of trail information, providing the hiker with an easy reference for both planning and actual walking. More detailed information on hiking trails is available in *Guide to Catskill Trails*, published by the Adirondack Mountain Club.

The Long Path traverses the Catskill Park in a north–south direction for 94 miles. It is overlaid on many of the trails described here. See the *Guide to the Long Path* for more details. In most places, the Long Path is designated only by its distinctive plastic marker at the trailheads and junctions.

Although a great deal of the forest land in the Catskills can be explored using marked trails, hikers can find out what the wilderness is really like only by "getting off the beaten path." Trailless travel, or bushwhacking, often leads to interesting discoveries—a little-known waterfall, a balanced rock, or one of the remains of the mountain industries of the last century. Best of all, bushwhacking heightens the hiker's awareness of the environment. Hikers who bushwhack should not blaze or otherwise mark the route. Such independent blazing is illegal, defaces the wilderness, and ruins the experience of hiking in a trailless area for those who follow.

Some trailless Catskill summits, such as Rocky or Balsam Cap, are thickly overgrown with spruce, making bushwhacking a physically demanding endeavor. Others, such as Halcott or Vly, are relatively open. Before leaving the trail, a hiker should have a compass and a topographic map and know how to use both. Most important, all hikers—but especially those who plan to bushwhack—should let someone know where they are going before setting out, and their expected time of return.

To provide an incentive for visiting mountain peaks and areas not usually

Figure 12-4. Southeastern Catskills from Wittenberg Mountain

seen by the average hiker, the Catskill 3500 Club was founded in 1962. Membership in the Catskill 3500 Club is limited to those who have climbed all thirty-five 3,500-foot Catskill peaks—including the trailless peaks—in any season, as well as four specific peaks (Slide, Blackhead, Panther, and Balsam) during the winter. The Club also recognizes as winter members those who have climbed all thirty-five mountains during the winter. Sign-in canisters, maintained by the Catskill 3500 Club, are at the summits of most of the trailless peaks. By 2001, over 1,300 hikers had qualified for regular membership, and more than four hundred hikers had met the requirement for becoming winter members. Club hikes and other functions are open to nonmembers, who are known as "aspirants." Current information on the 3500 Club can be obtained through the New York-New Jersey Trail Conference.

Trails in the Southern Catskills

Outside of the North/South Lake area, the Catskills' most-hiked trails are those that climb Slide Mountain, the highest peak in the range at 4,180 feet. It was not officially recognized as such, however, until Arnold Guyot's surveys in the 1880s, and even then, the owners of the hotels around North and South lakes hotly disputed it, claiming that the nearby Kaaterskill High Peak (3,655 feet) was actually higher. Slide Mountain was publicized by the writings of natural-

ist John Burroughs, who is fittingly memorialized by a plaque on the summit ledge. It may well be the most popular peak in the area, but Slide is far from the only offering. With two large wilderness areas covering about 80,000 acres—an area larger than some national parks—there are many other peaks and trails that offer a backcountry experience unparalleled within a hundred miles of Times Square.

Wittenberg-Cornell-Slide Trail (Burroughs Range Trail)

Length: 9.1 miles Blaze: red

The most challenging approach to the Burroughs Range (Wittenberg, Cornell, and Slide mountains) is from Woodland Valley, one of the deepest valleys in the Catskills. The trailhead is at a state campground at the end of Woodland Valley Road, which leaves NY 28 just west of Phoenicia. After following a winding course alongside Woodland Creek for about five miles, the road ends at the campground, where there is a large parking area for day hikers. A small fee is charged in season.

To reach the trailhead from the parking area, cross the road and follow the red blazes between two campsites to a bridge over the creek. The trail climbs steeply to the register—a preview of the four-mile, 2,580-foot ascent to the summit of Wittenberg Mountain. After winding through some hemlock groves and past some open ledges, ascending steadily all the way, the trail turns eastward and levels off for a while at a steady elevation of about 2,500 feet. There is a seasonal spring slightly uphill from the trail shortly after this bend.

At 2.6 miles, the trail comes to a T junction. Here, the Terrace Mountain Trail (yellow) leads north (left) 0.9 mile to the Terrace Mountain Lean-to. The Wittenberg-Cornell-Slide Trail turns right, at first undulating through a northern-hardwoods forest of maple and beech. Soon, however, a switchback heralds the beginning of the ascent up Wittenberg proper. The trail climbs up a series of steep ledges that require care and the use of hands as well as feet. Above these ledges, the forest changes to predominantly balsam fir, reflecting the harsh weather faced by the exposed slope. Although the most difficult part of the hike to the summit of Wittenberg is now over, there is more climbing to be done before reaching the sign marking 3,500 feet of elevation, and from there, another 280 feet of vertical elevation must be gained before the summit finally presents itself at 3.9 miles.

When it does, there is no mistaking it. A hundred-foot-long exposed rock ledge serves as a giant bench from which to view the Ashokan Reservoir and points to the east. It is well worth the significant effort to reach; indeed, the outstanding view is the primary reason why many hikers rate Wittenberg as their favorite of all the Catskill peaks.

Continuing on, the trail follows the narrow ridge known as Bruins' Causeway to Cornell Mountain. After descending to the col, the hiker confronts a steep V-shaped cleft—the only means to continue the ascent to Cornell. Extreme care must be exercised here, especially if proceeding downhill in the reverse direction. The summit of Cornell (3,860 feet), reached at 4.7 miles, is a few hundred feet further along, via a short yellow-blazed spur leading to the left. There are some limited views east from this clearing, but they are not as spectacular as Wittenberg's panorama.

After reaching a viewpoint over Slide Mountain, with the slide that gave the mountain its name visible on the mountain's north face, the trail drops down to a spruce grove, where there are several designated campsites at elevation 3,300 feet. This is a good place to rest before beginning the trail's uncompromising assault on Slide.

This rugged climb—quite steep in places—is relieved by a good spring coming out of a rock wall a quarter-mile below the summit, which is reached at 7.0 miles. It is marked by an open ledge and a plaque in memory of John Burroughs, placed by the Winnisook Club, which still owns part of the mountain's western slopes. There is plenty of space atop this outcrop, near which a shelter once stood, and a good day will usually find a number of people taking lunch here. The view has grown in somewhat in recent years, but it is still possible to see Connecticut, Massachusetts, and Vermont beyond the peaks to Slide's immediate east, including those the trail has just traversed.

The mountain's actual summit is just beyond, in a clearing where a concrete foundation is all that remains of a former fire tower. The trail now begins to descend, soon coming upon an open view to the north from which many Catskill peaks are visible. The trail continues along the summit ridge, its unusual white quartz pebble surface sometimes giving it the feel of a garden path. In the opinion of some geologists, this indicates that Slide Mountain was the only Catskill peak not covered by glaciers during the last Ice Age.

Figure 12-5. At the summit of Slide Mountain

At 7.7 miles, the Curtis-Ormsbee Trail (blue) leaves to the left, leading to a junction with the Phoenicia-East Branch Trail in 1.6 miles. The Long Path follows this longer but more scenic route, which has become a popular ascent route for day hikers. The Wittenberg-Cornell-Slide Trail continues ahead, winding around the mountain at the end of the ridge to follow an old bridle path. This section is actually New York State's oldest public path in the Forest Preserve, built in 1892 at a cost of $250.

At the base of the ridge, the Wittenberg-Cornell-Slide Trail ends at a junction with the Phoenicia-East Branch Trail (yellow). To the right, this trail leads in 0.7 mile to the Slide Mountain parking area on Slide Mountain Road (County 47)—the most popular starting point for day hikes up Slide Mountain.

Peekamoose-Table Trail   *Length: 7.2 miles Blaze: blue*

Peekamoose and Table mountains are the most southerly of the Catskills' major peaks. South of these mountains, no peak exceeds 3,500 feet in height until West Virginia. These two mountains are accessible via the Peekamoose-Table Trail, which can be hiked either from the northern trailhead, 1.2 miles from the end of Denning Road, or from the southern trailhead on Peekamoose Road (County 42). They are an attractive destination for an overnight, but can also be climbed as a day hike.

The southern end of the trail is at a parking area on the north side of Peekamoose Road (County 42), two miles north of the tiny hamlet of Sundown. The 2,640-foot ascent to Peekamoose Mountain begins with a steady climb up an old woods road to the trail register at 0.3 mile. The grade levels slightly, giving the hiker the chance to appreciate how quickly this land—pasture less than a century ago—has been reclaimed by the forest.

In less than a mile, at a red pine grove planted by the Civilian Conservation Corps during the 1930s, the trail bears left, leaving the old road, and begins to climb again, entering first-growth forest. Soon, the trail enters an area devastated by Hurricane Floyd in 1999. The heavy blowdown has opened a view over the Rondout Valley to Spencers Ledge and Little Rocky Mountain. The steady ascent continues, interrupted only by several steep rock ledges, which may require the use of hands as well as feet.

At 1.9 miles, the trail reaches Reconnoiter Rock, a tall glacial erratic perched on a flatter boulder. At one time, good views could be had from the top, but the views are now limited, due to the growth of the surrounding forest. However, an overlook on the opposite side of the trail offers a view of the northern Shawangunks.

Although the trail has now climbed 1,800 feet from its starting point, over 600 feet of additional climbing remains before the summit is attained. The forest now changes to stunted hardwoods, with spruce and white birch beginning to appear. After a short, steep climb, the trail passes the 3,500-foot sign and reaches, at 2.4 miles, an open rock ledge which offers an unobstructed 180° panorama to the south and west. There is no sign of civilization, and from here one can trace the course of the trail up from Peekamoose Road and appreciate how much climbing has been done. This is an excellent location for a lunch break.

The Peekamoose-Table Trail now continues through the nearby meadows and past a rare high-elevation stand of sugar maple. It goes by a seasonal spring and up short rock clefts, passing through a boreal forest of balsam fir and red spruce. Finally, at 3.4 miles, the trail reaches a large boulder which marks the summit of Peekamoose Mountain (3,843 feet). There is no view from the actual summit, but some views can be found nearby, reached by faint paths through the woods.

The trail now descends steeply to the col between Peekamoose and Table mountains (camping is permitted here only in the winter, since the elevation is over 3,500 feet). A gentler climb leads up to the long, flat ridge of Table Mountain. An unmarked spur trail (which may be difficult to locate) leads north to a viewpoint over Slide Mountain and the Burroughs Range. The actual summit (3,847 feet) is at the western edge of the ridge, 4.3 miles from the trailhead. It is marked by a tree with brackets that once held a Catskill 3500 Club canister (placed here before this trail was built).

From the summit, the trail descends rather steeply, with a good view to the west soon appearing. At 4.5 miles, a short spur trail to the left leads to the Table Mountain Lean-to, with a plaque honoring Frank Bouton, a long-time trail maintainer in the Catskills. There is a spring to the right of the Peekamoose-Table Trail a short distance below.

About a mile later, at elevation 2,900 feet, an open ledge south of the trail offers a striking view of Van Wyck Mountain, and on clear days, New Jersey's High Point stands out on the horizon beyond. The trail continues down the ridge, at one point dropping slightly to climb back up a small knob, with a view to the south. The trail now bends to the north, descending steadily, and it reaches the East Branch of the Neversink River at 6.8 miles.

Just before the Peekamoose-Table Trail crosses the river, an unmarked path leaves to the right. It parallels the river, reaching the col between Slide and Cornell in about five miles, and crossing the river several times along the way. This path, which may be difficult to follow in places, is most often used by hikers making bushwhack ascents of Lone, Rocky, Balsam Cap, and Friday mountains, all of which are trailless.

Although the East Branch of the Neversink River can easily be crossed on rocks, hikers face a greater challenge at the crossing of Deer Shanty Brook, about 200 feet further along the trail. Here, in 2001, the deep brook channel is crossed only on a single log. A more substantial bridge was washed away in spring floods, and efforts to build another bridge have been repeatedly frustrated by the brook's tendency to flood and the area's wilderness status. The brook can be crossed on rocks when the water is low, but the crossing can be a serious obstacle to hikers during high-water periods.

On the other side of the brook, the trail climbs to a junction with the Phoenicia-East Branch Trail (yellow). Here, at 7.2 miles, the Peekamoose-Table Trail ends. The Phoenicia-East Branch Trail may be followed to the left for 1.2 miles along a woods road to the parking area at the end of Denning Road.

Ashokan High Point Trail   *Length: 5.4 miles Blaze: red*
The summit of Ashokan High Point (3,080 feet) offers superb views from 2,500

feet above the Ashokan Reservoir. It can be climbed by a red-blazed trail that begins from Peekamoose Road (County 42), 3.9 miles southwest of the hamlet of West Shokan. The trailhead parking area is on the north side of the road.

The trail begins on the opposite side of the road, where it descends to a footbridge over Kanape Brook. The trail follows along the north side of the brook on a wide woods road to a large level area amid a white pine forest. Just beyond, at 2.5 miles, the road reaches the height of land between Mombaccus Mountain (2,840 feet) and Ashokan High Point. Here, the road proceeds ahead onto private property, while the red-blazed trail turns left. After passing a red-blazed trail coming in from the left (this is the return route of a loop), the Ashokan High Point Trail ascends steeply, with some views to the left over Spencers Ledge and Little Rocky Mountain.

The summit of Ashokan High Point, reached at 3.6 miles, is marked by old tower footings on a rock and survey markers. It once offered sweeping views over the reservoir, but the views are now obscured by encroaching vegetation. The trail descends to open meadows, with views of Slide Mountain and the Burroughs Range to the west. It soon resumes its descent, and it eventually loops back to join the ascending route 5.4 miles from the start. To return to Peekamoose Road, turn right and follow the red markers back to the parking area.

Red Hill Trail   *Length: 1.4 miles Blaze: yellow*
This short trail, blazed in 2001, provides access over state land to the restored fire tower on 2,990-foot Red Hill, with a 360° view over the Hudson River valley, the Shawangunks, and Slide, Peekamoose, and Table mountains to the east and north. The trailhead is on Dinch Road, where parking is available. The trail climbs steadily to the tower, an ascent of 800 feet in 1.4 miles. There is a spring to the right of the trail at 1.1 miles, where the trail turns left.

Trails in the Central Catskills

Two major north-south trail systems connect NY 28 with County 47 (Slide Mountain Road or West Branch Road). Although both of these trails are suitable for backpacking, they are most often used by day hikers, who hike sections of these trails to reach their destination.

Pine Hill-West Branch Trail   *Length: 14.9 miles Blaze: blue*

Although this trail has few viewpoints, it nevertheless offers an appealing wilderness sojourn, running mostly through first-growth forest and reaching (or nearly reaching) three major summits. Several lean-tos on or near the trail make it attractive for backpacking, and a network of side trails branching down to the valleys affords excellent day-hiking opportunities.

The trail's southern terminus is just opposite the Biscuit Brook parking area, on County 47, 12.8 miles south of its junction with NY 28 in the hamlet of Big Indian. The trail soon begins a steady climb, reaching an elevation of 2,500 feet on a ridge about a mile from the start. At this point, it turns sharply to the northeast and begins a gentle descent along an old woods road to the Biscuit Brook Lean-to, 1.9 miles from the trailhead.

After crossing the brook and several tributaries, the trail starts to climb once again. At approximately 3,000 feet, it levels off briefly and begins to veer away from the tributary it has been following. It goes up several broad switchbacks, climbs over some rock ledges, and levels off once again on a southerly spur of Big Indian Mountain.

Four and a half miles from the trailhead, near the sign marking 3,500 feet of elevation, a faint path to the right climbs 200 feet in a quarter-mile to the summit of Big Indian Mountain (3,700 feet), marked by a Catskill 3500 Club canister (a gray metal box on a tree). The trail proper continues along the side of the mountain, going through some balsam fir patches and offering views to the west over Graham and Doubletop mountains when the leaves are down.

From Big Indian Mountain, the trail descends moderately into a col where, at 5.8 miles, it reaches a junction with the Seager-Big Indian Trail (yellow). This trail leads southwest 0.9 mile to the Shandaken Brook Lean-to and continues for another 2.1 miles to the Seager trailhead at the end of Dry Brook Road. Continuing north, the Pine Hill-West Branch Trail resumes climbing, almost imperceptibly at times. After a few easy ledges, it passes the summit of Eagle Mountain (3,600 feet) at 6.9 miles. This wooded summit, with no views, is widely regarded as the least interesting of all the major Catskill peaks. The actual summit is a few hundred feet west of the trail.

An easy 1.4-mile stretch brings the hiker to Haynes Mountain (3,420 feet), again with no views. The trail now descends gently, losing about 500 feet in elevation, until it reaches a junction with the Oliverea-Mapledale Trail (red) at 9.1 miles. To the right, this trail descends, very steeply at one point, 1.9 miles to McKenley Hollow Road and Oliverea; to the left, it descends 1.8 miles to

Rider Hollow Road and Mapledale. Lean-tos are situated near each end of the Oliverea-Mapledale Trail.

The blue-blazed trail now ascends moderately to the summit of Balsam Mountain (3,600 feet), where it crosses a corner of private property. Just past the summit, a short side trail to the right leads to a viewpoint over Big Indian Hollow and Hunter, Plateau, and West Kill mountains. After a short level stretch, the Pine Hill-West Branch Trail begins to descend Balsam Mountain's north face, steeply in places.

The descent ends at the col between Balsam and Belleayre

Figure 12-6. Outcrop along the trail to Balsam Mountain

JACK FAGAN

mountains (at about 2,900 feet elevation), and soon afterwards the Pine Hill-West Branch Trail arrives at a junction with the Mine Hollow Trail (yellow) at 11.2 miles. This side trail descends for one mile to a junction with the Oliverea-Mapledale Trail in Rider Hollow. The Mine Hollow Trail can be combined with the Pine Hill-West Branch Trail and the Oliverea-Mapledale Trail to make a 5.2-mile loop hike over Balsam Mountain.

The Pine Hill-West Branch Trail now climbs to the eastern summit of Belleayre Mountain, with only a few easy ledges to surmount. It reaches the clearing at the summit, where a fire tower once stood, at 12.1 miles. Here, the Belleayre Ridge Trail (red) leaves to the left, following an old road for half a mile to a lean-to and ending at 1.0 mile on the mountain's true summit (3,420 feet)—the top of the Belleayre Mountain Ski Area. On the way, it passes the upper terminus of the Cathedral Glen Trail (blue), which descends 1.7 miles to the Village of Pine Hill, passing through the extensive hemlock grove after which the trail is named.

The Pine Hill-West Branch Trail turns eastward from this junction, following an old road down the ridge. Half a mile from the junction, it passes the

Belleayre Mountain Lean-to, and shortly afterwards, at 12.7 miles, it reaches a junction with the Lost Clove Trail (red), which descends 1.3 miles to a parking area near the end of Lost Clove Road. The Pine Hill-West Branch Trail now swings back to the north side of the ridge, remaining on the old road as it enters private property and reaches a gate at 14.1 miles. Although the road leading to this point is driveable, no parking is available here. The marked trail continues north along the road to the abandoned tracks of the Ulster & Delaware Railroad at the end of Station Road on the outskirts of Pine Hill.

Giant Ledge-Panther-Fox Hollow Trail   *Length 7.5 miles Blaze: blue*
This trail provides access to the 3,720-foot Panther Mountain from both the north and the south. The shorter southern approach, which traverses Giant Ledge on the way to the summit of Panther, is very popular with hikers. Fewer hikers choose to approach Panther from the north, but although this route is longer, it offers greater seclusion and several attractive vistas from a series of false summits.

The area bisected by the trail has a fascinating natural history. The lower-density rock found in the area and the circular drainage pattern traced around the mountain by Woodland and Esopus creeks has led a number of geologists to believe that the mountain sits atop an ancient meteor impact crater.

To reach the southern end of the trail, hikers should park at the parking area at a hairpin turn on County 47, 7.4 miles south of the hamlet of Big Indian and a mile north of Winnisook Lake. From the east side of the road, opposite the parking area, hikers should follow the Phoenicia-East Branch Trail, which crosses a bridge over a tributary of Esopus Creek and then climbs, reaching the beginning of the Giant Ledge-Panther-Fox Hollow Trail at 0.8 mile, in the col between Giant Ledge and the north ridge of Slide Mountain.

For the first half mile, the blue trail is relatively level. It then begins to climb, passing the site of a former lean-to, where a good spring may be found on a short side trail to the left. Beyond the lean-to site, the trail climbs even more steeply over rock ledges, finally leveling off at 0.8 mile on the top of the 3,200-foot Giant Ledge. A series of viewpoints along the trail rewards the hiker with broad views over Woodland Valley to the east. By crossing over to the west side of the ridge, hikers will find views over Big Indian Hollow and the Esopus headlands. Some of the viewpoints are at the edge of precipitous cliffs, and hikers should exercise caution. Giant Ledge is a popular place to camp (it is one of the few spots in the Catskills where ridgetop camping is legal, since its elevation is below 3,500 feet), and there are several designated campsites to the west of the trail.

The trail descends rather steeply from the north end of the ridge, and after leveling off briefly, it begins to climb Panther Mountain. For part of the way, the trail traverses a series of long switchbacks, which make the climb a little easier, and near the top of the switchbacks, there is an excellent view over Slide and Wittenberg mountains and Giant Ledge.

After passing through a flat area, with a seasonal spring to the right of the trail at 2.0 miles, the trail begins to climb more steeply over rock ledges. Upon reaching the 3,500-foot marker, the grade begins to moderate, and the trail continues through a dense evergreen forest. Finally, the summit itself—a small ledge with wide views to the north and east—is reached at 2.5 miles.

Most hikers choose to return to their cars by retracing their steps, and the trail north of here is much less traveled. By leaving a car at each end, though, one can continue along the trail, which takes the hiker slowly and sometimes steeply down a ridgeline of several false summits, some with expansive views. After passing the Fox Hollow Lean-to at 7.0 miles, the trail ends at a parking area on Fox Hollow Road, 1.6 miles south of NY 28.

Trails in the Northern Catskills

Although more populous and with fewer remote areas than the southern Catskills, the northern Catskills have many rewarding climbs, including four trailless peaks and the Devil's Path, a 24.6-mile trail that reaches five major summits and skirts 4,040-foot Hunter Mountain, second highest in the Catskills. This area may be approached via Platte Clove Road from West Saugerties or via NY 23A, which climbs through Kaaterskill Clove from Palenville. Both roads feature outstanding views, but Platte Clove Road is the more difficult approach. Driving this steep, narrow road (closed in winter) requires special caution.

Devil's Path   *Length: 24.6 miles Blaze: red*

According to a tradition attributed to the area's early Dutch settlers, the range of mountains traversed by the Devil's Path—with their steep, rocky slopes and deep gaps between them—were the devil's private preserve, specially adapted to his cloven hooves, where he could go when desiring to retreat from the world of man. Today, anyone with a pair of good boots can follow this trail up those peaks, although the steep and rocky ascents from the cols between peaks often require the use of hands as well as feet. However, the difficult climbs are more than offset by the outstanding views at or near the summits.

Most hikers cover this trail in short sections, using access trails through the cols for rewarding day climbs. A backpacking trip its entire length takes two or three days and is recommended only for those in excellent condition who are seeking a strenuous hike.

Figure 12-7. Devil's Kitchen Lean-to

Although the Devil's Path officially starts at the junction of Prediger and Platte Clove roads, several miles southeast of Tannersville, most hikers will choose to begin their hike at the end of Prediger Road, 0.4 mile to the south, where there is limited parking along the right side of the road. After crossing a small creek, the trail follows an old woods road. Half a mile from the end of Prediger Road, the first junction with the Jimmy Dolan Notch Trail (blue) is reached. To the right, this side trail leads 1.6 miles to Jimmy Dolan Notch, where it rejoins the Devil's Path, offering a shorter approach to the peaks on either side.

The Devil's Path proceeds east from the junction and follows a relatively level route until it reaches the Old Overlook Road, which comes in from the left at 2.3 miles. The Long Path now begins to run concurrently with the Devil's Path. (To the left, the blue-blazed Long Path leads to Platte Clove Road in 0.9 mile.) In another 300 feet, the Devil's Path reaches the northern end of the Overlook Trail (blue), which proceeds ahead along the road, reaching the Devil's Kitchen Lean-to in 0.1 mile and continuing to Overlook Mountain. Here, the Devil's Path leaves the road. It turns right (west) and begins a stiff climb of Indian Head Mountain, which gets its name from its ridgeline's resemblance to a stylized and somewhat stereotypical face of a Native American. The steep climb proceeds through a stand of old-growth hemlock—giant specimens that were too remote to be harvested during the height of the Catskill tanning industry in the mid-1800s.

After a steady climb of over a mile, the Devil's Path finally levels off, as fir and spruce begin to take over the surrounding woods. As it works its way along the mountain's east face—under the "Indian's chin"—it passes Sherman's Lookout, an open ledge to the left of the trail that looks eastward, through Platte Clove, over the Hudson River valley. The trail continues to follow a contour around the "Indian's chin," and soon reaches another viewpoint to the southwest.

After a short descent, the trail reaches a steep rock face which is a challenge to climb, requiring the use of both hands. The reward is a wide eastern overlook off an oblong rock overhang that offers a view even broader than that from Sherman's Lookout. Soon, the trail comes to another steep pitch, where exposed roots help to provide footing. The 3,500-foot level is reached just beyond. From here, the route to the summit—reached at 4.6 miles—is relatively easy.

From the summit (3,573 feet), the Devil's Path descends rather steeply to reach its second junction with the Jimmy Dolan Notch Trail (blue) at 5.1 miles. This trail can be followed back to Prediger Road for a 6.7-mile loop hike.

The Devil's Path proceeds ahead, soon beginning the climb of Twin Mountain. Switchbacks alternate with a series of rock chutes for the next 0.4 mile, ending shortly after the 3,500-foot elevation is reached. Here, the trail levels off and offers a view back to Indian Head Mountain, taking in Overlook Mountain as well.

In the next few hundred feet, the trail winds around slightly and reaches a particularly fine view from Twin Mountain's east summit (3,580 feet). The view extends from the Shawangunks and the Hudson Highlands in the far south to Sugarloaf Mountain and Twin Mountain's true summit to the west and Slide Mountain to the southwest. The panorama presents a vivid sense of the region's vastness.

From the east summit, the Devil's Path heads northwest, dipping gently into the low ground between the two summits, and then climbing to the west summit, beginning with a narrow switchback up a large rock face. Twin's west summit (3,640 feet)—the true summit of the mountain—is reached at 6.1 miles. Just beyond, an open ledge affords an impressive view, although not as expansive as the one from the east summit. A cave just below the summit affords shelter in bad weather.

The trail now steeply descends 800 feet to Pecoy Notch, reached at 6.8 miles. Here, the Pecoy Notch Trail (blue) leads for about two miles, past beaver meadows and old quarries, to a parking area on Elka Park Road. An attraction worth this detour is Dibble's Quarry—located 1.0 mile from the junction with the Devil's Path—which features impressive rock chairs built over the years by local residents from bluestone tailings.

Two hundred feet past the notch, the Devil's Path begins a steep climb up Sugarloaf Mountain, with occasional views back at Twin Mountain. About 3,500 feet in elevation, the trail levels off in a thick boreal forest. Soon, the climb resumes, somewhat more gently, but there is still half a mile to go before finally reaching the 3,800-foot summit at 8.0 miles, marked by a small boulder next to the trail. A yellow spur trail to the left leads to southern views, partially obscured by encroaching vegetation.

A large boulder with a view over Mink Hollow to Plateau Mountain marks the beginning of the steep descent of Sugarloaf's western face, where the trail descends 1,200 feet in a mile. Here the Devil's Path really earns its name, dropping through rock chutes and switching back past massive ledges of dark blackish shale. At the base of the mountain in Mink Hollow, the northern branch of the Mink Hollow Trail (blue) goes off to the right, leading in 2.8 miles to a parking area on Elka Park Road. The Mink Hollow Trail can be combined with the Pecoy Notch Trail and the Devil's Path to make an attractive—albeit strenuous—seven-mile loop hike up Sugarloaf Mountain.

A short distance beyond, at 9.0 miles, the southern branch of the Mink Hollow Trail leaves to the left. It leads in a few hundred feet to the Mink Hollow Lean-to and continues for three miles to a parking area at the end of the southern section of Mink Hollow Road (which leads to NY 212 in Lake Hill). To the right, a woods road (the route of the Mink Hollow Trail prior to a 1998 relocation) leads in 0.2 mile to a spring and continues for about half a mile further to the end of the northern section of Mink Hollow Road (which leads to Elka Park Road).

After another mile-and-a-half of steep climbing, the Devil's Path reaches an open rock, with views back to Twin and Sugarloaf, and about half a mile later, it arrives at the 3,840-foot summit of Plateau Mountain. Here, 10.9 miles from the start, the trail turns right and continues for the next two miles along the summit ridge of Plateau Mountain, in a level expanse of boreal forest.

The western end of Plateau Mountain is marked by two viewpoints: Danny's Lookout, to the north of the trail, and Orchard Point, where the trail begins its descent into Stony Clove Notch. The view from Orchard Point includes Hunter, Southwest Hunter, and West Kill mountains, as well as more distant peaks to the northwest and southwest. From Orchard Point, the Devil's Path begins a steady, rather steep descent. Although the trail drops 1,500 feet in only a mile, there are no chutes to descend on this route. At one point, the trail crosses a rocky area where only paper birch grow—the remains of an old landslide. There is a spring adjacent to the trail about half a mile from Orchard Point.

At the bottom, the Devil's Path joins an old road, crosses the right-of-way of the abandoned Ulster & Delaware Railroad, and reaches NY 214—the only paved road the trail crosses for its entire length—at the southern end of Notch Lake. Here, 13.4 miles from the start, the Long Path leaves the Devil's Path and proceeds south along NY 214 to Silver Hollow Road. Parking is available at the Devil's Tombstone State Campground, just to the south of the Devil's Path crossing of NY 214, with a fee charged in season.

The Devil's Path crosses the outlet of Notch Lake—which boasts a striking view of the notch—and begins its ascent of Hunter Mountain. First climbing through a pair of ledges known as the Devil's Portal, about a third of a mile from the notch, the trail ascends rather steeply for the next half mile. Beyond there, though, the grade eases. There are some steep climbs along the western section of the Devil's Path, but the challenging chutes and ledges that characterize the climbs east of NY 214 are absent.

The forest here is an eclectic mix of species, betraying the heavy logging done here in the early twentieth century. Just under 3,500 feet, over a mile up from Stony Clove Notch, the trail levels off in a forest of red spruce and paper birch, following the route of an old narrow-gauge railroad built in the early 1900s by the Fenwick Lumber Company to transport trees felled in its logging operations.

After about three-quarters of a mile of this smooth walking, the Devil's Path reaches a junction with the Hunter Mountain Trail (yellow). To the right, this trail leads in 1.6 miles to the fire tower on the 4,040-foot summit of Hunter Mountain—a worthwhile side trip. The Devil's Path turns left at the junction and a few hundred feet later, at 15.7 miles, it passes the Devil's Acre Lean-to, with a nearby spring. The unusual wetness of this area results from an old logging camp at this site, remnants of which can still be found in the woods near the trail.

A short distance beyond the lean-to, another old narrow-gauge railbed to the left is used by some hikers to access the elusive summit of trailless 3,740-foot Southwest Hunter Mountain. The Devil's Path now bends to the right and follows a contour around the west side of the mountain. At 16.1 miles, a short yellow-blazed trail leads left to an open ledge, with a fine view of Southwest Hunter Mountain.

From here, the Devil's Path begins a steady descent through a deciduous forest, finally reaching, at 17.6 miles, a trail junction at Diamond Notch Falls. Straight ahead, the Diamond Notch Trail (blue) leads in 0.7 mile to the end of the driveable Spruceton Road, with parking available a short distance beyond. The Devil's Path turns left here, joining the Diamond Notch Trail to cross a wooden bridge over the stream just above the falls. On the other side of the bridge, the Devil's Path turns right, while the Diamond Notch Trail continues for 2.3 miles through the narrow Diamond Notch Hollow to a parking area at the end of driveable Diamond Notch Road, near Lanesville, passing a lean-to along the way. After following the stream for a short distance, the Devil's Path bears left and begins an unrelenting two-mile climb of West Kill Mountain.

A spring offers relief about two-thirds of a mile up, but there is still much elevation to be gained before the peak can be claimed. There are a few rocky sections as the forest gradually changes to paper birch and balsam fir. Just below the 3,500-foot level (marked by a DEC sign), the trail levels off and passes by an interesting rock overhang (designated as a "cave" on the Trail Conference map). The climb soon resumes, but more gently. Finally, after a short, steep section, the Buck Ridge Lookout—the last great viewpoint on the Devil's Path—is reached at 19.7 miles. Little of civilization is in evidence in a view dominated by Hunter Mountain, but ranging as far south as Peekamoose Mountain. A nearby ledge on the opposite side of the trail looks out over 3,680-foot Rusk Mountain to the north.

West Kill Mountain's 3,880-foot summit—the only Catskill summit marked by an official DEC sign—is amid the balsam fir, about 500 feet west of the lookout. Relatively few hikers continue along the ridge west of here, and the trail may be narrower and more overgrown. After descending from the summit (passing a spring on the way down), the trail follows the ridge at about the 3,300-foot level, with some short ups and downs, for about a mile and a half. The Devil's Path then begins to climb again—up a tricky section of large rock slabs and then up two ledges—to the 3,420-foot viewless summit of St. Anne's Peak, also known as West West Kill Mountain.

From the western peak, the trail descends, at first intermittently, then steadily, to the boggy gap between St. Anne's Peak and North Dome, known as Mink Hollow (although it has the same name, this col is not the same as the one crossed by the Devil's Path between Sugarloaf and Plateau mountains).

Here, the trail turns north and descends gradually, along a creek and through a hemlock grove and large field of glacial erratics, to its western end at a parking area on Spruceton Road, 24.6 miles from Prediger Road.

Other Hunter Mountain Routes

The Devil's Path, described above, provides an attractive route up Hunter Mountain, the Catskills' second-highest peak, but the mountain may also be climbed by several other routes.

The most popular route up Hunter Mountain is the Spruceton Trail (blue), the former jeep road to the fire tower. Leaving from the parking area on Spruceton Road (County 6), 6.7 miles east of NY 42, this trail follows a woods road which ascends gently to Taylor Hollow, the gap between Rusk and Hunter mountains, in 1.7 miles. The next section is a good deal rougher and steeper. After passing a spring to the right of the trail, the John Robb Lean-to is reached at 2.3 miles, with a good view over Spruceton Valley. The sign marking 3,500 feet of elevation is just beyond.

In another 500 feet, the Colonel's Chair Trail (yellow) goes off to the left, leading in 1.1 miles to the chairlift at the summit of the Hunter Mountain Ski Area. The Spruceton Trail now levels off, traversing a pleasant boreal forest for the remaining mile to the summit. After passing a viewpoint to the left over the Blackhead Range and then a spring on a yellow-blazed spur trail to the left, the trail goes up a short, steep pitch and reaches the summit clearing, with the fire tower and adjacent cabin, at 3.4 miles. There are excellent views over the entire Catskills and beyond from the tower, which was restored in 2001.

From the summit, the Spruceton Trail continues through a dense evergreen forest to end, at 3.6 miles, at a junction with the Hunter Mountain Trail (yellow) and the Becker Hollow Trail (blue). To the right, a short yellow-blazed trail leads to a viewpoint over Southwest Hunter Mountain and Spruceton Valley from a rock ledge. The Hunter Mountain Trail continues ahead 1.6 miles to the Devil's Path.

A popular eight-mile loop hike of Hunter Mountain, starting from the parking area near the end of Spruceton Road, can be made by using the Spruceton Trail, the Hunter Mountain Trail, the Devil's Path, and the Diamond Notch Trail. This circular hike can be completed in one day, or one may choose to stay overnight at either the John Robb Lean-to or the Devil's Acre Lean-to.

The 2.1-mile Becker Hollow Trail, which begins from NY 214, 1.3 miles south of its junction with NY 23A and 1.6 miles north of the Devil's Path crossing at Notch Lake, offers the shortest route to the summit but has a well-earned reputation as the most difficult, due to its steady and steep grade.

It is also possible to reach the summit of Hunter Mountain by taking the ski area's chairlift to its highest level and following the Colonel's Chair Trail (yellow) and then the Spruceton Trail (blue) to the fire tower. The total one-way hiking distance for this route is 2.3 miles, with an elevation gain (from the top of the chairlift) of about 1,000 feet.

Overlook Mountain   *Length: 6.6 miles Blaze: red, blue*

Overlook Mountain, a 3,140-foot peak north of Woodstock, has been a popular climb since the eighteenth century. Its outstanding views over the Catskills and the Hudson River valley have been enhanced by the restoration in 2000 of the fire tower on its summit. Overlook Mountain may be approached either from Platte Clove Road to the north or from Meads Mountain Road to the south, with the shorter southern approach being favored by most hikers.

The southern trailhead is on Meads Mountain Road, about two miles north of Woodstock, at the top of a winding climb, where the road begins to turn to the west. Parking is available here. The hike proceeds up the Overlook Spur Trail (red)—a woods road still used to access the radio antennas atop the mountain—on a moderate grade. The surrounding forest is full of mountain laurel, which is particularly lovely when in bloom during the spring.

At elevation 3,000 feet, the trail reaches the radio antennas and the ruins of the Overlook Mountain House. This structure—the final attempt to establish a hotel here—burned in the 1920s before it was completed. Exploring the concrete-and-metal ruins can be hazardous, and extreme caution should be exercised.

The road becomes rougher for the remaining half mile to the junction with the Overlook Trail (blue), which leads ahead for 4.6 miles to Platte Clove Road (see description below). At the junction, the Overlook Spur Trail turns right and proceeds in another half a mile to the summit, 2.5 miles from the start. Here, a cabin, picnic table and a few balsam firs complement the fire tower. After climbing the tower to take in the view, be sure to follow the unmarked herd path to the north, which leads down to an open ledge with a sweeping view over the Ashokan Reservoir and the lowlands of eastern Ulster County.

The Overlook Trail proceeds north from the junction, descending gradually for 1.4 miles to reach the eastern end of the Echo Lake Trail (yellow), which leads down 0.6 mile to the lake itself. A lean-to and several designated campsites make this lake—the only natural one within a Catskill wilderness area—a popular place to spend the night. The Overlook Trail now begins to follow a contour around Plattekill Mountain, and it ends at the Devil's Path at 3.6 miles (from the junction with the Overlook Spur Trail), just past the Devil's Kitchen Lean-to. From here to Platte Clove Road it is another mile (via the aqua-blazed Long Path, which leaves to the right in 0.1 mile).

Kaaterskill High Peak

Rising between Plattekill and Kaaterskill cloves—the only passages through the Catskill Escarpment between Saugerties and Windham—is 3,655-foot-high Kaaterskill High Peak, once thought to be the highest in the Catskills.

Kaaterskill High Peak is technically a "trailless" peak, but a maintained snowmobile trail surrounds it, and an unofficial but well-established trail leads from the snowmobile trail to the summit. The easiest approach is from the south. There is a parking area at the start of the snowmobile trail on Platte Clove Road, just west of the end of its steep climb up the mountain from West Saugerties. For the first 3.5 miles, the Long Path (aqua) runs concurrently with the snowmobile trail on a relatively level route. About three miles from the trailhead, it passes through an area (known as Pine Plains) which is often very wet, even in relatively dry seasons. Hikers should prepare accordingly.

At 3.5 miles, the Long Path continues ahead as the snowmobile trail turns sharply left and ascends to the next level. The route to Kaaterskill High Peak follows the snowmobile trail, which soon reaches a T junction. Here, the summit route turns right, following the snowmobile trail for a short distance. The established trail to the summit soon leaves to the left at a junction marked by a cairn. The well-worn summit trail—unofficially marked with blue paint blazes and cairns—climbs steadily to the summit clearing, with a few rock faces and ledges along the way.

There is no view from the summit, but the real attraction—Hurricane Ledge—is a quarter-mile further along the trail. This open, treeless area faces south and offers an excellent view of the Devil's Path mountains and the Hudson River valley. It is an excellent place to have lunch.

The unofficial trail continues southward, but this portion of the trail is steep and not as well defined as the route coming from the north. It may be difficult to follow, and it is not recommended for inexperienced hikers.

Another section of the Long Path allows access to Kaaterskill High Peak from the north, beginning in Palenville off NY 32A. This six-mile approach route, which goes past several outstanding overlooks and scenic waterfalls, is longer than the route from the south and requires a climb of nearly 3,000 feet.

Long Path (Phoenicia to Silver Hollow Notch)

Length: 10.6 miles Blaze: red, blue

Combined with previously existing trails over Tremper Mountain, a relocation of the Long Path completed in 2000 makes it possible to follow a trail route from Phoenicia to Silver Hollow Notch, just south of the Devil's Tombstone State Campground on NY 214. This route—when combined with a proposed trail over Cross Mountain—will connect the Wittenberg-Cornell-Slide Trail with the Devil's Path, thus providing a link between the trail systems of the southern and central Catskills and the Devil's Path to the north.

This section of the Long Path begins at a parking area along Old Route 28 (County 40), 1.6 miles east of Phoenicia. Here, the Long Path begins to follow the Phoenicia Trail (red), which traverses a hemlock-covered slope to reach the old road to the Tremper Mountain fire tower. The trail follows the road as it switches back regularly over the next mile and a half, passing the remains of an old quarry on the way. (Hikers who wish to explore the quarry should exercise caution, as the area is frequented by rattlesnakes). At 2.3 miles, the Baldwin Memorial Lean-to is on a short side trail to the right, with a spring nearby.

In a birch and hemlock grove, the trail begins to level off. At 3.0 miles, the trail reaches the Tremper Mountain Lean-to, and a short distance beyond it arrives at the fire tower on the mountain's 2,740-foot summit. The forest here is a mix of oak and other pioneer species, reflecting the frequent fires that once plagued this area. From the fire tower (which was restored and reopened in 2001), there are views over the Slide Mountain area and the Devil's Path.

The Phoenicia Trail ends at the summit, but the Long Path continues ahead along the ridge on the Warner Creek Trail (blue). At 5.2 miles, after several brief descents, it reaches the col with neighboring Carl Mountain. Here, to the right, the Willow Trail (yellow) drops down sharply for 2.5 miles to the hamlet of Willow. The Long Path continues north, following the blue-blazed Warner Creek Trail.

Winding around below the summit of Carl Mountain, the trail finally reaches a tributary of Warner Creek over a mile from the junction. After crossing it below a waterfall, it drops down past an old quarry and some stone foundations to join an old road running along the creek. It then crosses Warner Creek at 7.3 miles.

On the other side, the trail reaches an old road in an area that is often wet and follows it for a short distance, crossing into Greene County along the way. A sharp turn to the north heralds the beginning of a sustained climb of a 3,000-foot peak known informally as Edgewood Mountain.

The trail runs for some distance along the level summit, with views of nearby Plateau Mountain from rock ledges in open areas. The trail then descends steadily to Silver Hollow Road, which is heavily rutted and eroded, and barely passable even for four-wheel drive vehicles. Here, the Warner Creek Trail ends, and the Long Path turns left on the road, now marked with aqua paint blazes. It follows the road for 0.9 mile, past the headwaters of Stony Clove Creek, down to NY 214. The Devil's Tombstone State Campground, where parking is available, is 1.4 miles north along NY 214.

Bluestone Wild Forest

Located on NY 28, three miles west of Exit 19 of the New York State Thruway, the 3,000-acre Bluestone Wild Forest was extensively mined for bluestone in the latter half of the nineteenth century. The bluestone was used for steps, curbing, and sidewalks in major cities. Although the industry collapsed in 1880, with the discovery of Portland cement, remnants of quarries and old wagon roads are scattered throughout the oak, white pine, and pitch pine forests. The 16-acre Onteora Lake offers fishing opportunities, and there are designated campsites around the lake.

The 1.8-mile Onteora Lake Loop Trail circles the lake and passes by several bluestone quarries. The Jockey Hill-Wintergreen Ridge Trail uses an old woods road to make a 1.8-mile loop. Both trails are open to mountain biking and cross-country skiing as well as hiking.

Trails in the Northeastern Catskills

The Catskill Escarpment—the so-called "Great Wall of Manitou," where the mountains suddenly rise up from the Hudson River valley—dominates this section of the Catskills. The striking view of the Escarpment from across the river inspired many of the early Hudson River School artists. For the hiker, there are two areas of particular interest in the northeastern Catskills—the North/South Lake area and the Blackhead Range—both of which are linked by the Escarpment Trail.

The North/South Lake State Campground near Haines Falls is adjacent to the site of the former Catskill Mountain House, frequented by the elite in the nineteenth century. Walking was a popular pastime in those days, and an extensive network of trails around the hotel was developed. Although the campground, picnic areas, and beaches are most heavily used by today's visitors, the hiking trails remain and provide attractive day hikes. All of the marked trails in the area are shown on Trail Conference Map 40. The major trail in the area is the Escarpment Trail, described below. A fee is charged in season at the gatehouse leading into the campground.

Kaaterskill Falls Trail   *Length: 0.4 mile Blaze: yellow*
This short trail (originally part of the Escarpment Trail) allows visitors to access the base of Kaaterskill Falls, the second highest waterfall in New York. The trailhead is on the north side of NY 23A, about two miles west of Palenville, and just east of the bridge over Bastion Falls. The parking area, however, is on the south side of the road, 0.2 mile further west. Caution should be exercised while walking along this narrow, busy highway.

The trail ascends steadily along Spruce Creek, passing through virgin hemlock growth, and climbing over rocks and alongside bluffs. Due to heavy use, the trail is severely eroded in some areas. At the falls, reached at 0.4 mile, a 20-foot lower cascade empties the pool below the spectacular upper falls. Although it is possible to continue on to the natural amphitheater behind the falls, extreme caution is required. The footing along the route can be treacherous, and a number of people have lost their lives here. There is no direct access from the base of the falls to the top.

Escarpment Trail   *Length: 23.0 miles Blaze: blue*
Although the Escarpment Trail is a continuous 23-mile trail, extending from Schutt Road at the North/South Lake State Campground to NY 23 near Windham, there are, in a sense, two Escarpment Trails—the first being the lower five miles, an appealing day trip around the North Lake area, and the second being the remainder of the trail, which is ideal for backpacking (but also offers many day-hiking opportunities).

The southern trailhead of the Escarpment Trail is opposite the parking area on Schutt Road, just before the North/South Lake State Campground gatehouse. Running roughly downhill and parallel to Schutt Road, it crosses two old railroad grades and then, at 0.5 mile, reaches the end of Schutt Road near a junction with the Schutt Road Trail (red). The Schutt Road Trail leads in 1.1 miles to another junction with the Escarpment Trail, and the two trails can be combined to make a 3.7-mile loop hike.

The Escarpment Trail now follows Spruce Creek through a hemlock grove, soon passing the site of the former Laurel House (to the right of the trail). A trail mileage sign at 0.7 mile marks the junction with the former route of the trail (now closed), which led to the base of Kaaterskill Falls. The trail continues gently downhill through a mixed forest and, at 1.2 miles, reaches the Layman Monument, a stone marker memorializing a firefighter who died at this spot in 1900. Fire has, in fact, been quite frequent in this area, as the plethora of mixed trees in the surrounding woods suggests. Just beyond, there is a viewpoint over Kaaterskill Clove and Kaaterskill High Peak.

After passing the southern end of a short yellow-blazed trail which leads north to the Schutt Road Trail, the trail reaches Inspiration Point—with broader views—1.9 miles from the start. Then, at 2.6 miles, the Sleepy Hollow Horse Trail joins from the left. A few hundred feet beyond, the Escarpment Trail turns sharply left and ascends a winding, laurel-bordered woods road, as the Harding Road Trail (red), which descends to NY 23A in 2.9 miles, continues ahead. The Long Path joins here, and it runs concurrently with the Escarpment Trail for the rest of the way to NY 23.

At 3.1 miles, a junction is reached with the Schutt Road Trail, which leads back to Schutt Road in 1.1 miles. Here, the Escarpment Trail turns right. After passing Boulder Rock—a viewpoint over Palenville and the Hudson River valley—the trail reaches Pine Orchard, the site of the legendary Catskill Mountain House, at 4.5 miles. Only the gates remain; after much debate about whether to preserve the structure, the DEC razed it on a winter night in 1963.

The roads leading west from the Mountain House site can be used to return to the parking lot on Schutt Road. For those who want to continue, Artists Rock, with its views of the Hudson River valley, is reached at 5.1 miles, and the trail goes by Newman's Ledge, another noted viewpoint, at 5.8 miles.

Now beginning to climb gradually, the Escarpment Trail passes the northern end of the Rock Shelter Trail (yellow) at 6.4 miles and the Mary's Glen Trail (red) at 7.1 miles. Each of these trails can be used to return to the starting point, making a loop hike of about eight or nine miles. After a short, steep ascent, the Escarpment Trail reaches North Point at 7.2 miles. This well-known spot offers broad views over the entire North/South Lake area, with Kaaterskill High Peak in the background.

Figure 12-8. North/South Lakes from the Escarpment Trail

Most day hikers go no further than here. Beyond this point, the trail is largely the domain of backpackers. The summit of North Mountain (3,180 feet) is reached at 7.7 miles, and Stoppel Point (3,420 feet)—with the remains of a wrecked airplane near the trail—is at 8.9 miles. From here, the trail descends to a junction at Dutcher Notch, 11.0 miles from the start. To the right, the Dutcher Notch Trail (yellow) passes a spring at 0.4 mile and continues to Floyd Hawver Road near the hamlet of Round Top in another two miles. To the left, the Colgate Lake Trail (yellow) leads in 4.3 miles to Colgate Lake on County 78.

The Escarpment Trail now begins a rather steep climb, gaining 800 feet of elevation in less than a mile. At the top of the climb, a viewpoint to the left of the trail overlooks Lake Capra and Colgate Lake. The hiker now enters a boreal forest area known, interestingly, as Arizona (due to its dryness). Over the next mile, Blackhead Mountain begins to loom in the distance, and there are occasional views to the right over the Hudson River valley.

After a relatively flat section, the Escarpment Trail begins a steep ascent of Blackhead Mountain. Almost as soon as it crests at the summit ridge, a viewpoint on the left—perhaps the best vista on the entire trail—provides views over the Hudson River valley, the Escarpment all the way back to North Point, and the hills of New England on the far eastern horizon. Blackhead's viewless 3,940-foot summit, 13.6 miles from Schutt Road, is a short distance beyond. Here, the Blackhead Mountain Trail (yellow)—which descends to Lockwood Gap (the col between Blackhead and Black Dome mountains) in 0.6 mile—continues ahead, while the Escarpment Trail turns right and descends steeply through some rocky chutes, dropping 1,100 feet of elevation in only a mile. This section can be particularly difficult to traverse in the winter, when covered with snow and ice.

At 14.6 miles, the base of the descent is reached. Here, the Batavia Kill Trail (yellow) comes in from the left. It leads in 0.3 mile to the Batavia Kill Lean-to, with water from the adjacent stream, and continues to a junction with the Black Dome Range Trail (red) in 1.0 mile.

The Escarpment Trail now traverses a relatively level ridge, reaching 3,100-foot Acra Point at 16.4 miles. A short distance beyond, there is a good view over Big Hollow. The northern end of the Black Dome Range Trail (which leads in 1.2 miles to a parking area on Big Hollow Road) is on the left at 17.2 miles. From here, the Escarpment Trail climbs steeply to Burnt Knob (3,180 feet), which has several good viewpoints.

After traversing several minor summits, the trail climbs to the summit of 3,524-foot Windham High Peak, reached 19.8 miles from the start. From this peak—the most northerly of the Catskill summits over 3,500 feet in elevation—there is an unobstructed view over Albany, the Helderberg Escarpment, and the lower Adirondacks and Green Mountains to the north. The trail now descends gradually, passing through an area that was once farmed (note the stone walls, grassy areas, and reforested Norway spruce groves). At 22.0 miles, it passes the Elm Ridge Lean-to and reaches a junction with the Elm Ridge Trail (yellow). This side trail, which departs to the left, passes a spring in 500 feet and continues for another mile to a parking area at the end of Peck Road. The Escarpment Trail turns right at the junction and descends for a mile to its terminus on NY 23, where parking is available.

Black Dome Range Trail   *Length: 6.6 miles Blaze: red*
A distinct trio of high peaks visible from a distance, the Blackhead Range forms the southern wall of Big Hollow Valley, east of Hensonville. The Black Dome Range Trail traverses two of these peaks, and it connects with the Blackhead Mountain Trail, which leads to the summit of its namesake.

The western trailhead of the Black Dome Range Trail can be reached from the hamlet of Maplecrest by driving south on Maplecrest Road to Elmer Barnum Road. The trail officially begins at this intersection, but cars can be driven along Elmer Barnum Road for another 0.9 mile to the end of the road, where parking is available.

The trail bears left from the road and, for the first quarter mile, follows a rocky dirt road. At the point where private property gives way to state land, there is a register box. Here, the trail bears left, leaving the road, and ascends moderately but steadily to a false summit known as Caudal, reached at 0.9 mile. Near the top, there are views to the south over the peaks of the Devil's Path. The trail descends slightly and soon begins a short, steep climb to the second false summit, the 3,520-foot Camel's Hump. From the top, there are views ahead over Thomas Cole Mountain—the first "real" summit of the hike.

The journey of nearly a mile to its summit begins with a short descent into a grassy col (with rather poor drainage) and continues with a steady climb at moderate to steep grades up the mountain, named for the painter most associated with the Hudson River School. There are no views from the 3,940-foot summit itself, reached at 2.4 miles from the end of the driveable road, but a yellow-blazed side trail leads to a ledge with limited views to the south.

Continuing eastward, the trail descends gently into the low point between Thomas Cole and Black Dome mountains—at 3,720 feet, the highest col in the Catskills. It then climbs to the summit of Black Dome, the Catskills' third-highest peak at 3,980 feet. Here, at 3.4 miles, an open area looking south—with a view of the entire Devil's Path—makes a nice lunch spot. From the summit, the trail soon begins a rather steep descent to Lockwood Gap, the Black Dome-Blackhead col. About halfway down, an open ledge just east of the trail offers a panoramic view over Blackhead Mountain, directly ahead.

At Lockwood Gap, reached at 4.0 miles, the Blackhead Mountain Trail (yellow) continues ahead to the peak after which it is named, while the Black Dome Range trail turns left (north), leaving the ridge. It begins by descending steeply on a rocky footpath, but after passing a spring about 0.3 mile from the col, the grade moderates. After paralleling a tributary, the Black Dome Range Trail crosses the Batavia Kill and, at 4.9 miles, reaches a junction with the Batavia Kill Trail (yellow), which leads uphill 0.3 mile to the Batavia Kill Lean-to and continues to the Escarpment Trail.

Turning left at the junction, the Black Dome Range Trail follows the stream downhill on a moderate grade, crossing the stream twice in the half-mile to the parking area at the end of Big Hollow Road, reached at 5.4 miles. This parking area is a popular location from which to begin a day hike. The trail continues ahead along the road, but it turns right in a short distance, crosses the Batavia Kill once more, and climbs to its terminus on the Escarpment Trail, 6.6 miles from the start.

The Black Dome Range Trail may be combined with the Batavia Kill, Escarpment, and Black-

Figure 12-9. Bridge across the Batavia Kill

head Mountain trails to make a 4.5-mile loop hike of Blackhead Mountain. For those seeking a weekend backpacking trip, the Black Dome Range Trail, together with the Blackhead Mountain, Escarpment, and Elm Ridge trails, may be used to form a 14-mile horseshoe-shaped hike which includes all four 3,500-foot peaks in the area.

Colgate Lake Trail   *Length: 4.3 miles Blaze: yellow*

The Colgate Lake Trail offers the hiker the rare opportunity to take in some beautiful woodland and views at a mostly level grade. It begins at a parking area on County 78, just east of Colgate Lake, and it immediately crosses a large field with a view of the Blackhead Range. Once in the woods, it follows old roads through land once farmed and crosses several tributary streams of the East Kill.

About 2.4 miles from the start, the trail goes through a towering grove of hemlocks next to a beaver meadow. It then begins to follow an old road, crosses the East Kill, and comes out on a wide meadow at 3.0 miles, with more views over the Blackheads. The trail continues up the old road to Dutcher Notch, where it ends at 4.3 miles, at a junction with the Escarpment Trail.

Trails in the West Central Catskills

Most of the peaks in the west central Catskills are not as high as those in the eastern area of the region. Nevertheless, the lands in Ulster County's western corner and nearby in Delaware County and northern Sullivan County offer many hiking opportunities, including several major peaks with superb views.

Dry Brook Ridge Trail   *Length: 13.6 miles Blaze: blue*
Like the Escarpment Trail, the Dry Brook Ridge Trail can be divided into two distinct sections. The northern section of the trail is a nine-mile traverse of the ridge for which the trail is named. It is lightly used, and does not go over or near any major peaks. The trail section south of Mill Brook Road is a woods road which provides access to Balsam Lake Mountain (via a side trail) and is used more extensively.

The northern terminus of the Dry Brook Ridge Trail is reached by turning south off NY 28, 0.4 mile southwest of the traffic light at Margaretville, and going 0.1 mile to South Side Road, which parallels NY 28. The trailhead is 0.1 mile to the left, on the right side of the road. For the first 1.8 miles, the trail climbs steadily on switchbacks to the top of the ridge's northern knob, Pakatakan Mountain. At 2.7 miles, the German Hollow Trail (yellow) comes in from the left. It descends to the German Hollow Lean-to in 0.8 mile and continues through abandoned farmland to the end of Chris Long Road.

For the next two and a half miles, the Dry Brook Ridge Trail takes a leisurely jaunt along the ridge, offering several westward views. The Huckleberry Loop Trail (red) leaves to the right at 3.3 miles. This trail—which lives up to its name, offering an abundance of berries for the passing hiker—makes a leisurely 8.3-mile loop, ending back at the Dry Brook Ridge Trail. The Dry Brook Ridge Trail passes just below the 3,460-foot summit of the ridge, with a small bog nearby, at 5.0 miles, and the lower end of the Huckleberry Loop Trail is reached about half a mile beyond. The Dry Brook Lean-to, with an adjacent spring, is passed at 8.3 miles. After going over another rise, the Dry Brook Ridge Trail descends to a trailhead parking area on Mill Brook Road at 9.6 miles. This trailhead, at elevation 2,600 feet, is the highest in the Catskills.

The Dry Brook Ridge Trail crosses the paved road at the western end of the parking area and continues uphill on an old town road which crosses private property still owned by descendants of the nineteenth-century rail magnate Jay Gould. For the next two miles, the walk is quite pleasant, with the trail climbing gradually to a spring at 3,100 feet in elevation (just beyond the one switchback on this section of the trail). The trail then levels off on the 3,200-foot contour.

At 11.6 miles (two miles from the Mill Brook Road trailhead), a woods road comes in from the east at a sharp angle. This road provides access to the 3,868-foot peak of Graham Mountain, about two miles from the junction. Although marred by deteriorating ruins of a concrete building constructed in the 1960s to house a television relay station, the summit offers excellent views to the west and northwest. Hikers who wish to follow this route should obtain advance permission from the caretaker of this private property.

A short distance beyond, the Dry Brook Ridge Trail reaches a signed junction. The main trail continues ahead on the old road (blocked by a yellow gate just ahead, where it enters state property), reaching its southern trailhead at the end of Beaver Kill Road at 13.6 miles. Most hikers, though, will want to follow the Balsam Lake Mountain Trail (red), which begins on the right and follows another road—quite steeply in places—for 0.8 mile to the summit of the mountain. The fire tower at the 3,721-foot summit offers excellent views in all directions, with the panorama extending from Graham Mountain just to the east to the Blackhead Range, far in the distance to the northeast. The trained eye can even pick out Elk Hill, the highest peak in northern Pennsylvania, standing all alone to the southwest. The boreal forest near the summit contains a sphagnum bog, rather unusual at this high elevation.

From the summit, the Balsam Lake Mountain Trail proceeds west on a footpath, soon reaching a junction with the Mill Brook Ridge Trail, which leads west 5.9 miles to Alder Lake. The Balsam Lake Mountain Trail then descends steeply to its second junction with the Dry Brook Ridge Trail in another 0.8 mile. On the way, it passes a spring and a side trail which leads to the Balsam Lake Mountain Lean-to. The parking area at the southern end of the Dry Brook Ridge Trail is another mile beyond the junction.

Mill Brook Ridge Trail   *Length: 5.9 miles Blaze: yellow*
The Mill Brook Ridge Trail is the longest route to the summit of Balsam Lake Mountain, but it is lightly used and provides a delightful approach to the peak. It also provides a link between the trails in the western Catskills and those in the central Catskills.

The trail's western terminus is at the eastern end of Alder Lake. The Alder Lake Loop Trail (red), which circles the lake, provides access from the parking area at its western end, reached by following County 54 north from Turnwood. The Mill Brook Ridge Trail heads into the woods, climbing only slightly as it runs along the valley between Mill Brook Ridge to the north and Cradle Rock Ridge to the south. The Beaver Meadow Lean-to, reached at 1.5 miles, is situated in a beautiful spot next to the meadow. Just beyond, the trail begins a sustained climb, and it reaches the highest point on the ridge (3,480 feet) at 2.9 miles. It then descends to a col and climbs to another high point on the ridge. Just before reaching this peak, a viewpoint to the right looks out over Beecher Lake to the southwest. As the trail continues along, Balsam Lake Mountain begins to loom in the distance.

After descending slightly, the trail reaches the base of Balsam Lake Mountain. It curves to the south along a contour and then ascends steadily on switchbacks. Just below the summit, there is a broad view to the west over the entire Mill Brook Ridge. The Mill Brook Ridge Trail ends at 5.9 miles at a junction with the Balsam Lake Mountain Trail (red). The fire tower on the summit is a short distance to the left, and the parking area at the southern end of the Dry Brook Ridge Trail is 1.7 miles to the right.

Long Pond-Beaver Kill Ridge Trail   *Length: 7.5 miles Blaze: red*
The Long Pond-Beaver Kill Ridge Trail connects the Neversink-Hardenburgh Trail (yellow) with the Mongaup-Hardenburgh Trail (blue). The southern trailhead is at the intersection of Black Bear and Basily roads (0.2 mile north of Round Pond), where parking is available. The trail proceeds west for two miles west along Basily Road, which is driveable (although no parking is available). It then turns left onto another road, which is passable by car only for the first 0.4 mile. At 3.6 miles, it reaches a junction with a short red-blazed spur trail which leads south to Long Pond and a lean-to.

Turning north, the Long Pond-Beaver Kill Ridge Trail crosses Willowemoc Creek on a footbridge at 4.4 miles and briefly runs along Flugertown Road. Here, the Mongaup-Willowemoc Trail (yellow) begins, with both trails running concurrently for half a mile. The Long Pond-Beaver Kill Ridge Trail then begins its ascent of the Beaver Kill Ridge. After following an old lumber road on easy grades, the trail ascends more steeply to the crest of the ridge, reached at 6.3 miles, with a view of privately-owned Sand Pond below on the left. The trail follows along the ridge for a little over a mile, ending, at 7.5 miles, at an intersection with the Mongaup-Hardenburgh Trail (blue). To the right, it leads in 3.2 miles to Beaver Kill Road. To the left, it is 3.2 miles to Mongaup Pond and the state campground.

Mongaup-Hardenburgh Trail
Length: 6.4 miles Blaze: blue
The Mongaup-Hardenburgh Trail begins at the north end of the Mongaup Pond State Campground between campsites 144 and 147 on Loop G. It ascends 1.6 miles to the middle peak of Mongaup Mountain (2,959 feet). The trail then follows the Beaver Kill Ridge over the east peak of Mongaup Mountain (2,928 feet), reached at 2.7 miles, and in another half a mile, it intersects the Long Pond-Beaver Kill Ridge Trail (red), which leads in 4.0 miles to Long Pond. After passing a spring, the trail reaches the highest point on Beaver Kill Ridge (3,224 feet) at 4.8 miles. It then descends north off the Beaver Kill Ridge and crosses the Beaver Kill on a footbridge to end at Beaver Kill Road. From here, the Neversink-Hardenburgh Trail (yellow) leads to the right, along the road, for two miles to the Balsam Lake parking area and the trailhead for the Dry Brook Ridge Trail (red).

Figure 12-10. Waterfall on the Neversink River

Neversink-Hardenburgh Trail
Length: 13.0 miles Blaze: yellow
The Neversink-Hardenburgh Trail connects the Mongaup-Hardenburgh Trail and the Dry Brook Ridge Trail with the Long Pond-Beaver Kill Ridge Trail. At each end, the trail runs along driveable roads, and it follows a woods road for most of the its route, crossing many small streams as it passes between the watersheds of the Beaver Kill and the West Branch of the Neversink River.

The Neversink-Hardenburgh Trail begins on Beaver Kill Road, at the northern terminus of the Mongaup-Hardenburgh Trail (blue). It proceeds west along Beaver Kill Road for 2.0 miles to the end of the road at the Balsam Lake parking area, where the Dry Brook Ridge Trail (blue) begins. The Neversink-

Hardenburgh Trail turns right and follows a footpath for about a mile and a half until it joins a woods road. After crossing the Beaver Kill at 5.3 miles, just a mile and a half below the source of this famous trout stream, the trail ascends gently to a height of land and then follows a contour to reach the Fall Brook Lean-to at 6.4 miles. About half a mile further, the trail enters the first of several clearings. At 7.9 miles, there is a small parking area; however, the road is still very rough, and those without four-wheel drive vehicles might want to park further south along the road.

At 10.9 miles, at a parking area, a junction is reached with the Long Pond-Beaver Kill Ridge Trail (red). The Neversink-Hardenburgh Trail continues along paved roads to its southern terminus at the bridge over the East Branch of the Neversink River southwest of Claryville.

Starting at the Balsam Lake parking area, the Neversink-Hardenburgh, Long Pond-Beaver Kill Ridge, and Mongaup-Hardenburgh trails may be combined to make a 21.7-mile circuit through gentle terrain, with the Long Pond Lean-to offering a convenient overnight stop.

West of Mongaup Pond

To the west of Mongaup Pond State Campground in the Town of Rockland, there is an extensive trail system, composed primarily of wide, grassy roads designed primarily for snowmobile and/or cross-country ski traffic. These gentle roads also make appealing hikes. Here, the Catskills show a slightly different face. The presence of many young trees, numerous stumps, and piles of sawlogs attests to the heavy logging that occurred here, continuing well into the twentieth century.

The trail system west of Mongaup Pond can be accessed via the snowmobile trail which heads west from the campground, or by driving up Beech Mountain Road to its end. The Flynn Trail (blue), which begins here, goes north and then west, reaching Hodge Pond at 2.2 miles. At 2,580 feet above sea level, this is the highest natural pond in the Catskills. Hodge Pond is part of the Beech Mountain Nature Preserve, a 288-acre preserve, named after the 3,118-foot peak, which is the highest in Sullivan County. The preserve is managed for research by the Open Space Institute, and hikers are requested to stay on the trails and not disturb any research equipment they may encounter.

From Hodge Pond, the Flynn Trail continues to its terminus, at 3.2 miles, at a junction with the Quick Lake Trail (red). The latter trail can be followed to the left back to the parking area, providing an alternate return route. To the right, the Quick Lake Trail leads in 4.1 miles to Quick Lake

Other trails in the area include the 1.7-mile Big Rock Trail (yellow) and the 1.8-mile Logger's Loop Trail (yellow). A map showing all the trails in the area appears on the reverse side of Map 43 of the Trail Conference's Catskill Trails map set.

Trails in the Western Catskills

The trails in this gentler area of the western Catskills are concentrated in the towns of Colchester and Andes in Delaware County, south of the Pepacton Reservoir. The mountains here show significant evidence of past settlement, and many of the trails follow old roads that serve as snowmobile trails in the winter.

The trails in the area can be combined to form a continuous 25-mile one-way hike, but since there are many road crossings, individual trails can be hiked in day trips. These trails are not as heavily used as those elsewhere in the Catskills; thus, they are ideal for the hiker who is seeking greater solitude.

Touch-Me-Not Trail

Length: 6.8 miles Blaze: red

The most easterly section of the Delaware County trail system, the Touch-Me-Not Trail begins at the Alder Lake parking area in Ulster County. It proceeds west and, at 2.9 miles, after crossing into Delaware County, it reaches Barkaboom Road, just south of Big Pond, where parking is available.

After briefly following the road to the north, the trail turns left and climbs Touchmenot Mountain, first gently, then more steeply. Near the summit (2,760 feet), at 4.0 miles, it reaches a junction with the Campground Trail (blue), which descends in 0.7 mile to the Little Pond State Campground. In another three-quarters of a mile, the Touch-Me-Not Trail reaches a junction with the Little Pond Trail (yellow), which also descends to the campground.

After ascending Cabot Mountain (2,970 feet), with a view near the summit, the Touch-Me-Not Trail descends steeply to Beech Hill Road at 6.8 miles, where it ends.

Middle Mountain Trail

Length: 2.0 miles Blaze: red

The Middle Mountain Trail begins on Beech Hill Road, 0.2 mile north of the western end of the Touch-Me-Not Trail (red), passing a spring not far from its start. It runs two miles west to Mary Smith Hill Road, going over Beech Hill (2,844 feet) and Middle Mountain (2,975 feet), with a viewpoint just east of the summit of Middle Mountain. It ends at Mary Smith Hill Road, where parking is available. The Mary Smith Trail (red) begins on the opposite side of the road.

Mary Smith Trail   *Length: 4.5 miles Blaze: red*
The Mary Smith Trail begins on the west side of Mary Smith Hill Road, opposite the western end of the Middle Mountain Trail (red). After climbing over Mary Smith Hill (2,767 feet), it descends to cross Holliday and Berry Brook Road, where parking is available, at 3.3 miles. It then ascends to end at a junction with the Pelnor Hollow Trail (blue) at 4.5 miles.

The trail system forks here. Those hikers who wish to follow the entire length of the Delaware County trail system should turn right on the Pelnor Hollow Trail and follow it northwest for 0.8 mile to a junction with the Campbell Mountain Trail (blue) and the Little Spring Brook Trail (yellow). Others may choose to turn left (south) and follow the Pelnor Hollow Trail along the ridgeline for 2.3 miles to the Pelnor Hollow Lean-to and, 0.9 mile beyond, to the end of Pelnor Hollow Road.

Campbell Mountain Trail   *Length: 5.5 miles Blaze: blue*
The Campbell Mountain Trail begins at a junction with the Little Spring Brook Trail (yellow) and the Pelnor Hollow Trail (blue). After crossing Brock Mountain (2,760 feet), the Campbell Mountain Trail crosses NY 206 at 3.4 miles. The Campbell Mountain Lean-to is located on a short side trail to the left at 4.7 miles, and the trail ends at a parking area on Campbell Mountain Road at 5.8 miles.

Trout Pond Trail   *Length: 5.4 miles Blaze: blue*
The last link in this chain of trails is the Trout Pond Trail. Starting at Campbell Mountain Road across from the west end of the Campbell Mountain Trail, it ascends to an unnamed peak (2,526 feet) and then descends somewhat steeply to Campbell Brook Road at 2.1 miles (no parking is available here). After passing a lean-to, the trail reaches Trout Pond (with another lean-to) at 4.0 miles. Though its southern end may be busy on summer weekends, few users go as far as the northern end of the pond. Trout Pond offers excellent fishing, and the lean-to at its northern end is a good choice for those seeking solitude.

Here, at the northern end of the pond, a junction is reached with the Mud Pond Trail (blue) which leads south for 3.7 miles to a parking area on Russell Brook Road, going around Mud Pond on the way (a short side trail leads to the pond). The Trout Pond Trail continues south along the eastern shore of the Trout Pond, and it ends at a parking area on Russell Brook Road (about a mile and a half north of the terminus of the Mud Pond Trail) at 5.4 miles.

Trails in the Northwestern Catskills

Although much of the state land in this section of the Catskills is outside the Blue Line that delineates the Catskill Park, there are a number of interesting hiking opportunities in this area.

Bearpen Mountain

Acquired by the State in 1999, Bearpen's 3,600-foot summit is the highest in New York outside the two Forest Preserves. Several decades ago, it was developed as a ski area, leaving it with both an easily walked road to the summit and two wide, cleared swaths that provide views to the northwest.

Ski Run Road, the easiest access to the peak, leaves County 2 about three miles south of its junction with NY 23 just west of Prattsville. Although this route is legally driveable, it is very rough and not recommended for automobiles. (Snowmobiles or all-terrain vehicles may be encountered on this road.)

The first two miles climb 1,200 feet, passing through an alternating checkerboard of state forest and private land, some of which has obviously been logged. At the head of the valley, in Delaware County, a hunter's cabin and picnic tables mark a three-way junction. Here, the hiker bound for Bearpen should turn sharply left.

This next section of road, less accommodating to automotive traffic, climbs gently. About a mile further on, a state forest sign on the south side marks the return to Greene County. Continuing on the road for another mile, the hiker will pass, on the right, a pond built to provide ice skating opportunities at the ski area. Soon, the remains of the ski trails come into view.

From the summit, amid young, shrublike trees and relics from the abandoned ski lifts, one can look back down to the junction where the hike began, as well as over the expanse of Schoharie Reservoir and the Blenheim-Gilboa power project to its north.

A shorter but steeper route to the summit starts from Halcott Mountain Road (County 3), reached from Halcott Center to the south. This rough dirt road is also legally driveable, but is not maintained in wintertime, and is not recommended for automobiles. A hunter's cabin marks the start of an old road that leads to the summit. There are many old roads in the area, so a compass and a map are essential to navigation. On the opposite side of the road is Vly Mountain, another trailless peak, with a Catskill 3500 Club canister on its summit, about a mile from the road.

Huntersfield Mountain

A little-used section of the Long Path allows hikers to climb this impressive peak, Schoharie County's highest at 3,423 feet. The trailhead is located near where Huntersmark and Macomber Road enters state forest lands, north of Red Falls. The Long Path's aqua blazes cross the road where it forks at a state forest sign and gate. This is a good place to park and start walking, as the road ahead becomes rougher as it goes on, and the gate can be closed at any time.

The trail to the north follows Huntersfield Creek through deciduous woods for 0.3 mile before reaching the road again and turning left. Here, it proceeds for 0.7 mile through some very muddy stretches in red pine plantations, finally turning right to climb the mountain. Crossing back and forth across the county line (the yellow blazes mark the state forest boundary, which follows the county line), the trail reaches an open viewpoint to the west at 1.4 miles. The climbing continues through mixed forest and up a succession of ledges until the summit—marked by a survey benchmark set in a stone—is reached at 2.4 miles. Here, a short loop trail blazed with yellow markers gives access to three cut views to the southwest, south, and east back to Windham High Peak. There is a lean-to at the second viewpoint.

Mount Utsayantha

Towering over the Town of Stamford, this 3,214-foot peak stands at the northwest corner of the range. It takes its name from an Indian princess who, according to one legend, drowned herself in a nearby lake rather than give up her European lover. Its main attraction to today's visitors is the fire tower that stands on the summit. Although modern communications equipment now surrounds the tower, the views still remain. Access to the summit is via an old road which begins at Mountain Avenue, just south of NY 23 in Stamford. It is an easy walk of just over a mile to the summit.

From the fire tower, there are views over much of Delaware County. Bearpen Mountain looms to the east over Utsayantha's neighboring peaks, and Hunter Mountain can sometimes be seen beyond. To the west, there is a panorama of the upper valley of the Susquehanna River as it works its way southwest from Cooperstown to Binghamton. To the north, the Scotch Valley Ski Area is visible. In the distance, the land gradually softens into the low hills of Schoharie, Otsego, and Chenango counties—the Leatherstocking country of James Fenimore Cooper's famous tales.

THIRTEEN

THE SHAWANGUNK MOUNTAINS

tanding high above the valleys on either side, the Shawangunk (pronounced SHON gum) Mountain range is a continuation of the ridge that is known as Blue Mountain in Pennsylvania and Kittatinny Mountain in New Jersey. It reaches from the New York-New Jersey line northeast to Rosendale. Referred to affectionately by hikers and climbers as the "Gunks," the area offers a hiking experience of great variety and beauty. Veteran hikers will find the challenge of rough trails and rock scrambles, while less ambitious hikers may enjoy spectacular views from gentle carriage roads. The dramatic landscape is fashioned of miles of white cliffs and ledges, clear mountaintop sky lakes, deep oak forests, and sparse ridgetop barrens of bonsai-shaped pitch pines.

The northern Shawangunks, from Ellenville north to Rosendale, comprise a 25,000-acre natural area that contains the majority of the Shawangunk trails. The area is divided into four major ownerships, each with its own trails, access points, and fees. At the north end is the Mohonk Preserve, which nearly surrounds the second area, the Mohonk Mountain House lands. The Minnewaska State Park Preserve occupies the wide mid-section of the ridge, and is the largest single ownership. To the south of Minnewaska is the Sam's Point Dwarf Pine Preserve. For reasons of clarity, the different sections are treated separately below, even though trails do not always respect the boundaries. The

Wallkill Valley Rail Trail, although not a mountain trail, is included here because of its proximity and because the Shawangunks are so much a part of its scenery. Also included in this chapter are two preserves along the Hudson River, northeast of New Paltz—Black Creek Forest Preserve and Shaupeneak Ridge Cooperative Recreation Area. While not part of the Shawangunks, these preserves are located nearby.

Hiking in the southern Shawangunks, from Ellenville south to the New Jersey border, is largely confined to the Shawangunk Ridge Trail. For hiking opportunities in the southern Shawangunks, see chapter 19, "Long Distance Trails," pp. 397-401.

Geology

At its northeastern end, the Shawangunk ridge rises gradually from the Hudson River valley near Rosendale as a series of low hills, suddenly dramatized by the "table rocks" near High Falls and by the spectacular Mohonk escarpments of Bonticou Crag, Sky Top, and Eagle Cliff. The first of the five successively higher lakes, Mohonk (1,245 feet), is cradled between the latter two cliffs. From this point southwestward, the ridge grows higher and broader, and at Gertrude's Nose it bends to the west toward Ellenville. The four other lakes, whose shores exhibit striking sculpture of cliff and fallen rock, in order are Minnewaska (1,650 feet), Awosting (1,865 feet), Mud Pond (1,842 feet), and Maratanza (2,242 feet). Near the last is Sam's Point, the southernmost promontory of the range. The widest point is near Mud Pond. Southwest of Sam's Point, the Shawangunks settle again into a lower and narrower ridge that continues to the New Jersey border at Port Jervis, where it is known as Kittatinny Mountain.

The narrow Shawangunk Mountain range is composed of Shawangunk Conglomerate, a rock so durable that it formed the basis of a substantial quarrying industry during the nineteenth century, providing millstones to grist mills around the country. It forms the slabs, cliffs, *talus* (rock debris), ice caves, and other distinctive features of the Shawangunks.

The Shawangunks were shaped by two orogenic episodes: the Taconian (about 410 million years ago) and the Acadian (about 360 million years ago). At the end of the Ordovician Period, a huge mountain range formed to the east of the present-day Hudson River. The subsequent erosion of this Taconian highland region produced sand-and-gravel sediment that was carried by streams and deposited in a shallow Silurian sea that extended from Pennsylvania to just south of Kingston, New York (the northern end of the Shawangunk Moun-

Figure 13-1. Cliffs of the Shawangunk Ridge

tains). This quartzose sediment eventually was transformed into the conglomerate which makes up today's Shawangunk Mountains.

In most places, the Shawangunk Conglomerate layers are gently dipping along several broad anticlines and synclines. These folds are the result of the Acadian Orogeny. The Ordovician shales which are exposed on lower slopes and underlie the conglomerate elsewhere are much more intensely folded. These shales had originally been folded during the earlier Taconian Orogeny, at the end of the Ordovician Period, and were further deformed during the Acadian Orogeny. As a result of the different ways in which they were formed, there is an angular discordance—called an unconformity—between the Silurian and Ordovician strata. The discordance may be seen in several places in the Shawangunks, including the most famous climbing location—the Trapps.

The Shawangunks are an especially fine place to study the effects of Ice Age glaciers. The extremely hard quartzose rock has tended to preserve most of the glacial grooves, striations, and chattermarks that were carved by boulder-laden glacial ice over 10,000 years ago. The glacial markings on rocks in the Shawangunks tend to be more frequent and clearer than those found on bedrock surfaces in the Hudson Highlands and the Catskills.

The mountaintop lakes of the Shawangunks also owe their existence, in part, to the Ice Age glaciers. The lakes are located in bedrock hollows which the overriding ice scoured and possibly deepened. Then, as the glacial ice melted, bouldery debris was deposited across drainage gaps, backing up waters to form the scenic "sky lakes." These lakes are now fed by rainwater falling directly on the lakes and draining off the surrounding higher ground.

History

Arrowheads from 6200 B.C.E. testify to the long relationship between humans and the Shawangunks. For centuries, Native American hunting bands undoubtedly roamed the ridge in search of game to bring to their villages below. In 1677, the New Paltz Patent brought French Huguenots to the area. Six of their original stone houses remain on Huguenot Street in New Paltz. They are open for tours seasonally.

As the valleys became settled, and farming inched up the mountainside, the forest along the ridge began a steady decline. First felled for fuel and lumber, trees were used for a variety of industries that peaked and passed during the nineteenth century. One important industry was charcoal production, which consumed trees voraciously, although the charcoal pits through which trails pass are scarcely recognizable now. Perhaps affecting the area more than any other was the tanning industry, which in the early 1800s began the systematic destruction of the hemlock forests, both here and in the Catskills. All that is left are two notable old-growth stands—the upper Palmaghatt at Minnewaska, and Glen Anna at Mohonk. Using the saplings, which were plentiful in the second growth, the barrel hoop industry followed the demise of the tanning industry, and millions of hoops were manufactured in the Shawangunks.

The thin soil that lies atop the ridge is good for blueberries. Berry-picking flourished as an industry into the 1950s, particularly between Sam's Point and Lake Awosting. The early commercial berry-pickers spent the summer in shacks whose remnants can still be seen near Smiley Road and Lake Maratanza. Remains of a network of trails, marked by cairns and leading to favored picking areas, are still visible as well.

The extremely durable Shawangunk "grit," as the conglomerate characteristic of the Shawangunks was known by local stonecutters, was shaped to create the grinding stones used by corn and flour mills in the nineteenth century. Occasionally, the conglomerate was used for building purposes, as well. The remains of many small quarries can be found throughout the northern Shawangunks.

As the West opened to settlers, many farms in this area were abandoned. Coal, and later oil and gas, reduced the demand for wood fuel, allowing the forests to make a gradual comeback. Coinciding with the start of this trend was a romantic fascination with the picturesque and the spiritual in nature, reflected in the painting, literature, and landscape architecture of the time.

"Wilderness" vacations became fashionable at luxurious resorts such as the Catskill Mountain House.

Enter the Smiley twins, Albert K. and Alfred H. In 1869, Albert acquired the original 310-acre parcel, comprising Mohonk Lake and the surrounding land, from John Stokes, who had run a tavern on the lake. The brothers, who had been teachers, entered the hotel business, and to maintain the character of the property they added adjoining farms and other private holdings to the estate as they became available. They also began to remodel and expand their small inn until, in 1910, it appeared much as it does today.

In 1879, Alfred H. Smiley opened his own hotel, the Lake Minnewaska House, which consisted of two buildings (now removed): Cliff House east of the lake and Wildmere at the north. Both estates expanded until Mohonk reached 7,500 acres, and Minnewaska more than 10,000 acres. Over the years, more than 200 miles of carriage roads and trails were created, all seeking out scenic view spots. As much as any single human factor, the pioneering work of the Smileys and their descendants in road-building techniques, conservation, and land management practices has set the direction and the standard for land stewardship and land conservation in the Shawangunks.

Natural History

Fires have had a prominent role in shaping the character of the Shawangunk forests. A complex interplay of species with environmental factors such as droughty soils, drying winds, summer lightning strikes, and millennia of human use has formed the fire-adapted forest communities of the Shawangunk ridgetop. These communities are characterized by pitch pine and oak forests with shrub layers of scrub oak, mountain laurel, and blueberries. Berry-pickers accentuated the trend by periodically setting fires rather than permitting the berries to be shaded out by competing vegetation. The ashes served as fertilizer, and the crop flourished. Since the most characteristic species of the Shawangunks are those that have benefitted from the history of fires, we can only wonder at the future of this magnificent landscape now that its popularity for recreation makes fire seem so unwelcome in its traditional role.

A particular legacy of fire ecology is the pitch pine plains atop the ridge in the Sam's Point and High Point areas. This forest community is, to the best of our knowledge, unique in the world. Sometimes described as a pygmy forest, the dense treetops in these pine plains are often no more than six to nine feet high, and frequently even lower—in some places less than two feet. Pine barrens and pine plains communities are found elsewhere, but typically they are found in coastal sand plains or glacial outwash plains, not rugged rocky ridgetops.

Once cleared for human uses, the forests returned to the slopes of the Shawangunks, bringing red cedar, birch, white pine, chestnut oak, red oak, striped maple, and red maple. Hemlock has returned to line shady streams and cool north-facing slopes. The second growth has also figured in the resurgence of white-tailed deer, which feed on the low brush not present in a mature forest. Lacking the timber wolf and mountain lion—predators that once roamed the rocky cliffs—deer are more numerous now than ever. Preferring other low bushes to mountain laurel, the increased deer population has indirectly contributed to the flourishing of that beautiful shrub amid the white rocks of the Shawangunks.

Other factors have helped shape the character of today's Shawangunk forests. During the 1910s and 1920s, chestnut blight decimated the American chestnut, previously an extremely important forest tree in many sites. It persists in the form of root sprouts that are sometimes prolific in the Shawangunk forests. Chestnut oak and other oaks have apparently replaced the American chestnut. Although it is fire-resistant, chestnut oak is vulnerable to gypsy moth defoliation, especially during periods of drought. In some mountainside areas, the gypsy moth infestation may result in nearly complete loss of the forest canopy, releasing a dense regrowth of shrubs and young trees from beneath.

The rugged cliff-and-talus areas are home to several distinctive species of wildlife, including the five-lined skink (a lizard), fisher (a member of the weasel family), and porcupine. After decades of absence, the fisher was reintroduced in the 1970s, and is a natural predator of porcupines. The Eastern woodrat, a dignified cousin to the urban species, disappeared from talus areas in the 1970s. A study in the 1990s found that reintroduced woodrats suffered from a debilitating parasite caught from raccoons.

In the mid-1970s, attempts were made to reintroduce the peregrine falcon to the cliffs of the Shawangunks, one of the last natural nesting places in the eastern United States. These efforts were unsuccessful at the time. Since then, however, the urban cliffs and canyons of New York City's bridges and skyscrapers have attracted a growing population of these majestic birds. Finally, in the late 1990s, a pair of peregrine falcons returned to the Shawangunks and successfully fledged young. To protect the habitat of these endangered birds, certain cliff areas may be closed to hikers during the spring and early summer nesting season.

Other species are becoming more common in the area, including the raven, coyote, and black bear, while still others, notably songbirds, appear to be in decline. Researchers at the Mohonk Preserve monitor many species. Detailed records begun by members of the Smiley family extend back to the 1920s. Checklists and additional information on wildlife and plants of the Shawangunk Mountains are available from the Mohonk Preserve, P.O. Box 715, New Paltz, NY 12561; (845) 255-0919; www.mohonkpreserve.org.

MOHONK PRESERVE

The Mohonk Preserve is New York State's largest non-profit privately owned nature sanctuary. Its 6,400 acres extend for nearly eight miles along the Shawangunk ridges, from Bonticou Crag to Millbrook Mountain. The original Mohonk estate was assembled by the many purchases of Albert K. Smiley and his descendants during the nineteenth and early twentieth centuries. The Mountain House itself and the lands immediately surrounding it remain in the ownership of the Smiley family, but much of the outlying land has been conveyed to the Mohonk Preserve, a non-profit organization (originally organized as the Mohonk Trust in 1963). Hiking on preserve lands is by day-use (or annual) permit, for which a fee is charged. Mohonk Preserve permits, which may be obtained at the visitor center or from rangers on patrol, also allow one to hike on Mohonk Mountain House lands.

To reach the Trapps Gateway Visitors Center of the Mohonk Preserve, take the New York State Thruway to Exit 18 and proceed west on NY 299 through the Village of New Paltz. Continue on NY 299 until it ends at US 44/ NY 55, at the base of the mountain. Turn right onto US 44/NY 55 and continue for 0.2 mile to the driveway leading into the visitors center on the right. The visitors center, built in 1998, contains exhibits on the unique geology, flora, and fauna of the Shawangunks. The larger Wawarsing parking area is 0.1 mile farther along US 44/NY 55, just before the "hairpin turn." The yellow-blazed East Connector Trail—an artfully constructed stairway of Shawangunk conglomerate—connects the visitors center and the Wawarsing parking area with Undercliff Road, providing access to hiking and climbing routes above. The trails may also be accessed from the West Trapps parking area, about 0.3 mile beyond the Trapps Bridge overpass on US 44/NY 55, and from a parking area on Clove Road, about a mile north of US 44/NY 55. Parking along the highway shoulder is no longer permitted.

The northern section of the Mohonk Preserve may be accessed from the Spring Farm parking area on Upper 27 Knolls Road. To reach this parking area, take NY 299 west through the Village of New Paltz. Immediately after crossing the bridge over the Wallkill River, turn right onto Mountain Rest Road. Continue on Mountain Rest Road for 0.8 mile beyond the entrance to the Mohonk Mountain House, and turn right onto Upper 27 Knolls Road.

On spring and fall weekends, parking areas at the Mohonk Preserve may fill to capacity early in the day. Thus, hikers should plan on alternate destinations during these busy periods. Maps and trail guides, as well as other information, may be obtained by contacting the Mohonk Preserve, P.O. Box 715, New Paltz, NY 12561; (845) 255-0919; www.mohonkpreserve.org.

Trails in the Mohonk Preserve

Walking ranges from easy, scenic strolls on carriage roads to rough scrambles over boulders, through crevasses, and across open ledges. Only a brief indication of the possibilities can be made here; hikers are encouraged to go, maps in hand, and make their own discoveries.

Bonticou Crag *Length: 1.8 miles Blazes: red, blue, yellow*
The top of Bonticou (1,194 feet) is a far more rugged and dramatic viewpoint than its modest height would suggest. *Bontecou* is from the Dutch for "spotted cow." The reason for the name is obscure and subject to dispute, but may refer to the mottled appearance of its lichen-covered white conglomerate cliffs. The hike to its summit passes through an interesting variety of terrain that includes upland woods, boulders, rocky ridgetop pine barrens, and a craggy cliff-top summit.

The hike to Bonticou Crag begins at the Spring Farm parking area on Upper 27 Knolls Road, off Mountain Rest Road. The shortest route is the Crag Trail (red), which begins across the road from the parking area. At first, the Crag Trail parallels Spring Farm Road, running jointly with the Table Rocks Trail (blue), but the two trails soon split, with the Crag Trail turning right,

Figure 13-2. Bonticou Crag

uphill. It climbs through several meadows and crosses, in quick succession, Cedar Drive and Spring Farm Road. The trail continues to climb through a hardwood forest until it ends, at 1.0 mile, at the intersection of Cedar Drive and Bonticou Road. Here the hiker should not take the hard left (which is the other side of the Cedar Drive loop) but rather the larger-angled left, which is Bonticou Road. Soon, the crest of Bonticou Crag appears on the left, and the Bonticou Ascent Path (yellow) leaves to the left. Turn left on this trail, which almost immediately intersects the Northeast Trail (blue).

Here the hiker has two options. The shortest route to the top of Bonticou Crag is to continue ahead on the Bonticou Ascent Path, which becomes a rock scramble that requires agility, confidence, and the use of hands as well as feet. For a longer but much easier ascent, turn left onto the Northeast Trail, which proceeds north, along the base of the boulder field. After about a quarter of a mile, the Cedar Trail (red) leaves to the left, and the Northeast Trail swings to the right and continues uphill through rocky woods. At the top of a short, steep section, the opposite end of the Bonticou Ascent Path appears on the right. Turn right on this yellow-blazed trail, which gradually ascends the ridge of Bonticou Crag, with views over the Catskills to the north. The route of the blue-blazed Northeast Trail may be visible along the base of the cliffs and boulders below to the right. At 1.8 miles, the yellow-blazed trail reaches the dramatic summit of Bonticou Crag, with its broad expanses of white conglomerate rock sparsely set with bonsai-shaped pitch pines. There are views northwest to the Catskills, northeast to Stissing Mountain in Dutchess County, and southeast to the Hudson Highlands.

For an alternative, slightly longer, return route, take the Bonticou Ascent Path north to the Northeast Trail (blue). Turn left onto the Northeast Trail, then bear right in a short distance onto the Cedar Trail. Follow the Cedar Trail to the Table Rocks Trail (blue), then turn left on the Table Rocks Trail, which leads back to the Spring Farm parking area.

Millbrook Ridge Trail
Length: 3.0 miles Blaze: light blue

The Millbrook Ridge Trail, at the southern end of Mohonk Preserve, is one of the loftiest in the Shawangunks, skirting along the crest atop some of the Shawangunks' tallest cliffs: the Near Trapps, Bayards, and Millbrook Mountain. The trail starts on the Trapps carriage road, 100 yards west of the Trapps Bridge over US 44/NY 55, accessible from the West Trapps parking area. Blue blazes on the left side of the road mark the beginning of a trail ascending steep rocky slabs, and framed by twisted pitch pines. Fine examples of glacial scratches, polishing, and chattermarks are evident on the smooth conglomerate slabs as the trail ascends.

The trail quickly crests the ridge at a north-facing viewpoint with a dramatic 270° panorama, known locally as the Hawk Watch. During the autumn, this airy spot is often occupied by birders monitoring the southward migration of hawks along the ridge. During the peak of migration, hundreds of hawks of various species may be seen from here in a day, riding the updrafts caused by strong winds deflected over the ridge. The tilted layer-cake structure of the white conglomerate is clearly revealed on the Trapps cliff directly across the highway gap to the northeast. The Dickie Barre cliffs are visible to the west, with the Catskills beyond to the north, and the Wallkill Valley sweeps away below to the east. The trail turns right, and soon emerges not far from the edge of the cliff, which it parallels for much of its way, occasionally offering views across the Wallkill Valley. Hikers should stay on the trail and exercise extreme caution; the many footpaths that trend left toward the cliff edge lead to the tops of rock climbs. *Do not attempt to follow them.*

At 0.8 mile, a small saddle known as Smedes Cove marks the division between the Near Trapps and the Bayards. At this point, the Bayards Path (red) branches right to return to Trapps Road. The blue trail continues, turning left to climb up a short ledge, soon passing a couple of cairns, and winding along the edges of conglomerate slabs. Views to the east show the wetlands of the Marakill.

Approaching the south end of the Bayards, glimpses of Millbrook Mountain become more frequent through the treetops ahead, until an opening atop a rounded conglomerate slab suddenly reveals a full view of Millbrook's sheer cliff and wave-shaped profile. The trail turns right to step down from the slab and traverse a second, wider saddle amid dense mountain laurel, soon passing a second red-blazed trail on the right, at 1.8 miles. This is a handy bail-out to the Coxing Trail, which provides an alternate return route.

From here, the trail wanders briefly among open slabs and sparse oak woods, until crossing an intermittent stream amid boulders and shady hemlocks. The trail then steps up onto boulders, and soon climbs out of the woods along an airy bedrock ridge, with the bedding planes of the conglomerate turned nearly vertical in places. The Millbrook cliff drops away to the left, with commanding views. From this elevated perspective, the view northeastward along the ridge toward the Sky Top tower clearly shows the structure of the Shawangunks: a wave-shaped serpentine ridge with sheer white cliffs along its southeastern flank.

The trail weaves steadily uphill among rock outcrops and pitch pines to terminate at a junction with red trails at the top of Millbrook Mountain, at 2.9 miles. Within a few steps to the left, following red blazes, the trail crosses into the Minnewaska State Park Preserve and gains a dramatic 360° view.

The return may be by the same route. An alternative begins along the Millbrook Mountain Trail, the red-blazed right fork of the junction. This heads downhill to the north, among slabs and pine barrens, reaching a junction with the Coxing Trail (blue) on the right at 0.2 mile. Turn right to follow the blue trail gradually downhill, first among open slabs, then into sparse oak forests, and finally into deep, moist woods. Rock rows indicate earlier agrarian use of this area; after crossing a wet forest area, the trail follows the route of an old farm road. The junction with the red-blazed cutoff trail, branching right, is at 1.3 miles. The Coxing Trail terminates on Trapps Road at 2.0 miles. A right turn along the carriage road leads back to Trapps Bridge.

Overcliff and Undercliff Roads   *Length: 5.4 miles Signs: directional only*
This easy and level walk on carriage roads loops around the dramatic scarp of
the Trapps cliffs, the hub of the southern preserve. Built around 1903, with the
aid of few machines, Undercliff Road is especially remarkable, considering that
it was built solely to capture the scenic panoramas of the Wallkill Valley and
the cliff above. Overcliff Road, which completes the circuit hike, also completes the views toward the remaining compass points, including Coxing Clove,
Rondout Valley, and Catskill Mountains.

The hike begins from the West Trapps parking area on US 44/NY 55. The
footpath from the upper end of the parking area proceeds uphill to the Trapps

JACK FAGAN

Figure 13-3. Along Undercliff Road

Bridge, passes portable
outhouses, and continues
up rustic stairs to the level
of the carriage road. A left
onto the carriage road
brings the hiker in a few
yards to a carriage road
intersection, with a large,
flat-topped boulder in its
center. The route turns
left again here, onto
Overcliff Road. Although
the name of Overcliff is

misleading (it is not along the top of a cliff), it nonetheless offers sustained
panoramic views of the Dickie Barre cliffs, the Rondout Valley, and the Catskill
Mountains as it weaves between oak woods, open slabs, and pitch pines. At
2.2 miles, Overcliff Road turns right to meander through a small pass and
descend along the face of a low bluff. Overcliff Road continues for another 0.1
mile, bearing right to reach a junction of carriage roads at Rhododendron Bridge
at 2.5 miles. At this point, the loop turns right onto Undercliff Road. At 3.3
miles, Undercliff Road makes an S turn, revealing the broad face of the Trapps
that will loom above on the right until the carriage road again reaches the
Trapps Bridge. Along the way, the carriage road traverses open talus, with wide
views across the Wallkill Valley. Rock climbers become more prevalent on the
carriage road as well as on the rocks above, up to the Uberfall, their traditional
congregating place on the carriage road, marked by a kiosk, bulletin board,
first aid box, and usually a helpful ranger on patrol.

MOHONK MOUNTAIN HOUSE

The Mohonk Mountain House, together with the landscape surrounding it, was designated a National Historic Landmark in 1986. Its 2,200-acre grounds, extending from Copes Lookout on the south to the Mountain Rest Golf Course on the north, feature miles of trails and carriageways ideally suited for hiking. Mohonk's hallmark is the rustic gazebo (known locally as a summerhouse) situated atop a cliff or amid boulders to capture an artful setting or view. With the seasons of mountain laurel bloom and autumn foliage seeming to draw the most visitors, other times of the year are best for quiet contemplation of Mohonk's rugged and varied scenery.

Day visitor passes, parking, maps, and information are available at the gatehouse. A limited number of day visitor passes is sold each day. The day pass entitles the bearer to hike the carriageways, trails, and paths, and to tour the grounds, and is also honored on the adjoining Mohonk Preserve lands. Day visitors are not permitted to enter the Mountain House or to use the lake and its facilities unless purchasing a meal.

In winter, when trails are open for skiing, hiking is not permitted. On busy spring and fall weekends, parking areas may fill up by mid-morning, and the

Figure 13-4. Mohonk Mountain House

267

gate closes. To find out whether Mountain House trails are open for hiking or skiing or filled to capacity and closed, call (845) 255-1000. Hikers should plan on alternate destinations during these busy periods.

Access to the Mohonk Mountain House itself is reserved for overnight guests and guests who purchase a meal there. The hiker choosing one of these options may drive up the mountain to the Mountain House, and start the walk there, also earning the opportunity to enjoy the distinctive character of the hotel, as well as certain of its special programs. Reservations for meals are required, and should be made in advance by calling the dining room at (845) 256-2056. One overnight program of particular note is the "Hiker's Holiday" package offered each May. Information about reservations for overnight stays may be obtained by calling (800) 772-6646.

To reach the Mohonk Mountain House, leave the New York State Thruway at Exit 18. Turn left onto NY 299 and follow Main Street through the Village of New Paltz. Immediately after crossing the bridge over the Wallkill River, turn right at the MOHONK sign. After 0.25 mile, bear left at the fork and continue up Mountain Rest Road to the Mohonk Mountain House gate at the crest of the ridge.

For more information, contact the Mohonk Mountain House, 100 Mountain Rest Road, New Paltz, NY 12561; (845)255-1000; www.mohonk.com.

Trails at Mohonk Mountain House

The center of activity for day users is the Picnic Lodge Day Visitor Center, where rest rooms, snacks, and additional information are available in season. On some weekends, a shuttle bus may be available for a fee. The walk to Picnic Lodge begins on the Huguenot Trail, at the back of the parking lot west of the gatehouse. The 1.7-mile route includes both trails and carriage roads, and is marked by signs. Beginning at the parking area, the Huguenot Trail turns right onto Whitney Road at 0.3 mile, follows this road gradually downhill, and then turns left onto North Lookout Road at 0.5 mile. The route then follows North Lookout Road as it loops around, and turns left onto a trail leading uphill, marked by a sign to Picnic Lodge.

At Mohonk Mountain House, the term "carriageway" that is more familiar to state park visitors is replaced with the historic term "carriage road." They are the same, but hikers should be aware that Mohonk maps and directional signs name carriage roads as "Road" or "Drive." Carriage roads are

Figure 13-5. Along Humpty Dumpty Road, looking up at a summerhouse on Eagle Cliff

soft-surfaced, closed to motorized use except for patrol and maintenance, and offer very favorable hiking. *Please note:* The Mountain House area is densely laced with trails and carriage roads, so constant attention to trail signs and landmarks is required, and a good map is essential.

Additional walks and guidelines for visitors are described in maps and brochures provided with the Mohonk day-use pass. More ambitious hikes extend onto Mohonk Preserve lands and include the Trapps (Undercliff and Overcliff roads), Duck Pond Trail, and Plateau Path. Notable hikes on rough paths that involve rock scrambles, agility, and the use of hands as well as feet include Arching Rocks Path, Labyrinth Path, and Rock Rift Path.

Eagle Cliff Road *Length: 1.7 miles Signs: directional only*
The Eagle Cliff carriage road is a loop road that offers a great variety of scenery in a relatively short and easy walk. The walk is beautiful in either direction, but the tradition is to walk up the western side, beginning by the tennis courts, and return along the bluff overlooking the lake.

Humpty Dumpty Road *Length: 1.9 miles Signs: directional only*
This easy carriage road walk traverses the Humpty Dumpty talus, a slide rock area nearly 900 feet in height, extending from Eagle Cliff to Rhododendron Swamp. The sparse trees in the talus are among the oldest in the Shawangunks, dating from pre-colonial times. From the west side of the Mountain House, the route proceeds along Copes Lookout Road, then turns left on Humpty Dumpty

JACK FAGAN

Figure 13-6. The Crevice

Road. The hike returns to the Mountain House via Short Woodland Drive and Lake Shore Road, making a loop of 1.9 miles.

Labyrinth Path

Length: 0.5 mile Blaze: red

The route through the talus at the base of the Sky Top cliff is a rough path known as the Labyrinth. Don't let the brief length of this trail fool you! The most rugged way to Sky Top, it winds through narrow defiles, scrambles over boulders, and climbs a rustic ladder, requiring agility and the use of hands as well as feet. From the Mountain House, Lake Shore Road heads south for 0.1 mile to the sign for Labyrinth Path on the left. The hiker is quickly immersed in a tumble of boulders that create a kind of inner sanctum of the Shawangunks. At 0.4 mile, the exhilarated hiker reaches the Crevice, formed by a massive block of con-glomerate that since glacial times has separated from the main body of Sky Top cliff by several feet. A system of rustic ladders climbs through it to join Sky Top Road, which forms a loop at the top. The Crevice is a tight squeeze in places. Travel light, or be prepared to pass your pack separately. (Those electing not to climb the Crevice may quickly descend from the talus on a red-blazed trail to Spring Path and Lake Shore Road, which returns to the Mountain House.) Once on Sky Top Road, hikers reach the tower by turning left toward Sky Top

Path, reached in 0.1 mile. The return trip to the Mountain House is via Sky Top Path.

Sky Top Path   *Length: 0.4 mile Signs: directional only*
One of the most popular objectives for hikers at Mohonk is Sky Top, a prominent cliff whose stone tower, the Albert K. Smiley Memorial Tower, is easily visible from as far as the New York State Thruway. From the Mohonk Mountain House, hikers should head east, past the golf putting green, to Sky Top Path (marked by a sign). The path passes the Council House and Conference Center building, climbing and crossing a loop of a carriage road, Sky Top Road, at 0.3 mile. Another loop of the road is reached at the tower.

A winding stairway inside the tower leads to the observation deck. The views of the nearby valleys and distant mountains from there are well worth the climb. On a clear day, parts of six states are visible. The gentler Sky Top Road and the Reservoir Path may be combined for an alternate return route.

Sky Top Road   *Length: 1.5 miles Signs: directional only*
This especially leisurely and indirect carriage road loop to Sky Top is attractive during mountain laurel bloom. From the Picnic Lodge, Bruin Path switchbacks briefly uphill to Huguenot Drive atop a low bluff at Garden Overlook. From the Mountain House, hikers can depart directly on the Huguenot Drive carriage road. From Garden Overlook, it's an 0.1-mile walk north on Huguenot Drive to the intersection with Sky Top Road.

The pond along the way often proves productive for watchers of frogs, turtles, birds, and dragonflies. Originally built as a reservoir for the hotel, it now serves as a home for many animals. (Today's drinking water supply uses a sanitary underground tank nearby.) A second reservoir at the base of the Sky Top tower still provides a supply of water for the hotel's sprinkler system. These mountaintop reservoirs obviated the need for an unsightly water tower at Mohonk, leaving the stone tower as a solitary landmark. The carriage road forks at the lower pond to form a loop to the tower. For the uphill climb, hikers should take the right fork, which is more direct, reaching Sky Top tower at 1.5 miles. For the return trip, hikers should follow the other leg of the Sky Top Road loop back to the pond, from which they can return to the Mountain House or Picnic Lodge the way they came.

MINNEWASKA STATE PARK PRESERVE

The 11,630-acre Minnewaska State Park Preserve was once the site of two mountaintop hotels. Many miles of scenic trails and historic carriageways wind their way around Lake Minnewaska and Lake Awosting and beyond. The original section of the park, which centered on Lake Awosting, was created in 1971 by the State of New York and The Nature Conservancy. The 1,200-acre section that includes Lake Minnewaska was added in 1987, at the conclusion of a long and spirited legal battle over the proposed development of the site by the Marriott Corporation that might have resulted in the construction of a 450-room hotel and conference center, 300 condominiums, and an 18-hole golf course on the site. A broad coalition of conservation groups, led by the local Friends of the Shawangunks and including the New York-New Jersey Trail Conference, was successful in demonstrating that the site could not support the proposed development, and in establishing the area as a premier state park preserve.

The Shawangunk "sky lakes" of Lake Minnewaska and Lake Awosting are the scenic centerpieces of the park preserve, from which most other scenic attractions can be reached. These lakes are well known for the exceptional clarity of their water and their aquamarine color. Both lakes are set into white conglomerate cliffs and encircled with carriageways that provide ready access to many views. The numerous scenic overlooks in the park are destinations by themselves, with varied and sweeping views of the lakes, cliffs, expanses of pine barrens, and valleys below. They include Hamilton Point, Castle Point, Gertrude's Nose, Millbrook Mountain, Murray Hill, Margaret Cliff, Beacon Hill, and the High Peters Kill cliffs. Many are accessible by both trail and carriageway.

For more information, contact Minnewaska State Park Preserve, P.O. Box 893, New Paltz, NY 12561; (845) 255-0752; www.nysparks.com.

Trails in Minnewaska State Park Preserve

In addition to providing easy access to scenic areas, the old carriageways that crisscross Minnewaska provide essential linkages. A number of the trails described below begin with a carriageway walk of up to three miles. To provide their guests with access to the most scenic spots, the Minnewaska hotels built and maintained over 50 miles of roads on which only horse-drawn vehicles were permitted. In so doing, they left a rich legacy to us all. The carriages are gone, but hiking, horseback riding, cross-country skiing, and bicycling are permitted. In recent years, the carriageways have become the domain of mountain bicyclists in the warmer seasons and of footprint-sensitive cross-country skiers when there is snow. Some abandoned carriageways are partially overgrown, while others are well maintained and sustain heavy use.

Minnewaska contains other trails not described below and carriageways that are not maintained as trails. The most notable of the latter are the Awosting Falls Carriageway, which offers a brief and popular walk to the waterfall; the Old Smiley Road, a Palisades Interstate Park Commission-owned linkage from Lake Awosting to the base of the ridge at Ellenville; and Stony Kill Carriageway, which links Lake Awosting to Stony Kill Falls.

Beacon Hill Trail   *Length: 0.8 mile Blaze: yellow*
The Beacon Hill Trail is one of the most scenic short hikes in the immediate area of Lake Minnewaska. It begins at the end of the Beacon Hill Carriageway, 0.7 mile from the Lake Minnewaska parking area. From the parking area, hikers can reach the path by walking back down the paved entrance road, heading northward for approximately 0.1 mile, and watching on the right for the Beacon Hill Carriageway marker (orange with a black B). A right turn onto the carriageway to its end at 0.6 mile leads to views northward over the High Peters Kill cliffs and Dickie Barre.

The Beacon Hill Trail begins at the end of the orange-blazed carriageway, where it bears right and enters the woods. The trail descends briefly, then climbs gradually, soon reaching (at 0.3 mile) an opening atop a rock ledge with views to the left, extending across the Coxing Clove. The trail leads generally uphill, winding among low blueberries, pitch pines, woodlands, and rock slabs. Landmarks visible along the way include Dickie Barre, the Sky Top tower, and the backsides of the Trapps and Millbrook Mountain, with the Village of New Paltz visible beyond. The trail turns right to re-enter the woods, and soon turns left and drops down to cross a small stream at 0.7 mile. Shortly before reaching its end, the trail winds around a large boulder on the left where sharp eyes will spy the remains of two metal braces that once anchored one of Minnewaska's wooden gazebos, built to capture the view. The Beacon Hill Trail ends at an open field that once was the ballfield of the Minnewaska mountain houses. The parking area is reached by crossing the field and turning right on the red-blazed carriageway or turning left for a longer walk around Lake Minnewaska.

Blueberry Run Trail *Length: 2.2 miles Blaze: blue*

The Blueberry Run Trail begins at the crest of Castle Point, where the Long Path joins the Castle Point Carriageway, 3.2 miles from the Lake Minnewaska parking lot. The trail heads north, away from the cliff edge, along a scenic upland route, with views of the Catskills in the distance. It descends to cross two carriageways and the Peters Kill, and it ends on the Long Path, 3.1 miles from the Jenny Lane parking area.

At Castle Point, blue blazes across the carriageway from the overlook mark the start of the Blueberry Run Trail. After climbing a low conglomerate bluff, the trail begins a long, gradual descent. It crosses a small stream at 1.0 mile, just before an intersection with a yellow trail that branches to the left, leading to the Upper Awosting Carriageway. It then turns sharply right and traverses dense mountain laurel, beautiful around early June when it is usually in bloom. Sounds from the nearby carriageway may be audible to the left. The trail crosses another small stream and passes beneath a power line at 1.3 miles.

After crossing the Upper Awosting Carriageway at 1.7 miles, the Blueberry Run Trail heads downhill. Soon, the Mossy Glen Trail (yellow) leaves to the right, and the Blueberry Run Trail crosses the Peters Kill on a footbridge. A short climb up then brings the trail to the Peters Kill or Lower Awosting Carriageway at 2.0 miles. Heading directly across the carriageway, the trail remains level for a short distance and crosses a small stream before making a brief ascent. The Blueberry Run Trail ends at a junction with the Long Path, between Jenny Lane and Lake Awosting, at 2.2 miles. Hikers may continue in either direction on the Long Path. To return to Lake Minnewaska, hikers can retrace their steps either to the Mossy Glen Trail or to the Upper Awosting Carriageway. A left turn on the Mossy Glen Trail leads to the Awosting parking area on US 44/NY 55; turning left on the Upper Awosting Carriageway returns the hiker to Lake Minnewaska.

Castle Point Carriageway *Length: 4.3 miles Blaze: blue*

The Castle Point Carriageway is the highest within the Minnewaska State Park Preserve, skirting along the tops of the series of bluffs that define the western rim of the Palmaghatt Ravine, with lofty outward views. It is popular with mountain bicyclists. The Castle Point Carriageway begins from Lake Shore Drive on the west side of Lake Minnewaska, 0.4 mile from the parking area. It departs westward, soon crossing a grassy hilltop area (a former golf course), with sweeping views northward to the Catskills. The route then enters a sparse oak-and-pine forest that is characteristic of the ridge, and it turns generally southward. At 0.7 mile, a carriageway ascends to join from the left, connecting to the Hamilton Point Carriageway, below. Views open to the southeast, across the Palmaghatt Ravine and the Wallkill Valley beyond. The first of the major views, at 1.0 mile, is over Kempton Ledge.

The carriageway gradually ascends in a westerly direction, passing beneath a power line at 1.8 miles, then meandering through miniature cliffs known as the Castles, with frequent vistas. At 3.2 miles, the carriageway crests the top of the escarpment at Castle Point. Here, at an elevation of 2,200 feet, is a beautiful area where the hiker may pause for lunch or just to enjoy the panorama. Extensive flat ledges offer nearly 360° views of the immediate area. On clear days, Schunemunk, Black Rock Forest, and Storm King may be seen to the south, while the Catskills dominate the view to the north. Closer by are views of Lake Awosting, Margaret Cliff, Murray Hill, Sam's Point, and the Wallkill Valley. The Long Path ascends the bluff from the Hamilton Point Carriageway below, and it follows the top of the bluff downhill for a short distance.

From Castle Point, the carriageway winds downhill and around a hairpin turn where the Long Path departs to the right, and it soon passes beneath the dramatic cliffs of Battlement Terrace that overhang the carriageway. At 4.3 miles, the Castle Point Carriageway ends at the Hamilton Point Carriageway (yellow), which can be used as an alternate return route.

Gertrude's Nose Trail
Length: 3.4 miles Blaze: red

The Gertrude's Nose Trail begins on Millbrook Drive, at a point 2.1 miles from the parking area at Lake Minnewaska. From the parking area, the route passes along the right (west) side of the lake, following the red-blazed Lake Shore Drive until Millbrook Drive (yellow) forks to the right near the end of the lake, at 0.7 mile. A right turn onto Millbrook Drive leads to the Gertrude's Nose Trail. At 1.0 mile, the carriageway to Hamilton Point and Castle Point forks off to the right, marking the inconspicuous beginning of the Palmaghatt Ravine. Millbrook Drive stays left and eventually skirts along the eastern rim of the ravine. A large boulder, known as Patterson's Pellet, is perched on the brink of the cliff on the right side of the carriageway at 1.6 miles. From here, the Palmaghatt Ravine is visible as a narrow, cliff-lined gorge that widens and deepens to the southwest. A small stream, the Palmaghatt Kill, flows through the bogs and forests at its bottom. Several hundred yards farther on, at 2.1 miles, a low cairn with red blazes along the right side of the carriageway marks the

JACK FAGAN

Figure 13-7. Along the Gertrude's Nose Trail

beginning of the Gertrude's Nose Trail.

Departing the carriageway into pitch pine woods, the trail soon comes to an opening on the right, where an exposed bedrock outcrop affords views across the Palmaghatt Ravine toward the Hamilton Point and Castle Point carriageways on the opposite rim. Continuing through the woods, the trail soon makes an abrupt descent that ends in a shady hemlock stand at the base of the slope. The trail leaves the stand to pass under a power line at 0.5 mile, where it crosses a small stream. A few steps up a low rock ledge brings the trail to a bedrock slab that is open to the top of a low cliff on the right. From here, the trail climbs gradually, following the top of a series of broad, open conglomerate ledges of increasing height that form the rim of the Palmaghatt Ravine. The trail weaves in and out along the edge of the pine barrens forest and the open slabs.

At Gertrude's Nose, reached at 1.3 miles, one stands atop the prow-shaped apex of the cliffs, with views across the Palmaghatt Ravine to Hamilton Point and Castle Point, and southward across the Wallkill Valley. Boulders left by the glaciers are strewn across the open expanses of bedrock. The trail turns left, continuing along the cliff top, with views of the Wallkill Valley. At 2.3 miles, the trail makes a gradual descent and passes beneath the power line once again.

It then makes a short, steep climb to meander through open slabs and scrubby pitch pines on the southwest shoulder of Millbrook Mountain. Eventually, Millbrook Drive (yellow) approaches the trail from the left and runs parallel until both terminate at a viewpoint at the summit of Millbrook Mountain (3.4 miles). The carriageway ends at a small turnaround circle. At the trail junction near the circle, blue blazes mark the terminus of the Mohonk Preserve's Millbrook Ridge Trail to Trapps Bridge, and red blazes heading downslope to the north mark the terminus of the Millbrook Mountain Trail to Lake Minnewaska. The 3.2-mile Millbrook Drive (yellow) or the 1.2-mile Millbrook Mountain Trail (red) lead back to Lake Minnewaska.

Hamilton Point Carriageway   *Length: 4.0 miles Blaze: yellow with black* H
The Hamilton Point Carriageway follows the northern rim of the Palmaghatt Ravine, an immense V-shaped ravine whose side walls consist of a double row of high, vertical cliffs. This is one of the most scenic routes between Lake Minnewaska and Lake Awosting. From the Lake Minnewaska parking area, Lake Shore Drive (red) proceeds for 0.7 mile to the south end of the lake, where a yellow-blazed carriageway forks right and a sign indicates the way to Millbrook Mountain and Hamilton Point. The yellow-blazed carriageway leads to Palmaghatt Junction, at 1.0 mile, where Millbrook Drive (also blazed yellow) leaves to the left. The Hamilton Point Carriageway continues ahead and soon reaches another junction, with the fork ascending to the right leading to the Castle Point Carriageway, above. This time, hikers take the left fork (yellow-blazed), continuing into a deep hemlock forest. The carriageway soon emerges from deep woods, and views begin to open across the Palmaghatt Ravine. Patterson's Pellet, a large white glacial erratic, can be seen perched on top of the opposite wall. The carriageway begins to skirt the top of the cliffs, with views across the ravine. The upper section of the ravine visible from here supports a growth of large hemlock trees, which appear to have survived the tanning industry's quest for hemlock bark. The lower, southwestern part of the Palmaghatt is private land and is closed to hikers, but the cliffs and ravine northeast of the power line are within the park preserve.

At 2.2 miles, a power line swath is carved across the ravine, and wires, oddly out of place here, pass overhead. After skirting the tops of the cliffs, the carriageway swings away from the cliffs and passes through a stand of small trees, until it emerges near Hamilton Point at 3.4 miles. Here, at an elevation of 2,020 feet, hikers get a panoramic view of Gertrude's Nose visible above to the

JACK FAGAN

Figure 13-8. Along the Hamilton Point Carriageway

southeast, the Wallkill Valley to the south, and Margaret Cliff and Murray Hill to the west. Leaving Hamilton Point, the road makes a sharp bend to the north. Soon, the Long Path joins the carriageway for a short distance as it proceeds from Castle Point above on the right to Margaret Cliff on the left. The Castle Point Carriageway (blue) forks right at 3.8 miles, and the Hamilton Point Carriageway ends at an intersection with the Lower Awosting Carriageway (black) half a mile later.

High Peters Kill Trail

Length: 3.5 miles Blaze: blue

The High Peters Kill Trail is a scenic up-and-down route that starts near the Peters Kill in Minnewaska State Park Preserve and ends at the Coxing Kill in the Mohonk Preserve. Of the trails described here, it is the only one north of

US 44/NY 55, in a part of the park that is notably free of carriageways.

The trail starts at the end of the Lower Awosting parking area that is nearest the highway. It immediately crosses US 44/NY 55 and heads into the woods, bearing right. The woods here are mostly oak and maple, with a healthy undergrowth of mountain laurel. The trail soon reaches the ridge line, with views of the highway below on the right. After passing through a split rock, the views open up, revealing the low cliffs of Dickie Barre ahead on the right. From here, the path begins a gradual descent along the tops of the Peters Kill cliffs, amid sustained outward views. The cleared areas visible on the slopes below to the east are the remains of the ski area once operated by the Minnewaska resort. Along the way, the cliffs to the right gradually diminish in stature, giving way to rocky slopes. At 1.6 miles, the trail steepens downhill and bears right to approach the Peters Kill. After crossing a set of two bridges over the Peters Kill at 1.7 miles, a junction is reached with the Low Peters Kill Trail (red). This trail, which leaves to the right, follows along the east bank of the Peters Kill, then loops back to end at a parking area on the north side of US 44/NY 55. The High Peters Kill Trail now begins to ascend the northwest slope of the rounded section of ridge known as Dickie Barre.

Once on top of Dickie Barre, at 2.1 miles, views of the Catskills open up on the left. The trail then leads left and passes large rocks on the right, soon leveling off for a short distance before beginning a steep descent, following a route known in the 1800s as the "Dug Way." It was a road built or dug to transport millstones quarried atop Dickie Barre down to the Coxing Clove, and thence to High Falls or Alligerville, for shipment on the Delaware and Hudson Canal. Millstones were dragged behind oxen or draft horses on a flat wooden sledge called a stone boat.

At the base of the Dug Way, the trail crosses onto the Mohonk Preserve, where a separate fee is required for day use. Hikers who prefer to remain entirely on state park land may return by the same route with full, open views. Otherwise, hikers can continue downhill onto the lands of the Mohonk Preserve. At 3.3 miles, the High Peters Kill Trail turns right, onto a woods road, at an opening in an old stone wall. To the left, the road, known as the King's Lane, is blazed yellow and leads uphill to a set of cliffs and crevices called the Lost City—a favorite spot for rock climbers. The High Peters Kill Trail ends at the Coxing Kill parking area on Clove Road, about one mile north of US 44/NY 55.

Hikers who choose to use Mohonk Preserve lands should prepare in advance by purchasing a day pass at the Mohonk Preserve Trapps Gateway Visitors Center on US 44/NY 55. This day pass also enables hikers to spot a car at the Coxing Kill parking area.

Long Path (Jenny Lane to Mud Pond)   *Length: 9.5 miles Blaze: aqua*
Rather than taking a direct route across Minnewaska State Park Preserve, the Long Path meanders through the park on a winding course, passing ridge-top viewpoints and waterfalls, and scrambling up and down rocky cliffs. Since it crosses many of the park's trails and carriageways, the Long Path can be combined with them to make a variety of loop hikes.

The Jenny Lane parking area is a convenient place to begin a hike on the Long Path in Minnewaska. Jenny Lane is an obscure dirt road which leads north from US 44/NY55, 1.2 miles west of the entrance to Minnewaska State Park Preserve. To reach the parking area, turn right onto Jenny Lane and then right again in a short distance.

The Long Path turns west just before the parking area and soon crosses US 44/NY 55. After re-entering the woods, it crosses the Sanders Kill, which may be flooded or completely dry, depending on the season. The trail ascends gradually, shaded for the most part by stunted hardwoods whose roots encounter only a thin layer of soil, with solid rock just below. In June, the abundant clusters of mountain laurel provide a spectacular display.

At 2.2 miles, the Blueberry Run Trail (blue) leaves to the left. Soon, several open ledges provide views to the south over Litchfield Ledge, Huntington Ravine, the Peters Kill, and the Lower Awosting Carriageway. Then, at 2.6 miles, the Long Path reaches a power line, where it briefly jogs to the right, then re-enters the woods. The trail turns right onto the Lower Awosting Carriageway at 3.3 miles, crossing an earthen causeway over Fly Brook, the outlet of Mud Pond. A side trip to Lake Awosting is possible by continuing for half a mile on the Lower Awosting Carriageway.

After re-entering the woods to the left, the Long Path ascends ledges and crosses the Peters Kill, the outlet of Lake Awosting. A little farther along the trail, there is a view to the east of Litchfield Ledge and Huntington Ravine. Descending through hemlock and mountain laurel into Huntington Ravine, the trail reaches Rainbow Falls, with its cool mist, at 4.0 miles.

Ascending from the ravine, the Long Path crosses the Upper Awosting Carriageway and continues to climb. It follows close to the edge of Litchfield Ledge, passing through dense stands of mountain laurel, with openings that provide views to the north over the Catskills. It soon reaches an area with stunted pine trees scattered among conglomerate outcrops—a classic pine barrens landscape.

At 5.0 miles, the Long Path emerges onto a cliff top, rewarding the hiker with dramatic views of Lake Awosting. Now heading toward Castle Point, the Long Path descends to the Castle Point Carriageway. It turns left and follows the carriageway for a short distance along the cliff edge, crossing the top of Battlement Terrace. Then, at 5.8 miles, the Long Path reaches the crest of Castle Point, the highest point in the area (2,200 feet). There are views of the Wallkill Valley and the Hudson Highlands beyond. Here, the Blueberry Run Trail (blue) leaves to the left.

From Castle Point, the Long Path descends very steeply to the Hamilton Point Carriageway. It turns right and follows the carriageway for about 600 feet, then re-enters the woods on the left. Continuing to descend, the trail passes a small cave and goes through an interesting natural tunnel in the rocks. After crossing a brook and Slate Bank Road, an old carriageway, the trail ascends steeply to Margaret Cliff at 7.2 miles. Descending gradually over ledges, with views to the south, the Long Path makes a sharp left turn from the ledges and soon turns right onto Spruce Glen Road, which it follows for a short distance before turning off to the left. The trail then ascends Murray Hill, which offers a 360° view. Descending from the summit, the Long Path approaches Lake Awosting, with a short side trail leading to Awosting Lake Shore Drive. The Long Path curves to the southwest and soon enters a region of open ledges, stunted pine trees, and frequent clumps of blueberry bushes mixed with laurel. The ledges are not continuous—in places, they break up into jumbled rock, or split to form deep crevices. To the south, the ledges terminate as vertical cliffs.

After reaching a series of open ledges that come down to the water's edge, with views over Mud Pond, the Long Path bears right through hemlocks and, at 9.5 miles, crosses Fly Brook, the outlet of the pond. Beyond this point, the trail has been closed by the landowner, and hikers must retrace their steps at least as far as Lake Awosting, where the black-blazed carriageway can be used as an alternate return route to the causeway over Fly Brook.

Lower Awosting Carriageway
Length: 3.0 miles Blaze: black

The Lower Awosting Carriageway, also known as the Peters Kill Carriageway, provides the most direct route between the Lower Awosting parking area at the park entrance and Lake Awosting. The route was originally cleared to a considerable width, making a straight, uninteresting, and very exposed lane. However, nature has begun to heal this affront; the forest is beginning to shade the edges of the road. Because of its directness and the popularity of Lake Awosting, there is usually much foot and bicycle traffic on this route.

Hikers may prefer to take the parallel Mossy Glen Trail (yellow), a pleasant footpath which runs alongside the Peters Kill for the first part of the route from the parking area. At the end of the Mossy Glen Trail, hikers should turn right onto the Blueberry Run Trail (blue), then left

Figure 13-9. Millbrook Mountain, looking toward Sky Top

on the Lower Awosting Carriageway. The carriageway crosses Fly Brook on a causeway, then immediately climbs a steep hill just before reaching Lake Awosting.

Millbrook Mountain Trail   *Length: 1.2 miles Blaze: red*

This footpath begins at the south end of Lake Minnewaska, 0.9 mile from the Lake Minnewaska parking area. Lake Shore Drive (red), on the right side of Lake Minnewaska, leads to the start of the trail. Lake Shore Drive continues past the intersections with the Upper Awosting Carriageway (green), Castle Point Carriageway (blue), and Hamilton Point Carriageway (yellow) (a sign at this intersection mentions Millbrook Mountain), and descends on a switchback to reach the level of the shoreline at the south end of the lake. Here, at 0.9 mile, on the right side of the carriageway is the sign for Millbrook Mountain Trail.

The trail departs the carriageway and crosses a rocky, wooded area that is sometimes wet and difficult to traverse because of overflow from the lake. It soon crosses the outlet stream. In dry years, only water gurgling below the rocks may be heard. Shortly after, at 0.1 mile, the trail narrows to run alongside a rock face that is covered with rich lichen. The dropoff to the left may be dangerous in snow and ice, so hikers should exercise extreme caution in winter and early spring. Soon, the trail opens to cross a rock slab with an open view on the left, across the Coxing Clove toward the Sky Top tower and New Paltz. Continuing on, the trail descends gradually and enters a shady hemlock stand. After crossing a stream at 0.7 mile, it begins the ascent of Millbrook Mountain. The first section is very rocky and wet most of the time. The sloping conglomerate slabs, smoothed by glacial action and thinly covered with algae and crustose lichen, can be slippery underfoot. The forest gives way to sparse stands of chestnut oak and pitch pine, as exposed bedrock replaces soil underfoot. Nearly halfway up the slope, at 1.0 mile, the Coxing Trail (blue) departs left. The Millbrook Mountain Trail continues uphill, following red blazes, until, at 1.2 miles, the Millbrook Ridge Trail departs left at the top of Millbrook Mountain. This junction marks the terminus of the Millbrook Mountain Trail; a red-blazed path to the right crosses a sloping conglomerate slab to reach the summit, with a 360° view, in about 100 feet.

The return hike to Lake Minnewaska can be via the same route, or along the 3.2-mile Millbrook Drive (yellow), which ends at a turnaround circle at the base of the summit slab.

Stony Kill Falls

Stony Kill Falls, which drops 87 feet over conglomerate ledges, is one of the outstanding features of Minnewaska State Park Preserve. The most direct access to the falls is from below, by following Rock Haven Road (which intersects US 44/NY 55 just east of Kerhonkson) south for 2.5 miles and turning left onto Shaft 2A Road (also known as Shaft Road), which is gated about half a mile from the falls. However, until recently, this approach required the hiker to cross private property. The only approach to the falls through park property—via the Old Smiley Road and the Stony Kill Carriageway—required a hike of over five miles from the Lower Awosting or Lake Minnewaska parking areas.

In January 2001, the Open Space Institute—with the assistance of the New York-New Jersey Trail Conference—purchased a 90-acre parcel of land just below Stony Kill Falls, thus making it possible to approach the falls from Shaft

2A Road without crossing private property. It is anticipated that this parcel will eventually be acquired by the Palisades Interstate Park Commission. There are plans to construct a parking area at the end of Shaft 2A Road and a trail from the parking area crossing the Stony Kill and continuing to the base of the falls, with a branch connecting to the Stony Kill Carriageway. For more current information, contact the Trail Conference, 156 Ramapo Valley Road, Mahwah, NJ 07430; (201) 512-9348; www.nynjtc.org.

Upper Awosting Carriageway

Length: 3.3 miles Blaze: green
The Upper Awosting Carriageway, also known as the Awosting Lake Carriageway, is the most direct route between Lake Minnewaska and Lake Awosting, following an almost-level grade for its entire length. It begins at Lake Shore Drive (red) on the west side of Lake Minnewaska, 0.1 mile from the Lake Minnewaska parking area, at the lake's swimming area. From here, the Upper Awosting Carriageway proceeds westward, crossing an old orchard area before entering sparse oak woodlands. At 1.4 miles, the Blueberry Run Trail (blue)

Figure 13-10. Stony Kill Falls

crosses, and at 2.0 miles, the Upper Awosting Carriageway crosses a power line swath. The carriageway then curves to the left and begins to enter Huntington Ravine, defined by the overhanging cliffs of Litchfield Ledge on the left and the Overlook cliffs on the opposite side. At 2.4 miles, the Long Path crosses from above Litchfield Ledge on the left, and descends toward Rainbow Falls on the right. The Upper Awosting Carriageway crosses a stream amid deep forest, then winds around beneath the Overlook cliffs on the left. It ends at a junction with the Awosting Lake Shore Drive (black) at 3.3 miles.

SAM'S POINT DWARF PINE PRESERVE

The southernmost promontory of the Shawangunks is a rock outcrop called Sam's Point, which affords broad views extending from the Hudson Highlands in the southeast to High Point State Park and the Kittatinnies in the southwest. The name "Sam's Point" has also been used to designate the plateau-like mountainscape north of this promontory, formed of thick slabs of Shawangunk conglomerate. A miniature forest of evergreen heaths, blueberries, and pitch pines finds a tenuous foothold in this harsh, rocky environment. This is the highest and wildest part of the Shawangunks.

The Sam's Point area was formerly owned by the Village of Ellenville, with Lake Maratanza—the highest of the Sky Lakes—serving as the village's water supply. For three decades, some 4,600 mountaintop acres were leased to Ice Caves Mountain, Inc., a private corporation, and public access was limited to the Ice Caves on the escarpment, southeast of the Sam's Point promontory. In 1997, the land was acquired by the Open Space Institute, and it is once again open for hiking, under the management of The Nature Conservancy. The name that the conservancy has chosen for this area—Sam's Point Dwarf Pine Preserve—emphasizes the unusual mountaintop habitat.

Lake Maratanza, near Sam's Point, is still part of the water supply system of the Village of Ellenville, and no recreational use of the lake is permitted. While there are plans to reopen the Ice Caves in 2001, visitors will have to walk in a distance of 1.5 miles from the parking area.

To reach the Sam's Point Dwarf Pine Preserve, take NY 52 south from Ellenville. In about five miles, at the crest of the ridge, turn left at a sign to Cragsmoor. Proceed north for 1.4 miles, turn right in front of the Cragsmoor post office, then immediately turn right again onto Sam's Point Road. Follow Sam's Point Road for 1.5 miles to the parking area for the preserve. A parking fee is charged. A three-mile partially paved Loop Road leads uphill from the parking area, circling Lake Maratanza and providing access to the various hiking routes. This road is closed to private vehicles (although it is still kept open for administrative use).

The trails in the southeastern part of the preserve are open to the public

Figure 13-11. Sam's Point

for hiking (bicycles are not permitted), but access to the more fragile area in the northwestern part of the preserve is by permit only. For further information, contact the Eastern New York Chapter of The Nature Conservancy, 251 River Road, Troy, NY 12180; (518) 272-0195 or (845) 647-7989; www.nature.org.

High Point Road to High Point *Length: 2.9 miles Blaze: none*
To reach the High Point Road from the parking area, follow the Loop Road straight ahead. At 1.0 mile, the road curves to the right and reaches the level of Lake Maratanza, which can be glimpsed to the right. A short distance beyond, after passing the last communications tower, turn left (north) onto High Point Road. This level road proceeds through a dwarf forest of pitch pine and mountain crest shrubbery. Wild cranberry and bog cotton may be observed in the shallow, wet areas near the road. At 2.3 miles, a yellow-blazed trail to the left leads in 0.7 mile to Indian Rock, a large mass of bedrock shaped by glaciers and left perched on the cliff edge. From a rock outcrop at 2.7 miles, a rough road to the right climbs to the site of the former High Point fire tower. Despite its name, this point (2,240 feet) is not the highest point in the Shawangunks (the unmarked highest point, 2,289 feet, is located somewhere between Lake Maratanza and the promontory of Sam's Point). However, the fire tower site offers a panoramic view to the south, west, and north.

Long Path to Verkeerder Kill Falls *Length: 3.0 miles Blaze: aqua*
Beginning at the parking area, take the right branch of the Loop Road. At 1.0 mile, turn right onto the road that leads to the Ice Caves, and almost immediately turn left onto a footpath. For the first three-quarters of a mile, the dwarf pitch pines along the trail allow for views over the Wallkill Valley and toward Lake Awosting in Minnewaska State Park. After crossing the outlet of Lake Maratanza in a small birch-and-oak meadow, the trail enters an area of taller deciduous trees. It soon bears right, joining an older, more heavily worn path which descends toward the falls at the edge of the escarpment. After a heavy rain, the roar of the falls can often be heard long before reaching them. At 3.0 miles, the Long Path reaches the Verkeerder Kill, a multi-channeled stream which can be difficult to cross in wet weather. The best views of the spectacular falls can be obtained by crossing the stream and proceeding south along the escarpment for about 100 feet. Use caution when approaching the cliff edge, as the dropoff is very steep. There is no access to the base of the falls.

High Point Trail   *Length: 2.3 miles Blaze: red*
The High Point Trail connects the site of the former High Point fire tower, just off High Point Road, with the Long Path north of Verkeerder Kill Falls. It crosses a remote and wild area known as the Badlands or the Pine Plains, with bonsai-like pitch pines that are among the oldest trees in the Shawangunks. This open, relatively level trail follows the ledges and outcrops of a south-facing escarpment.

From the site of the fire tower, the High Point Trail heads south. At 0.2 mile, it passes the highest point of the route—2,246 feet, as indicated by the USGS survey markers—which offers a panoramic view to the north, east, and south. The trail descends from this outcrop and heads southeast, ending at 2.3 miles at a junction with Long Path (aqua). To reach Verkeerder Kill Falls, turn right and follow the Long Path downhill for 0.3 mile. (The Long Path heading north from the trail junction is closed as of spring 2001.)

High Point Road, the High Point Trail, and the Long Path can be combined to make an attractive 8.5-mile loop hike around the Sam's Point Dwarf Pine Preserve.

WALLKILL VALLEY RAIL TRAIL

Running through the valley at the base of the Shawangunks, mostly within view of the many southeast-facing cliffs, is the 12.2-mile Wallkill Valley Rail Trail. Until 1977, the Wallkill Valley Railway brought freight through the Wallkill Valley between Montgomery and Kingston. With rails and ties now gone, the fine cinder trail surface offers flat and easy walking. Also open to mountain bikers and horseback riders, it rambles through farms and forests, streams and wetlands, and the towns of Gardiner and New Paltz—almost always within view of the Shawangunks. First opened in 1991, the rail trail is managed and maintained by the Wallkill Valley Rail Trail Association, Inc.

To reach the Wallkill Valley Rail Trail, take Exit 18 from the New York State Thruway and turn west on NY 299 (Main Street) through New Paltz until intersecting the rail trail just before the Wallkill River bridge. The southern terminus, on Deniston Road, may be reached by proceeding south on NY 208 and then turning right onto Deniston Road. Ample parking is available adjacent to the trail in New Paltz, and limited parking is available at most road crossings. For more information, contact the Wallkill Valley Rail Trail Association, P.O. Box 1048, New Paltz, NY 12561-1048; www.gorailtrail.org.

From the southern trailhead on Deniston Road, the trail proceeds northward as a tree-lined corridor between fields. Soon, Sand Hill Road begins to parallel the trail to the west, and the profile of the Shawangunks is visible across fields and through breaks in the trees. Sand Hill Road crosses at 1.4 miles, and it continues to parallel the trail to the east until the hamlet of Gardiner is reached at 2.5 miles.

At Gardiner, the trail crosses US 44/NY 55 in the downtown area. The former railroad station, dating from 1868, is now an antique shop. North of Gardiner, the trail again traverses open fields with views, crosses a small road at 3.3 miles, and at 3.5 miles reaches the intersection of Phillies Bridge Road and Old Ford Road. North of Phillies Bridge Road, the trail enters woodlands, crossing a trestle over Forest Glen Road at 4.3 miles, and it crosses Bridge Creek Road at 4.5 miles. From Bridge Creek Road, it is another 0.8 mile through the woods to Old Ford Road.

A short distance north of Old Ford Road, the trail enters the Town of New Paltz. It traverses orchards and looks out on scenic farmlands that extend to the west toward the Shawangunk Mountains. The trail's elevated bridge over the Plattekill Creek at 6.3 miles offers a broad panorama, with Mohonk's Sky Top tower crowning the horizon.

After crossing Cedar Drive at 7.0 miles, the trail passes a pond and wetland to the west. It crosses Plains Road at 8.2 miles and soon overlooks a flood plain forest along the Wallkill River to the west, with a side trail descending steeply to the riverbank.

At 8.5 miles, the trail crosses Main Street (NY 299) in the Village of New Paltz. A mile later, after crossing Huguenot Street, the trail leaves the village, traversing woodlands and passing a gun club to the east. At 10.5 miles, the 413-foot-long Wallkill River bridge is crossed.

Just beyond the bridge, the trail crosses Springtown Road and passes a horse farm on the east, with the cliffs of Bonticou Crag looming above to the west. The trail intersects a small lane at 10.8 miles and then enters woodlands until it reaches Cragswood Road at 11.9 miles. It continues north for another 0.3 mile to a sign marking the line between the towns of New Paltz and Rosendale, where the trail officially ends.

OTHER AREAS IN EASTERN ULSTER COUNTY

Although not part of the Shawangunk Mountains, these two delightful preserves, acquired by Scenic Hudson, Inc. in the 1990s, afford visitors to the area the opportunity to hike in the eastern part of Ulster County, with views over the Hudson River.

Black Creek Forest Preserve

The Black Creek Forest Preserve, located just off US 9W in the Town of Esopus, is a 130-acre woodland tract acquired in 1999 by Scenic Hudson, Inc. It features a hemlock forest mixed with hardwoods, old stone walls, and vistas up the Hudson River from a riverfront viewpoint. The parking area for the preserve is on Winding Brook Road, on the east side of US 9W, 5.3 miles north of the intersection of US 9W and NY 299.

There are three marked trails in the preserve, and these trails may be combined to make an attractive 2.3-mile loop hike. From the parking area, follow the Black Creek Trail (yellow), which briefly parallels the access road and turns right to cross Black Creek on a 120-foot suspension bridge. The trail climbs on switchbacks, crosses a tributary stream, and reaches a junction with the Vernal Pool Trail (red) at 0.5 mile. Turn right on the Vernal Pool Trail, which passes several seasonal ponds and runs along an old stone wall. At 0.8 mile, turn right onto the Hudson River Trail (blue) and follow it as it rises to a rocky promontory and then descends to the river. The trail runs along the hemlock-lined riverfront for 500 feet and reaches the Pitch Pine Overlook, which offers broad views over the Hudson River to the north, at 1.0 mile. Only the occasional passage of a train on the opposite shore disturbs the tranquility of this quiet spot.

The Hudson River Trail swings upward and ends at the Vernal Pool Trail at 1.3 miles. Turn right on this red-blazed trail, which heads north, then turns sharply left and proceeds south on an old farm road. The Vernal Pool Trail ends at 1.8 miles at a junction with the Black Creek Trail. Follow this trail straight ahead for the return to the parking area.

For more information, contact Scenic Hudson, Inc., 9 Vassar Street, Poughkeepsie, NY 12601; (845) 473-4440; www.scenichudson.org.

Figure 13-12. Shaupeneak Ridge: Hudson River Overlook on the Red Trail

Shaupeneak Ridge Cooperative Recreation Area

The 500-acre Shaupeneak Ridge Cooperative Recreation Area in the Town of Esopus was acquired by Scenic Hudson, Inc. in 1994 and is currently managed under an agreement between Scenic Hudson, the New York State Department of Environmental Conservation, and the West Esopus Landowners Association. The parcel includes a portion of the ridge line of the Marlboro Mountains, with a viewpoint over the Hudson River. Canoeing is permitted in Louisa Pond, which lies within a glacially-carved bowl. Two parking areas provide access to the property. To reach Shaupeneak Ridge, take US 9W north 5.8 miles from its intersection with NY 299 and turn left (west) onto Old Post Road. The lower parking area is 0.2 mile from US 9W, on the right side of the road. The upper parking area is 2.5 miles from US 9W, on the left side of Poppletown Road (which continues ahead where Old Post Road makes a sharp bend to the left).

Shaupeneak Ridge has four major trails—the Blue, Red, White, and Orange trails—each of which is about 1.5 miles long. The Blue Trail starts from the upper parking area and circles Louisa Pond. The Red Trail, which makes a loop to the east of Poppletown Road, features two overlooks—a broad viewpoint over the Hudson River, with the eastern shoreline of the river visible from Hyde Park to Rhinebeck, and another viewpoint over the Catskills and

Shawangunks. By combining these two trails, a 2.6-mile loop, with relatively little elevation gain, can be made from the upper parking area. The hike can be further lengthened by taking in the Orange Trail, which makes a loop to the west from the Blue Trail.

Those who are looking for a more ambitious excursion can take a 5.7-mile loop hike covering most of the trails in the preserve, with an elevation gain of about 700 feet. From the lower parking area, follow the White Trail, which first runs along the base of the ridge and then turns uphill. At 0.4 mile, turn right onto the Yellow Trail, which soon reaches the Waterfall Spur (purple). Follow this short trail to an attractive waterfall, then return to the Yellow Trail and turn right. At the next junction, turn right onto the White Trail, which continues to climb to the crest of the ridge.

At 1.8 miles, the White Trail ends at a junction with the Red Trail. Turn right and almost immediately reach the Hudson River Overlook. Continue ahead on the Red Trail, passing the Catskill Overlook. The Red Trail crosses Poppletown Road at 2.5 miles and soon ends at a junction with the Blue Trail. Turn right at this junction and follow the Blue Trail as it loops around Louisa Pond, crossing a wet area on puncheons and passing through an attractive hemlock grove. At the upper parking area, proceed ahead, crossing Poppletown Road, and continue on the Red Trail. Turn right at the junction with the White Trail at 4.2 miles, and follow the White Trail downhill to the lower parking area.

For more information, contact Scenic Hudson, Inc., 9 Vassar Street, Poughkeepsie, NY 12601; (845) 473-4440; www.scenichudson.org.

FOURTEEN

SCHUNEMUNK MOUNTAIN

est of Black Rock Forest in the northern Hudson Highlands, a land formation rises that has several unique and striking features. Usually pronounced skun-uh-munk, the name means *excellent fireplace* in the Algonquin tongue. This name was given to the Lenni Lenape village that once existed on the northern spur of the mountain. A peaceful people, they were variously known as the "Original People," "Chosen People," and "People of the Stony Country." The white settlers referred to them as "the Delaware." Hikers on Schunemunk have much to marvel at, from the continuous views along the ridge to the unforgettable rock beneath their feet.

The area around the northern half of the ridge is a diverse mixture of land uses—industry, the fine arts, and open space. To preserve this magnificent ridge from development, the Mountainville Conservancy was organized by Star Expansion Industries, the Ogden Foundation, and the Storm King Art Center, with its chief architect H. Peter Stern, president of Star Expansion Industries and of the Storm King Art Center. With the Conservancy's future uncertain, the Open Space Institute, in 1996, with a grant from the Lila Acheson and DeWitt Wallace Fund for the Hudson Highlands, purchased 2,100 acres of Schunemunk Mountain and additional lands. This acquisition ensured access to the mountain and the preservation of the mountain background for the sculpture of Storm King Art Center. In March 2001, Governor George Pataki announced that this property would be acquired by the State of New York and become a state park, to be managed by the Palisades Interstate Park Commission. The

Nature Conservancy owns 163 acres on the northern end of the ridge.

Car access is by NY 17 or the New York State Thruway to Exit 16 (Harriman), then north on NY 32 to Highland Mills, Woodbury, or Mountainville. Short Line buses, from the Port Authority Bus Terminal in Manhattan, stop at these towns.

Geology

Schunemunk Mountain features a number of unusual geologic features. Soaring well above the surrounding region, its summit reaches an elevation of nearly 1,700 feet above sea level. A striking feature of the mountain is its double crest. For nearly three miles, there are two ridges running parallel to each other, separated by the valley of Baby Brook. Each ridge consists of layers of the same conglomerate sloping inward towards each other, thus forming a geologic downfold or syncline (Figure 14-1). This dip continues into the sandstones below the conglomerates on each flank. Schunemunk is therefore as much a part of the Appalachian Fold Belt as the older, softer, and much more eroded Great Valley to the north and northwest.

The caprock of the ridges is a reddish-purple matrix, studded with pebbles of white quartz and pink sandstone, some of which reach diameters of eight inches. Both this conglomerate and the sandstones that underlie it are Devo-

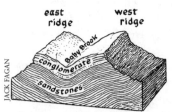

Figure 14-1. Schunemunk syncline

nian in age. Because of the similarity of the Schunemunk strata to those of the Catskills, over 30 miles away, it is reasonable to assume that, during the Devonian period, the Catskill deltaic sediments must have extended over the surrounding region—that part of the Fold Belt now eroded to form the Great Valley. The folding episode that produced the synclinal structure of Schunemunk was the Alleghenian Orogeny, about 260 million years ago—the last to affect eastern North America. Figure 14-2 depicts the probable original continuity of the Catskill and Schunemunk strata. The Devonian-age reddish conglomerate may be traced southward to Bearfort Ridge near Greenwood Lake and onward into New Jersey.

When standing on the ridgetops of Schunemunk Mountain, one can see a line of hills made up of Precambrian bedrock, including Woodcock Hill and Bull Mine Hill. The Precambrian knobs are largely surrounded by Paleozoic

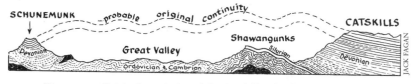

Figure 14-2. Original continuity of the Catskill and Schunemunk strata

strata and, like Stissing Mountain (see page 188), their origin is unclear. Whether they are protruding basement rock that is continuous *at depth* with the distant Hudson Highlands, or whether they are masses separated from other Precambrian rock by complex faulting—*i.e.*, overthrust blocks carried eastward to their present location—has not yet been determined.

Trails on Schunemunk Mountain

With over 25 miles of trails, Schunemunk Mountain offers hikers opportunities to walk along ridges, view cascading streams, and investigate megaliths.

On Schunemunk Mountain, there are different ways of trail blazing—painted blazes on trees and rocks, *cairns* (rock piles), and plastic rectangles nailed to the twisted trunks of the pines. The hiker must be alert to sudden changes in the trail's direction, especially as there are so many distracting views along the ridge.

Barton Swamp Trail   *Length: 2.1 miles Blaze: red dot on white*
Because the Barton Swamp Trail follows the wooded trough that separates the central and western ridges of Schunemunk, it provides a sheltered exit to Taylor Hollow, where it connects with the Jessup Trail, the Trestle Trail, and the Long Path.

The Barton Swamp Trail starts at the Long Path (aqua), a short distance west of Barton Swamp. At 0.2 mile, the Western Ridge Trail (blue dot on white) comes in from the right and leaves from the left after another 0.1 mile. The Barton Swamp Trail continues northeast through the forest, paralleling the headwaters of Baby Brook. At 1.6 miles, the Barton Swamp Trail crosses the Sweet Clover Trail (white), then continues for a distance, crossing the brook occasionally, following one bank for a while, then the other. There are large stands of white birch trees and, at drier spots, mountain laurel. The Barton Swamp Trail meets the Jessup Trail (yellow) at 1.7 miles and veers west, climbing steeply

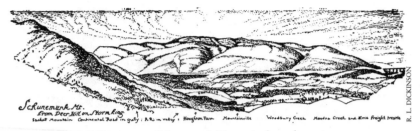

Figure 14-3. Schunemunk Mountain from the east

over rocks to the western ridge where, at 2.0 miles, the Trestle Trail leaves to the right. The Barton Swamp Trail ends in another 300 feet at a junction with the Long Path.

Dark Hollow Trail *Length: 1.6 miles Blaze: black on white*
The Dark Hollow Trail begins at the southern end of the Otterkill Trail, 2.2 miles from the parking area on Otterkill Road. The trail climbs through a hemlock grove, makes a sharp right turn, and continues to climb. At 0.9 mile, an unmarked trail goes right to Dark Hollow Brook through a thicket of mountain laurel. After passing views of the Hudson River and Storm King at 1.1 miles, the Dark Hollow Trail ends at the Jessup Trail (yellow) at 1.6 miles. The summit of Schunemunk is 0.4 mile south on the Jessup Trail.

Jessup Trail *Length: 8.6 miles Blaze: yellow*
As the main north–south trail on Schunemunk, the Jessup Trail traverses the full length of the mountain from the parking area on Taylor Road in Mountainville to its terminus on Seven Springs Road in Monroe. From NY 32 in Mountainville, hikers can walk or drive one-third of a mile west on Taylor Road to the parking area on the right. From the parking area, the Jessup Trail (together with the Sweet Clover and Highlands trails) crosses Taylor Road and continues south along paved Shaw Road, paralleling the New York State Thruway and passing a barn and a garage. In 0.2 mile, it curves west and passes a caretaker's cottage, where the paving ends. Soon, at the second road gate, the Sweet Clover and Highlands trails leave to the left, while the Jessup Trail continues west over a culvert and crosses a plowed field. It climbs to a woods road paralleling the railroad tracks and continues north for about half a mile. The

Jessup Trail then turns left, crossing the tracks, and immediately turns right onto the Otterkill Trail (red diamond). In 150 feet, it reaches Baby Brook and turns left, leaving the Otterkill Trail. The Jessup Trail now heads west, paralleling the brook. It climbs steadily, about 700 feet in the next 0.8 mile, reaching an intersection with the Barton Swamp Trail (red) in Taylor Hollow at 1.8 miles. From Taylor Hollow, the Jessup Trail ascends a ridge among pitch pines. The ridge displays the marvelous and unique conglomerate bedrock that makes Schunemunk so fascinating.

For 0.5 mile along the ridge, there is a continuous series of panoramic views of meadows, fields, and Beaver Dam Lake to the north, the Hudson River to the northeast, and Storm King Mountain and the hills of Black Rock Forest toward the east. There are also views of the western ridge of Schunemunk, parallel to the main ridge. Between the ridges—which represent the two limbs of the Schunemunk syncline—lie Baby Brook and the Barton Swamp Trail (see Figure 14-1).

At 2.5 miles, the Jessup Trail intersects the Sweet Clover Trail (white), and the two trails turn together to the south. The cracks in the bedrock on the ridge here afford fine blueberry picking in season, usually from middle to late July. The pitch pines exposed on the ridge, stunted into rugged beauty by the winter winds, display their ability to survive the stringent conditions that nature imposes. At 2.7 miles, the Jessup Trail drops into a forested cleft in the ridge, and the Sweet Clover Trail (white) diverges to the left. The Jessup Trail then climbs the ridge again, continuing south. At 3.4 miles, the Dark Hollow Trail (black on white) goes off to the left. Both the Sweet Clover and the Dark Hollow trails are convenient for returning to a starting point at the north end of the trail.

The Jessup Trail continues on the ridge, reaching, at 3.7 miles, a short spur trail, marked by cairns, which leads to the Megaliths, a group of huge blocks that have split off from the bedrock. There is a view here toward the western ridge, overlooking Barton Swamp. The highest elevation in the area, which is marked by paint on the bedrock, is reached at 3.8 miles. At 1,664 feet, this vantage point provides views of the neighboring summits in Harriman State Park, Black Rock Forest, and the Hudson Highlands from Storm King to the Beacons. There are views of several fire towers and the Perkins Memorial Tower atop Bear Mountain to the southeast. On a clear day, the higher peaks of the Catskill Mountains are identifiable across the horizon to the north: Slide, Cornell, Wittenberg, Plateau, Sugarloaf, and Indian Head. Toward the west are the Kittatinny Mountains with the monument atop High Point, the highest

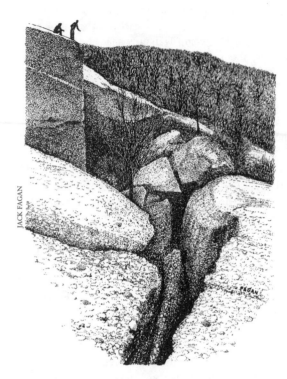

JACK FAGAN

Figure 14-4. At the Megaliths

elevation in New Jersey at 1,803 feet. The Shawangunks, part of the same ridge that forms the Kittatin-nies, can be seen toward the northwest, stretching from Sam's Point to Mohonk.

The Jessup Trail continues southward, passing the end of the Western Ridge Trail (blue dot on white) at 3.9 miles, and reaching one lookout point after another. Hawks can often be seen circling in the updrafts from the cliffs, occasionally swooping down into the woods below for a meal. At 4.5 miles, another high point, at 1,662 feet, is reached, with more views east and west. The trail continues, occasionally dropping down through gaps in the ridge, before ascending again. At times, the ridge is as smooth as a sidewalk, ground down by the friction of moving glaciers. Occasionally, large erratics are found, carried from distant locations by the same glaciers that ground the bedrock smooth. Indeed, a huge boulder of Schunemunk conglomerate can be found on the grounds of Arden House, over ten miles to the south. At 4.8 miles, the Long Path, running northwest and southeast, crosses the Jessup Trail at the widest part of the ridge.

Over the next 1.9 miles, crossing ridges alternating with forested areas, the Jessup Trail gradually descends over a series of small rises. Views toward the east and west can occasionally be seen through the trees. The trail passes a strange white boulder at 6.7 miles—a glacial erratic of dolomitic limestone originating somewhere to the north and deposited on Schunemunk by the last glacier to grind south across the land. The last good lookout point is at 8.0 miles, where the elevation is 1,320 feet. Farther down, the grade steepens, descending through forests near the end. At 8.6 miles, the Jessup Trail terminates at Seven Springs Road. The Highlands Trail (teal diamond) is co-aligned for the southern 5.8 miles.

Long Path   *Length: 6.9 miles Blaze: aqua*

The Long Path leaves NY 32 at the railroad trestle about 1.6 miles north of the Highland Mills bus station. Parking is available on the west side of NY 32 about 0.2 mile south of the trestle. The route follows the trestle to the top and heads north along the railroad tracks for about 0.4 mile. It turns left through a gravel pit and then turns right, crossing a small stream as it enters the woods. The trail climbs steadily for over half a mile, then turns up a rocky defile to Little Knob. It ascends a wooded incline, a talus slope, and the edge of a cliff bordered with twisted pitch pines to reach High Knob at 1.4 miles, with views to the east, north, and south.

From High Knob, the Long Path descends north along the top edge of the high, pine-bordered cliff above an impressive ravine. At the saddle of this ravine, the trail climbs steeply to the top of another rock wall. High Knob and its cliffs are visible from here. The trail then heads northwest, ascending gradually in 0.5 mile to a view to the north. It then descends slightly and crosses the headwaters of Dark Hollow Brook. From here, it climbs steadily northwest, until, at 2.6 miles, it joins the Jessup Trail (yellow), with views east and west.

The Long Path continues northwest down a gentle slope, enters the woods, and descends a series of ledges overlooking Barton Swamp and the western ridge; the last ledge is steep. The trail plunges down a talus slope into Barton Swamp, crosses a brook, jogs left onto a woods road, and then goes right. The trail then gently ascends the ridge, only to descend into a saddle, passing the southern end of the Barton Swamp Trail (red on white) at 4.1 miles.

Continuing on the western ridge, the Long Path darts back and forth across the exposed conglomerate, passes over some deep crevasses, and ducks behind scraggly growths, into forested areas and across treeless surfaces. At 5.1 miles, it intersects the Sweet Clover Trail (white). At the end of the western ridge, the Long Path enters land belonging to The Nature Conservancy, set aside to protect rare species of moths and timber rattlers. At 5.6 miles, the Long Path meets the 100-yard spur of the Barton Swamp Trail (red on white) which connects to the main portion of the Barton Swamp Trail.

Turning left, the Long Path begins its descent. Within minutes, the geology and ecology change. No longer is the ground covered with the pinkish-white conglomerate. The stunted and gnarled vegetation of the windswept ridgetop gives way to a forest of taller trees. After some switchbacks, at times utilizing woods roads, the trail ends at the Hil-Mar resort, where parking is available.

Otterkill Trail   *Length: 2.2 miles Blaze: red diamond*
To reach the Otterkill Trail, take NY 32 to Orrs Mills Road. After crossing the New York State Thruway, turn left on Otterkill Road and proceed under the railroad trestle. The trailhead parking area is 0.3 mile west of the trestle.

At first, the Otterkill Trail runs jointly with the Trestle Trail (white), ascending steeply along a woods road. In 500 feet, the Trestle Trail leaves to the right, while the Otterkill Trail continues straight ahead, continuing uphill until it reaches the level of the tracks. At 0.3 mile, there is a sweeping pastoral view over the valley, with the railroad tracks visible in a rock cut below. The Jessup Trail (yellow) crosses at 1.1 miles and, after meandering through an open hardwood forest, the Otterkill Trail crosses the Sweet Clover Trail (white) at 2.1 miles. It then turns away from the tracks, dips down to cross Dark Hollow Brook, and ends at the Dark Hollow Trail (black on white) at 2.2 miles.

Sweet Clover Trail   *Length: 2.8 miles Blaze: white*
This trail is a good approach to the east and west ridges of Schunemunk. From the hikers' parking area on Taylor Road, the Sweet Clover Trail (together with the Jessup Trail) proceeds south along paved Shaw Road, paralleling the New York State Thruway and passing a barn and a garage. Turning west into the meadow, the trail becomes a dirt road. Soon, the Sweet Clover Trail turns left (south), leaving the Jessup Trail, which continues straight ahead. At 0.8 mile, the Sweet Clover Trail turns west into the woods. The trail leaves the dirt road to cross the railroad tracks a mile from the start and then shortly crosses the Otterkill Trail (red diamond).

The Sweet Clover Trail climbs steadily, crossing a slope of flaggy sandstone that plunges down to Dark Hollow Brook far below. This section of the trail is reminiscent of western trails. The trail switchbacks up past the northernmost branch of Dark Hollow Brook, crosses a swampy stretch, then heads uphill again. At about 1,450 feet, the trail meets the Jessup Trail (yellow) and runs north with it for 0.2 mile on conglomerate rock. It then turns west, drops steeply into Barton Swamp, and crosses the headwaters of Baby Brook. After reaching the Barton Swamp Trail (red on white) at 2.7 miles, it climbs steeply to terminate at the Long Path (aqua) 0.1 mile later. The Highlands Trail (teal diamond) is co-aligned with the Sweet Clover Trail from Taylor Road to the Jessup Trail (yellow), which it then follows south.

Trestle Trail   *Length: 1.4 miles Blaze: white*
The Trestle Trail begins on Otterkill Road, 0.3 mile west of the railroad trestle. At first, the Trestle Trail runs jointly with the Otterkill Trail (red diamond), ascending steeply along a woods road. In 500 feet, the Trestle Trail leaves to the right, continuing to climb steeply, with seasonal views through the trees. At 0.6 mile, there is a view to the north over the valley, and at 1.2 miles, there is a panoramic view to the north and east, with the northern Hudson Highlands visible in the distance. As it goes along the western side of the ridge, the Trestle Trail passes through scrub oak, blueberry bushes, and pitch pine. It ends at the Barton Swamp Trail (red) at 1.4 miles.

Western Ridge Trail   *Length: 0.6 mile Blaze: blue dot on white*
This short trail serves as a crossover for the eastern/western ridges of Schunemunk Mountain. The eastern end is on the Jessup Trail, 0.1 mile south of the 1,664-foot-high summit of Schunemunk Mountain. At first, the Western Ridge Trail descends sharply into the Barton Swamp. At 0.4 mile, it joins the Barton Swamp Trail (red on white) for 0.1 mile and then ascends the western ridge to end 0.2 mile later at the Long Path (aqua).

FIFTEEN

STORM KING AND BLACK ROCK FOREST

torm King Mountain looms above
the Hudson River like a fortress, dominating the rugged river gorge on the
west. Originally considered to be part of the adjacent Butter Hill, Storm King
Mountain was named in the mid-nineteenth century by the romantic journalist
Nathaniel Parker Willis. Its glowering eastern end rises sheer from the river to
more than 1,300 feet and is the dominating feature of Storm King State Park.
Just behind it, to the southwest, lies Black Rock Forest, the largest sustained
area over 1,200 feet in the Highlands. There, the mountains plunge for more
than 1,000 feet to the west, north, and south and provide the hiker with sweeping vistas and strongly contrasting habitats.

STORM KING STATE PARK

Much of the terrain in the northern Highlands was preserved for hikers by Dr.
Ernest Stillman, a New York physician. In 1922, Stillman gave about 800 acres
in Storm King Clove to the Palisades Interstate Park to ensure the preservation
of the scenic surroundings of the old Storm King Highway. Subsequent purchases and gifts have added an additional 1,000 acres to the park. This tract
forms the foreground for the eastward view from US 9W before it turns west
for its descent to Cornwall.

Hikers have long enjoyed the views from Storm King, but few ventured onto
the trailless area to the south—Storm King Clove and the North Ridge of Crows
Nest. In 1993, volunteers from the New York-New Jersey Trail Conference built a

JACK FAGAN

Figure 15-1. Storm King Mountain

trail in the heart of Storm King State Park, providing hikers with views and points of interest that had been virtually inaccessible. The trail is named after William Thompson Howell, legendary explorer of the Hudson Highlands.

Born on April 12, 1873, in Newburgh, New York, William Thompson Howell was a man of seemingly boundless energy who would often hike 30 or more miles a day, no matter what the weather. Writer, amateur photographer, and pathfinder, he was best known for his rambles in the Hudson Highlands. Perhaps no man or woman ever loved the Highlands as much as he. With unbridled enthusiasm, he explored their hills and hollows, forests and crags, and abandoned farms and mines. He proposed that the Highlands be protected in a great park that would benefit many. Although, in time, some of the hills and vistas that he loved became part of the Palisades Interstate Park, Howell never lived to see his dream fulfilled, dying of tuberculosis on April 26, 1916. One of Howell's favorite haunts was a mountain he called "Old Cro' Nest." He explored this rugged area thoroughly, making several camps in its forest. Many narratives describe this exceptionally beautiful Highlands peak.

Storm King is more than just a serene mountain. Its name is associated with a watershed court case that became the basis for environmental law in the United States. In the early 1960s, conservationists renewed their interest in preserving the Hudson Highlands. Since Storm King was part of the Palisades Interstate Park, the mountain was considered "safe," and so conservationists decided to focus their efforts on preserving the eastern Highlands. At the same time, Consolidated Edison announced elaborate plans for Storm King. They wanted to build a powerhouse at the base of the mountain, a 260-acre reservoir within Black Rock Forest, and ten-story transmission towers running across the river to Putnam County. Conservation efforts shifted back to the west side of the Hudson. In 1963, a small group of people met and formed the Scenic Hudson Preservation Conference. The Nature Conservancy, the New York-New Jersey Trail Conference, the Natural Resources Defense Council, and the Hudson River Fishermen's Association joined with Scenic Hudson to contest the project. Over the next seventeen years, the battle raged, with national and international support. Legal testimony ranged from the esthetical to the practical. Con Edison's efforts to mitigate the negative visual effects were not acceptable, as the threat to fisheries remained. A new threat appeared—possible harm to the Catskill Aqueduct and New York City's water supply.

Finally, in December 1980, a negotiated settlement was worked out, calling for Con Ed to drop its plans for the project. The *New York Times* hailed the resolution of this conflict as a "peace treaty for the Hudson." The outcome of the conflict established the right of citizen groups to sue a government agency to protect natural resources and scenic beauty. It set a precedent for national environmental issues dealing with the question of whether commercial developers could carry out development to meet one need at the expense of others.

In the course of extinguishing a forest fire in the park during a dry spell in the summer of 1999, firefighters encountered exploding ordnance. The ordnance had apparently been fired well over a century ago to test cannons manufactured at the West Point Foundry in Cold Spring, across the river, and it exploded due to the heat generated by the fire. Because of the danger presented by other unexploded ordnance, Storm King State Park was closed to the public. Subsequently, it was determined that artillery shells fired from the West Point Military Reservation may also have landed in the park. Although efforts have been made to locate and remove all ordnance adjacent to the trails, the park remains closed to the public as of summer 2001. It is hoped that it will be reopened in the near future.

For more information, contact the Palisades Interstate Park Commission, Administration Building, Bear Mountain, NY 10911; (845) 786-2701; www.nysparks.com.

Trails in Storm King State Park

Aside from the Bobcat Trail, there is nothing easy about the trails in Storm King State Park. However, views of the Hudson Highlands and the Hudson River reward hikers far beyond the effort required to arrive at a viewpoint. Since the network of trails is small, hikers can minimize retracing their steps, especially if a car shuttle is used.

Bluebird Trail   *Length: 0.6 mile Blaze: blue and red*
This trail, which is a shortcut across the Stillman Trail (yellow), was not named for the bird that may be found in this area. Rather, before the trail was blazed, hikers used the acronym BLUBRD—bear left up, bear right down—to help them remember which way to go.

The lower end of the Bluebird Trail is on the Stillman Trail, 0.9 mile from the gate on Mountain Road, at a point where the Stillman Trail turns sharply left, leaving a woods road. The Bluebird Trail follows a rock-edged sidehill path through a hemlock grove and ascends Storm King on a series of switchbacks and rock steps. At 0.3 mile, it bears left at a T junction with a woods road. It turns right off the woods road at 0.4 mile and reaches a viewpoint at 0.5 mile. The Bluebird Trail ends at the Stillman Trail in the saddle bewteen Butter Hill and the summit of Storm King. The upper end of the Howell Trail is just over the rise to the left.

Bobcat Trail   *Length: 0.4 mile Blaze: white*
Hikers wishing to enjoy the views at the North Peak of Crows Nest without a climb should use the Bobcat Trail. It begins on the north side of a small parking lot off the northbound lanes of US 9W, about two miles north of its intersection with NY 218 and NY 293. Unfortunately, there is no access to or from the southbound lanes of US 9W. After leaving the parking lot, the trail descends gently, loops to the left, and terminates at the Howell Trail (blue) in 0.4 mile.

By-Pass Trail   *Length: 0.4 mile Blaze: white*
The By-Pass Trail connects the Howell Trail (blue) on the southern flank of Storm King to the Stillman Trail (yellow) near the brow of the mountain. Starting 0.4 mile from the northern terminus of the Howell Trail, the By-Pass Trail makes a short descent, ascends rather steeply, and soon reaches a view of Crows

Nest, the Hudson River, and Constitution Island. The trail continues northeast, ascending gradually, with two more views to the south. Just after the third view, the trail ends at a junction with the Stillman Trail (yellow).

Howell Trail
Length: 3.6 miles Blaze: blue

The Howell Trail begins just to the left of the Stillman Memorial Spring on NY 218, about one mile north of the Lee Gate at West Point. Parking is available on both sides of the road at the spring, with additional parking on the east side of NY 218 both north and south of the trailhead.

Behind the spring, the trail turns left and begins a gradual ascent up the north slope of Crows Nest. After several switchbacks, it turns left on a woods road that comes in from the right and gently descends toward the river. At 0.4 mile, the trail turns sharply right off the road and ascends rock steps. Staying on the road gives a short side trip to the "pitching point," where, at the beginning of the twentieth century, logs were tossed down into the Hudson. After a series of switchbacks and rock steps, the trail continues its ascent of the pine- and hemlock-covered spine of Crows Nest's north peak. Along the way it passes several northward views of Storm King, the Hudson River, Breakneck Ridge, and Beacon Mountain. On a clear day, the distant Shawangunks and Catskills can be seen. The higher the hiker climbs, the more expansive are the views. At the North Peak (1,000 feet) there is another view just before the trail turns sharply right at 1.4 miles. Occasional cairns mark the trail as it proceeds along the ridge, and more viewpoints open up on both sides, including views to the south of the South Peak of Crows Nest and Constitution Island. The trail begins a gradual descent toward North Point, reaching it at 1.8 miles, with a view of the Hudson River in the distance and the pine and hemlock ridge just traversed.

The Howell Trail continues to descend gradually until, at 2.1 miles, it reaches the terminus of the Bobcat Trail (white), coming in from the left. The trail then follows a woods road and continues its descent into The Clove. At 2.5 miles, it turns left at a junction with the Stillman Spring Trail (white), coming in from the right. After crossing The Clove, the trail begins its 700-foot ascent in 0.9 mile in a series of switchbacks and rock steps up to the saddle between Butter Hill and Storm King. At 3.1 miles, it turns right on a woods road coming in from the left. The southern terminus of the By-Pass Trail (white) and views to the south are at 3.2 miles. Leaving the woods road, the trail turns left toward the saddle and passes another viewpoint at 3.5 miles. At 3.6 miles, the Howell Trail terminates at a junction with the Stillman Trail (yellow).

Stillman Trail   *Length: 3.3 miles Blaze: yellow*

This trail, originally known as the Schunemunk-Storm King Trail, was renamed in honor of Dr. Ernest Stillman. Two large stone pillars mark the Stillman Trail's entrance to Storm King State Park on Mountain Road, about a mile north of US 9W. Limited parking is available at the trailhead.

From the stone pillars. the trail goes east along a woods road which once carried pony-riding New Yorkers to views at the top of Storm King Mountain. Leaving the woods road to the left at 0.5 mile, the trail descends to a viewpoint to the north at 0.6 mile. Ascending, the trail goes on and off short segments of woods roads. It turns left and leaves the woods road at 0.9 mile. Here the Bluebird Trail (blue and red) begins to the right. The Stillman Trail sidehills its way across a steep slope and then ascends on switchbacks to the brow of the hill, passing several viewpoints over the Hudson River valley to the east and Schunemunk Mountain, the Shawangunks, and the Catskills to the northwest. The By-Pass Trail (white) leaves to the left at 1.7 miles. As the Stillman Trail wends its way to the summit of Storm King, it passes views to the south and east over Crows Nest and Bull Hill (Mount Taurus). After reaching the summit at 1.9 miles, the trail goes west and then southwest along the ridge, with limited views to the north and west. At 2.6 miles, in the saddle between Storm King and Butter Hill, the Stillman Trail passes the northern terminus of the Howell Trail (blue) to the left and then the southern end of the Bluebird Trail to the right. After ascending Butter Hill, with 360° views, at 2.8 miles, the trail drops over rocky ledges, with views to the south and east. At 3.1 miles, the trail passes stone pillars, the remains of Spy Rock House, the summer cottage of Dr. Edward L. Partridge, a commissioner of the Palisades Interstate Park. The Stillman Trail continues to descend and, at 3.3 miles, reaches a large parking lot on US 9W, with views over the Hudson River through the clove between Butter Hill on the left and Crows Nest on the right. The trail crosses US 9W through a gap in the center divider, follows the road south, and soon enters Black Rock Forest. The description of the trail continues in the Black Rock Forest section of this chapter (page 319). The Highlands Trail (teal diamond) is co-aligned for the entire length of this section.

Stillman Spring Trail   *Length: 0.7 mile Blaze: white*

Since many hikers do not wish to reclimb Crows Nest after hiking the Howell Trail, the Stillman Spring Trail offers a quick return to cars parked on NY 218. It begins at the Howell Trail (blue) in The Clove and starts its gradual descent to NY 218. Along its way there are seasonal views of Crows Nest, Breakneck Ridge, and Bull Hill (Mount Taurus) on the right, and Butter Hill and Storm King on the left. At 0.3 mile, the trail crosses a small stream and continues its descent. At 0.5 mile, it turns sharply right and after a short, but steeper descent, it crosses a stone bridge over a stream, turns, and descends more gradually again. At 0.7 mile, it reaches NY 218, adjacent to the Stillman Memorial Spring.

BLACK ROCK FOREST

Linked to Storm King by the Stillman Trail, the 3,700-acre Black Rock Forest has served as a field station for scientific research and education for more than seven decades. The forest was originally set aside in 1928 by Dr. Ernest Stillman for experimentation in forest management and for demonstration of forestry methods. These efforts continued after the forest was donated to Harvard University in 1949, but the focus shifted when it was acquired in 1989 by the not-for-profit Black Rock Forest Preserve. The forest is administered by the Black Rock Forest Consortium, a group of public and private educational and research institutions ranging from the neighboring Storm King School to New York City institutions such as the American Museum of Natural History and Columbia University. The mission of the Black Rock Forest Consortium is to promote scientific research and excellence in education while carefully managing the ecosystem of the forest. Several scientific studies are in progress at any given time, and thousands of students visit the forest each year for a variety of educational programs.

In 1999, the Consortium opened a new Center for Science and Education on Whitehorse Mountain, about one mile from US 9W. The Center, which is designed to allow students, teachers, and researchers to take increased advantage of Black Rock Forest's resources, has laboratory, classroom, and data management facilities. The building is open to the public, but no exhibits are provided.

Despite this primary educational emphasis, the consortium is dedicated to keeping Black Rock Forest open to the public for recreational pursuits such as hiking. Visitors are not charged for access, but the consortium is dependent on voluntary contributions to cover a portion of the expense of maintaining the forest.

Natural History

Black Rock Forest represents a characteristic slice of New York's Hudson Highlands. The area is completely underlain by resistant Precambrian granite and gneiss more than one billion years old.

Botanists have described a number of distinctly different ecological zones in Black Rock Forest. The most widespread plant community is an oak forest, dominated by three species: red, white, and chestnut. Red oak is by far the most common canopy tree in the forest, but at higher elevations and especially on rocky terrain, chestnut oak dominates, due to its greater drought tolerance and fire resistance. Associated hardwood trees include red and sugar maple, pignut and mockernut hickory, and black birch. Common understory trees include the American chestnut, formerly the dominant canopy tree, which was reduced to a nonreproductive status by the chestnut blight fungus. The most common shrubs are witch hazel and mountain laurel, the latter erupting in a sea of white and pink flowers each June. Lowbush blueberry is also common.

A slightly different variant of this community type is found in wetter areas and stream bottoms. Here the canopy is more diverse, with sugar maple more common and a greater component of American beech, basswood, tulip tree, and sweet gum. Common understory trees include ironwood and striped maple, with spicebush in the shrub layer. Yellow birch and sycamore are also found along the stream bottoms. Primarily along north-facing stream drainages, this community gives way to a third type—the dark, dense groves of American hemlock. The year-round shade cast by the hemlocks results in a community with lower species diversity and very little vegetation in the shrub and ground layers. Yet the climatic amelioration provided is a critical factor for much of the forest's wildlife.

As one ascends the ridges toward the summits, the chestnut oak forest gives way to a ridgetop plant community of much smaller stature and different composition. The characteristic trees are scrub oaks and pitch pine, species not able to persist elsewhere in the forest. Soils here are extremely shallow, and these areas are subject to the full impact of wind and weather, as well as the brunt of frequent acid deposition in the form of rain, snow, and fog. Many areas are covered by barren rock or a meadow community of lichens, mosses, and grasses. Hikers are asked to tread delicately in these fragile environments.

Black Rock Forest also possesses several large wetland areas, some open and others covered by trees such as red maple and alder that can tolerate a flooded rooting zone. Shrub cover by species such as leatherleaf is especially dense in many of the wetlands, while other areas are dominated by sphagnum moss. These wetlands fulfill a variety of critical ecosystem functions, such as water recharge, flood control, and nutrient recycling, provide breeding grounds for a wide array of species, and are some of the most productive and biologically diverse areas in the Highlands.

Finally, the forest also contains numerous ponds and reservoirs, which supply local communities with water and the hiker with refreshing vistas. Around the perimeters one can often find gray birch, a light-loving species not able to survive in much of the rest of the forest, alder trees, and some spectacular azaleas. Water lilies and spatterdock grow in some of the ponds, providing a beautiful floating floral display in mid-summer. Visitors may be able to see a variety of fish in the ponds, as well as bullfrogs, pickerel frogs, newts, and painted and snapping turtles. Stick lodges and gnawed trees provide evidence of ongoing beaver activity, although the animals themselves are seldom seen. Even rarer are sightings of environmentally sensitive species such as mink and river otter, which have been able to live in this area in small populations.

Deer are the most common large mammal in the forest, most often seen around dawn or dusk. Other common mammals include raccoons, opossums, red and gray foxes, gray, red, and flying squirrels, and longtailed weasels. Coyotes have made a great comeback in this area since about 1985, and their presence can be detected through their tracks, scat, or occasionally the sound of their plaintive calls. Poisonous snakes such as copperheads and timber rattlesnakes have been reported in the forest, but they are seldom encountered. More often seen are black racers, pilot black snakes, garter snakes, and water snakes. In shallow woodland pools and swamps, the calls of a variety of highly vocal frogs may be heard sequentially through the breeding season, from wood frogs and spring peepers, to American toads and gray tree frogs. Beneath moist logs and leaf litter are redbacked and slimy salamanders, while the streams are inhabited by two-lined salamanders and beautiful northern red salamanders.

Finally, the birdlife of the forest is diversified, especially during the spring and fall migratory periods when as many as ninety different species can be seen. Several of the more exposed summits in Black Rock Forest, as well as Storm King Mountain itself, are excellent vantage points from which to observe the autumn migrations of thousands of hawks, including rare peregrine falcons, and of golden and bald eagles. And just as each season features different avian fauna, at the same time each habitat provides different food, cover, and nesting capabilities that support distinctly different birds.

History

Black Rock Forest's cultural history dates from about the time of the American Revolution. The Continental Army used Continental Road, which bisects the forest, as a direct route across the mountains from West Point to New Windsor and Newburgh. From Spy Rock, sentinels from Washington's camp at Newburgh monitored British vessels sailing up the Hudson from Haverstraw Bay. On the west side of Continental Road, in the central part of the forest, stands a solitary stone house sheltered by tall spruces. Dating from the 1830s, the Chatfield Stone House is the first building shown on early maps of this area and the only building still existing on the property. A fire in 1912 gutted the Chatfield House, but it was reconstructed in 1932 and has been used since that time for storage and, more recently, as a focal point for educational activities.

More than one dozen other residences are known to have existed within the forest boundaries. The inhabitants of these widely scattered farms eked out a subsistence living by pasturing a few acres, cultivating small gardens, and cutting wood as a means of earning cash. Hunting and trapping wild game also added food and revenue sorely needed by these isolated families. An observant hiker can locate these old homesteads by looking for old cellar holes, remnant lilac bushes, stone walls, or dense stands of coniferous trees. Along Continental Road, a number of apple trees remain from the orchards that were planted in the 1800s.

The various stands of trees provide evidence of forest operations in the Stillman era. Most of the conifers represent plantings from the 1930s, including stands of red pine, and Norway and white spruce. Other areas were clearcut in blocks or strips, and today these areas can be detected by looking for stands of trees with nearly uniform diameters. Some of the longest recorded experiments in the entire region can be found marked by blue-staked corner posts and numbered trees. Many of these are long-term forest growth plots under continuous study since the 1930s. Finally, most of the roads and artificial ponds are also legacies from this intensive era of forest management.

Access

Black Rock Forest is open year-round, during daylight hours only, for recreational pursuits. However, it may be closed during periods of fire danger, deer hunting, and other times as posted. No motor vehicles of any kind are allowed in the forest without a permit. Bike riding in the forest is restricted to members of the Black Rock Mountain Bike Club; information may be obtained at the

Black Rock Forest Headquarters, located north of US 9W at 129 Continental Road in the Town of Cornwall. No fires are permitted at any time, and camping by the public is not permitted. Anything encountered in the forest, including scientific and educational materials, must be left undisturbed. All organized groups (hiking, birding, and so forth) are required to register with the Black Rock Forest Headquarters prior to visiting by calling (845) 534-4517. During deer-rifle season, Black Rock Forest is closed to hikers.

Short Line bus service to within two miles of the forest is available from New York City's Port Authority terminal to Mountainville (on the west side of the forest) or to Cornwall-on-Hudson (on the north side). The main parking area is 0.2 mile south of US 9W on the northern side of the forest. Coming from the south, drivers take the first right turn onto Mountain Road, 0.4 mile after the Storm King parking area on US 9W. A sharp right leads through a tunnel under the highway. (The tunnel is passable by small vehicles only; larger vehicles should proceed as below.) The road passes a T intersection and continues to the main parking area. Larger vehicles, or those that miss the Mountain Road turnoff, can proceed north on US 9W to the Angola Road exit to the southbound lanes of US 9W, and proceed as described below.

For visitors coming from the north on US 9W, the entrance to the forest is 1.6 miles south of Angola Road. A right turn on the entrance road and another right turn at the T junction leads to the main parking area. Limited parking is available at other forest entrances, with the largest area immediately adjacent to US 9W, south of Old West Point Road. Parking on the west side for the major trails is noted in the trails descriptions in this chapter. For more information, contact the Black Rock Forest Center for Science and Education, 129 Continental Road, Cornwall, NY 12518; (845) 534-4517.

Trails and Woods Roads in Black Rock Forest

More than 30 miles of forest trails and woods roads crisscross Black Rock Forest. The trails, with steep ups and downs, lead to lookout points, while the roads wind among the reservoirs. Hikers can easily avoid the multi-use roads. When using the roads, keep an eye out for bicycles, forest maintenance trucks, and vehicles driven by scientists and visiting student groups.

The two main forest trails, which run approximately southwest to northeast, are the Stillman Trail (yellow) and the Scenic Trail (white). The Sackett

Figure 15-2. Causeway over Jim's Pond

Trail (yellow circle) is also a ridge trail with outlooks to the west and north. Crossing these trails, which are maintained by the New York-New Jersey Trail Conference, are a number of short trails running roughly north to south that can be combined in a variety of long and short walks. To understand the connections, consult Map 7 of the Trail Conference's West Hudson Trails map set.

Along the floor of the forest meander scenic gravel roads from which hikers can enjoy the reservoirs at closer range. However, to protect the public water supply, swimming, fishing, or other public use of these reservoirs is not allowed. Circular walks in different combinations are possible on these woods roads, which survive from the days when this area was populated by families scattered on small farms.

Arthur Trail
Length: 0.7 mile Blaze: yellow

This trail is named after the son of Jim Babcock, woodsman, rattlesnake hunter, and first forester and caretaker of Black Rock Forest. It starts and ends on Jim's Pond Road. Going north, after 0.3 mile, the Scenic Trail (white) comes in from the left and runs jointly with the Arthur Trail for 0.1 mile. The Arthur Trail crosses the outlet of Sutherland Pond on unique puncheons—cross-sections of a two-foot-diameter tree, laid down like pie plates. It ends at the junction of

Jim's Pond Road and the Compartment Trail (blue). The Highlands Trail (teal diamond) is co-aligned for 0.1 mile.

Black Rock Hollow Trail
Length: 1.5 miles Blaze: white

The Black Rock Hollow Trail provides the quickest access to Black Rock Mountain from US 9W. The trail starts from a parking area on southbound US 9W less than a mile from the Angola Road entrance (and just beyond Old West Point Road) and follows a dirt road for 0.6 mile. At the filter plant, it turns right and goes into the woods. Heading upstream along Black Rock Brook for 0.9 mile, it ends at the Stillman Trail (yellow). A right-hand turn on the Stillman Trail leads to the top of Black Rock Mountain in 0.4 mile.

Chatfield Trail
Length: 0.7 mile Blaze: blue

This trail, named for a hamlet that is now a part of Cornwall, begins at the Scenic Trail (white), midway from the Arthur and Eagle Cliff trails. Heading northeast, it crosses a brook and ascends steeply through mountain laurel and mixed hardwoods. The grade changes to a gentle ascent while the route goes along a large rock formation, passing a marsh area on the right. After the Chatfield Trail passes the Secor Trail (yellow) at 0.5 mile and the Ledge Trail (yellow) at 0.6 mile, it descends gently to end at Chatfield Road at 0.7 mile near Tamarack Pond.

Compartment Trail
Length: 1.1 miles Blaze: blue

From the northern junction of the Arthur Trail and Jim's Pond Road, this trail travels on a woods road, running jointly with the Highlands Trail (teal diamond) for the first 0.4 mile. The Compartment Trail soon turns right, leaving the woods road, and at 0.3 mile the Split Rock Trail (white) goes off to the right. At 0.4 mile, the Compartment Trail turns left, leaving the Highlands Trail and joining the Stillman Trail (yellow) for 600 feet. The Compartment Trail then turns right, and it ends on Hall Road at its junction with the Sackett Trail (yellow circle).

Duggan Trail
Length: 0.4 mile Blaze: red

Named in honor of the Duggan family who donated land to Black Rock Forest, the Duggan Trail provides the primary access to the Black Rock Forest trail system. From the left end of the parking lot on Reservoir Road, the Duggan Trail winds gently downhill to end at the Reservoir Trail (blue) near Ben's Bridge.

Eagle Cliff Trail *Length: 0.1 mile Blaze: blue*

This short trail leads from the Scenic Trail (white), 0.4 mile from the junction with the Arthur Trail (yellow), to views of the Manhattan skyline at Eagle Cliff. The Rut Trail (red/orange) leads down the other side of Eagle Cliff to the Stropel Trail (yellow).

Hill of Pines Trail *Length: 0.6 mile Blaze: white*

This trail connects Carpenter Road with the Swamp Trail (blue), shortly before the latter emerges on Old West Point Road.

Ledge Trail *Length: 0.3 mile Blaze: yellow*

The remains of a fire tower are on this link between the Scenic Trail (white) and Chatfield Trail (blue). Dr. Stillman had a wooden tower built on the rocky outcroppings at the highest point of the trail. It was hit by lightning shortly after it was finished and burned to the ground.

Mine Hill Trail *Length: 0.2 mile Blaze: yellow diamond*

This trail provides access to Black Rock Forest from the west. Parking is available for two or three cars just above the steep hairpin turn on Mine Hill Road, 0.9 mile from Angola Road. The beginning of the Mine Hill Trail is across the road. The Mine Hill Trail starts steeply up a rocky slope, reaching open views to the north and northwest at 0.1 mile. Leaving the viewpoint, the trail doubles back to the south, ascending on a more moderate grade to end at 0.2 mile at the Sackett Trail (yellow circle).

Reservoir Trail *Length: 0.5 mile Blaze: blue*

Starting at the Stillman Trail (yellow) just west of the Upper Reservoir, the trail follows the reservoir outlet brook. At 0.5 mile, it crosses the brook on Ben's Bridge. The Duggan Trail (red) comes in from the right, and the Reservoir Trail soon ends at the filter plant.

Rut Trail *Length: 0.2 mile Blaze: red/orange*

This short trail leads from the Stropel Trail (yellow) to the Eagle Cliff Trail (blue), with views of the Manhattan skyline from Eagle Cliff.

Ryerson Trail *Length: 0.3 mile Blaze: yellow*

This trail branches right (southeast) from the Scenic Trail (white), 0.2 mile from Jupiter's Boulder in the southwest part of Black Rock Forest, and short-cuts over to Jim's Pond Road, where it ends.

Sackett Trail   *Length: 1.6 miles Blaze: yellow circle*

The Sackett Trail offers several viewpoints with wide vistas to the west and northwest as it winds along the crest of Sackett Mountain. It is accessible from the Mine Hill and Stillman trails and Continental Road. Its southern terminus is on the Stillman Trail (yellow), 0.2 mile from Hall Road. It passes a viewpoint in just over 0.1 mile and then passes the Mine Hill Trail (yellow diamond) coming in on the left at 0.3 mile. The Sackett Trail continues north and then east, crossing two brooks. At 1.1 miles, the trail arrives at the crumbling walls and chimney of the old Beattie cabin, built as a family camping retreat before Dr. Stillman owned the forest. Less than a tenth of a mile later, the Sackett Trail passes the northern terminus of the Compartment Trail (blue). For about 150 feet, the trail uses Hall Road, named for a family formerly living at the junction of Continental Road and US 9W. After leaving Hall Road from the east side, the trail winds around a hill with rocky outcroppings. It heads east and uphill, ending at Continental Road at 1.6 miles.

Scenic Trail   *Length: 5.9 miles Blaze: white*

This aptly named trail is appealing at any time of year. As the Scenic Trail meanders across Black Rock Forest, it crosses numerous woods roads and short trails, thus lending itself to forming interesting loop hikes. The trail is south of and generally parallel to the Stillman Trail (yellow) until it intersects it, ending at the foot of Mount Misery. The Highlands Trail (teal diamond) is co-aligned with the Scenic Trail for 1.9 miles as the two trails enter Black Rock Forest from the west. Access for hikers coming by Short Line bus from New York City is via the Highlands Trail from the bus stop in Mountainville at the junction of NY 32 and Angola Road.

The Scenic Trail begins just south of the northern junction of Mineral Spring and Old Mineral Spring roads. Parking is available 0.3 mile farther south, at the southern end of Old Mineral Spring Road. The trail enters Black Rock Forest on a dirt road. At 0.3 mile, the trail approaches Mineral Spring Falls, a triple cascade flowing over a series of ledges through a dark hemlock grove. Continuing ahead, the trail climbs up the ravine, paralleling the stream. After turning left near the top of the grade, the trail winds through hemlock groves and over varied terrain to approach the slopes of Mount Rascal.

After a few short diago-
nal rises, the Scenic Trail
begins to parallel the ridge
line and, at 1.4 miles, comes
to Jupiter's Boulder, the first
of two outlooks to the
northwest, which on a clear
day afford distant views to
the Shawangunks and the
Catskills. The route continues generally northeast-

Figure 15-3. Jupiter's Boulder

ward, passing the western terminus of the Ryerson Trail (yellow) at 1.6 miles.
After passing through a laurel lane (in full bloom in mid-June), the Scenic Trail
reaches Jim's Pond Road at 1.9 miles. Here, the Highlands Trail (teal diamond)
leaves to the left. The Scenic Trail continues south on the road until it turns
sharply east. It coincides for a short distance with the Arthur Trail (yellow) and
then leaves to the right. At 2.5 miles, the Scenic Trail passes the southern terminus of the Chatfield Trail (blue), which leads across the forest to Chatfield
Road, and then passes the Eagle Cliff Trail (blue) at 2.9 miles. The next junction is with the Stropel Trail (yellow) at 3.1 miles, and then a short distance
afterwards the Scenic Trail passes the Ledge Trail (yellow), leading to the
Chatfield Trail. Soon, the Spy Rock Trail (blue), which leads to Spy Rock (at
1,461 feet, the highest elevation in Black Rock Forest), leaves to the left. After
crossing Continental Road at 3.7 miles, the Scenic Trail continues northeast on
Bog Meadow Road, and in less than half a mile it abruptly turns right off the
road to meander up Rattlesnake Hill. As the trail continues north over the hill,
it crosses Carpenter Road at 4.2 miles, then goes up and over Hill of Pines.
Soon after crossing the Swamp Trail (blue), the Scenic Trail ends at 5.9 miles at
the Stillman Trail (yellow), on a slope at the southern base of Mount Misery.

Secor Trail   *Length: 0.3 mile Blaze: yellow*
The Secor Trail is named for a family residing in Cornwall. Starting on Chatfield
Road due south of Sphagnum Pond, it is a shortcut over to the Chatfield Trail
(blue).

Shortcut Trail   *Length: 0.4 mile Blaze: yellow triangle*
Aptly named, this trail eliminates 0.75 mile along the Stillman Trail (yellow). It

begins where the Stillman Trail joins Hall Road, goes south along Hall Road for 0.1 mile before turning west into the woods, and ends at the Stillman Trail at 0.4 mile.

Split Rock Trail   *Length: 0.4 mile Blaze: white*
This short spur trail leads from the Compartment Trail (blue), reaching the lookout at Split (or Echo) Rock at 0.2 mile. It continues past the views of the Manhattan skyline (visible on a clear day), Sutherland Pond, and the hills to the south, and ends on Sutherland Road at its intersection with Chatfield Road.

Spy Rock Trail   *Length: 0.2 mile Blaze: blue*
This short spur trail leads from the Scenic Trail (white), 0.1 mile east of its junction with the Ledge Trail (yellow), over rock outcroppings to Spy Rock. One pitch pine marks the summit (1,461 feet), which offers views north toward the Catskills and northwest to the Shawangunks. This is the highest elevation in Black Rock Forest.

Stillman Trail   *Length: 5.3 miles Blaze: yellow*
From the Butter Hill-Storm King parking lot on the northbound side of US 9W, the Stillman Trail crosses the road and follows it south for 0.2 mile. It is co-aligned with the Highlands Trail (teal diamond) for the next 4.3 miles. Turning right, the trail continues up a steep, rocky ravine. Emerging from the ravine, the grade moderates as the climb continues to a small rocky area at the top of the ridge at 0.5 mile. The trail then winds along the top of the ridge, with no well-defined summit. After passing through a dense stand of laurel, it descends steeply, then levels off before beginning a gradual descent to the Upper Reservoir. At 1.0 mile, the trail passes the Black Rock Forest boundary sign. The descent continues over an easy grade, with the reservoir visible through the trees to the left. The trail passes close to the north end of the dam and spillway before turning south below the dam.

At 1.3 miles, the trail reaches Reservoir Road, historically known as Old West Point Road, below the Upper Reservoir dam. It turns right and follows the road to a point opposite the triple blaze marking the southeastern end of the Reservoir Trail (blue). Here, the Stillman Trail turns left from Reservoir Road, crosses the outlet from the Upper Reservoir, and then diverges left from the Reservoir Trail, which heads northwest. The Stillman Trail continues southwest up a steep grade over a rocky path and crosses White Oak Road at 1.5

miles. The steep ascent continues and, at 1.6 miles, the
Stillman Trail reaches the
summit of Mount Misery.
The bare rocks at the summit
offer views to the north and
west, with Aleck Meadow
Dam and part of the reservoir
visible.

A tenth of a mile later,
the steep descent off the ridge
begins. At the bottom of the
descent, the trail levels off,
turns right, and enters a boulder field. At 1.9 miles, in the
middle of the boulder field,
the route passes the northern
end of the Scenic Trail
(white), climbs briefly, and
then descends over an easy
grade. The trail again crosses
White Oak Road near Aleck
Meadow Reservoir at 2.1

Figure 15-4. Woods road near Split Rock

miles. After passing the east end of the dam and the spillway, the trail descends,
turns left below the dam, and then crosses the bridge over the outlet of Aleck
Meadow Reservoir. Downstream from the bridge, the stream cascades through
a narrow ravine in a hemlock grove. The trail continues west along the foot of
the dam and leaves the reservoir at the northwest corner at 2.3 miles. The
gradually ascending trail passes the southern end of the Black Rock Hollow
Trail (white) on the right at 2.4 miles, and within 300 feet makes a sharp right
turn within sight of White Oak Road. Hikers should take care, as the terrain is
open between the turn and the road, giving the impression that the path is
straight ahead. After the turn, the trail climbs gradually to the summit of Black
Rock Mountain at 2.8 miles. There are views to the west, north, and northeast.
A blue-blazed trail leads a short distance north over rocks to more open ledges.

The descent on the west side is, at first, steep over rocks and then moderate
to a major intersection. The Stillman Trail first joins Hulse Road shortly before

the intersection at 3.2 miles, then turns right on Continental Road for a few paces to where the Sackett Trail (yellow circle) begins. The Stillman Trail turns left into the woods, while the Sackett Trail goes straight ahead. It is easy to become confused here, as both trails use yellow blazes: the Stillman's are rectangles, while the Sackett's are circles. There are small black-and-white signs to help find each trail. Proceeding southwest, the Stillman Trail ascends an easy grade along a ridge and, at 3.6 miles, reaches the western end of the White Oak Trail (white) on the left.

At 4.3 miles, when the Stillman Trail reaches the Compartment Trail (blue) at a large rock with a cairn, the Highlands Trail (teal diamond) continues ahead on the Compartment Trail, while the Stillman Trail turns right. The Stillman and Compartment trails join together for slightly over 0.1 mile until the Compartment Trail turns sharply off to the right in sight of Hall Road. Less than 100 feet later, the Stillman Trail meets Hall Road at a bend in the road and turns right. The Shortcut Trail (yellow triangle) follows Hall Road to the left. At 4.5 miles, the Stillman Trail turns off to the left and then meets the Sackett Trail (yellow circle) on the right at 4.7 miles. Turning south from this junction and proceeding over easy grades, the Stillman Trail reaches the western end of the Shortcut Trail (yellow triangle) at 5.0 miles.

The Stillman Trail continues south, then turns west and descends a moderate grade as it approaches its western terminus—a viewpoint 5.3 miles from the parking lot on US 9W.

Stropel Trail *Length: 0.2 mile Blaze: yellow*
The Stropel Trail begins at Jim's Pond Road. After climbing ledges, the Rut Trail (red/orange), which leads to the Eagle Cliff lookout, leaves to the left. The Stropel Trail ends at the Scenic Trail (white), a short distance east of the Eagle Cliff Trail (blue).

Swamp Trail *Length: 0.5 mile Blaze: blue*
The Swamp Trail begins on White Oak Road, just south of its intersection with the Stillman Trail (yellow). It heads east between Mount Misery and Hill of Pines to the Old West Point Road, crossing the Scenic Trail (white) not quite halfway. The trail ends just past the northern terminus of the Hill of Pines Trail (white).

Tower Vue Trail   *Length: 0.7 mile Blaze: yellow*

The Tower Vue Trail lives up to its name and rewards the hiker with views of the site of the old fire tower. Leaving the White Oak Trail (white) near the east end of Arthurs Dam, this trail parallels the eastern shoreline of Arthurs Pond. Going up and down many times before reaching Bog Meadow Road, it is reminiscent of a roller-coaster ride.

White Oak Trail   *Length: 1.2 miles Blaze: white*

The White Oak Trail begins at the Stillman Trail (yellow) northwest of Sphagnum Pond. After crossing Sutherland Road, the trail skirts the outlet of Sphagnum Pond. At 0.4 mile, it joins a woods road for a short distance. The trail then turns right onto Continental Road. (To the left is the white oak tree for which the trail and road are named.) The trail soon turns left, leaving the road, and skirts the northern end of Arthurs Pond. It then passes the northern end of the Tower Vue Trail (yellow). The White Oak Trail ends on White Oak Road south of Aleck Meadow Reservoir.

SIXTEEN

BEAR MOUNTAIN-HARRIMAN STATE PARKS

he variety of trails looping across the rugged landscape, draped upon the Highlands, is a major part of the appeal of Bear Mountain-Harriman State Parks. This network of infinite combinations is unmatched in the area surrounding metropolitan New York. The hiker may choose to climb through the crevices of the Lemon Squeezer, savor the views of the Hudson from high on Dunderberg, or ramble on old woods roads past sleepy swamps and abandoned mining villages.

Harriman State Park perpetuates the name of Edward H. Harriman, the railroad builder who conceived the idea of establishing a park in the Hudson Highlands, and of his widow, Mary A. Harriman, who carried out his intention by giving 10,000 acres to the state in 1910. With that nucleus, additional acquisitions over the years expanded the jointly operated Bear Mountain and Harriman State Parks to approximately 52,000 acres. For more information, contact the Palisades Interstate Park Commission, Administration Building, Bear Mountain, NY 10911; (845) 786-2701; www.nysparks.com.

For a history of the park and a complete guide to the marked and unmarked trails, see *Harriman Trails—A Guide and History*, by William Myles (New York-New Jersey Trail Conference, 2d ed. 1999).

Geology

The Hudson Highlands and their extension southwesterly into the Ramapo Mountains along the New York-New Jersey border constitute a major

Figure 16-1. Bear Mountain and the Hudson Highlands from Long Mountain

topographic feature of our region. The bedrock is entirely Precambrian and consists mostly of a variety of gneisses, many of which represent metamorphosed sedimentary rocks. The Highlands of Bear Mountain-Harriman State Parks probably were once more than 10,000 feet high, and the present hills are mere remnants of what was formerly a mountain range comparable to the present-day Rockies.

Among the striking evidences of glaciation in Bear Mountain-Harriman State Parks are the abundant bedrock surfaces that were scratched, polished, or grooved by rock debris carried by Ice Age glaciers. Erratic boulders—some of immense size—were carried from the Catskills and elsewhere to the north. Left behind when the glaciers melted, they are widely distributed throughout the park.

Natural History

Like the rest of the Hudson Highlands, the Bear Mountain-Harriman State Parks harbor a wide range of plant and animal life. The variety of habitats range from the brackish Iona Island marsh at sea level to the mountainous interior. The latter reaches more than 1,300 feet, with thirty-six lakes, numerous swamps, open fields, hemlock forests, and hardwood ridges.

DICKERSON·SPITZENBERG·DUNDERBERG·BALD·TIMP·WEST·MOUNTAIN

TURKEY MOUNTAIN 900

Southeast

AND DOWN COUNTRY
trail, where now stands a plaque for Raymond Torrey
Foreground · "SEVEN LAKES DRIVE" QUEENSBORO LAKE
BEAR BETWEEN THE TORNE AND THE TIMP R C Dickinson 1923 50

R. L. DICKINSON

Observers can find roughly forty species of mammals, twenty-five species of reptiles, and more than ninety species of nesting (breeding) birds in this area. Squirrel, deer, raccoon, and woodchuck probably are seen the most often, although beaver, otter, mink, and bobcat are present in limited numbers. While black bear are rare, they have been reported. Hikers may encounter a variety of snakes including garter, water, milk, ring-necked, and hog-nosed. In rocky, open areas, milk snakes and ring-necked snakes can be found, while hog-nosed snakes are occasionally seen sprawled out on sandy roads, trails, and exposures. Copperhead and timber rattlesnakes are less likely to be found, as they tend to avoid human contact. Five-lined skinks, which belong to the lizard family, may also scamper across a hiker's path.

With more than 240 species of birds visiting the area, there is plenty of activity to watch in the sky. Among the more exciting birds are wood duck, goshawk, red-tailed hawk, broad-winged hawk, ruffled grouse, woodcock, screech owl, great horned owl, pileated woodpecker, tree swallow, veery, blue-gray gnatcatcher, hooded warbler, black-throated green warbler, prairie warbler, Louisiana water thrush, and scarlet tanager. The two most common and characteristic nesting birds are catbird and towhee, which seem to be everywhere during summer hikes. Iona Island is excellent for birding, with ducks, herons, bitterns, and marsh wrens in summer and its winter ducks and occasional bald eagle in winter. Wild turkeys are becoming more numerous, and turkey buzzards are frequently seen.

The mature forests in the park are a blend of evergreen and deciduous varieties. Principal evergreens are red cedar, hemlock, and white pine. The deciduous trees include oak, maple, hickory, ash, tulip, beech, and sour gum. Laurel, rhododendron, witch hazel, spicebush, wild azalea, sweet pepperbush, alder, blueberry, and sumac are among the shrubs found in the park. Iona Island hosts prickly pear cactus. In addition to the well-known flowers of meadow and forest, the hiker can find others less known and even more rare. Ferns, lichens, and mosses abound in the forest, including evergreen species such as polypody, Christmas, and evergreen wood ferns.

The Trailside Museum and Zoo, across US 9W from the Bear Mountain Inn, contains a selection of many local plants, birds, animals, and reptiles. A visit here will help the hiker identify much of the flora and fauna within the park.

Iron Mines in the Highlands

The abandoned shafts, pits, and dumps of old iron mines are among the most fascinating features of the Highlands, including Bear Mountain-Harriman State Parks. Over twenty known mines were worked at one time or another. The iron ore consists of veins of magnetite (a variety of iron oxide) that are interlayered with the Highland gneisses. Mining began in colonial times, about 1730. At its height, during the Civil War, the industry controlled the life of the region and supported a sizable population.

After the iron-ore deposits of the Great Lakes region were discovered, the center of iron mining in the United States shifted away from the New York-New Jersey region. Because the ores near Lake Superior were so abundant and more easily mined, the iron industry of New York and New Jersey declined, and

Figure 16-2. *Old iron furnace at Arden*

JACK FAGAN

by 1890, almost all the mines in what is now Bear Mountain-Harriman State Parks had been abandoned. Many of the inhabitants drifted away from the region when there was no more work, leaving houses to fall into the cellar holes still visible along many old roads now overgrown. Apple trees, lilac bushes, and daffodils remain as evidence of these homes.

Refer to William Myles's book, *Harriman Trails,* and Edward Lenik's, *Iron Mine Trails,* for specific characteristics of each of the mines.

Dunderberg Spiral Railway

This uncompleted and abandoned scenic venture is a curiosity of the Highlands. Work on the railway began in the spring of 1890. Less than a year later, after a substantial sum had been spent on construction and a significant portion of the line graded, the enterprise faltered for lack of funds. For part of their routes, the Ramapo-Dunderberg and Timp-Torne trails follow sections of the old railway grade.

Each section ends abruptly and gives little impression of a unified scheme. Complete details and an illus-

Figure 16-3. Dunderberg railway tunnel

tration of the railway layout can be found in *Harriman Trails*, by William Myles. The whole railway can be explored in a day by bushwhacking from one section to the next, once the general plan is understood.

Trails in the Bear Mountain-Harriman State Parks

There are more than 235 miles of marked trails in the parks. This chapter includes most of the marked trails. Parking is noted in specific trail descriptions. Public transportation to Bear Mountain-Harriman is available from the New York Port Authority Bus Terminal. Short Line buses to the Bear Mountain Inn also stop, if requested, along US 9W at Tomkins Cove and Jones Point.

Short Line buses and Metro-North trains to Suffern, Sloatsburg, Tuxedo, Southfields, and Arden give access to trails on the west side of the parks.

Anthony Wayne Trail   *Length: 2.8 miles Blaze: white*

The midpoint of this trail, accessible from the north end of the Anthony Wayne parking lot (Exit 17 on the Palisades Interstate Parkway), forms a loop with the Popolopen Gorge Trail (red on white) at Turkey Hill Lake and the Timp-Torne Trail (blue) on the west end of West Mountain. Named for "Mad Anthony" Wayne, a hero of the American Revolution, the trail starts from Turkey Hill Lake and heads south until it crosses US 6 at 0.7 mile. The trail crosses Seven Lakes Drive at 1.0 mile and then continues gently uphill. It crosses the 1779 Trail and shortly thereafter descends to cross the Palisades Interstate Parkway at 1.8 miles. East of the parkway, the trail follows the old Beechy Bottom Road to the left a short distance; then it turns off to the right over the shoulder of West Mountain to end at the Timp-Torne Trail (blue).

Appalachian Trail   *Length: 18.8 miles Blaze: white*

This major long-distance trail traverses the northern section of the park, extending from the Bear Mountain Bridge to NY 17. On the way, it intersects or runs jointly with ten other marked trails, and it can be combined with these trails to make a variety of loop hikes. The section through Bear Mountain-Harriman State Parks was the first section of the 2,160-mile-long Appalachian Trail (AT) to be completed, and much of the AT through the park still follows the original route.

Both ends of the trail in the park are readily accessible. The west end is at the Bear Mountain Inn, which is served by buses from New York City's Port Authority Bus Terminal and where ample parking is available (fee charged in season). The east end is at NY 17 and Arden Valley Road, where buses from New York City will stop on request. Cars may be parked at the Elk Pen parking area, just south of Arden Valley Road, 0.3 mile east of NY 17. Parking is also available near several intermediate points along the trail.

Before proceeding west on the AT from the Bear Mountain Inn, hikers may wish to follow the trail east, through a pedestrian tunnel under US 9W, into the Trailside Museum and Zoo, which features native plants, animals, reptiles, and birds. A sign on the AT, as it passes through the museum, marks the lowest point on the entire trail from Maine to Georgia—124 feet above sea level.

To head west on the AT from the Inn, follow a paved path west to a playground near the southern tip of Hessian Lake. Here, the Appalachian, Cornell Mine (blue), Major Welch (red dot on white), and Suffern-Bear Mountain (yellow) trails converge. The AT proceeds uphill, following a joint route with the Suffern-Bear Mountain Trail (yellow). At 0.6 mile, the AT turns right and begins to climb Bear Mountain in earnest, gaining 700 feet in elevation in the next 1.2 miles. It turns right onto the paved Scenic Drive at 1.0 mile, with views to the right over the Hudson River, Bear Mountain Bridge, and Iona Island. After turning left, leaving the road, and then crossing it twice, the AT arrives at 1.8 miles at the summit of Bear Mountain (1,305 feet), where it crosses the Major Welch Trail (red dot on white). The stone Perkins Memorial Tower (built in 1934 in memory of George W. Perkins, first president of the Palisades Interstate Park Commission) has historical exhibits.

The AT descends to the Perkins Memorial Drive and turns left, following the paved road for 0.5 mile. It then bears left and re-enters the woods. At 3.4 miles, it crosses Seven Lakes Drive and briefly joins the 1777W Trail (red 1777 on white circle). (A parking area is located on a short access road just south of Seven Lakes Drive, 0.2 mile west of the AT crossing.) After passing the west end of the Fawn Trail (red), the AT steeply ascends to the ridge of West Mountain. It reaches a viewpoint to the east, joins the Timp-Torne Trail (blue), then crosses the ridge and arrives at a viewpoint over Black Mountain to the west. For the next 0.6 mile, it runs along the crest of the ridge, with many views to the west. At 5.0 miles, the Timp-Torne diverges to the left, and the AT begins a steady descent, crossing Beechy Bottom East Road and then paralleling it for a short distance. At the bottom, the AT crosses Beechy Bottom Brook, then turns sharply right to join the Ramapo-Dunderberg Trail (R-D) (red dot on white). Both trails cross the Palisades Interstate Parkway at 6.2 miles, then cross a woods road and the 1779 Trail (blue 1779 on white circle) and begin their ascent of Black Mountain.

At 6.9 miles, the AT/R-D comes out on open rocks at the summit of Black Mountain, with views over the Hudson River to the east. On a clear day, the Manhattan skyline is visible to the south. Continuing west, a viewpoint over Silvermine Lake is reached at 7.3 miles, and the AT/R-D descends steeply to cross the Silvermine Ski Road. After climbing over a ridge, the trails descend to reach the William Brien Memorial Shelter at 8.3 miles. Here, the Menomine Trail (yellow) leaves to the left. The AT/R-D now climbs over Letterrock Mountain. At 9.1 miles, near a wooden footbridge at the base of the descent, the AT diverges to the right, leaving the R-D.

The AT crosses Seven Lakes Drive at 10.3 miles and ascends to a rocky promontory, with views to the south over Lake Tiorati. It briefly joins several woods roads and, after climbing over a knoll, crosses Arden Valley Road at 12.5 miles. To the left, 0.3 mile downhill, is Tiorati Circle, where parking is available. The R-D now rejoins the AT, and both trails continue southward, climbing the ridge of Fingerboard Mountain (1,328 feet). At 13.6 miles, the Hurst Trail (blue) leaves to the right, with the Fingerboard Shelter visible immediately below. Just beyond, the AT turns right, leaving the R-D, and begins to descend, steeply in places, passing through a mixed forest of hardwoods and hemlocks broken by several laurel thickets. At 14.2 miles, at the base of the descent, the AT turns left along Surebridge Brook, passing the remains of the Greenwood Mine, a major source of iron ore during the Civil War.

The AT climbs the ridge of Surebridge Mountain and, at 15.1 miles, it crosses the Long Path (aqua). It climbs to the summit of Island Pond Mountain and then descends. On the way down, at 15.7 miles, it goes through the Lemon Squeezer, a narrow, steep passage between large boulders. A side trail to the right provides an alternative route to bypass a very steep section. At the base of the Lemon Squeezer, the Arden-Surebridge Trail (red triangle on white) joins briefly. The AT crosses the inlet of Island Pond, climbs to a viewpoint over the pond, and then descends to cross the pond's outlet, channeled into a spillway of cut stones (constructed by the Civilian Conservation Corps in 1934).

After briefly following Island Pond Road (a woods road, built by Edward Harriman about 1905), the AT turns right at 16.5 miles and climbs Green Pond Mountain. The trail runs along the summit ridge for a short distance, and just before it begins its descent on switchbacks, there is a view to the west from open rocks. At 17.5 miles, the AT turns right on the Old Arden Road, which once connected the Arden estate of the Harriman family with Tuxedo. (The Arden-Surebridge Trail begins here and proceeds south on this road.) In 500 feet, the AT turns left on the paved Arden Valley Road, which it follows over the New York State Thruway and the Norfolk Southern Railroad to reach NY 17 at 18.0 miles.

Arden-Surebridge Trail   *Length: 6.3 miles Blaze: red triangle on white*
This trail is readily accessible at both ends. Short Line buses from New York City's Port Authority Bus Terminal will stop at the park entrance on NY 17 and Arden Valley Road, and car parking is available at the Elk Pen, just south

of Arden Valley Road, a short distance east of NY 17. The west end of the trail is at a fishermen's parking lot off Seven Lakes Drive at Lake Skannatati.

The trail starts where a dirt road going east from the Elk Pen parking area reaches the Old Arden Road. The Arden-Surebridge Trail proceeds south along Old Arden Road. In 150 feet, the Appalachian Trail (white) turns left over Green Pond Mountain. The Arden-Surebridge Trail leaves the road at 0.4 mile, turning left and climbing gently onto a plateau. At 0.8 mile, it turns left on the route of the former Green Trail and begins a steep ascent of the south end of Green Pond Mountain. Leveling off, it joins Island Pond Road for 0.3 mile and then turns left, looping south for 2.0 miles around a swamp below Island Pond. The Arden-Surebridge Trail meets the Appalachian Trail 3.5 miles from the Elk Pen, just before the Appalachian Trail heads north through the Lemon Squeezer, a curious rock formation. It is worth a quick side trip to climb through the crevices.

After the brief meeting with the Appalachian Trail, the Arden-Surebridge Trail turns right and in 0.2 mile joins the Long Path (aqua) coming in from the left. Immediately beyond, the north end of the White Bar Trail will be seen on the right at 3.7 miles. Following the "Lost Road," the Arden-Surebridge Trail passes the southern end of Dismal Swamp and goes up Surebridge Mountain. At 4.0 miles, the Arden-Surebridge Trail goes by the northern end of the Lichen Trail (blue L on white) and then through a hemlock grove to the Surebridge Mine Road. Extensive fire damage in the area will be discernible for years.

The Arden-Surebridge Trail and Long Path reach "Times Square" at 4.6 miles. Hikers must take care to follow the red triangles on white, as the Ramapo-Dunderberg Trail, blazed with a red dot on white, also crosses this multi-trail junction. Just beyond "Times Square," the Long Path leaves the Arden-Surebridge Trail to the right, heading south and east. The Arden-Surebridge continues to follow the now descending road to the beginning of the Dunning Trail (yellow) at 5.0 miles.

After crossing a brook, the Arden-Surebridge Trail continues for several hundred feet past water-filled holes of the Pine Swamp Mine on the left and then makes a sharp right turn off the road. It goes on past the northeast corner of Pine Swamp, where the temperature can be 20 degrees cooler than the surrounding areas. Following another old woods road, the trail makes another sharp right turn and climbs gently through a glen to the top of Pine Swamp Mountain. Here are views to the south over Lake Skannatati, Lake Kanawauke, Little Long Pond, Lake Sebago, and the Ramapo ridge. At 6.0 miles, the Red

Figure 16-4. View from Pine Swamp Mountain: Lakes Skannatati and Kanawauke

Cross Trail (red cross on white) begins on the left. After descending Pine Swamp Mountain, the Arden-Surebridge Trail ends at Lake Skannatati on Seven Lakes Drive, 6.3 miles from the Elk Pen.

Beech Trail   *Length: 3.9 miles Blaze: blue*
The Beech Trail connects the Red Cross Trail with the Long Path east of Seven Lakes Drive. It provides an easy hike without much change in elevation. From the Red Cross Trail (red cross on white), the Beech Trail heads south through deciduous woods, passing over a low shoulder of Flaggy Meadow Mountain, runs along Tiorati Brook for a short distance, crosses the brook on a highway bridge, and briefly turns right to parallel Tiorati Brook Road (closed in winter) at 0.9 mile. When the road is open, parking is permitted here.

The trail gently rises along the eastern slope of Nat House Mountain before crossing Hasenclever Road (a fire road), and it continues south through level woods. It comes to an area of stone walls, old fruit trees, lilacs, wisteria, and barberries—all reminders of one-time human presence. Stone foundations and a small family burying ground give a feeling of once-active farm life.

At 2.7 miles, the trail joins a woods road and passes under the east flank of Rockhouse Mountain. At 3.3 miles, it crosses County 106 and then passes

Green Swamp on the left and an imposing hill of boulders on the right before reaching its end at the Long Path (aqua).

The Bicentennial Trails

The 1777 and 1779 trails were blazed in 1975 for the bicentennial celebration to commemorate the strategically important military events occurring in the Hudson Highlands during the American Revolution. Under the direction of the Palisades Interstate Park Museum staff, these trails were drawn up following the routes used by the British and American armies in 1777 and 1779, respectively. Where private property restrictions interfered, portions were rerouted, but overall the trails remain faithful to the general routes. The maps consulted were the ones made for General Washington by his official map maker, Major Erskine. The Boy Scouts of America created a special blaze for the trails and marked them with the respective year.

1777 Trail   *Length: 10.6 miles Blaze: red 1777 on white circle*

The 1777 Trail comprises three portions: a joint section of 3.0 miles, the 1777E Trail (Fort Clinton branch) of 2.3 miles, and the 1777W Trail (Fort Montgomery branch) of 5.3 miles. The joint portion of the trail begins on US 9W, 0.7 mile south of its intersection with Old Ayers Road, which leads to Jones Point.

There is a small parking area 200 feet south of the trailhead on the east side of US 9W. Starting from the highway, the trail leads to the abandoned hamlet of Doodletown, where it splits into its east (1777E) and west (1777W) sections. The 1777E passes the Bear Mountain Inn, goes through the tunnel under US 9W, and ends at the Trailside Museum and Zoo. The western portion is an undulating path that ultimately ends at the Popolopen Gorge viaduct on US 9W.

1779 Trail   *Length: 8.5 miles*
Blaze: blue 1779 on white circle

The 1779 Trail begins at the north end of the Popolopen Gorge viaduct, with parking available 0.8 mile to the south by following US 9W

Figure 16-5. Old burying ground on the Beech Trail

JACK FAGAN

to the Bear Mountain Inn. The trail is mostly a low-level wooded route that starts by running concurrently with the 1777W (red 1777 on white) and Timp-Torne (blue) trails. At 1.3 miles, the Timp-Torne Trail turns right to ascend the 941-foot Popolopen Torne, with its 360° view. At 1.5 miles, the Timp-Torne Trail rejoins the 1779 Trail from the right and the two trails cross Popolopen Creek on a footbridge (as of spring 2001, the bridge is out). Just beyond a fireplace at 1.7 miles, the Popolopen Gorge Trail (red on white) joins from the left. Four trails run concurrently for about a mile until the combined 1779/Popolopen Gorge trails turn right and the combined 1777W/Timp-Torne trails continue straight.

Figure 16-6. Claudius Smith's Den

Queensboro Lake appears on the left at 3.1 miles, and the 1779 Trail veers left, leaving the Popolopen Gorge Trail, at 3.5 miles. Now free of the concurrent trails, the 1779 Trail crosses the Anthony Wayne Trail (white) at 4.5 miles and the combined Appalachian/Ramapo-Dunderberg trails at 6.0 miles. After crossing the Palisades Interstate Parkway at 7.0 miles, the 1779 Trail turns left onto the Red Cross Trail (red cross on white) at 7.6 miles and a tenth of a mile later is joined by the Suffern-Bear Mountain Trail (yellow). Within a tenth of a mile, in quick succession, the Suffern-Bear Mountain Trail leaves to the right and the Red Cross Trail leaves to the left. The 1779 Trail finally emerges at the park boundary on Queensboro Road in the community of Bulsontown. One-quarter mile from the trail's end, paved Queensboro Road intersects Mott Farm Road, with limited parking available on the east side of the latter road.

Blue Disc Trail

Length: 2.8 miles Blaze: blue dot on white

This trail begins on the gas pipeline right-of-way just west of the parking area in the circle at the end of Johnsontown Road in Sloatsburg. The trail turns left on a woods road after 0.2 mile and crosses the Kakiat Trail at 0.5 mile. It then proceeds over Almost Perpendicular, which offers views to the south and east. The trail continues north along the ridge and descends gradually to Elbow Brush. It crosses the Tuxedo-Mt. Ivy Trail (red dash on white) at Claudius Smith's Den. Next it continues north over Big Pine Hill, with an all-around view, to its terminus at Tri-Trail Corner at the foot of Black Ash Mountain.

Cornell Mine Trail   *Length: 2.5 miles Blaze: blue*
This trail extends from the Bear Mountain Inn to the Ramapo-Dunderberg Trail near the summit of Bald Mountain. The first section of the Cornell Mine Trail is fairly easy walking on woods roads. Beginning at a trail junction about 100 yards behind and west of the Bear Mountain Inn, the trail travels south along the east side of the ice-skating rink, where it is joined by the 1777E Trail. Together they pass through two tunnels under Seven Lakes Drive and the South Entrance Road.

At 0.8 mile, the Cornell Mine Trail diverges left from the 1777E Trail, descends, and intercepts abandoned Doodletown Road. The trail turns left onto the old road, reaching US 9W at 1.0 mile, at Doodletown Brook. Parking is available on the east side of the road. From an elevation of 20 feet, the trail reenters the woods and ascends nearly 1,000 feet in the next 1.4 miles, at first following the top of a deep stream embankment. At about 2.1 miles, the final climb becomes steeper. The Cornell Mine Trail ends at the Ramapo-Dunderberg Trail (red dot on white) in the col between Dunderberg and Bald mountains. To the west (right), a short climb along the Ramapo-Dunderberg Trail leads to the Cornell Mine and views of Bear Mountain, the Hudson River, and the Bear Mountain Bridge.

Dunning Trail   *Length: 3.8 miles Blaze: yellow*
Accessible only via other trails, the Dunning Trail starts at the north end of Stahahe High Peak east of Lake Stahahe on the Nurian Trail (white) after the latter has ascended steeply past the Valley of Boulders. Heading southeast, it threads its way between the north shore of Green Pond and an overhanging wall of stone over a jumble of boulders. It turns east and re-crosses the Nurian Trail before turning left onto Island Pond Road (a woods road) for a short distance. The Dunning Trail turns right and reaches the Boston Mine, where it turns right again and goes up the hill behind the mine.

In another 0.5 mile, the Dunning Trail turns left and joins the White Bar Trail. It soon leaves the White Bar Trail and turns right onto Crooked Road, a woods road. Several ascents and 0.4 mile farther east, the trail crosses the Ramapo-Dunderberg Trail (red dot on white). It goes southeast, passing over slabs of bare rock, and then begins to head eastward. Soon the Crooked Road goes off to the right, providing a shortcut to County 106.

The Dunning Trail turns in a northeasterly direction on a woods road. A large swamp on the right is edged by mounds of tailings from the Hogencamp Mine up the hill to the left. The Long Path (aqua) soon comes in from the left and coincides with the Dunning Trail briefly before turning downhill to the right toward Lake Skannatati. From here, the Dunning Trail becomes straighter and more level and continues in a northeasterly direction. It skirts the west side of Pine Swamp as tall hemlocks form a canopy. The impressive Pine Swamp Mine is up on the left, but only large piles of tailings from it are visible from the trail. The Dunning Trail continues to follow the woods road until it ends at the Arden-Surebridge Trail (red triangle on white).

Figure 16-7. Pine Swamp Mine

JACK FAGAN

Hillburn-Torne-Sebago Trail
Length: 4.8 miles Blaze: orange

The Hillburn-Torne-Sebago Trail extends from Seven Lakes Drive at the Lake Sebago dam south to the Ramapo Torne, connecting with six other trails along its length. At the north end, parking is available at the Lake Sebago parking area off Seven Lakes Drive, 0.7 mile past the start of the trail and about 4.3 miles from NY 17.

The trail begins on the north side of the brook. It follows Woodtown Road, turns off to the right (south) on a path, crosses the Tuxedo-Mt. Ivy Trail (red dash on white), and continues on the unmarked Stony Brook Trail for a short distance. Turning off left, it steeply climbs Diamond Mountain, which has a good lookout over Lake Sebago near the top. At the summit, the Seven Hills Trail (blue dot on white) joins from the left, and both trails continue along the ridge, soon passing at 1.0 mile the Diamond Mountain-Tower Trail (yellow), which descends left to the Pine Meadow Trail (red on white). The Hillburn-Torne-Sebago and Seven Hills trails continue over the summit, then go their separate ways down to Pine Meadow Brook. At the base of the mountain, the Hillburn-Torne-Sebago Trail turns left onto the Kakiat Trail (white). After a few feet, the Hillburn-Torne-Sebago Trail turns off the Kakiat Trail to the right and crosses the brook on a footbridge over the Cascade of Slid. It meets the Pine Meadow Trail (red on white), joins it going left for a short distance, then turns off right up Chipmunk Mountain. At 2.4 miles, the Seven Hills Trail joins from the left, coincides briefly, and leaves to the right. The Hillburn-Torne-Sebago Trail crosses the Raccoon Brook Hills Trail (black R on white) at 3.2 miles and, after descending from the view on the Russian Bear cliff, it crosses a brook in a hollow. On the opposite slope, the Seven Hills Trail joins again from the right, then leaves to the right. The Hillburn-Torne-Sebago Trail continues to its terminus on the Ramapo Torne and its scenic overlook at 4.8 miles.

Kakiat Trail *Length: 7.4 miles Blaze: white, or black* K *on white*
Although this trail touches no high or open viewpoints, it offers a considerable variety of terrain. Named after one of the oldest land grants on the east side of the Ramapos, *Kakiat* is a corruption of a Native American word that appears on the land grant patent of 1696. The trail crosses the park, going from the Ramapo-Dunderberg Trail near Tuxedo to the entrance to Kakiat County Park off US 202 in Rockland County.

To reach the Kakiat Trail, hikers follow the Ramapo-Dunderberg Trail (red dot on white) from the Tuxedo railroad station, passing under the New York State Thruway, turning left on Grove Drive, and following it until the Ramapo-Dunderberg turns right into the woods. The Kakiat Trail begins at a sharp right turn and follows a woods road and an abandoned utility line around Daters Mountain. At 1.3 miles, as Kakiat bends sharply right, a path goes left toward Daters Mine. The Kakiat Trail continues on, and the Blue Disc Trail (blue dot on white) joins briefly at 1.5 miles. In 0.3 mile, the Kakiat Trail crosses a gas pipeline, then crosses Spring Brook, and briefly joins the White Bar Trail. Either the Blue Disc or the White Bar trails can be followed to the right for parking at Johnsontown Circle.

JACK FAGAN

Figure 16-8. Ruined farmhouse along the Kakiat Trail

At 2.3 miles, the Kakiat Trail crosses Seven Lakes Drive. After passing the foundation of an old farmhouse, it reaches a bridge over Stony Brook at 3.0 miles and then crosses over Pine Meadow Brook. The trail then makes a sharp right turn along the north bank of Pine Meadow Brook. It becomes quite rugged as it goes over and around large boulders along the ravine. At 3.4 miles, the Kakiat Trail passes the Cascade of Slid, a spectacular sight during the spring runoff. It then briefly joins the Hillburn-Torne-Sebago Trail (orange).

Farther on, the Kakiat meets the Seven Hills Trail (blue on white), and both are joined by the Pine Meadow Trail (red on white). All three cross Pine Meadow Brook on a footbridge. The Seven Hills and Pine Meadow trails then head right, while the Kakiat Trail turns left, soon passing the start of the Raccoon Brook Hills Trail (black R on white), which heads left. The Raccoon Brook Hills Trail is crossed again at 4.6 miles, where the two trails join briefly. The Kakiat crosses several ridges and the deep ravine of Torne Brook, as well as the Suffern-Bear Mountain Trail (yellow) on Cobus Mountain at 6.0 miles. The Kakiat Trail comes down the mountain, mostly on woods roads. Where it passes directly under the power line, the trail makes a sharp left. At the base of the mountain, the Kakiat Trail follows along dirt roads in Rockland County's Kakiat Park, crossing the Mahwah River on a footbridge. The trail ends near the entrance to the park on US 202. Parking is available near the entrance.

Long Path   *Length: 25.7 miles Blaze: aqua*

The Long Path, a major long-distance trail, traverses the park from Mt. Ivy to Central Valley. Along the way, it crosses nine other marked trails, making possible a variety of circular hikes. A popular hike is the short section of the Long Path from the parking area on US 6 to the Torrey Memorial on Long Mountain.

Although the Long Path does not actually enter Bear Mountain-Harriman State Parks until it reaches Calls Hollow Road, many hikers choose to begin their hike from the intersection of US 202 and NY 45, just east of Exit 13 of the Palisades Interstate Parkway. On weekends and holidays, parking may be available in the Mt. Ivy commuter parking lot; for further information, call the Haverstraw Police at (845) 354-1500. The Long Path follows US 202 under the Parkway and then turns right (north), following the entrance ramp and then running along a narrow forested strip parallel to the Parkway. After crossing the South Branch of Minisceongo Creek at 1.4 miles, it joins a woods road and climbs to Cheesecote Town Park, passing Cheesecote Pond. It then skirts the Letchworth Village Cemetery and reaches Calls Hollow Road at 3.5 miles. Parking at this road crossing is not recommended.

The Long Path turns left and follows the road for about 500 feet, then turns right and re-enters the woods. At 4.5 miles, it crosses the Old Turnpike, now the right-of-way for a buried telephone cable. At 5.3 miles, the Suffern-Bear Mountain Trail (yellow) joins from the right, and both trails climb over ledges to reach the Big Hill Shelter, built in 1927. Here, the Long Path bears right, leaving the Suffern-Bear Mountain Trail. It descends to cross the Old Turnpike, bears left and parallels it for about half a mile, then turns right onto a woods road. Soon, it bears sharply left, uphill. After crossing Lake Welch Drive near its intersection with St. John's Road at 7.6 miles, the Long Path continues along a woods road. The Beech Trail (blue) leaves to the right at 8.2 miles. Then, at 8.8 miles, the Long Path crosses County 106 (Gate Hill Road).

At 9.3 miles, the Long Path crosses Seven Lakes Drive, where parking is available. It goes north along the eastern side of Lake Skannatati, then swings left to follow the northern side of the lake, as the Arden-Surebridge Trail (red triangle on white) begins to the right. The Long Path briefly joins the Dunning Trail (yellow) at 1.3 miles. It bears right, leaving the Dunning Trail, and passes just above an abandoned shaft of the Hogencamp Mine and below an overhanging rock known as Cape Horn. The Long Path follows an old mining road over a rise and then descends to reach "Times Square," a major trail junction,

JACK FAGAN

Figure 16-9. Stockbridge Shelter

at 11.3 miles. Here, the Ramapo-Dunderberg Trail (red dot on white) crosses, and the Long Path joins the Arden-Surebridge Trail (red triangle on white). Both trails run briefly along the wide Surebridge Mine Road, then turn left and climb gently through a hemlock grove.

At 11.9 miles, near the crest of Surebridge Mountain, the Lichen Trail (blue L on white) begins to the left. The Long Path descends, following the route of the "Lost Road," and reaches a marsh at the base of the descent. Here, the White Bar Trail (horizontal white bar) leaves to the left. In another 30 feet, the Long Path turns right, leaving the Arden-Surebridge Trail, which continues straight ahead. The Long Path now runs between a marsh on the right and a steep, hemlock-covered slope on the left. At 12.9 miles, the Appalachian Trail (white) crosses, and then the Long Path climbs a knob, goes down to a marsh, and ascends another knoll. After a partial view of Upper Lake Cohasset appears to the left, the trail passes an old shelter which is not available for public use and descends to cross Surebridge Mine Road and a stream.

The Long Path crosses Arden Valley Road at 15.0 miles and continues along a woods road, passing a swamp to the right. It then leaves the woods road and begins its ascent of Stockbridge Mountain, steeply at times. It follows the crest of the ridge, with some gentle ups and downs, passing under Hippo Rock—a large overhanging boulder—at 17.0 miles. After a short descent, the Menomine Trail (yellow) leaves to the right at 17.2 miles, and the Long Path climbs over ledges to reach the Stockbridge Shelter, with views to the south.

Soon, the Long Path descends another ledge, with the Cave Shelter (formed by an overhanging rock) just to the right. The Long Path continues to descend gradually and turns left on a woods road (the Nawahunta Fire Road) at 18.8 miles. Reaching US 6 at 19.3 miles, the Long Path crosses the highway and continues along the exit road from the adjacent parking area (this exit road is the old US 6, which was replaced by the present road in 1967). The parking area is a convenient place to begin a hike to the Torrey Memorial on Long Mountain.

From the parking area, the Long Path proceeds north on a woods road. At 19.7 miles, the Popolopen Gorge Trail (red dot on white) begins on the right, and the Long Path climbs steeply over ledges to the summit of Long Mountain, which is reached at 20.0 miles. The 1,155-foot summit offers 360° views, with Bear Mountain to the east and Turkey Hill Lake directly below. Carved into the rock on the summit is a memorial to Raymond H. Torrey, one of the authors of the first edition of the *New York Walk Book*. In another 500 feet, the Long Path turns left and descends on switchbacks. It crosses Deep Hollow Brook and soon reaches a wide firebreak, the boundary of the United States Military Academy at West Point. The Long Path follows this boundary for about a mile and then bears left to ascend Howell Mountain. It reaches a viewpoint to the west over Brooks and Blackcap mountains at 21.6 miles. The Long Path descends steeply into Brooks Hollow, where it crosses the outlet stream from Lake Massawippa. It climbs Brooks Mountain on switchbacks and runs along its crest, with views over the valley below, then descends to cross NY 293 at 23.1 miles. The Long Path now ascends to a shoulder of Blackcap Mountain and follows it to the southwest, closely paralleling the West Point boundary, until it descends to US 6 at 24.5 miles. It follows the highway for 0.6 mile, then turns right, passing through a gap in a chain-link fence. It descends along the abandoned route of US 6, reaching the dead-end of Estrada Road in Central Valley, where limited parking is available, at 25.7 miles.

Major Welch Trail   *Length: 2.6 miles Blaze: red dot on white*
This trail, which ascends Bear Mountain's north slope, was named in 1944 in memory of Major William A. Welch, the first general manager of the Palisades Interstate Park. Major Welch was basically responsible for launching Harriman's trail network, and it was he who convened the first meeting of the Palisades Interstate Park Trail Conference, which soon became the New York-New Jersey Trail Conference.

(boathouses) Hessian Lake

R. L. DICKINSON

Figure 16-10. Hessian Lake at the foot of Bear Mountain

The Major Welch Trail starts behind the Bear Mountain Inn and follows the asphalt path along the western shore of Hessian Lake nearly to its north end before making a sharp left (west) into the woods. Climbing gently for a short distance, it then makes another sharp left turn and begins a steep, steady ascent of about 900 feet to the summit at 1,305 feet. There are panoramic vistas to the north along this stretch. Before reaching the summit, the trail crosses Perkins Memorial Drive. Near the top, it goes through a picnic area and turns right onto Perkins Drive, passing Perkins Memorial Tower. The trail descends the south slope of Bear Mountain via a weathered ridge with many viewpoints. At 2.6 miles, it ends on a lower section of Perkins Memorial Drive, meeting the Appalachian Trail (white). Parking is available at the Bear Mountain Inn, which is also a destination for a New York City bus.

Menomine Trail   *Length: 2.9 miles Blaze: yellow*
Blazed in 1994, this trail connects the Long Path (aqua) to the Appalachian Trail (white), linking shelters located at both ends. The midpoint is the Silvermine Lake parking lot off Seven Lakes Drive, where rest rooms are available.

Starting on the Long Path on Stockbridge Mountain about 0.1 mile southwest of the Stockbridge Shelter, the trail drops gradually on a woods road, which is crossed by other faint old roads, before passing through a picturesque grove of pines on the shore of Lake Nawahunta. Just beyond the grove, the trail crosses the lake inlet and makes a sharp right at the 1.0-mile point onto a fire road leading to Seven Lakes Drive. It crosses the road, passes the Lewis family grave site, and continues through a picnic area to the base of the old Silver Mine downhill ski slope. Going through a section of small boulders, it continues along the west shore of Silvermine Lake. After a short distance, the trail proceeds uphill on an old road to intersect a fire road. It turns left on the fire road and crosses Bockey Swamp Brook, the inlet of the lake. After climbing up to the William Brien Memorial Shelter, it ends at an intersection with the joint Appalachian (white) and Ramapo-Dunderberg (red dot on white) trails.

Nurian Trail   *Length: 3.4 miles Blaze: white*
This trail goes from the former Southfields railroad station to the Ramapo-Dunderberg Trail, terminating about 0.4 mile north of the Ramapo-Dunderberg Trail's crossing of County 106, where there is parking. Parking spaces are available in Southfields at the Red Apple Rest, away from the restaurant. Hikers should follow along the railroad tracks to the north. About 100 yards past the site of the former train station, the trail turns right and descends.

After crossing the Ramapo River, the Nurian Trail crosses the New York State Thruway on a pedestrian bridge. After the bridge, the trail makes a left turn, follows Old Arden Road north for about 0.3 mile, makes a sharp right, and starts the ascent up the west side of Green Pond Mountain. Passing the summit at 1.1 miles, the trail descends to the north end of Lake Stahahe and circles that end of the lake on an asphalt road. In about 200 yards, the Nurian Trail leaves the road and goes up the ravine of the Island Pond outlet brook, which has numerous falls, proceeding through an area covered with large rocks called Valley of the Boulders. A few spots are difficult to negotiate, especially in winter. The trail turns right (south) near the head of the ravine and goes up along a long sloping rock, passing an outlook point. Shortly beyond, it meets the western terminus of the Dunning Trail (yellow) at 2.0 miles. The Nurian Trail turns left and passes down and through a small valley, crossing the Dunning Trail again before meeting Island Pond Road.

The Nurian Trail goes south briefly on Island Pond Road and then makes a left turn. In another 0.5 mile, the White Bar Trail (horizontal white bar) joins from the left. The trails run jointly for 0.1 mile; the Nurian Trail then turns left and goes downhill. It crosses a brook and climbs steeply up the west slope of Black Rock Mountain to end at 3.4 miles at the Ramapo-Dunderberg Trail (red dot on white). The last half of the trail passes through extensive mountain laurel.

Pine Meadow Trail   *Length: 5.5 miles Blaze: red on white*

Those who arrive at Sloatsburg by bus or train may walk to the start of the Pine Meadow Trail, on the south side of Seven Lakes Drive, 0.7 mile east from NY 17. The most convenient car access is from the parking area at the Reeves Meadow Visitor Center on Seven Lakes Drive, 1.4 miles east of NY 17.

From its western terminus, the trail enters a scrub-filled field on the south side of Seven Lakes Drive at its crossing of Stony Brook, curves left, and follows Stony Brook. It crosses a telephone cable route, and at 0.7 mile passes the terminus of the Seven Hills Trail (blue on white) on the right. In another 0.2 miles, the trail passes the Reeves Meadow Visitor Center. Just beyond, the Reeves Brook Trail (white) begins to the right. The Pine Meadow Trail parallels Stony Brook to a fork,

JACK FAGAN

Figure 16-11. Pine Meadow Lake: Rock formation near the dam

where it swings to the right uphill. Here the Stony Brook Trail (unmarked) continues straight ahead.

The Hillburn-Torne-Sebago Trail (orange) comes in from the left at 2.1 miles, coincides with the Pine Meadow Trail for about 100 yards, and then turns abruptly right. The Pine Meadow Trail levels off and meets the Seven Hills Trail (blue dot on white) coming in from the right at a fireplace. Both trails run together for a short distance. Soon the Kakiat Trail (white) comes in from the right, and all three trails turn left and cross a bridge over Pine Meadow Brook. The Kakiat and Seven Hills trails turn left, while the Pine Meadow Trail turns sharply right along the brook. At 2.7 miles, the trail reaches the large boulders called *Ga-Nus-Quah* ("stone giants") by the Native Americans.

A short distance later, the Diamond Mountain-Tower Trail (yellow) goes left, climbing Diamond Mountain. Here the Pine Meadow Trail takes a sharp right turn onto a woods road to Pine Meadow Lake. It follows the north shore of the lake and passes the remains of an old pumphouse at 3.7 miles. At the end of the lake, the Conklins Crossing Trail (white) starts and goes right. About 0.4 mile farther on, the Pine Meadow Trail crosses Pine Meadow Road East and continues for another mile until it reaches its terminus at 5.5 miles on the Suffern-Bear Mountain Trail (yellow).

Popolopen Gorge Trail   *Length: 4.5 miles Blaze: red on white*
Providing a pleasant walk through the Popolopen Gorge to Turkey Hill Lake, this trail can be reached from the Bear Mountain Inn parking area by walking north on the paved path along the east shore of Hessian Lake and proceeding north, past a traffic circle, to US 9W. The trail begins on the left, just before the Popolopen Gorge viaduct. The western terminus of the trail can be reached by heading north on the Long Path (aqua) from the parking area on the north side of Long Mountain Parkway (US 6), located 1.2 miles west of Long Mountain traffic circle.

From US 9W, the Popolopen Gorge Trail leads gently down along a woods road 0.2 mile to Roe Pond, where there is an old dam. It continues to follow the steep southern side of the gorge, passing the area called Hell Hole, picturesque in early spring with water dashing over and around the boulders in the brook. The trail then climbs steeply for about 100 feet to the old Bear Mountain Aqueduct, which it follows until joining the Timp-Torne (blue), 1777W, and 1779 trails at 1.4 miles. This area is dominated by a hemlock forest.

The four trails cross Queensboro Brook on a footbridge at 2.1 miles. After 2.6 miles, the Timp-Torne and 1777W trails continue straight ahead, while the Popolopen Gorge and 1779 trails turn right and skirt the north shore of Queensboro Lake. At 3.2 miles, the 1779 Trail leaves to the left. The Popolopen Gorge Trail then passes the dam of Turkey Hill Lake. It follows the south shore of the lake until it meets the Anthony Wayne Trail (white) at 4.0 miles. Turning uphill, away from the lake, after a short climb the trail turns right on an old road, continuing through a small ravine to end at the Long Path (aqua).

Ramapo-Dunderberg Trail   *Length: 22.0 miles Blaze: red dot on white*

The Ramapo-Dunderberg Trail (R-D), which goes from Tuxedo to Jones Point, is the oldest of the Bear Mountain-Harriman trails. Built by the walking clubs, it offers diverse terrain and many views. Intersecting twenty-one different trails, it can be combined with them to form interesting circular hikes. Cars can be parked at the Tuxedo railroad station on weekends, and both Metro-North trains from Hoboken and Short Line buses from New York City stop here.

From its start at the Tuxedo railroad station, the R-D crosses the Ramapo River on a footbridge, turns left on the other side, turns right on East Village Road to an underpass of the New York State Thruway, and turns left on Grove Drive. In a few hundred feet, it turns right into the woods, climbing around a ridge and passing, in 0.2 mile from the road, the terminus of the Triangle Trail (yellow). At 1.3 miles, the Tuxedo-Mt. Ivy Trail (red dash on white) begins, diverging to the right. The R-D continues northeast to the crossing of Black Ash Swamp Brook. Here is a natural rock dam formed by the last glacier. Here also is Tri-Trail Corner, where three trails—the R-D, the Blue Disc (blue dot on white), and the Victory (blue V on white)—meet. The R-D climbs northward to the summit of Black Ash Mountain, with a view near the top over the swamp to the south. The White Bar Trail (horizontal white bar) crosses the R-D in the dip between Black Ash and Parker Cabin mountains. Soon after, the terminus of the White Cross Trail (white cross) is passed on the right.

The R-D continues north up to the top of Parker Cabin Mountain, which it reaches at 3.5 miles. Here, on the level summit, the Triangle Trail (yellow) comes in from the left, coincides with the R-D for about 150 feet, and then bears right (east). The R-D descends the north side of Parker Cabin Mountain to a gap where it crosses the Victory Trail. From the gap, the trail ascends steeply up Tom Jones Mountain. Near the stone shelter on the summit, there is a view east and south. The trail drops steeply down the northeast slope, where it crosses a brook and then County 106. Parking is available for three or four cars.

North of the paved road, the trail climbs steadily up Black Rock Mountain. Between rock walls, the Nurian Trail (white) begins at the left, while the R-D bears right over a rock ledge. Much of the next section of trail traverses open rock. The Bald Rocks Shelter, at 6.1 miles, is off the trail to the right about a mile north of the Nurian Trail. To the left of the trail at Bald Rocks is the location reported to be the highest in the park (elevation 1,382 feet). A U.S. Coast and Geodetic Survey marker is anchored in the rock here. ʻ

Farther along, the R-D crosses the Dunning Trail (yellow), and then about

[handwritten annotation:] From 106 No, very Nice, not too difficult fine views

another half-mile northward, the Lichen Trail (blue L on white) meanders north-west over ledges, some with views, and offers a shortcut to the Arden-Surebridge Trail. The R-D winds down from Hogencamp Mountain through woods to "Times Square," where it crosses the Long Path (aqua) and the Arden-Surebridge Trail (red triangle on white). Hikers should be careful here, as it is easy to go on the wrong trail. After going over several ledges, the R-D begins to climb Finger-board Mountain. As it levels off at the top, the Appalachian Trail (white) comes in from the left at 8.9 miles. Shortly thereafter, the trail passes the west end of the Hurst Trail (blue), which leads in a few hundred feet to the Fingerboard Shelter and then goes down to Seven Lakes Drive.

At Arden Valley Road, the Appalachian Trail continues straight ahead (north) while the R-D turns right (east), following the paved road past the Tiorati Circle. About 0.3 mile east of the circle, the trail turns left into the woods and proceeds east over Goshen Mountain. It descends and then joins the Appalachian Trail again at a plank bridge 1.3 miles from the circle. An-other 0.8 mile later, the R-D comes to the William Brien Memorial Shelter and the southern terminus of the Menomine Trail (yellow). At 0.9 mile farther north-east, the R-D crosses the Silvermine Ski Road, which can be followed left to Silvermine Lake.

The trail crosses a streambed and heads steeply up Black Mountain, with views to the west. The trail then levels and winds along the top. Another climb to a rock ledge at 13.8 miles provides views to the south, including the Man-hattan skyline when weather permits. A descent, fairly steep at first, leads down the mountain's east slope, crossing the 1779 Trail, then a woods road, and finally the Palisades Interstate Parkway. East of the parkway, the Appalachian Trail leaves sharply to the left, while the R-D goes down to cross Beechy Bot-tom Brook. Past the brook, the trail turns left and briefly follows a woods road, now marked as a bike trail. At 15.1 miles, the R-D turns right, climbs to Beechy Bottom East Road, and then ascends steeply to the southern end of West Mountain. On an open area near the top, the trail meets the Suffern-Bear Mountain Trail (yellow) just above the ledge called Cats Elbow, with views to the south into the interior of the park.

After coinciding briefly, the Suffern-Bear Mountain Trail turns north (left), while the R-D swings east across the summit. It descends into Timp Pass where, at 16.7 miles, it meets the eastern terminus of the Red Cross Trail (red cross on white). Here also, the unmarked Timp Pass Road heads north to Doodletown.

Rising above is The Timp, a striking cliff with a pronounced overhang, one of the most picturesque rock faces in the park. From Timp Pass, the R-D descends slightly, then ascends the southern slopes of the mountain. At 17.6 miles, it crosses the Timp-Torne Trail (blue). To the left, Timp-Torne leads 0.2 mile to a striking overlook from the top of The Timp, with its sweeping views south and the Manhattan skyline in the distance.

The R-D Trail continues east and enters the saddle between The Timp and Bald Mountain, where it crosses the 1777 Trail, then climbs steeply up Bald Mountain to the summit, with views west and north. Just off the summit to the left of the trail is the Cornell Mine, from which iron ore was taken. Continuing east, the trail soon passes the terminus of the Cornell Mine Trail (blue), which comes up from the left. In another 0.9 mile, the R-D passes the unmarked Bockberg Trail on the right.

Continuing across and then down Dunderberg Mountain, the R-D passes by several beautiful viewpoints and crosses several grades of the unfinished Dunderberg Spiral Railway. At 21.0 miles, the R-D turns right and follows a section of the graded railbed for half a mile. It then turns left at a freestanding stone wall and descends steeply along the route of the proposed cable incline that would have pulled the cars up the mountain. At the bottom of the incline, the R-D joins the Timp-Torne Trail just above a 100-foot-long masonry tunnel (through which the final descending leg of the railway was supposed to have passed), and it follows the Timp-Torne Trail for 0.2 mile to its terminus on US 9W. Ample parking is available on the west side of the road, a short distance to the east, opposite the intersection with Old Ayers Road, which leads to Jones Point. Short Line buses from the Port Authority Bus Terminal to Bear Mountain will stop at this intersection to pick up or discharge passengers.

Red Cross Trail *Length: 7.9 miles Blaze: red cross on white*
The Red Cross Trail goes through the middle of the park, generally southwest, from the Ramapo-Dunderberg Trail (red dot on white) at Timp Pass to the Arden-Surebridge Trail, 0.25 mile north of the Lake Skannatati parking area on Seven Lakes Drive.

From its eastern terminus, the Red Cross Trail descends steeply along a woods road and at 0.5 mile briefly joins the North "Ski" Trail. At 0.9 mile, a trail leads off to the left toward the Addisone Boyce Girl Scout Camp. Shortly thereafter, the Red Cross Trail goes right, away from the woods road, and crosses Beechy Bottom Road at 1.4 miles. It turns right at 1.9 miles, joining the 1779 Trail. Within the next 0.2 mile the Suffern-Bear Mountain Trail (yellow) joins and leaves, and the 1779 Trail leaves.

At the Palisades Interstate Parkway (2.2 miles), the trail jogs left along the northbound lane before crossing it, the center median, and the southbound lane. It turns left down the southbound lane before entering the woods to the right. The trail goes through a wet section, where Owl Swamp Brook comes down from the right and skirts a marsh to the left. About 1.2 miles from the parkway, an unmarked woods road leads right (north) toward the William Brien Memorial Shelter at the north end of Letterrock Mountain. At 4.7 miles, the trail passes the northern end of the Beech Trail (blue). It encounters another swampy area before crossing Tiorati Brook on rocks at 5.4 miles. Depending on water flow, hikers may have to seek an alternative crossing up- or downstream.

From the brook, the trail ascends to a grassy ballfield and crosses it and paved Tiorati Brook Road. Some parking is available off the north side of the road just left (east) of the trail. The Red Cross Trail continues south on a prominent woods road until it passes the Hasenclever Mine at 6.0 miles on the left. The trail turns right on a cross road and then right again off the road before ascending Hasenclever Mountain. Shortly after crossing a telephone line, it goes south, then briefly north, before passing the north end of Lake Askoti, where a beautiful point of rock juts into the water. Crossing Seven Lakes Drive at 7.5 miles, the Red Cross Trail climbs Pine Swamp Mountain to terminate at the Arden-Surebridge Trail (red triangle on white).

Reeves Brook Trail   *Length: 1.7 miles Blaze: white*
This trail begins at the Pine Meadow Trail (red on white) about 100 yards from the Reeves Meadow Visitor Center (parking available), 1.4 miles east of NY 17 on Seven Lakes Drive.

The trail makes a gradual ascent, approaching Reeves Brook at 0.2 mile, with the brook on the left for some distance. After a woods road leaves to the right at 0.5 mile, the trail ascends fairly steeply. At 1.4 miles, it crosses the Seven Hills Trail (blue dot on white). It terminates at its junction with the Raccoon Brook Hills Trail (black R on white) 0.3 mile later.

Seven Hills Trail   *Length: 6.6 miles Blaze: blue dot on white*
The trail starts on the east side of Seven Lakes Drive, 4.0 miles from NY 17, opposite the entrance to the Lake Sebago parking area. It ascends Conklin

JACK FAGAN

Figure 16-12. View of Pine Meadow Lake from Diamond Mountain

Mountain, joins Woodtown Road, and crosses Diamond Creek. The Seven Hills Trail then turns right, off Woodtown Road, and starts its traverse of Diamond Mountain. It soon crosses the Tuxedo-Mt. Ivy Trail (red dash on white). The trail briefly follows a fire road and passes views of Lake Sebago. The Diamond Mountain-Tower Trail (yellow) begins at the left at 1.4 miles. In another 0.1 mile, the Hillburn-Torne-Sebago Trail (orange) comes in from the right and joins the Seven Hills Trail. At 1.7 miles, the other end of the Diamond Mountain-Tower Trail leaves to the left. The Hillburn-Torne-Sebago and Seven Hills trails continue together and go over the summit of Diamond Mountain.

Past the summit, the Hillburn-Torne-Sebago Trail diverges sharply right. The Seven Hills Trail continues ahead, making a steep descent to Pine Meadow Brook, where it turns left onto the Kakiat Trail (white). The joint trails meet the Pine Meadow Trail (red on white) coming in from the left, and all three trails cross Pine Meadow Brook on a footbridge. The Kakiat Trail then turns off to the left, while the joint Seven Hills and Pine Meadow trails turn right. Shortly, at a fireplace, the Seven Hills Trail turns off left and goes uphill; the Pine Meadow Trail continues straight ahead. At 3.0 miles, coming from the right, the Hillburn-Torne-Sebago Trail rejoins and soon leaves to the left.

After a steep descent, the Seven Hills Trail briefly follows a gas pipeline. It then crosses the Reeves Brook Trail (white) and passes the start of the Raccoon Brook Hills Trail (black R on white) on the left at about 4.0 miles. Soon afterwards it reaches Torne View. After another 0.4 mile, the Hillburn-Torne-Sebago Trail joins once more, coming in from the left. The trails run together for 0.2 mile, after which the Seven Hills Trail turns right to go down the mountain, while the Hillburn-Torne-Sebago Trail continues ahead. The Seven Hills Trail turns north, crosses Beaver Brook, skirts a large swamp, and finally reaches its terminus on the Pine Meadow Trail. To the right, a short hike on the Pine Meadow Trail leads to parking at Reeves Meadow.

Suffern-Bear Mountain Trail   *Length: 23.5 miles Blaze: yellow*
This trail from Suffern to Bear Mountain is quite rugged in many places. The southern terminus is just north of the commuter parking lot off NY 59 and US 202, just south of the New York State Thruway overpass (hiker parking permitted on weekends only). Access to the southern portion of the Suffern-Bear Mountain Trail is also possible from the parking lot off US 202 at the southern terminus of the Kakiat Trail in Kakiat County Park.

About 500 feet north of the Thruway overpass on NY 59, the trail turns sharply right from the sidewalk and goes steeply up to a viewpoint on the slope of Nordkop Mountain. Joining a woods road for a time, it follows north along the ridge of the Ramapo Rampart. After leaving the woods road, the trail continues over the fairly level mountaintop, crossing a gas line.

About 1.5 miles from Suffern, the trail climbs out of a hollow, goes up a rock formation known as the Kitchen Stairs, and soon crosses another gas line and then a power line. At 3.2 miles, the Suffern-Bear Mountain Trail reaches the Valley of Dry Bones, an area of giant boulders. Continuing on, the trail crosses yet another gas line and passes two big boulders called Grandma and Grandpa Rocks. Shortly beyond, at 4.5 miles, the Kakiat Trail (white) crosses. The Suffern-Bear Mountain Trail proceeds north over Cobus Mountain, then descends to the Conklins Crossing Trail (white). It continues up a steep slope to the Stone Memorial Shelter. A mile after the shelter, the Suffern-Bear Mountain Trail passes the terminus of the Pine Meadow Trail (red on white) on the left.

The Suffern-Bear Mountain Trail reaches the summit of Panther Mountain at 7.7 miles, with a view toward the Hudson River and surrounding villages. After a descent, the trail crosses the Tuxedo-Mt. Ivy Trail (red dash on white) at a stone fireplace almost a mile farther on. At 9.4 miles, the Red Arrow Trail (red) comes in from the right. The Suffern-Bear Mountain Trail, going northwest, crosses Woodtown Road and reaches the Third Reservoir at 10.1 miles. Climbing Breakneck Mountain, the trail meets the beginning of the Breakneck Mountain Trail (white), where it turns right (northeast). There are views to the east as the trail follows the crest to Big Hill Shelter at 11.2 miles. The trail then encounters the Long Path (aqua) briefly, drops along some ledges, and crosses a woods road and the Old Turnpike, which is now a buried telephone cable right-of-way. The Suffern-Bear Mountain Trail reenters the woods, climbing gradually up the south side of Jackie Jones Mountain (1,276 feet) to the microwave relay tower and old fire tower. The trail then leaves the road and goes northeast over Panorama, a viewpoint over High Tor and the Hudson River. The Suffern-Bear Mountain Trail descends northward past the large glacial erratics known as the Three Witches. It enters the ruined Buchanan estate, ORAK (KARO spelled backwards—the estate was built by an executive of the company that made the syrup), before rejoining the blacktop road just before County 106 (Gate Hill Road). This point is 13.2 miles from Suffern. Parking is on the south side of the road.

The Suffern-Bear Mountain Trail turns right to cross a brook on the highway bridge, and then turns left onto a woods road. Soon it veers right, climbs a ridge, and passes a large boulder on the left known as the Irish Potato at 13.8 miles. The trail descends, with Upper Pound Swamp visible to the right, and then goes down to Lake Welch Drive. Parking is possible a half-mile west on Tiorati Brook Road, which is closed in winter. At 15.6 miles, the Suffern-Bear Mountain Trail turns right, parallels the road, and then goes over and across the Palisades Interstate Parkway.

After paralleling the Parkway a short distance, the Suffern-Bear Mountain Trail makes a sharp right turn and starts an extremely steep ascent of the south side of Pyngyp Mountain. At 16.0 miles, halfway up the mountain, is a memorial tablet to Harold Scutt, who first scouted the trail in 1925.

At and near the summit (1,016 feet), there are panoramic views to the southeast. Descending to a woods road in the notch beyond, the trail turns right for 100 yards, then goes left across a brook, past a fireplace, and up to the summit of The Pines, with viewpoints to the north.

Beyond The Pines, the Suffern-Bear Mountain Trail turns left onto a woods road, the route of the Red Cross (red cross on white) and 1779 trails. After 400 feet, the Suffern-Bear Mountain Trail turns right, leaving the road, and in another 0.5 mile it crosses Beechy Bottom Road. It next climbs Horn Hill (930 feet) and, after a gradual descent, crosses another woods road (the North "Ski" Trail) at 18.8 miles and then climbs up the southern spur of West Mountain.

After climbing steeply and making a turn called the Cats Elbow, the Suffern-Bear Mountain Trail meets the Ramapo-Dunderberg Trail (red dot on white) at an open ledge. The two trails join for a short distance, and then at 19.2 miles the Ramapo-Dunderberg swings east, while the Suffern-Bear Mountain Trail goes left, northward into the hollow between the two summits of West Mountain. After the Suffern-Bear Mountain Trail climbs again to the crest of West Mountain, the Timp-Torne Trail (blue) enters from the left at 19.8 miles and departs right 0.3 mile later. (On the latter trail, a little way to the east, is the West Mountain Shelter, with views of the Manhattan skyline.)

The Suffern-Bear Mountain Trail then climbs to another high point. It curves left down a steep talus slope to a gully where, after crossing a brook, it follows its left bank to the Doodletown Bridle Path, a woods road. It briefly goes left on the bridle path, then swings right to cross the 1777W Trail. The Suffern-Bear Mountain Trail then rejoins the bridle path for about 0.5 mile until it reaches a bend in the path, where it goes left uphill to Seven Lakes Drive. As it continues up and over the shoulder of Bear Mountain, it is joined by the Appalachian Trail (white) from the left at 23.0 miles. Both trails pass the ski jump and continue to the terminus of the Suffern-Bear Mountain Trail at the signpost 100 yards behind the Bear Mountain Inn. Parking is available at the Inn, where Short Line buses from New York City also stop.

Timp-Torne Trail   *Length: 11.2 miles Blaze: blue*

The trail begins on the west side of US 9W just south of its intersection with Old Ayers Road, which leads to Jones Point. Buses from New York City will stop to discharge or pick up passengers here. Parking is available on the west side of US 9W, just north of the trailhead.

Soon after entering the woods, the trail passes the lower tunnel of the Dunderberg Spiral Railway and begins its initial steep ascent up the southeastern slope of Dunderberg Mountain. At the top of this ascent, the Ramapo-Dunderberg Trail (red dot on white) (which has run concurrently with the Timp-Torne up to this point) continues ahead, while the Timp-Torne bears left. The Timp-Torne Trail meanders past massive rock outcroppings and occasional views of the Hudson River before it turns left on a completed grade of railway bed at 0.7 mile. It briefly turns right, then left on another grade, to approach the huge but never completed upper tunnel. After looping around the tunnel and past a small seasonal watercourse, it crosses the unmarked Jones Trail at 1.2 miles. It then begins to ascend again, with more views of the Hudson River. At 2.7 miles, the Timp-Torne Trail crosses the 1777 Trail and passes an overlook on the left atop a large rock outcropping. The trail drops a bit until it crosses the Ramapo-Dunderberg Trail. The Timp-Torne Trail now proceeds to the summit of The Timp, with its sweeping view to the south. After passing a

[handwritten annotation:] Parking is just S. of Jones Pt turnoff. Went to 1777 trail, then to T-T trail, nice views of Hudson, Steep ascent & descent before 9 W.

353

Anthony's Nose ~ Manitou ~ City of Peekskill ~ Iona Island ~ Dunderberg ~ Bear Mt.

more vertical geography

Queensboro trail

Hessian Lake
Popolopen Creek and its viaduct
Fort Montgomery road past the Torne
Views from Popolopen Torne
down the River and up the
Queensboro Valley

R. L. DICKINSON

Figure 16-13. Hudson Highlands south from Popolopen Torne (prior to the Bear Mountain Bridge)

viewpoint to the north over the Bear Mountain Bridge, the trail descends to the unmarked Timp Pass Road, which it crosses at 3.9 miles. The Timp-Torne Trail then climbs, first moderately and then steeply, to the West Mountain Shelter at 4.6 miles. Weather permitting, the Manhattan skyline can be seen on the southern horizon from this point.

Continuing along the ridge of West Mountain, the Timp-Torne Trail is joined from the right by the Suffern-Bear Mountain Trail (yellow) at 4.7 miles, which coincides for 0.3 mile and then departs left. The Timp-Torne Trail joins the Appalachian Trail (white) after another 0.1 mile and, following the west ridge of West Mountain, offers vistas of the park and the Hudson River. At 5.9 miles, it diverges left from the Appalachian Trail and gradually descends West Mountain, crossing the Fawn Trail (dark F on pink) and reaching the terminus of the Anthony Wayne Trail (white) on the left at 6.9 miles. At Seven Lakes Drive, the Timp-Torne joins the 1777W Trail, crosses the Drive and the Palisades Interstate Parkway, and turns right onto the old Fort Montgomery Road. The Popolopen Gorge (red on white) and 1779 trails join from the left at 7.5 miles. All four trails gradually descend into the Popolopen Gorge. At 8.7 miles, the Timp-Torne, 1777W, and 1779 trails turn left and cross Popolopen Creek on a footbridge (as of spring 2001, this bridge is out), while the Popolopen Gorge Trail continues straight ahead. At 0.1 mile beyond the bridge, the Timp-Torne Trail leaves the 1777W and 1779 trails, turns left into the woods, crosses Mine Road, and climbs very steeply to the summit of Popolopen Torne (941 feet), which offers a 360° view.

The trail then drops 500 feet, recrosses Mine Road, and rejoins the 1777W and 1779 trails on the route of an old aqueduct. The three trails eventually terminate on US 9W just north of the Popolopen Gorge viaduct. Parking for these trails is at the Bear Mountain Inn, 0.8 mile to the south, which also serves as a stop for Short Line buses from New York City.

Triangle Trail   *Length: 5.3 miles Blaze: yellow triangle*
The Triangle Trail makes an easy loop from the Ramapo-Dunderberg Trail near Tuxedo to the Tuxedo-Mt. Ivy Trail near the Dutch Doctor Shelter. Parking is available on weekends at the Tuxedo railroad station, which is accessible by Short Line bus from New York City or Metro-North train from Hoboken.

From the station, the Ramapo-Dunderberg Trail (red dot on white) leads to the start of the Triangle Trail on the left in 0.7 mile. After 2.6 miles, the White Bar Trail (horizontal white bar) joins the trail from the left on the side of Parker Cabin Mountain. The trails coincide for a short distance, until the Triangle diverges left. The Triangle Trail then climbs steadily to the top of Parker Cabin Mountain, where it joins the Ramapo-Dunderberg at the summit. After about 100 feet, the Triangle Trail diverges right to the sharp eastern edge of the mountain, where there is an outstanding lookout over Lakes Skenonto and Sebago. The trail starts down steeply and then continues more easily over low ridges and level areas, crossing the Victory Trail (blue V on white) at 4.1 miles.

The Triangle Trail skirts Lake Skenonto and, farther on, Lake Sebago, and ends at its junction with the White Bar Trail (horizontal white bar) at 5.3 miles. To the left, the White Bar leads in about 0.2 mile to the Dutch Doctor Shelter and, just beyond, meets the Tuxedo-Mt. Ivy Trail (red dash on white). The triangle is completed by following the Tuxedo-Mt. Ivy Trail sharply right and hiking 2.8 miles back toward Tuxedo.

Tuxedo-Mt. Ivy Trail   *Length: 8.2 miles Blaze: red dash on white*
The Ramapo-Dunderberg Trail (red dot on white) leads to the start of the Tuxedo-Mt. Ivy Trail (red dash on white) on the right in 1.3 miles. In 0.3 mile, the Tuxedo-Mt. Ivy Trail reaches Claudius Smith's Den, an overhanging rock

formation used as a hideout during the Revolutionary War. The trail climbs alongside the caves, crossing the Blue Disc Trail (blue dot on white). At the top of the hill, the White Cross Trail (white cross) starts, heading left. The Tuxedo-Mt. Ivy Trail then goes over the shoulder of Blauvelt Mountain and down into the valley to cross Spring Brook. Shortly after, the White Bar Trail (horizontal white bar) joins from the left. The Dutch Doctor Shelter is 0.1 mile to the left on the White Bar Trail.

The Tuxedo-Mt. Ivy and White Bar trails continue together on a woods road for 500 feet. The Tuxedo-Mt. Ivy Trail then turns off to the left. It goes over the ridge, crosses a camp service road, and skirts the south shore of Lake Sebago, arriving at Seven Lakes Drive. The trail crosses the drive, turns left over the dam at 2.4 miles, and drops down the embankment on the right. Here is the start of the Hillburn-Torne-Sebago Trail (orange). The Tuxedo-Mt. Ivy Trail veers right on a wide path and shortly crosses the Hillburn-Torne-Sebago Trail again, which makes a broader loop to reach this point. The Tuxedo-Mt. Ivy Trail heads uphill on the north side of Diamond Mountain, crossing the Seven Hills Trail (blue dot on white) at 3.3 miles.

The Tuxedo-Mt. Ivy Trail descends and crosses Woodtown Road (3.5 miles), Pine Meadow Road West (4.3 miles), and Pine Meadow Road East (5.1 miles). A few hundred feet farther on, the Breakneck Mountain Trail (white) begins, branching to the left. The Tuxedo-Mt. Ivy Trail continues east and then follows a woods road to Woodtown Road, on which it turns right briefly. It diverges left, goes through a swampy area, and, at a fireplace, crosses the Suffern-Bear Mountain Trail (yellow) at 6.6 miles.

Descending gradually, the trail passes the start of the Red Arrow Trail (red) on the left, continuing down over some rocky footing. The trail leaves the woods at a power line, turns left on a service road, crosses under the power line, and heads back right on another service road, finally turning left down a dirt road to a paved road where parking is available.

The parking area is reached from US 202 (heading north) by turning left at the light at the junction of US 202 and NY 306. A short right and a left turn onto Mountain Road at the church, and then left again on Diltz Road, leads to the parking area, in a field to the right.

White Bar Trail   *Length: 7.7 miles Blaze: horizontal white bar*
One of the oldest trails in the park, the White Bar Trail connects the joint Arden-Surebridge Trail (red triangle on white)/Long Path (aqua), approximately

0.2 mile east of the Lemon Squeezer, with the Johnsontown Road Circle parking area in a fairly direct north–south line.

After leaving the Arden-Surebridge Trail/Long Path, the White Bar Trail goes south on a woods road, then meets and for a short distance coincides first with the Dunning Trail (yellow) and then with the Nurian Trail (white). After crossing County 106 at 2.1 miles, where parking is available, the trail goes over the top of Carr Pond Mountain at 2.7 miles. It drops steeply down into Parker Cabin Hollow at 3.1 miles. It again follows a woods road and then starts a long, steady climb up the shoulder of Parker Cabin Mountain. At 3.5 miles, the Triangle Trail (yellow) joins it from the right.

In the saddle between Parker Cabin and Black Ash mountains, the Triangle Trail turns left at 3.7 miles, while the White Bar Trail continues south and in another 0.2 mile crosses the Ramapo-Dunderberg Trail (red dot on white). After crossing the White Cross Trail (white cross), the White Bar Trail crosses the shoulder of Blauvelt Mountain. The White Bar Trail passes the terminus of the Triangle Trail (yellow) at 5.7 miles and then the Dutch Doctor Shelter. The Tuxedo-Mt. Ivy Trail (red dash on white) briefly joins from the right at 5.9 miles. The White Bar Trail turns right off the Tuxedo-Mt. Ivy Trail and continues south on a woods road. At 6.8 miles, the trail approaches Seven Lakes Drive at a vehicular gate, turns right into the woods, and joins unpaved Old Johnsontown Road to end at the Johnsontown Road Circle parking area.

SEVENTEEN

ROCKLAND COUNTY

lthough Rockland County is
one of the smallest counties in New York State, it is home to many state, county,
and town parks and is nearly one-third parkland. Most of the northwestern
boundary of the county runs along Bear Mountain-Harriman State Parks (see
chapter 16, "Bear Mountain-Harriman State Parks").

One of the most striking features of the county is the Palisades cliffs. This
unique geological formation begins at the Rahway River in New Jersey, crosses
the western edge of Staten Island, continues north along the river into Rockland
County, New York, turns inland at Haverstraw Bay, and then ends abruptly at
Mount Ivy.

Well-documented Palisades events began on September 13, 1609, when
Henry Hudson, sailing on the *Half Moon*, made his second anchorage of the
day opposite the present location of Fort Lee, New Jersey. Hudson sailed north
on the river as far as the present site of Albany in search of the Northwest
Passage, and returned on finding no outlet up the river.

Today, the Palisades cliffs comprise an almost continuous greenway that
extends along the eastern edge of Rockland County, from Tallman Mountain
State Park in the south to Mount Ivy in the north. Much of the Palisades lies
within several units of the Palisades Interstate Park system, and the Long Path
follows the Palisades ridge. When combined with the numerous intersecting or
nearby trails and byways, the Long Path offers many opportunities for circular
routes encompassing not only woods and meadows but also local history and
interesting architecture.

For the convenience of the reader, the parks and trails in this chapter are presented in geographic order, running from south to north along the Palisades. Several parks located elsewhere in the county are described at the end of the chapter.

History of Palisades Interstate Park

The beginning of the Palisades Interstate Park dates from the time when the residents of New York City were slowly aroused to the devastations of the quarrymen blasting along the cliffs for traprock. About the middle of the nineteenth century, much of the loose and easily accessible talus was removed to be used as ships' ballast. The real menace to the Palisades came with the demand for more concrete to build skyscrapers and roads. Quarries were opened from Weehawken to Hook Mountain. To check this activity, New York and New Jersey jointly created the Palisades Interstate Park Commission (PIPC) in 1900. Enabling legislation in New Jersey was advanced by the New Jersey Federation of Women's Clubs. In New York, Andrew H. Green, founder of the American Scenic and Historic Preservation Society, worked for the necessary legislation with the support of Governor Theodore Roosevelt and other conservation-minded officials. Land was acquired and developed as parks, with the appropriate facilities.

In the early days, most of this development was accomplished through gifts of money by the commissioners and other interested individuals, with funds for development projects also having been provided by the two states. Of the many individuals who contributed of their time, talents, and funds to create this park system, special recognition must be given to George W. Perkins, Sr., who was the Commission's first president and the organizing genius of its development. With the story of his leadership should be coupled the generosity of J. Pierpont Morgan at a critical time, and other notable gifts of land and funds, both private and public. As a result, quarrying of the river faces of much of the Palisades in Rockland and Bergen counties was stopped. Subsequently, the PIPC was also charged with preserving the natural beauty of the lands lying in New York State on the west side of the Hudson, including the Ramapo Mountains as well as state park lands in Rockland and Orange counties and those in Sullivan and Ulster counties outside the Catskill Forest Preserve.

In 1933, John D. Rockefeller, Jr. offered to the PIPC certain parcels of land on top of the Palisades that he had been assembling for some time. He wanted to preserve these Palisades' ridgetop lands from uses that were inconsistent with PIPC's ownership and to protect the Palisades themselves. He also hoped that an adequately wide strip of the land might ultimately be developed as a parkway. At the time, there seemed little likelihood of finding funds for a parkway, but various options were explored. In 1935, legislation was passed that enabled the Commission to accept deeds to the land offered. Additional properties were donated by the Twombleys and by the trustees of the estate of W. O. Allison. The parkway, completed to Bear Mountain in 1958, is a tree-lined, limited-access drive for noncommercial traffic only. Since 1937, both the New York and the New Jersey sections of the Palisades Interstate Park have been administered by the PIPC under a compact that legally cemented a uniquely successful tradition of cooperation between the two states.

Geology

The cliffs across the Hudson River from New York were named "the Palisades" because of the distinctive vertical lines that can be seen along their face. These vertical lines were thought to resemble the vertical log fences, called

JACK FAGAN

Figure 17-1. Rock columns and talus blocks

"palisades," which protected the local settlements. These vertical lines actually are long, narrow fissures that extend far down into the diabase rock, separating it into near vertical polygonal columns. The fissures were formed as shrinkage cracks when the intruding molten mass cooled and contracted. As the columns were exposed by the erosion of the sill, they separated into pinnacles and collapsed to form great talus blocks (Figure 17-1). This columnar structure is responsible for the dramatic cliff edge and the cliff-base scenery of the Palisades.

The Palisades cliffs begin in New Jersey and continue along the Hudson River to Hook Mountain in New York. Both in the Palisades State Park, which incorporates the New Jersey section of the Palisades, and in Hook Mountain State Park in New York, hikers can follow the ridgetop and view its polygonal columns or walk across the talus accumulations of diabase blocks alongside the river. In High Tor State Park, the Palisades reach their highest point (832 feet above sea level). Here. the igneous sill has turned westward, cutting across the sedimentary layers into which it intruded. This is called an intrusive dike.

TALLMAN MOUNTAIN STATE PARK

The southernmost component of the Palisades Interstate Park system in New York, 687-acre Tallman Mountain State Park stretches along the Hudson River from the hamlet of Palisades to the Village of Piermont. The main entrance to the park is on the east side of US 9W, 1.3 miles north of its intersection with Oak Tree Road/Washington Spring Road. The trails may also be accessed from the southern entrance to the park, located on the east side of US 9W, 0.3 mile north of this intersection (this parking area is not marked with a park sign). For more information, contact Tallman Mountain State Park, P.O. Box 491, Piermont, NY 10968; (845) 359-0544; www.nysparks.com.

Bordering the park to its south, the old-time charm of the hamlet of Palisades makes it seem hardly credible that it should still exist so close to New York City. Old Dutch houses with greenswards and gardens, and former artists' cottages, are scattered up and down the park-like hillsides.

Washington Spring Road leads east to Snedens Landing, the western end of the Dobbs Ferry route established in 1719. In 1775, Mollie Sneden, whose house still stands under the cliff, piloted the ferryboat carrying Martha Washington across the river on her way to join her husband in Cambridge. Also on this road is the site where the American flag received, by order of Parliament, its first salute from the British in May 1783. Snedens Landing currently serves as an enclave of many stars of stage and screen. Oak Tree Road leads west to the Village of Tappan, with its DeWint House (Washington really did sleep there), the Old '76 House, and André Hill—the execution and temporary burial site of John André, the British major and spy during the American Revolution who plotted with Benedict Arnold for the surrender of West Point.

Two north-south trails extend the length of the park—the Long Path and the Tallman Bike Path. These two trails may be combined to make a loop hike.

Long Path   *Length: 2.2 miles Blaze: aqua*
This section of the Long Path begins at the southern entrance to Tallman State Park. For the first 0.3 mile, it proceeds east on a gravel road, running concur-

Dickinson '21

Sneden's Landing where the British fleet lay, 1776-1783.

The revolutionary rampart where the American flag was first saluted by the British, 1783.

R. L. DICKINSON

Figure 17-2. Snedens Landing

rently with the Tallman Bike Path. The Long Path then turns left off the bike path and follows a woods road through a network of berms. These berms— elevated mounds of earth—were originally built to retain seepage from an oil tank farm that was to have been established in this area. Fortunately, because of public opposition, the project was abandoned. The areas between the berms are now filled with rainwater and, although shallow, make good birding sites. This entire area is a haven for frogs and salamanders, which breed in the ponds each spring. It is a wildflower paradise in April and May, with spring beauties, anemones, Dutchman's breeches, mayflowers, and many other species.

After about a mile, the Long Path crosses the Tallman Bike Path and turns left, paralleling the cliff edge, with views of the Piermont Marsh below. It then enters the main picnic area of the park, goes around the Tallman Park swimming pool, and heads uphill to the North Picnic Area, first gradually and then more steeply. From the edge of the escarpment along the picnic area there is an expansive view over the Hudson River, from the Tappan Zee to the north to the Piermont Marsh to the south.

At 2.2 miles, the Long Path leaves the North Picnic Area and begins to descend steeply. At the base of the descent, it turns left, briefly rejoining the

Tallman Bike Path, crosses a bridge over Sparkill Creek, and enters the Village of Piermont.

Tallman Bike Path   *Length: 2.1 miles Blaze: directional signs*
The Tallman Bike Path begins at the southern entrance to Tallman State Park. It proceeds east on a gravel road, at first running concurrently with the Long Path. At 0.3 mile, the Long Path leaves to the left. The bike path soon curves to the left and begins to parallel the Hudson River. At 0.9 mile, the Long Path crosses, and in another third of a mile, the road becomes paved. Soon afterwards, after descending an incline, the bike path reaches a gate at the entrance to a picnic area. A seasonal comfort station is located here. The bike path turns left on a paved road and continues for 600 feet to the main park road, where it turns right, following signs to the swimming pool. At 1.6 miles, the bike path reaches a traffic circle. Here, at another crossing of the Long Path, the bike path follows the park road to the right and descends to the river. (A detour to the left, up to the North Picnic Area along the escarpment, leads to beautiful views over the Hudson River and the Piermont Marsh.) At the bottom of the descent, the bike path proceeds straight ahead, passing through a barrier of wooden posts and continuing on a gravel road that runs alongside the tall reeds of the Piermont Marsh. At 2.1 miles, the Long Path joins from the left, and soon afterwards, the bike path ends on Ferdon Avenue in Piermont, just before crossing a bridge over Sparkill Creek. The Village of Piermont, originally known as Tappan Slote, is across the bridge.

PIERMONT

Piermont was once the bustling terminus of the Erie Railroad, whose original charter stipulated that it had to be built entirely within New York State. A mile-long pier was built in the shallow part of the river in 1840 so that passengers could transfer directly from trains to boats for New York. Eleazar Lord, the railroad's founder, renamed the village in honor of his pier. His mansion, The Cedars, known as Lord's Castle, still stands on the hillside almost directly west of the pier. The village-owned pier and its extensive development make an interesting diversion, with views up and down the river. The oblique right turn off of the bike path at the beginning of the business district leads to the pier. On the way to the end of the pier, hikers can see a variety of bird life, including herons, ducks, rails, swallows, and wrens, and a variety of trees, including white mulberries, cottonwoods, and willows. The Piermont Marsh is preserved as an estuarine sanctuary.

Piermont has many interesting arts and crafts shops and art galleries. A stop at a restaurant or coffeehouse makes a delightful pause. The hourly Red & Tan Lines (Coach USA) 9A bus to New York stops on Main Street.

Old Erie Railroad Bed   *Length: 3.0 miles Blaze: unmarked*
In 1870, the Nyack spur of the Northern Railroad of New Jersey was opened with great fanfare and much real estate speculation. The line eventually came under the control of the Erie Railroad. Passenger service on this line ended in 1965, with the Tappan Zee Bridge, which opened in December 1955, having siphoned off much of its ridership. The line was abandoned entirely several years later. The right-of-way from Piermont to Nyack, which runs along the mountainside just below the level of US 9W, is now owned by the villages through which it passes.

To reach this trail—with its seasonal views of the river and adjacent Westchester—from Piermont, hikers should follow the Long Path (aqua) up the hill to the old Piermont station. The Old Erie Railroad Bed is entered alongside the chain-link fence. It proceeds north, crosses a trestle, passes the Grandview station site, and finally emerges onto the southern end of Broadway in South Nyack. There is space for parking here. The right-of-way continues across the New York State Thruway into Nyack.

To return to Piermont, hikers can take the Long Path south from the intersection of NY 59 (Main Street) and Mountainview Avenue in Nyack, or catch the hourly Red & Tan Lines (Coach USA) 9A bus along Broadway. Nyack and Upper Nyack offer a collection of antiques and crafts shops, restaurants, and preserved Victorian and other architectural buildings.

CLAUSLAND MOUNTAIN

On the ridge above Piermont and Grandview, known as Clausland Mountain, several parks combine to create a continuous greenway. Tackamack and Nike town parks and Clausland Mountain County Park contain an interconnecting network of trails. The Long Path meanders through these parks as it continues northward, mostly along the ridgeline. Clausland Mountain is named after

Jans Claus, who acted as an agent for the sale of land to the Dutch settlers. His Native American name was Tackamack.

Long Path
Length: 3.3 miles Blaze: aqua

From Piermont, the Long Path winds uphill along paved roads, finally reaching the historic Rockland Cemetery. This cemetery is the final resting place of Henry Honeychurch Gorringe, who transported Cleopatra's Needle from Egypt to its current location in Central Park in New York City. His grave is marked by an obelisk. Also buried here is General John Charles Fremont, known as the "Pathfinder," who was a United States Senator from California, territorial governor of Arizona, and the first Republican candidate for President of the United States (losing the election to James Buchanan in 1856).

At 1.3 miles (from the center of Piermont), the Long Path leaves the cemetery and continues north, soon entering Clausland Mountain County Park. At 2.3 miles, the Long Path turns sharply left, heading downhill, as an orange-blazed trail continues straight ahead, leading in 0.3 mile to a parking area on Nike Lane and rejoining the Long Path at 2.7 miles. The Long Path then enters Tackamack Town Park and follows a stream downhill. It crosses the stream and ascends to reach Clausland Mountain Road, where parking is available, at 3.3 miles.

Clausland Mountain County Park

This 532-acre park is heavily wooded, with hardwoods predominating, along with thick stands of hemlock and dense growth of mountain laurel. In 2000, the County of Rockland, in partnership with the Town of Orangetown, Scenic Hudson, Inc., and several other organizations, purchased a 50-acre tract of land which has been added to the park, permitting several new trails to be blazed. Access to these trails is from a parking area on Nike Lane, which leads west from Tweed Boulevard (also known as Highland Avenue or County 5) north of Piermont. The 0.4-mile Blue Trail, which begins at a signboard on the east side of the road, forms a loop and offers seasonal views over the Hudson River to the east. The 0.6-mile U-shaped Orange Trail connects at both ends with the Long Path, and a short spur near its midpoint leads to the parking area on Nike Lane. The Orange Trail, together with the Long Path, can be combined to make a one-mile loop hike. For more information, contact the Rockland County Parks Department, 50 Sanatorium Road, Pomona, NY 10970; (845) 364-2670.

Nike Town Park

This town park, located at the highest point on Clausland Mountain, was once the location of a Nike missile base. The complex, a remnant of the Cold War, served as a radar station for the Nike-Hercules missiles which were located in the valley below. Many of the original buildings remain. There are several picnic areas in the park, and camping is allowed by permit only. For more information, contact the Town of Orangetown Parks Department, 81 Hunt Road, Orangeburg, NY 10962; (845) 359-6503.

Tackamack Town Park

This park is located on both sides of Clausland Mountain Road, with parking available on the north side of the road at the Long Path crossing. To reach the park from NY 59, take NY 303 south to Spruce Street, turn left, and continue ahead uphill as the road becomes Clausland Mountain Road. For more information, contact the Town of Orangetown Parks Department, 81 Hunt Road, Orangeburg, NY 10962; (845) 359-6503.

BLAUVELT STATE PARK

The 590-acre Blauvelt State Park is a component of the Palisades Interstate Park system. (*Blauvelt* is Dutch for "blue field.") In 1910, the area served as a rifle range for the New York National Guard. Designed to replace a facility at Creedmoor, Long Island, it was abandoned within three years after many complaints about—and equally many attempts to remedy the problems of—bullets landing in Grand View, on the east side of the ridge. The camp was turned over to the Palisades Interstate Park Commission and since then has been used as a YWCA summer camp (Camp Bluefields), an ROTC training center during World War I, and again as a military training ground for the soldiers from nearby Camp Shanks, a troop staging center during World War II. Today, there is no evidence of these intervening uses. Only the shadowy tunnels, decaying target support walls, and a few small buildings remain. Patricia Edwards Clyne, a Hudson Valley author, used Camp Bluefields as the setting for her children's book, *The Curse of Camp Gray Owl*.

Access to Blauvelt State Park is from the south or west. The southern end of the park is reached through Tackamack Town Park, with parking available on the north side of Clausland Mountain Road. At the western end, parking is available on Greenbush Road, just south of its intersection with NY 303. Blauvelt State Park is administered by Tallman Mountain State Park. For more information, contact Tallman Mountain State Park, P.O. Box 491, Piermont, NY 10968; (845) 359-0544; www.nysparks.com.

Long Path   *Length: 2.9 miles Blaze: aqua*

From the parking area on Clausland Mountain Road, the Long Path proceeds northward. After skirting a water impoundment and crossing a creek, the trail passes through a residential development and, at 0.5 mile, enters Blauvelt State Park. Half a mile later, after passing through a pine forest, the trail reaches an embankment—the former firing line for the 1,000-yard range. Here an orange blaze appears to the left, marking the start of a mile-long trail that circumnavigates the western portion of the old range, again intersecting the Long Path in the midst of a white pine forest. Part of this trail consists of the original paved access road running east-west, which can be followed westward to Greenbush Road, just off NY 303, where there is parking for several cars.

Farther north along the Long Path and beyond the last remnants of the firing range, a white-blazed trail departs to the left. It leads to a series of red-, white-, and red-and-white-blazed trails, mostly on woods roads, which may be difficult to follow. At 2.0 miles, the Long Path crosses Tweed Boulevard and climbs to a viewpoint over the Tappan Zee, Piermont Pier, New York City, and the Hackensack River valley, including Newark in the distance. The Long Path then winds its way to Bradley Boulevard where one can either continue north along the trail or follow the road east, downhill, to reach the Old Erie Railroad Bed, which can be used as an alternative return route to Piermont.

BUTTERMILK FALLS COUNTY PARK

This 72-acre park is located off Greenbush Road in West Nyack. The park is primarily steep woodland, with Buttermilk Falls cascading down the mountain in a westerly direction. A trail ascends the hillside along a gorge, leading to numerous scenic overlooks. Around 1900, President Theodore Roosevelt frequently rode horseback in this area. To reach the park from NY 59, take Greenbush Road south for about a third of mile to a parking area on the left side of the road. For further information contact the Rockland County Parks Department, 50 Sanatorium Road, Pomona, NY 10970; (845) 364-2670.

HOOK MOUNTAIN, ROCKLAND LAKE, AND NYACK BEACH STATE PARKS

Hook Mountain State Park (676 acres), Rockland Lake State Park (1,079 acres), and Nyack Beach State Park (61 acres) are also part of the Palisades Interstate Park system. Just north of the Nyacks, the Palisades ridge, which had moved inland to form a shallow bowl, returns to the river's edge. The familiar columnar formations reappear as Hook Mountain, jutting its massive curved and quarried face into the river and demarcating the Tappan Zee from Haverstraw Bay. The name is derived from the Dutch *Verdrietige Hoogte* (tedious or troublesome point), named for the contrary winds that sailors encountered while trying to round it. Hook Mountain's southernmost summit rises to 728 feet, the second highest (after High Tor) along the Palisades ridge.

In the last quarter of the nineteenth century, quarrying—which started on the Jersey Palisades—spread upriver, threatening to deface Hook Mountain on the Tappan Zee and the entire riverfront. There was a bustle of new activity at some landings, such as Snedens, Tappan Slote (Piermont), Rockland Landing, and Waldberg (Snedekers), where ferries plied across the river or steamers docked en route to New York. In 1872, the erection of a stone crusher at Hook Mountain signaled the beginning of large-scale operations. By 1900, this and 31 smaller quarries between Piermont and Nyack were operating. Sentiment was growing to stop this defacement, as had been done on the Jersey Palisades.

George W. Perkins, president of the Palisades Interstate Park Commission, played an instrumental role in influencing the philanthropists of his time as to the importance of preserving the Palisades. He believed the forested Highlands of the Hudson, famous for their scenery and as Revolutionary strongholds,

Figure 17-3. Hook Mountain and the Palisades ridge, from the north

would become a recreational resource for the people of the metropolitan district. The acquisition of Hook Mountain by the Commission was made possible by generous contributions by members of the Harriman, Perkins, and Rockefeller families, who have been adding to park holdings even up to the present time.

The first of the purchases at Hook Mountain was in 1911, with the acquisition of the large quarry at the south end of the mountain. By 1920, the last of the quarries ceased operations, and the public had a six-mile-long park along the river, where once such a park seemed only a dream.

From 1831 to 1924, Rockland Lake was the hub of another great industry that broke the serenity of the riverfront—the harvesting of ice. The discoverer of the superiority of ice from spring-fed Rockland Lake is unknown, but its renown spread to New York City, where the better restaurants would accept no other. In 1711, John Slaughter purchased land at Rockland Landing, including Trough Hollow. A dock was built, and gradually some commercial traffic appeared, but Nyack and Haverstraw had better natural facilities. As ice was harvested, it was conveyed to Rockland Landing by a sort of "escalator" and loaded onto riverboats. Later, the giant Knickerbocker Ice Company was formed, at one time employing four thousand men. Icehouses measuring more than 350 feet long, 100 feet wide, and 50 feet high, each with up to a 100,000-ton capacity, were situated at the northeast corner of the lake. In 1860, a cog railway was built through Trough Hollow, connecting lake and dock. A spur line of the West Shore Railroad also ran to the icehouses. Nevertheless, the growth of mechanical refrigeration permanently halted ice-harvesting operations in 1924. Rockland Lake then became a popular, privately owned recreation center for summer swimming and picnicking and winter ice-skating. In 1958, the Commission acquired 256-acre Rockland Lake and the surrounding upland areas. Later, additional acreage was purchased to include the entire "bowl."

The Long Path runs along the escarpment above, while a bike path follows the river's edge from the ruins of Haverstraw Beach State Park in "Dutchtown," a quaint section of Haverstraw, to Nyack Beach State Park in Upper Nyack. Three connecting paths to the Long Path—one each at the north, south, and middle points of the magnificent facade of the Hook—allow for circular hikes of varying lengths. The full loop of the Long Path and bike path is 12 miles.

For more information, contact Rockland Lake State Park, 87 Lake Road, Congers, NY 10920; (845) 268-3020; www.nysparks.com.

Long Path   *Length: 6.9 miles Blaze: aqua*
From the intersection of Christian Herald Road and US 9W, where parking is available, the Long Path follows US 9W uphill for 0.4 mile, before turning right into the woods and beginning its climb of Hook Mountain. Soon, the white-blazed Upper Nyack Trail—the most southerly of the three connecting trails to the Hook Mountain Bike Path—leaves to the right. The Long Path continues its climb of Hook Mountain where, at 1.2 miles, the open, rocky summit affords an excellent view up and down the Hudson River. At 1.5 miles, a yellow-blazed trail leaves to the left and proceeds downhill to the Executive Golf Course. The Long Path then continues north along the ridge line. At 3.5 miles, after a steep descent, the Long Path crosses a road which, downhill to the right, provides the second connecting link to the Hook Mountain Bike Path. The Long Path now begins to climb, passing a tiny old cemetery. It continues along the ridge, with several views of the Hudson River and Croton Point. At 6.5 miles, the Long Path makes a sharp left, up a slight grade, with the trail ahead providing the northernmost connection to the Hook Mountain Bike Path. The Long Path crosses under a power line and descends to reach US 9W, just east of its intersection with NY 304, at 6.9 miles.

Hook Mountain Bike Path   *Length: 4.9 miles Blaze: unmarked*
The northern terminus of the Hook Mountain Bike Path has two access points. The first is where the Long Path crosses US 9W, just north of NY 304. From US 9W, hikers should follow the Long Path (aqua) south and then bear left on a white-blazed connector trail. This trail descends steeply alongside a quarry to a paved road and an abandoned and vandalized stone ranger cabin. Fifty yards to the right, the unpaved bike path leads south along the cliffs, 60 feet above the river.

The other access is from Dutchtown. Continue north on US 9W past the NY 304 intersection, and turn right on Short Clove Road, immediately crossing the railroad tracks. Make a hairpin right turn onto Riverside Avenue and proceed south, passing through the quarrying operations into Dutchtown. Continue south to a barricade and a small parking area. From here south, the paved road—closed to automobile traffic—is marked as a bike path.

The bike path is at first level and then descends gradually. Where it begins to ascend again, a little-used trail diverges left. This trail leads to Haverstraw Beach State Park, where there once was a thriving settlement known, at various times, as Waldberg Landing, Snedekers Landing, or Red Sandstone Dock. At low tide (about two-and-a-half-hours later than at Sandy Hook), hikers can walk north about 200 yards along the river's edge toward the next jutting point to a large granite boulder just below the high water mark. Inscribed on this rock are the words ANDRÉ THE SPY LANDED HERE SEPTEMBER 21, 1780. The low land projecting from the opposite shore almost to the middle of the Hudson is Croton Point, with Tellers Point at its southern tip.

The paved bike path continues south and up a mild incline to reach the abandoned ranger cabin across from the connector trail with the Long Path, mentioned above. Shortly after leaving the paved section, the bike path comes to the first of the abandoned quarries in Hook Mountain State Park. The princess tree grows here on the diabase talus slopes resulting from old rock slides.

At the end of the second quarry, a path bears left to Rockland Landing North (two miles from the ranger cabin at the end of the paved road). Descending to the river, the overgrown path leads past stone comfort stations and picnic tables, all in various stages of decay. Immediately beyond, another abandoned stone building sits on the cliff side of the path.

After passing a third quarry (once landscaped as part of the park development), the bike path (now again paved) descends steeply to the remains of Rockland Landing South, with pier pilings visible in the river. It was here that the ice blocks from Rockland Lake reached the river's edge via the "escalator."

The bike path now goes up a gentle incline to reach a woods road 3.5 miles from the northern connector trail. The route to the right leads past an occupied stone ranger cabin and sharply up a paved road to the top of the ridge, crossing the Long Path, into the hamlet of Rockland Lake. This road to the ridge top is the middle of the three connector paths. To return to the parking area on US 9W near NY 304, hikers should follow the Long Path north from the top of the ridge.

To the left, after ascending from Rockland Landing South, the woods road runs along the riverside edge of the largest of the quarries. The cliffs here rise 400 feet or more, with columnar fluting noticeable at the south end. However, the path quickly drops down to the river's edge at a small point, with several picnic tables. It continues south close to the sandstone cliffs, where a park lean-to was built of the plentiful talus. South of the last of the quarries, at 4.9 miles, is Nyack Beach State Park, now a picnic area, with parking available (a seasonal fee is charged). The Works Progress Administration (WPA) built a red sandstone building, now only open for special events, underneath the concrete conveyor bunkers left over from the quarrying operations.

From the entrance kiosk of the park, the south connector trail (white) travels briefly south on Broadway before turning right onto Larchmont, alongside Marydell Camp, to Midland Avenue. It turns south on Midland Avenue and, within 100 yards, turns right into the woods. It gradually ascends to join the Long Path, 100 yards from where it leaves US 9W.

HIGH TOR STATE PARK

High Tor, one of Rockland County's most striking landmarks, was used as a signal point by colonists during the Revolution. Long cherished as part of the Van Orden farm on its south side, High Tor was threatened by quarrying for its trap rock, as Elder Van Orden grew older without descendants. Maxwell Anderson's picturesque play, *High Tor*, and local attachment to this peak—the highest along the Palisades (832 feet)—roused the Rockland County Conservation Association, the Hudson River Conservation Society, and the New York-New Jersey Trail Conference to action. Their efforts led to the purchase of the ridge and its presentation in 1943 to the Palisades Interstate Park Commission.

High Tor State Park (564 acres), the most northern component of the Palisades Interstate Park system on the Palisades proper, is located off South Mountain Road. Although the park serves primarily as a summer swimming facility, it is traversed by a 3.5-mile section of the Long Path. In addition, a woods road leads north from the parking lot to cross the Long Path along the ridge top and continues north to the top of the promontory known as Little Tor.

In 1995, Scenic Hudson, Inc. purchased the former vineyard property south of High Tor, which is now part of the park. The Deer Path (unmaintained) begins on the west side of US 9W just south of the Riverside Nursing Home (parking is limited). It follows a woods road and then switchbacks steeply up the escarpment, intersecting the Long Path just south of High Tor.

For more information, contact High Tor State Park, 417 South Mountain Road, New City, NY 10956; (845) 634-8074; www.nysparks.org.

Long Path   *Length: 5.7 miles Blaze: aqua*
The Long Path leaves South Mountain Road (County 90) off US 9W south of Haverstraw and climbs steeply to High Tor in 1.1 miles. High Tor has 360° views, with the peaks of Harriman State Park to the north readily visible. At 2.5 miles, the Long Path crosses a dirt road. To the right, this road leads up to

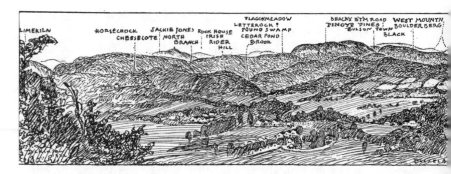

Figure 17-4. View north from Little Tor, to the Highlands

the summit of Little Tor, which offers a view of Garnerville, West Haverstraw, and clay banks once used in brick making—a profitable local industry of the 1800s. The advent of quick drying cement, the Panic of 1893 (which caused many facilities to close), and a disastrous mud slide in the early 1900s sealed the demise of the industry. To the left, this road leads downhill to the High Tor Pool, with water and restroom facilities available in season.

Continuing ahead on the Long Path, at 3.5 miles, the trail crosses Central Highway, where limited parking is available, and enters South Mountain County Park on a gravel road. Almost immediately, it leaves the road to the right and climbs steeply on a footpath. It soon recrosses the gravel road and then joins it briefly. At 5.4 miles, a precipice to the right affords views over several peaks in Harriman State Park. A short distance beyond, a view over an old quarry shows the end of the Palisades, as they dip into the ground. The Long Path follows the curving ridge downhill until, at 5.7 miles, it reaches NY 45 and turns north towards Harriman State Park. Limited parking is available here, and additional parking is available on weekends at the commuter parking lot at the intersection of NY 45 and US 202.

OTHER PARKS AND PRESERVES

Several county parks and preserves elsewhere in Rockland County also provide hiking opportunities. For more information, contact the Rockland County Parks Department, 50 Sanatorium Road, Pomona, NY 10970; (845) 364-2670.

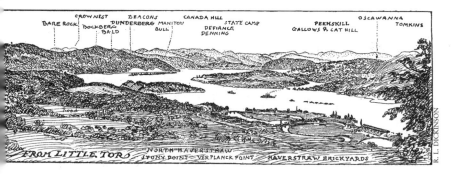

CROW NEST DEACONS CANADA HILL
BARE ROCK DUNDERBERG MANITOU STATE CAMP OSCAWANNA
DOCKBERG BULL DEFIANCE PEEKSKILL TOMKINS
BALD DENNING GALLOWS & CAT HILL

FROM LITTLE TOR NORTH HAVERSTRAW
STONY POINT VERPLANCK POINT HAVERSTRAW BRICKYARDS

R. L. DICKINSON

Kakiat County Park

Covering 353 acres adjacent to the southeastern side of Harriman State Park, this remnant of a land patent from the King of England consists of diverse topography, ranging from flat wetlands, to rolling hills, to the steep mountainside of the Ramapo Escarpment. Wildlife here is also varied, with deer, fox, and other mammals, in addition to numerous birds and reptiles, including the timber rattlesnake.

The Kakiat Trail, maintained by the Trail Conference, begins just northwest of the parking area and climbs the escarpment, where it enters Harriman State Park, on its way to Dater Mountain Nature Park. For a description of this trail, see pp. 337-38. A short section of the Suffern-Bear Mountain Trail crosses the western portion of Kakiat County Park. Two short trails in the park are maintained by the Rockland County Parks Department: the Old Mill Trail (blue), which runs along the Mahwah River to the ruins of an old electric-generating plant, and the Mountain Trail (orange), which ascends the escarpment to a beautiful viewpoint from where the Manhattan skyline is visible.

Access to Kakiat County Park is from US 202, opposite the Viola School. Parking is available just north of the entrance, and picnicking facilities are nearby.

Monsey Glen County Park

Located off NY 59 at the north end of Summit Avenue in Monsey, this 24-acre park contains several sandstone Native American caves where numerous artifacts—some over 3,000 years old—have been discovered. These artifacts are now archived at the Trailside Museum at Bear Mountain. A series of steps cut out of the sandstone rock—the purpose of which is unknown—leads to a platform. A white-blazed trail loops around the park and passes by these features. To reach the park, take NY 59 to Saddle River Road, and proceed south on Saddle River Road for 0.1 mile to the park entrance on the right.

Samuel G. Fisher Mount Ivy Environmental County Park

Composed primarily of marshland which serves as an aquifer for the Minisceongo Creek, this 270-acre park has been designated as a protected wetland area. Bisecting the park from north to south is an abandoned railroad bed which is now a hiking trail. This area is teeming with wildlife, especially birds—over 80 species have been sighted.

The park can be accessed from a parking area located at the southwest quadrant of the intersection of US 202 and the Palisades Interstate Parkway, adjacent to Exit 13 of the Parkway. Parking is also available at the end of Firemen's Memorial Drive, at the southern end of the park.

Kennedy Dells County Park

Owned in the early 1900s by the well-known movie producer Adolph Zukor, this 177-acre park offers a fitness trail, hiking trails, horseback riding, a horse corral, nature study, soccer, and cross-country skiing. The rolling topography makes for an enjoyable walk through open fields, while the extreme western portion is heavily wooded and abuts Crum Creek. To reach the park, take NY 304 to Main Street in New City and follow Main Street north for about one mile, past the County Court House, to the park entrance on the left.

Mountainview Nature County Park

With access off Strawberry Hill Lane in West Nyack, this 87-acre park is a mountainous tract, heavily wooded, with numerous short hiking trails and scenic views. The Long Path traverses the portion of the park on the east side of Mountainview Avenue, and Bear Swamp supports a variety of animal and bird life. To reach the park, take NY 303 to North Greenbush Road and follow it to Strawberry Hill Lane. Parking is available off Strawberry Hill Lane.

EIGHTEEN

STERLING FOREST

he Sterling Forest area includes over 20,000 acres of parkland, featuring dense second-growth woodlands, lakes, and marshes. The southwest-trending ridges are faced on the west by steep, rugged cliffs, hidden in dense forest and invisible from any outside point, but striking to encounter at close vantage. The area is home to bobcat, bear, grouse, and bald eagles, as well as rare and endangered species of flora and fauna. Sterling Forest is also the source of the Ramapo watershed, which provides pure drinking water to over two million New Jersey residents.

Sterling Forest lies on a bedrock of Precambrian gneisses, similar to those of Bear Mountain-Harriman State Parks. Veins of magnetic iron ore are interlayered with the gneisses. Thus, Sterling Forest played an important role in the early history of the mining and smelting industry, and it contains the remains of over 20 old mines and several furnaces. Many of the mine shafts have been filled in and closed. Sterling Mine, one of those that can no longer be seen, opened in 1750. Its shaft sloped nearly 1,000 feet under Sterling Lake. Sterling Mine was the principal producer of iron ore in the area from 1900 to 1921, when it closed down, along with the other Sterling Forest iron mines.

Once owned by the Harriman family, Sterling Forest was sold in the late 1940s to private investors. In the late 1980s, a massive development was proposed for the area, but after a 15-year effort to preserve the forest for public recreation, the bulk of Sterling Forest was purchased by the Palisades Interstate Park Commission in 1998. For details of the fight to save Sterling Forest from development, see chapter 1, "Trails and Trails Development," pp. 8-9.

This chapter describes not only the lands administered by the Palisades

Interstate Park Commission as Sterling Forest State Park, but also other contiguous parklands, including the Appalachian Trail corridor, owned by the National Park Service. Also included is a description of the trails in the New Jersey portion of Sterling Forest, now protected as the Wanaque Wildlife Management Area, Long Pond Ironworks State Park, and Passaic County Park.

For more information about Sterling Forest State Park, contact the Palisades Interstate Park Commission, 115 Old Forge Road, Tuxedo, NY 10987; (845) 351-5907; www.nysparks.com. For more information about the Wanaque Wildlife Management Area, contact the New Jersey Department of Environmental Protection, Division of Fish, Game and Wildlife, 501 East State Street, P.O. Box 400, Trenton, NJ 08625; (609) 292-2965.

🥾 Trails in Sterling Forest

There are two distinct components of the trail system in the Sterling Forest area. In addition to a number of hiking trails, blazed and maintained by volunteers of the New York-New Jersey Trail Conference, the park has marked a network of woods roads which offer the opportunity to explore other areas of Sterling Forest. These blazed woods roads, which are described below together with the hiking trails, include the Fire Tower Trail, the Lake-to-Lake Trail, the Long Swamp Loop Trail, the McKeages Meadow Trail, the Sterling Lake Trail, the Sterling Valley Trail, and the West Valley Trail. In some cases, the blazing along these roads may be infrequent.

As of summer 2001, the Palisades Interstate Park Commission is in the process of developing a master plan for Sterling Forest State Park. Once this plan is adopted, new trails may be established, and the routes of existing trails may be changed. For updated information, contact the Palisades Interstate Park Commission, 115 Old Forge Road, Tuxedo, NY 10987; (845) 351-5907; www.nysparks.com.

Allis Trail   *Length: 4.1 miles Blaze: blue*
The Allis Trail, which connects the Sterling Ridge Trail (blue on white) with the Appalachian Trail (white), was named for J. Ashton Allis, a pioneer hiker and trail builder in the metropolitan area. The southern end of the trail is on the north side of NY 17A, 1.8 miles east of the intersection of NY 210 and NY 17A in the Village of Greenwood Lake, and 2.8 miles west of the traffic light at

the Sterling Forest Ski Area. A small parking area is on the south side of NY 17A, directly across from the trailhead. After entering the woods on a foot-path, the trail joins an old woods road and descends gradually, running paral-lel to and just west of NY 17A. At 1.6 miles, the trail crosses a gas pipeline and heads away from NY 17A. It soon crosses under a power line and continues north along the ridge of Sterling Mountain, with a view of Schunemunk Moun-tain from the summit. The Allis Trail ends at 4.1 miles at a junction with the Appalachian Trail (white). To the right, the Appalachian Trail leads 0.7 mile to Mombasha High Point and 1.4 miles to West Mombasha Road. The High-lands Trail (teal diamond) is co-aligned for the entire length of the Allis Trail.

Appalachian Trail (NY 17 to Lakes Road)   *Length: 8.4 miles Blaze: white*
This major long distance trail traverses the northern section of Sterling Forest, following a trail corridor acquired by the National Park Service. At the eastern end, parking is available 0.3 mile east of the trail crossing of NY 17, at the Elk Pen parking area, on the south side of Arden Valley Road in Harriman State Park. At the western end, parking is available at the trail crossing of Lakes Road.

From NY 17, the Appalachian Trail (AT) steeply ascends the Agony Grind, arriving at an east-facing viewpoint over Harriman State Park in 0.4 mile. At 0.6 mile, a blue-blazed trail leaves to the left. This side trail descends in 0.4 mile to the Indian Hill Loop Trail (yellow), which offers the possibility of a less strenuous approach to the AT than the Agony Grind. The AT now ascends more moderately to the summit of Arden Mountain (1,180 feet), with limited views. At 1.6 miles, rock ledges provide good views of Mombasha High Point and Bellvale Mountain to the west and southwest, with the Catskills visible to the north.

The AT descends to cross Orange Turnpike at 1.8 miles. Here, the trail turns left, following the road for 250 feet, then turns right and reenters the woods. After a short, steep climb, the AT descends to Little Dam Lake, cross-ing its outlet on a wood-truss bridge at 2.9 miles. The trail reaches East Mombasha Road, where parking is available, at 3.2 miles. After climbing through a hemlock forest to a secondary summit, the AT descends very steeply on switchbacks and then climbs Buchanan Mountain (1,142 feet), where there is an excellent viewpoint to the southwest at 4.0 miles. The AT runs along an escarpment and then descends to cross West Mombasha Road at 5.2 miles. On the opposite side of the road, the trail enters an open field, designated as a butterfly refuge. After ascending on switchbacks, the AT reaches Mombasha High Point (1,280 feet), with views over Schunemunk Mountain and Harriman State Park. The Allis Trail (blue) departs to the left at 6.9 miles. In 100 feet, the Allis Trail reaches a westward viewpoint, with High Point Monument visible in the distance, and it continues 4.1 miles to the Sterling Ridge Trail (blue on white). Continuing ahead, the AT passes the pleasant cascade of Fitzgerald Falls at 8.1 miles, and it reaches Lakes Road (County 5), where parking is available, at 8.4 miles. The Highlands Trail (teal diamond) is co-aligned with the AT from the Allis Trail west to Lakes Road.

Fire Tower Trail   *Length: 5.3 miles Blaze: red*
The Fire Tower Trail, which follows woods roads for most of its length, runs in an east-west direction across Sterling Forest State Park, connecting Long Meadow Road (County 84) with Sterling Forest Road, and passing by the Sterling Forest Fire Tower along the way. The eastern trailhead is at a gated roadway on the west side of Long Meadow Road (County 84), 2.7 miles north of its intersection with Sterling Mine Road (County 72). The trail starts beyond the gate and follows a paved road for 0.6 mile, then bears left and ascends on a curving woods road to the fire tower, reached at 2.1 miles. The tower provides an impressive 360° panorama of Sterling Forest and the surrounding area, with Sterling Lake in the foreground to the northeast.

At the tower, the Fire Tower Trail joins the Sterling Ridge Trail (blue on white), and both trails continue south through a hemlock forest, with additional viewpoints before steep descents. At 2.7 miles, the Fire Tower Trail turns right, leaving the Sterling Ridge Trail, and proceeds west on a level woods road. At a T junction, reached at 3.2 miles, the Fire Tower Trail turns left and proceeds south on an eroded woods road, while the West Valley Trail (green) begins to the right, heading north on the same woods road. The Fire Tower Trail continues to descend along various woods roads until, at 5.3 miles, it reaches its western trailhead, in a parking area on East Shore Road, 0.8 mile north of the New York-New Jersey state line. The Lake-to-Lake Trail (white) begins just to the left, at another woods road.

Furnace Loop Trail   *Length: 0.9 mile Blaze: red*
To reach the Furnace Loop Trail from the trailhead of the Indian Hill Loop Trail (yellow), proceed for 0.4 mile in a counter-clockwise direction on the Indian Hill Loop Trail. The Furnace Loop Trail begins just beyond a ridgetop

viewpoint. It descends steeply on switchbacks through mixed hardwoods and hemlocks, with a limited southwest view over Sterling Forest. The trail passes to the right of a massive rock outcrop and crosses a boulder field. It then levels off and approaches the furnace area at 0.3 mile.

Beyond a fence is the historic Southfields Furnace, one of the most intact iron furnaces in the Highlands. Although recently stabilized, in 2001 it is still undergoing repair. Built in 1805 and rebuilt in 1836, this furnace was last fired in 1887. Besides the furnace itself, the stone-arched loading ramp and several walls of the casting room still stand. To the right, a stream runs through the furnace area, with a dam just upstream. As of summer 2001, plans are under-way to bridge this stream, thus enabling hikers to connect with the nearby Wildcat Mountain Trail (white) south of Orange Turnpike (County 19).

From the furnace, the Furnace Loop Trail bears left and ascends gently on woods roads. At 0.8 mile, it crosses a boulder field, turns left on a footpath that hugs the wall of an outcrop, and ascends steeply. The Furnace Loop Trail ends at the ridgetop at 0.9 mile, where it rejoins the Indian Hill Loop Trail.

Indian Hill Loop Trail   *Length: 3.6 miles Blaze: yellow*
Located on land owned by Scenic Hudson, Inc., the Indian Hill Loop Trail offers several viewpoints of the surrounding areas, traversing abandoned farm-lands with numerous old stone walls. To reach the Indian Hill Loop Trail from NY 17 in Southfields, proceed north on Orange Turnpike (County 19) for 1.3 miles to the park entrance on the right, follow the dirt road north for 0.2 mile, then turn right into the parking area.

The trail, described here in a counter-clockwise direction, starts at the information kiosk in the parking area. After turning right and proceeding through a hemlock grove, the trail ascends to reach a south-facing ridgetop at 0.4 mile. From a granite ledge, there are views of Harriman Park, the Ramapo Valley, and Sterling Forest. Just beyond, the Furnace Loop Trail (red) descends to the right. After following cairns along the ridgeline, with seasonal views to the south, the Indian Hill Loop Trail descends, crosses several stone walls, and turns right at a woods road. A 100-yard detour to the left on the road leads to a dam and a picturesque pond. The trail soon turns left off this woods road and reaches the eastern trailhead of the Furnace Loop Trail at 1.2 miles. The Indian Hill Loop Trail then ascends along a bouldery route, at times steeply, to reach the eastern face of the ridgetop at 2.0 miles.

Now headed in a northerly direction, the trail provides views across the

Ramapo Valley to Harriman State Park. Green Pond Mountain dominates the view, with the grassy Elk Pen in the foreground. The trail descends steeply on switchbacks and eventually turns left at a woods road between wide stone walls. Soon, at 2.5 miles, the trail turns sharply right onto a footpath, passing

Figure 18-1. Stone walls along Indian Hill Loop Trail

massive oak and maple trees. At 2.8 miles, the trail turns left, slightly uphill from a parallel stone wall. Here, to the right, a blue-blazed trail heads north for 0.4 mile to connect with the Appalachian Trail (white). Continuing west, the Indian Hill Loop Trail crosses more stone walls while passing through an old field and second-growth woodlands. The trail joins a woods road and, at a T junction, turns right (south) on the park entry road, soon passing the barrier gate to arrive back at the parking area at 3.6 miles.

Jennings Hollow Trail   *Length: 3.0 miles Blaze: yellow*
The Jennings Hollow Trail is a "lollipop"-shaped loop trail which follows woods roads through bottomland with numerous stream crossings, including Jennings Creek and several of its tributaries. A highlight of the trail is a view across an extensive wetland along the return segment of the loop. The trail is located within the Wanaque Wildlife Management Area.

The Jennings Hollow Trail starts from the Sterling Ridge Trail (blue on white), 1.1 miles north of the parking area at the intersection of County 511 and East Shore Road. From its junction with the Sterling Ridge Trail, the Jennings Hollow Trail proceeds northwest. At 0.7 mile, beyond a plank bridge over a stream, the end of the loop is reached. Taking the right-hand branch, the trail passes a stone wall, keeping to the right of Jennings Creek. Then, at 1.7 miles, the trail swings west through a hemlock ravine to cross the creek at a cataract.

Now on the return portion of its loop, the trail follows uneven terrain and crosses several feeder streams before turning south. At 2.0 miles, the trail joins a woods road that comes in from the right, and it descends to skirt the edge of a broad wetland with an extensive stand of drowned trees. The Jennings Hollow Trail then crosses the outlet of the wetland and rejoins the woods road before turning left to re-cross Jennings Creek at 2.6 miles. (The woods road, now unblazed, continues ahead for another 0.3 mile to a gate on East Shore Road, 1.7 miles north of County 511.) The Jennings Hollow Trail completes its loop at 3.0 miles, where it rejoins the "tail" of the loop.

Lake-to-Lake Trail   *Length: 5.1 miles Blaze: white*

The Lake-to-Lake Trail follows a woods road running east-west across Sterling Forest State Park. To reach its eastern trailhead, follow Long Meadow Road (County 84) 2.5 miles north from its intersection with Sterling Mine Road (County 72). After turning left toward Blue Lake, the parking area is immediately on the right.

The Lake-to-Lake Trail starts at the rear of the parking area and proceeds west over a hill. At 1.0 mile, the trail turns right at a gravel road and continues beyond a cable barrier to a woods road at the far end of a seasonal hunters' parking area. Ascending gradually, the trail crosses the Sterling Ridge Trail (blue on white) at 2.3 miles. The Lake-to-Lake Trail now descends westward, eventually passing another seasonal parking area at 4.2 miles. The trail ends at 5.1 miles at a parking area on the east side of East Shore Road, 0.8 mile north of the New York-New Jersey state line. The Fire Tower Trail (red) starts just to the right, beyond boulders blocking a woods road.

Long Swamp Loop Trail   *Length: 3.4 miles Blaze: orange*

To reach the Long Swamp Loop Trail from NY 17, follow Sterling Mine Road (County 72) west for 1.8 miles and turn right onto Eagle Valley Road. There is a parking area on the left in 0.1 mile, and in another 0.1 mile, the trail starts at a cable barrier on a power line service road and ascends to the left. Although the trail is well blazed, the hiker should be alert to numerous directional changes as the trail follows various woods roads.

Just before a power line pylon, the trail turns left onto a woods road. Soon, at a T intersection, the trail turns left again onto a gravel road, beginning the loop (in a clockwise direction). Just beyond this intersection is a dangerous open pit mine shaft which should be avoided. The trail soon turns right, reaches an open area, and descends to cross the outlet of Long Swamp on a wooden bridge at 0.5 mile. Proceeding northward along high ground, the trail continues ahead at 1.2 miles, as an unmarked woods road forks left and ascends to Pine Hill, with views from open rock ledges. The Long Swamp Loop Trail eventually descends to cross an intermittent stream at 2.2 miles. Now on the southbound section of the loop, the trail skirts to the left of Long Swamp and arrives back at the beginning of the loop at 3.4 miles. The hiker should then backtrack to reach Eagle Valley Road in another 0.3 mile.

McKeages Meadow Trail   *Length: 2.2 miles Blaze: yellow*
Parking for the McKeages Meadow Trail is on the right side of Long Meadow Road (County 84), at a gate 3.0 miles north of its intersection with Sterling Mine Road (County 72). The trail starts beyond the gate and turns right, going south along a power line service road. Beyond a culvert, a stream parallels the trail on the right. At 0.4 mile, the trail turns left onto a woods road, going east to cross the outlet of a swamp. After passing an open area, the trail bears left at 0.6 mile onto a less-used woods road. The trail proceeds north along the base of a hill, with McKeages Meadow off to the right.

At 1.1 miles, the trail bears left and ascends steeply. The road now becomes rougher, and it moves away from wetland vegetation and into an area of mixed hardwoods. Then, at 1.5 miles, the trail begins to descend. In another 750 feet, it turns sharply left onto an intersecting woods road and soon continues to descend, passing a lake visible through the trees on the right. At 2.1 miles, it levels off and crosses a causeway between two lakes. The trail then goes around a metal gate and ends, at 2.2 miles, at the Laurel Ponds parking area. (The road ahead leads in 0.2 mile back to Long Meadow Road.) In summer 2001, there are plans to construct the missing 0.6 mile needed to connect the two ends of the trail, making possible a loop hike.

Sterling Lake Trail   *Length: 1.6 miles Blaze: yellow*
The Sterling Lake Trail starts from a parking area on the south side of NY 17A, 1.8 miles east of the junction of NY 210 and NY 17A in the Village of Greenwood Lake, and 2.8 miles west of the traffic light at the Sterling Forest Ski Area. The trail proceeds south on a woods road, joined at first by the Sterling Ridge Trail (blue on white), which departs to the right at 0.1 mile. The Sterling Lake Trail continues straight ahead, gradually descending through mixed hardwoods to end at 1.6 miles on the west shore of Sterling Lake. Here, it meets the Sterling Valley Trail (blue), which follows a dirt road in both directions along the scenic shoreline.

Sterling Ridge Trail   *Length: 8.6 miles Blaze: blue on white*
The Sterling Ridge Trail traverses the Tuxedo Mountains of Sterling Forest from Greenwood Lake Turnpike (County 511) in Hewitt, New Jersey to NY 17A, east of the Village of Greenwood Lake. The New Jersey section of the trail traverses Long Pond Ironworks State Park and Passaic County Park, while the New York section goes through Sterling Forest State Park, administered by the Palisades Interstate Park Commission. The southern trailhead is at the junction of Greenwood Lake Turnpike (County 511) and East Shore Road. Parking is available on the south side of Greenwood Lake Turnpike, opposite the trailhead. Public transportation to the trailhead is available via NJ Transit buses 196 and 197. For information, contact NJ Transit at (800) 772-2222 within New Jersey or (973) 762-5100 outside the state, or visit their web site, www.njtransit.com.

From the southern trailhead, the Sterling Ridge Trail proceeds northeast on a woods road and intersects another old road at the ruins of a building, formerly the company store. It bears left, then soon turns right and crosses the Wanaque River on a wooden footbridge. Before crossing the bridge, continue straight ahead to see the ruins of the Long Pond Ironworks complex.

The complex contains the ruins of three furnaces, the oldest of which was built by Peter Hasenclever in 1766. A stone arch survives from a second furnace, built in 1862 by Peter Cooper and Abram S. Hewitt. The ruins of the Hasenclever furnace were discovered under a leaf-covered mound in 1956 and were excavated in 1967. Two original 25-foot waterwheels were burned in 1957. One has been stabilized in its ruined condition; the other was reconstructed on its original hub in 1994, with a grant from the New Jersey Historic Trust and Green Acres funds. The Friends of the Long Pond Ironworks are spearheading restoration efforts and offer public tours and programs. For more information, contact them at P.O. Box 809, Hewitt, NJ 07421; (973) 657-1688.

After crossing the bridge, the Sterling Ridge Trail bears left and follows an old road that soon veers away from the river to follow a tributary. At 1.1 miles, the trail passes the beginning of the Jennings Hollow Trail (yellow), which goes off to the left. Soon, the Sterling Ridge Trail curves to the left as the woods road continues ahead, leading to the Patterson Mine. The Sterling Ridge Trail now ascends Big Beech Mountain, leveling off, at 2.0 miles, at a false summit which offers views to the south. Ascending more steeply, the trail reaches the actual summit at 2.2 miles, with views of Bearfort Mountain and the Wyanokies.

Figuure 18-2. View of Sterling Lake from the Sterling Forest Fire Tower

After a steep descent, the trail reaches the New Jersey-New York line at 2.6 miles.

The Sterling Ridge Trail now crosses several woods roads, including the Lake-to-Lake Trail (white), at 2.7 miles. The Sterling Ridge Trail then ascends and, at 3.1 miles, it reaches a high point with views to the south. Descending from this viewpoint, the trail reaches a west-facing viewpoint at 3.4 miles. At 3.9 miles, the trail makes a right turn followed by a steep ascent and then level ridge walking. The Fire Tower Trail (red) joins from the west at 4.4 miles, in a hemlock grove.

At 5.0 miles, the Sterling Ridge Trail makes a sharp left turn and ascends to reach the fire tower, built in 1922. The tower offers spectacular 360° views of Sterling Forest. Here, the Fire Tower Trail leaves to the right, descending to the east on a woods road. The Sterling Ridge Trail continues ahead, with many ups and downs over the next two miles. Granite outcrops at 5.9 and 6.4 miles provide views to the east, with Sterling Lake visible in the foreground and the mountains of Harriman State Park in the distance.

The trail crosses a power line at 7.5 miles and reenters the woods. At 8.5 miles, the Sterling Ridge Trail joins the Sterling Lake Trail (yellow), which comes in from the right on a woods road. After passing a cable barrier across the road, the trailhead is reached at 8.6 miles, at a gate and parking area on the south side of NY 17A, 1.8 miles east of the junction of NY 210 and NY 17A in the Village of Greenwood Lake, and 2.8 miles west of the traffic light at the Sterling Forest Ski Area. The Allis Trail (blue), which leads in 4.1 miles to the Appalachian Trail (white), begins on the opposite side of NY 17A. The Highlands Trail (teal diamond) is co-aligned with the Sterling Ridge Trail for its entire length.

Sterling Valley Trail   *Length: 1.5 miles Blaze: blue*
The Sterling Valley Trail may be reached near its midpoint by following the
Sterling Lake Trail (yellow) to its southern end. To the right (south), the Sterling Valley Trail goes along a mostly-level woods road, following the scenic
shoreline of Sterling Lake for 0.7 mile to end at a gate. West Lake Road, which
continues ahead, leads to a private residential community. To the left (north)
(from the junction with the Sterling Lake Trail), the Sterling Valley Trail follows the woods road past an old canoe-launch area and crosses an earthen
causeway at the northern end of the lake, with abundant seasonal bird activity,
interesting foliage, and broad views over the lake. A quiet, picturesque pond,
which contains a beaver lodge, is to the left. The trail ends at a power line at
1.5 miles, just before reaching an intersection with a woods road that leads
north through a hemlock grove.

West Valley Trail   *Length: 2.6 miles Blaze: green*
The northern trailhead of the West Valley Trail is at a parking area on the south
side of NY 17A, 1.2 miles east of the junction of NY 210 and NY 17A in the
Village of Greenwood Lake, and 3.4 miles west of the traffic light at the Sterling Forest Ski Area. The trail proceeds south from a gate and runs along a
woods road in the valley west of the Sterling Ridge. At first, the trail is wide
and graveled. After a seasonal hunters' parking area is reached at 1.4 miles, the
trees close in and the road narrows. It soon passes through a swampy area,
with Jennings Creek to the left. The West Valley Trail ends at 2.6 miles at a
junction with the Fire Tower Trail (red). To the left, the Fire Tower Trail leads
in 1.1 miles to the Sterling Forest Fire Tower.

Wildcat Mountain Trail   *Length: 3.5 miles Blaze: white*
The Wildcat Mountain Trail traverses a wide variety of terrain, including maple-
shaded lowlands, boulder fields, several stream crossings, and a picturesque
pond. It features an outstanding south-facing view from an 800-foot-high open
rock ledge atop Wildcat Mountain.

The southern trailhead is at the intersection of NY 17 and NY 17A, about
2.5 miles north of the Village of Tuxedo. Parking is available on the west side
of the ramp leading north from NY 17A to NY 17 (at the northwest corner of
the intersection).

The trail begins on a woods road beyond a cable barrier at the north end
of the parking area, just to the left of the paved road. The trail soon turns left,

passes through a gap in a low stone wall, loops southwest through a dense stand of maple trees, and crosses a stream. Ascending Wildcat Mountain on a narrow woods road through a boulder-filled ravine, the trail levels off after two stream crossings. Soon, the trail narrows to a footpath, and at 0.6 mile, amid shrubby ridge foliage, it arrives at an 800-foot-high ledge, with a magnificent south-facing view over Harriman Park, the Ramapo Valley, and Sterling Forest.

The trail now turns right to run along the ledge and then begins a gradual descent. Turning generally north, with some ups and downs, the trail crosses a rock outcrop at 1.5 miles and, at 2.1 miles, passes a series of boulders aligned as cairns along a rock exposure. At 2.3 miles, the trail reaches a granite dome with a split glacial erratic on the right.

The trail continues to descend gradually through stands of laurel and, at 3.2 miles, it passes a boulder field and turns sharply right to join a woods road. About 200 feet beyond the woods road is a dam at the north end of a lily pond. The woods road continues north until, at 3.5 miles, it crosses a stream and emerges onto Hall Drive, a residential loop on the south side of Orange Turnpike (County 19), about 0.8 mile south of the Indian Hill parking area. The Southfields Furnace is on the opposite side of the road. As of summer 2001, plans are underway to bridge the stream north of Orange Turnpike, thus enabling hikers to connect to the Furnace Loop Trail (red), which provides access to the Indian Hill Loop Trail (yellow) and its link to the Appalachian Trail (white).

NINETEEN

LONG DISTANCE TRAILS

ost trails that cannot be walked comfortably from end to end in one day are considered long distance trails. These trails, typically spanning multiple chapters within this book, can be completed by hiking one section at a time or by backpacking. Hikers need to plan for transportation at the end point. Alternately, hikers can cover a segment of the trail out to a point and then hike back to the starting point the same way they came or on a different trail, if one is available.

The New York area boasts two premier long distance trails—the Appalachian Trail and the Long Path. The Long Path Trail System includes the Shawangunk Ridge Trail, which connects the Appalachian Trail at High Point State Park in New Jersey with the Long Path in the Shawangunks.

As of 2001, two other long distance trails are growing. One hundred twenty miles of the Highlands Trail are open and blazed. Eventually, it will extend from Storm King Mountain on the Hudson River to the Delaware River. The Hudson River Greenway Trail will run from New York City to Albany on both sides of the Hudson River.

Long distance trails that are contained within a single region are described in the relevant chapter of this book. The Long Island Greenbelt, Pine Barrens, and Nassau-Suffolk Greenbelt trails are examples of this type of long distance trail.

APPALACHIAN NATIONAL SCENIC TRAIL

The Appalachian Trail, known by hikers as the AT, runs from Springer Mountain in Georgia to Mount Katahdin in Maine, a distance of about 2,160 miles. In the New York area, it runs from the Delaware Water Gap to Connecticut. In general, it follows the spine of the Appalachian Mountains and seemingly goes over every mountain along the way.

Benton MacKaye, a regional planner, first proposed the trail in the *Journal of the American Institute of Architects* in 1921, in an article entitled "An Appalachian Trail, a Project in Regional Planning." He foresaw the large concentration of an urban population along the east coast and their need to retreat to nature for spiritual renewal.

The first section of the Appalachian Trail was built by volunteers from the New York-New Jersey Trail Conference in 1922-23, from the Bear Mountain

JACK FAGAN

Figure 19-1.
Appalachian Trail blaze

Bridge to the Ramapo River south of Arden in Bear Mountain-Harriman State Parks. The following year, they completed the section from Arden to Greenwood Lake. The entire trail from Georgia to Maine was completed in 1937; however, much of it was on private land and subject to interruptions as landowners changed. In 1968, Congress passed the National Trails System Act, which designated the Appalachian Trail and the Pacific Crest Trail as the first official National Scenic Trails. As of 1997, there are twenty National Scenic and Historic Trails. Additional provisions of the Act included assigning responsibility for the National Scenic Trails to the National Park Service and the U.S. Forest Service, acquiring rights-of-way for the trail where it is outside federal or state lands, and protecting the trails from incompatible uses—specifically, limiting the Appalachian Trail to primarily foot traffic. Funding for land purchases first became available in amendments to the Act in 1978. In 1982, New Jersey became the first state to acquire a complete corridor on protected lands.

In 1984, the U.S. Department of the Interior signed an agreement with the Appalachian Trail Conference (formed in 1925) to manage the trail and the newly purchased corridor. The Appalachian Trail Conference delegates its responsibilities to trail clubs along the length of the trail. In this area, the

New York-New Jersey Trail Conference has responsibility for the 162 miles in New York and New Jersey. This cooperative agreement among national, state, and local governments and volunteers serves as a model for efficient use of resources in an era of declining budgets. In 2001, only 20 miles of the entire AT, from Maine to Georgia, remain unprotected.

Every year, several hundred people *thru-hike* the Appalachian Trail, that is, they hike it continuously from end to end, generally taking from five to seven months to complete it. Many other people complete the trail over several years or decades, doing it a section at a time.

The *Appalachian Trail Guide to New York-New Jersey* and similar guides for other states describe the trail in great detail, with comments about trail features every few tenths of a mile. These guides are revised every three to five years. The *Appalachian Trail Data Book*, published by the Appalachian Trail Conference, is revised yearly and covers the whole trail in less than a hundred pages. It lists only major features along the trail, such as road crossings, shelters, rivers, and mountain tops. The trail is uniformly marked with a 2"x 6" painted white, vertical blaze. Most major road crossings are well marked, and the basic trail route appears even on most commercial road maps, although not always accurately.

Orange and Rockland Counties

From the New Jersey state line to the Bear Mountain Bridge, the Appalachian Trail crosses a series of ridges in 36.6 miles. The result is a trail that rewards its hikers with sights ranging from sweeping vistas to more contained pockets of beauty. Along the way, hikers pass unique geologic features and historic sites, many from the Revolutionary era.

The southernmost section of the Appalachian Trail (AT) in New York, which extends from NY 17A to the New Jersey-New York state line, is described below. For a description of the section from NY 17 to Lakes Road, see chapter 18, "Sterling Forest," pp. 379-80. The section from the Bear Mountain Bridge to NY 17 is described in chapter 16, "Bear Mountain-Harriman State Parks," pp. 328-30.

NY 17A to NY-NJ State Line *Distance: 5.9 miles Blaze: white*
From the AT crossing of NY 17A, where parking is available, the trail proceeds south through thick woods. After about two miles, the trail opens out onto the magnificent "sidewalks" of Bellvale Mountain, consisting of Devonian sand-

Figure 19-2. View of Greenwood Lake from Bellvale Mountain

stones and reddish conglomerate puddingstone. This ridge is the southern continuation of the Schunemunk Mountain syncline. However, as may readily be
seen along the crest of Bellvale Mountain, its angle of dip is much steeper—the
result of tighter folding in this area. The ledges offer views over Greenwood
Lake, which follows a valley mainly underlain by earlier Paleozoic-aged shales
and limestones. On a clear day, the skyscrapers of Manhattan may be seen in
the distance.

After about four miles of ridgetop walking along these ledges, the AT crosses
the state line into New Jersey. No direct road access to the AT is available at
this point, but hikers may choose to follow the State Line Trail (blue dot on
white) 0.9 mile down to County 511.

Putnam and Dutchess Counties

From the Bear Mountain Bridge, the Appalachian Trail proceeds in a northeast
direction to the New York-Connecticut state line. It traverses Hudson Highlands State Park and Fahnestock State Park, but for the most part this 52-mile
segment of the trail follows a trail corridor acquired by the National Park Service, with many views along the way.

For a description of the 5.1-mile section from NY 9D, just north of the
Bear Mountain Bridge, to US 9, which traverses the southern area of the East
Hudson Highlands, see chapter 9, "East Hudson Highlands," pp. 165-66. A
description of the 7.8-mile section which goes through Fahnestock State Park,
just to the north, may be found in chapter 8, "Fahnestock State Park,"
pp. 128-30. Several sections of the Appalachian Trail in Dutchess County are
included in chapter 10, "Dutchess County," pp. 178-80.

· LONG PATH

When Vincent and Paul Schaefer originally conceived the idea of the Long Path in the 1930s as New York's version of the Long Trail in Vermont, they had a unique vision. The trail would consist of an unmarked route through backcountry and wilderness corridors loosely linking points of interest. Today's Long Path Trail System—with town walks and wilderness, interconnections and co-alignments with other trails, and an extension into new territory to the north and west—is a tribute to those who have added their own vision to that of the founders.

The Long Path (LP) obtained its name from Raymond Torrey's weekly column, "The Long Brown Path," in the *New York Post*. Torrey was one of the founders of the New York-New Jersey Trail Conference in 1920. The Schaefers' idea, nurtured by Torrey, gained momentum, and in the 1930s construction of the trail in the area of the Palisades was begun. With the death of Torrey in 1938, the initial burst of energy faded, and it was not until the 1960s that Robert Jessen and Michael Warren took up the challenge and began laying out the Long Path that currently exists.

The Long Path Trail System comprises over 350 miles of trail, making it longer than Vermont's Long Trail—and more mileage is under way. While the business of building trails has not changed appreciably since the Long Path's beginnings, contemporary legal hurdles make bridging streams and moving boulders seem like child's play. Nonetheless, many dedicated members of the hiking community are willing to work not only at protecting what is already there, but also proposing improvements and additions. Thus, the Long Path represents a living trail system, one whose size and shape are ever changing, one that responds to environmental challenges and takes advantage of emerging opportunities.

While problem areas remain along the way—mostly on private lands, but even parklands are not immune from trouble—the trail affords a rich variety of hiking experiences: short hikes to isolated spots, full-day hikes across ridges and mountaintops, and backpacking adventures in wilderness areas. Thus, the Long Path is emblematic of all that the Trail Conference stands for—the building, maintaining, and preserving of hiking trails in New Jersey and New York—and provides access to the pleasures and rewards of hiking to an enormous and diverse population in the metropolitan area and beyond.

The *Guide to the Long Path* covers the Long Path from the George Washington Bridge to Altamont, just west of Albany. The trail is blazed in a shade of turquoise called aqua. However, the Long Path runs concurrently with other trails in many areas, especially the Catskills. In these areas, it is usually marked only with a plastic Long Path logo at the trailheads. Several hikes are given below, and other sections of the Long Path are described in the appropriate sections of this book.

New Jersey State Line to Schunemunk Mountain

The Long Path wends its way along the Palisades and through Bear Mountain-Harriman State Parks before heading west to cross Schunemunk Mountain about 65 miles from the state line. Bear Mountain-Harriman State Parks contain over 20 miles of the Long Path. It intersects, and sometimes coincides with, many trails within the park, making good loop hikes. One crossing is with the Appalachian Trail. Taking the Appalachian Trail 52 miles south to High Point State Park in New Jersey leads to the beginning of the Shawangunk Ridge Trail, an alternate route which rejoins the Long Path in the Shawangunks.

For a description of various sections of the Long Path as it winds its way along the Palisades in Rockland County, see chapter 17, "Rockland County." The 25.7-mile section of the Long Path from US 202 in Mount Ivy to Estrada Road in Central Valley is described in chapter 16, "Bear Mountain-Harriman State Parks," pp. 339-41. A description of the 6.9-mile section which traverses Schunemunk Mountain may be found in chapter 14, "Schunemunk Mountain," pp. 299-300.

Schunemunk Mountain to the Shawangunks

Much of this section of the Long Path consists of roadwalking. One exception is a 4.1-mile traverse of Highland Lakes State Park. An 8.6-mile section of the Long Path which follows the Shawangunk Ridge just south of NY 52 is described under the Shawangunk Ridge Trail (pp. 401-02). For a complete description of this portion of the Long Path, see the *Guide to the Long Path*. Relocations, which would eliminate much of the roadwalking in this section, are being considered; for updated information, contact the New York-New Jersey Trail Conference.

The Shawangunks to the Catskills

The Long Path wiggles its way through the "Gunks," providing hikers with panoramic vistas. Since it crosses other trails in Minnewaska State Park Preserve, there are ample opportunities for loop hikes. With the Open Space Institute's purchase of the Ellenville watershed lands, a portion of the Long Path, has been reopened. However, the route of the Long Path from Mud Pond to just east of Verkeerder Kill Falls has been closed by the landowner. For current information on this segment, contact the New York-New Jersey Trail Conference.

The exceptionally scenic 9.5-mile section of the Long Path in Minnewaska State Park Preserve, from Jenny Lane to Mud Pond, is described in chapter 13, "The Shawangunk Mountains," pp. 280-81. A three-mile section of the Long Path which goes through the Sam's Point Dwarf Pine Preserve and leads to Verkeerder Kill Falls is described on page 287 of this chapter.

The Catskills

The Long Path follows a winding 85-mile route through the Catskills, for the most part running concurrently with other trails. It traverses a number of mountains, and several circular hikes are possible in combination with other trails. Most of the route of the Long Path through the Catskills is described in chapter 12, "The Catskills."

From Peekamoose Road, the Long Path follows the Peekamoose-Table Trail (blue) north for 7.2 miles to the Phoenicia-East Branch Trail (yellow) (pp. 221-23). It then turns right and proceeds north on the Phoenicia-East Branch Trail for 1.7 miles to a junction with the Curtis-Ormsbee Trail (blue), which it follows for 1.6 miles up Slide Mountain. Just below the summit of the mountain, it turns right, follows the Wittenberg-Cornell-Slide Trail for 7.7 miles over Slide, Cornell, and Wittenberg Mountains, and descends to Woodland Valley (pp. 219-21).

The Long Path turns right onto Woodland Valley Road and follows it to Phoenicia, where it crosses the Esopus Creek and continues east on Old Route 28 (County 40). Next, it proceeds over Tremper, Carl, and Edgewood Mountains, following the Phoenicia (red) and Warner Creek (blue) trails. (This 10.6-mile portion of the Long Path route through the Catskills is described on pp. 237-38.) After a short roadwalk on NY 214, it proceeds east on the Devil's Path (red), which it follows for 11.1 miles over Plateau, Sugarloaf, Twin, and Indian Head mountains (pp. 228-32). It then follows the Old Overlook Road to Platte Clove Road, briefly turns right, then turns left and continues around Kaaterskill High Peak and down to NY 23A in Kaaterskill Clove. Next, it ascends on the Harding Road Trail (red) to a junction with the Escarpment

Trail (blue), which it follows for 20.4 miles over North Mountain, Stoppel Point, Blackhead Mountain, Acra Point, Burnt Knob, and Windham High Peak to NY 23, near East Windham (pp. 239-42).

North of the Catskills

The Long Path continues north of the Catskills, temporarily ending at NY 146 in Altamont, within 15 miles of Albany. This portion of the Long Path features parklands with views of the Schoharie Valley and reforestation areas. Two particularly interesting sections are described below, but see the *Guide to the Long Path* for a complete description of this section.

Vroman's Nose   *Length: 2.0 miles Blazes: various*
As evidenced by the initials in the rocks, people have been coming to the top of Vroman's Nose for over a hundred years. Once on top, hikers will see why—a sweeping view across the Schoharie Valley and Vroomansland to the Catskills. The Vroman's Nose Preservation Corporation, which owns the mountain, is dedicated to keeping it forever wild.

From a parking area on West Middleburgh Road, a green-blazed trail ascends 600 feet to meet a red-blazed trail and the Long Path (aqua), which comes in from the right. The red trail ends, and hikers continue on the Long Path and the green trail. The view to the right on the way to the summit is across the Schoharie Valley towards the Catskills. The joint trails reach the summit at 1.0 mile and then follow the escarpment, with views along the edge. At 1.2 miles, the trails reach an overhanging promontory, with views up and down the valley. Here, the green-blazed trail ends, and the Long Path joins a blue-blazed trail to descend, sometimes steeply, through the woods. The return to the parking area on West Middleburgh Road is via the yellow-blazed trail on the left at 1.5 miles.

Elm Road to Thacher State Park   *Length: 5.5 miles Blaze: aqua*
This section of the Long Path affords the hiker an opportunity to view working farms and travel along hedgerows; it ends with spectacular views and dramatic cliffs. To reach this section of the Long Path, take the New York State Thruway to Exit 22 (Selkirk). Turn right on NY 144 and continue south to NY 396. Turn right on NY 396 for six miles to South Bethlehem, where NY 396 ends and becomes County 301. Stay on County 301 for another six miles to its end at NY 443 in Clarksville. Turn left and follow NY 443 west for 4.2 miles to

Pinnacle Road (County 303), then turn right and follow Pinnacle Road for 0.3 mile to Elm Road. Turn left and follow Elm Road for 1.0 mile to the trailhead, on the right side of the road. Parking is available along the road, but hikers are requested not to park in the adjacent field.

The Long Path proceeds east, following a hedgerow along a field. After crossing a pipeline, the trail reenters the woods and descends to a stream. At 0.4 mile, the trail reaches a larger stream and then turns left to follow the stream through the woods. After passing through a small spruce plantation, it emerges into a larger spruce plantation and leaves the stream at 0.8 mile. The trail now begins to ascend. At 1.1 miles, it reaches Roemer's High Point, with its 270° views of the Catskills to the south and the Adirondacks to the north. It follows the ridge, descends gradually, ascends a small hill, and finally descends steeply. Entering John Boyd Thacher State Park at 2.2 miles, the trail descends along a series of switchbacks into a ravine, then follows a ski slope downhill.

After crossing Beaver Dam Road at 2.8 miles, the Long Path turns left on a trail that parallels the road and then turns right to follow a gravel park road. At 3.4 miles, the trail joins a nature trail which comes in from the right and continues its gradual descent into the ravine. After turning right and crossing the ravine, the Long Path turns left and, at 3.8 miles, leaves the nature trail. At 4.1 miles, the Long Path turns left and follows a woods road along the edge of a picnic area. It descends right along a gravel path to reach a paved access road which it follows to NY 157. After crossing NY 157, the trail marking changes from aqua paint blazes to round plastic Long Path discs. The Long Path reaches the overlook parking area, turns left, and follows the escarpment. At 5.0 miles, it arrives at a viewpoint over Mine Lot Falls, then follows the unblazed Indian Ladder Trail (when it is open, from mid-May to late fall) to the bottom of the falls. It then ascends rock steps, reaching the terminus of the Indian Ladder Trail, where parking is available, at 5.5 miles. At other times, when the Indian Ladder Trail is closed, the Long Path continues along the escarpment to the parking area at the end of the Indian Ladder Trail.

THE SHAWANGUNK RIDGE TRAIL

The Shawangunk Ridge Trail (SRT), part of the Long Path Trail System, begins at the junction of the Appalachian and Monument trails in High Point State Park. When the northbound Appalachian Trail turns east, the SRT continues

28 miles northeast to join the Long Path on the Shawangunk Ridge, one mile north of Old NY 17. Southwest of this point is the SRT; to the north and southeast is the Long Path. (The Long Path section immediately to the north of this junction, which follows the Shawangunk Ridge, was originally laid out as part of the Shawangunk Ridge Trail, but became part of the Long Path proper due to a 1995 relocation. For convenience, it is described in this section.)

Hikers are rewarded with a rich variety of geological formations and diverse ecosystems along the route. In a twenty-mile section, a dramatically exposed ridgetop rises 900 feet above an expansive thriving 17,500-acre wetland. The following sections are representative of the trail, but see the *Guide to the Long Path* for a complete description.

Otisville Road to Old NY 17 (County 171)   *Length: 10.0 miles Blaze: aqua*
This section of the Shawangunk Ridge Trail is appealing for hikers who are rail buffs or birders. The trail follows a converted railbed along the Basha Kill, a lake or wetlands depending on the season. To reach the southern trailhead, take NY 17 to Exit 122 and follow NY 211 west through Middletown and Otisville. Continue on NY 211 beyond Otisville to the intersection of NY 211 and Otisville Road (County 61), where limited parking is available. To reach the six parking areas within the Bashakill Wildlife Management Area, take NY 17 to US 209. Go south on US 209, and turn left onto Haven Road to reach South Road. The parking areas are north and south along South Road. To reach parking at the north end of this section, take NY 17 to Exit 114 (Highview). Turn left on Old NY 17, and proceed downhill for 0.7 mile. When the road makes a hairpin turn to the left, turn right onto a gravel road which leads to the VFW post.

From the intersection of NY 211 and Otisville Road (County 61), the Shawangunk Ridge Trail proceeds north on Otisville Road, descending below steep cliffs on the right. It passes over the western portal of the Otisville Tunnel, formerly the route of the main line of the Erie Railroad, and still used today by Metro-North passenger trains and Norfolk Southern freight trains. At 1.6 miles, it turns right onto Indian Orchard Road. Almost immediately, the trail crosses into Sullivan County, and the name of the road changes to South Road. Just past a parking area to the left at 1.8 miles, the trail turns left, leaving the road, and descends to the Basha Kill Rail Trail.

Over the next 5.5 miles, the trail follows an abandoned railbed that, when active as a railroad, was part of the New York, Ontario & Western (O&W)

Railroad system, but originally was allied with the competition, the Erie Railroad. Because the O&W initially refused to blast its way through to Monticello, the town financed another line to connect with the Erie at Port Jervis. This line was eventually expanded to include a branch to Ellenville and then extended all the way to Kingston. It dealt a severe blow to the Delaware & Hudson Canal, which could not compete with the greater flexibility and all-weather capabilities of the railroads.

The trail hugs the shore of the Basha Kill—a six-mile-long shallow lake in the springtime, and a thriving wetland in the summer and fall. The Basha Kill is home to a wide range of birds, including many migratory species. There are numerous bird-feeding stations along the way. The parking areas along this route make it readily accessible to the public, including hunters in season and birders. Nonetheless, it offers an unusual perspective, since the hiking trails are generally located on the highest lands.

After passing through the main parking area for the New York State Department of Environmental Conservation's Bashakill Wildlife Management Area, a short nature trail leads to an elevated platform that allows a view of several bird-feeding stations. Along the way, signs identify species of trees. The railbed is regained north for another 1.5 miles until it reaches a paved road on the outskirts of Wurtsboro. The trail goes to the left and continues on town streets, turning right onto Old Route 17. A railroad station on the right has been converted into a private residence which houses O&W railroad memorabilia, including a caboose. Continuing, the road begins to climb to yet another section of the abandoned O&W railroad. The bridge abutments where the tracks would have crossed the road are still visible. This portion was known as the High Line because of the tunnel that was blasted halfway up the Shawangunk Mountains. This railroad line ran from Weehawken, New Jersey, through the West Shore railroad junction in Cornwall to the western Catskills. This section of the trail ends at the old train station that has been converted to a VFW post. For a side trip, hikers can follow the railbed eastward, which leads to the Highview Tunnel. Though the tunnel is impassable, the brickwork of the tunnel portal is still in evidence.

Old NY 17 (County 171) to NY 52 *Length: 9.6 miles Blazes: various*
As one of the more dramatic stretches along the Shawangunk Ridge, this section has frequent views in all directions, and is dotted with pitch pine, scrub oak, and blueberry bushes. Outcroppings and boulders of the white conglom-

Figure 19-2. Shawangunk Ridge Trail at its intersection with the Long Path

erate that is characteristic of the northern Shawangunks add bright color and open vistas to the hiking experience.

To reach this section, take NY 17 to Exit 114 (Highview). Turn left onto Old NY 17, and proceed downhill for 1.0 mile. When the road makes a hairpin turn to the left, turn right onto a gravel road which leads to the VFW post, where parking is available. A short white-blazed trail connects the parking area at the VFW post with the Shawangunk Ridge Trail.

After leaving the O&W railbed by the VFW post, the trail ascends through the forest. At 1.0 mile, the Shawangunk Ridge Trail reaches the top of the ridge. Here, the Long Path comes in from the right and continues north along the ridge. The forest thins out, and different vegetation begins to predominate. The gnarled, dwarfed scrub oak and the windswept pitch pine are a testament to the harsh conditions on this exposed ridgetop. Views from here include the Catskills and the northern reaches of the Shawangunks, with the Basha Kill spreading out to the south.

The Long Path crosses seasonally spreading streams and woods roads, some of which lead to abandoned mines. After crossing Ferguson Road at 4.1 miles, where limited parking is available, the trail regains the ridgetop, passing more scrub oak and reaching additional viewpoints. From here, the monument at High Point State Park can be seen. The trail continues north along the ridgetop, through blueberry and mountain laurel. A knoll just off the trail at 6.4 miles offers a 360° view. To the north are the white rock outcroppings of Gertrude's

Nose and Sam's Point. In the more distant north are the jagged profiles of the Catskill Mountains. To the east, the gap of the Hudson River formed by Breakneck Ridge and Storm King Mountain can be seen.

Continuing north, the trail begins to descend, heading into the deeper woods below the ridgetop. The distinctive scrub oak and pitch pine cover are left behind for the next half mile. When the trail enters DEC property at 6.7 miles, the blazes change to blue discs. After crossing a dirt road that leads to Cox Road, and passing through an area crisscrossed with stone walls, the Long Path begins a gentle ascent. It leaves the DEC property and climbs to the open ridgetop, weaving in and out of the dense growth for well over a mile.

At first, the trail skirts the eastern cliffs, running parallel to some deep crevices. There are seasonal views to the east before the trail crosses to the western slopes of the ridge. The large open slabs of the distinctive white rock of the Shawangunks allow prolonged glimpses of the grandeur to the north and west, including the rounded peaks in the Catskills and the stark cliffs of Bear Hill Preserve. At 8.3 miles, the Long Path begins a long descent with a brief view before it drops steeply into the woods. After crossing a woods road and a significant stream, it begins to climb steadily, reaching, at 9.4 miles, a view of the Rondout Valley below and the Delaware & Hudson Canal and the O&W railbed to the west. The trail descends to reach NY 52 at 9.6 miles, where parking is available at a pullout 0.1 mile from the trailhead.

HIGHLANDS TRAIL

The Highlands Trail highlights the natural beauty of the New York and the New Jersey Highlands region, and draws the public's attention to this endangered resource. It is a cooperative effort of the New York-New Jersey Trail Conference, conservation organizations, state and local governments, and local businesses. When completed, it will extend over 150 miles from Storm King Mountain on the Hudson River in New York south to Phillipsburg, New Jersey, on the Delaware River. The route will connect major scenic attractions in both states. Ultimately, a network of trails, including alternate routes and multiuse paths, is envisioned.

The Highlands Trail is a combination of co-alignment on established trails, new trails, and road walking. The co-aligned route bears both blazes, except for the Appalachian, Sterling Ridge, and Allis trails, which have plastic Highlands Trail logos at critical points. Hikers must pay attention at intersections and turns, as the Highlands Trail often leaves one trail to join another. See individual trail descriptions for more details of the co-aligned trails.

Black Rock Forest requires all organized groups (hiking, birding, and so forth) to register prior to visiting by calling (845) 534-4517. During deer rifle season, there is no entry to either Black Rock Forest or Black Rock Fish and Game lands.

Since camping is not permitted along the Highlands Trail, thru-hikers should plan to stay in bed-and-breakfast facilities. Additional information about the Highlands Trail and accommodations along the trail, and a trail guide, may be obtained from the New York-New Jersey Trail Conference, 156 Ramapo Valley Road, Mahwah, NJ 07430; (201) 512-9348.

Storm King to County 511 *Length: 43.4 miles Blaze: teal diamond*
From Mountain Road in Cornwall, the Highlands Trail heads along the Stillman Trail (yellow) over the top of Storm King Mountain. It continues to US 9W, where there is parking, crosses US 9W, and enters Black Rock Forest. At 7.6 miles, the Highlands Trail goes straight on the Compartment Trail (blue) while the Stillman Trail turns right, running jointly with the Compartment Trail in the opposite direction. Over the next 0.7 mile, hikers need to watch for blazes indicating turns as the Highlands Trail leaves and joins three trails. The Highlands Trail follows the Compartment Trail for 0.4 mile until the latter ends at a junction with the Arthur Trail (yellow) on Jim's Pond Road. The Arthur and Highlands trails run jointly along the woods road for the next 0.1 mile, with the Highlands Trail staying on the road when the yellow blazes leave to the left. The Highlands Trail follows Jim's Pond Road for another 0.1 mile until it reaches the Scenic Trail (white) at 8.1 miles. Turning right off the road onto the westbound Scenic Trail, the Highlands Trail begins a steady descent. It follows the Scenic Trail for 1.9 miles to Mineral Spring Road, where the Scenic Trail ends. The Highlands Trail then turns left, follows the road for a short distance, and turns right. It now follows its own route, with the teal diamonds the only blazes, across Black Rock Fish and Game lands. The Highlands Trail soon begins a steady descent, and it reaches NY 32 in Mountainville at 11.6 miles.

The teal blazes follow NY 32 north for 1.0 mile and then make a left onto Taylor Road. After crossing the New York State Thruway, the trail reaches the parking area for the Schunemunk trails at 12.9 miles from the start. From the parking area, the trail joins the Sweet Clover Trail (white) up to the Jessup Trail (yellow), which the Highlands Trail now follows to the left, running south for 5.8 miles to Seven Springs Road (21.0 miles), where it turns right.

For the next 7.8 miles, until it reaches the Appalachian Trail (white), the teal diamonds are the only blazes. After following Seven Springs Road for 0.5 mile, the Highlands Trail turns off the road, through the woods and up and over a ridge to cross NY 208 at 22.0 miles. After following the shore of Orange-Rockland Lake, it reaches Museum Village Road, which it follows, crosses NY 17, and reaches a commuter parking lot at 22.6 miles. The Highlands Trail runs along the Orange Heritage Trail, which follows the abandoned main line of the Erie Railroad, for a mile as it heads west, crossing back over NY 17. Just before a bridge, the Highlands Trail turns right and heads down an embankment. Making a left under the bridge onto Oxford Road (County 51), the Highlands Trail follows the road and reaches NY 17M at 24.3 miles. (As of September 2001, the Oxford Road bridge over NY 17 is closed for reconstruction. Until the new bridge is opened, hikers who wish to follow the Highlands Trail south from Museum Village Road should continue on that road beyond the commuter parking lot to reach NY 17M, then turn right onto NY 17M and continue west to Lazy Hill Road.) After a quick jog across NY 17M, the trail makes a right turn onto Lazy Hill Road. The trail then follows an abandoned paved road through undeveloped Goose Pond Mountain State Park. At 25.9 miles, it goes left at Laroe Road (County 45), where there is parking.

The Highlands Trail follows Laroe Road for 1.0 mile and then turns right onto Gibson Hill Road, which it follows for 0.7 mile. After going under a power line, it turns left onto McGinnesberg Mountain Road, a dirt road. The Highlands Trail follows this road, which eventually becomes a woods road, for 1.2 miles as it climbs Bellvale Mountain and finally joins the Appalachian Trail (white). The Highlands Trail turns left to follow the northbound Appalachian Trail 0.4 mile to Lakes Road, where parking is available. The co-aligned trails continue to Fitzgerald Falls at 29.5 miles and then separate at 30.7 miles at the northern terminus of the Allis Trail (blue), which the Highlands Trail then follows, crossing NY 17A and reaching the north end of the Sterling Ridge Trail (blue on white) at 34.8 miles. The Highlands Trail continues for 8.6 miles on the Sterling Ridge Trail, ending at 43.4 miles at the junction of East Shore Road and Greenwood Lake Turnpike (County 511), where parking is available.

For the continuation of the Highlands Trail through the rest of New Jersey, see chapter 14, "Long Distance Trails," in the *New Jersey Walk Book*, a companion to this book.

HUDSON RIVER GREENWAY TRAIL

The Hudson River Greenway Trail is a trail as diverse as the valley, crossing urban, suburban, and rural areas to connect the valley's historic, cultural, and recreational resources. This trail system includes riverside walking trails and routes, countryside rail-trail corridors, a water trail, a bike route, and an auto route. On the west shore, the riverside routes extend from Battery Park in the Village of Waterford (north of Albany) to the New Jersey border (where it links with the Shore Trail to the George Washington Bridge and the New Jersey Hudson River walkway extending north from Liberty State Park in Jersey City); on the east shore, they extend from the Troy Dam to Battery Park in Manhattan. Industries, public works, railroad tracks, and private homes at the river's edge prevent the trail from following the shoreline for its entire length. The exact location of the trail will depend on the voluntary participation of public and private landowners.

As of 2001, just over 160 miles of trail of interest to hikers have been designated. These designated sections are almost entirely on public lands and utilize existing trails, some of which are described in this book, or are along village or city streets. For more information, contact the Greenway Conservancy for the Hudson River Valley, Capitol Building, Room 254, Albany, NY 12224; (518) 473-3835; www.hudsongreenway.state.ny.us.

FURTHER READING

This list of books is meant to be a starting point for those people wishing more information. Many of these books, particularly the trail guides, have frequent revisions, so be sure you use the latest versions. For additional historical information, consult a local history room in a public library, a local museum, or an historical society.

Backcountry Ethics

Hampton, Bruce, David Cole, Molly Absolon, and Tom Reed. *Soft Paths: How to Enjoy the Wilderness without Harming It.* 2nd ed. Mechanicsburg, PA: Stackpole Books, 1995.

Harmon, Will. *Leave No Trace: Minimum Impact Outdoor Recreation: The Official Manual of the American Hiking Society.* Helena, MT: Falcon, 1997.

Hodgson, Michael. *The Basic Essentials of Minimizing Impact on the Wilderness.* Merrillville, IN: ICS Books, 1991.

Waterman, Laura, and Guy Waterman. *Backwoods Ethics: Environmental Issues for Hikers and Campers.* 2nd ed. Woodstock, VT: Countryman Press, 1993.

———. *Wilderness Ethics: Preserving the Spirit of Wildness.* 2nd ed. Woodstock, VT: Countryman Press, 2000.

Flora and Fauna

Barbour, Anita, and Spider Barbour. *Wild Flora of the Northeast.* New York: Overlook Press, 1991.

Boyle, Robert H. *The Hudson River: A Natural and Unnatural History.* 2nd ed. New York: Norton, 1978. Out of print.

Cobb, Boughton. *A Field Guide to Ferns and Their Related Families: Northeastern and Central North America.* Boston: Houghton Mifflin, 1999.

Conant, Roger. *A Field Guide to Reptiles and Amphibians: Eastern and Central North America.* 3rd ed. Boston: Houghton Mifflin, 1998.

Fadala, Sam. *Basic Projects in Wildlife Watching: Learn More About Wild*

Birds and Animals through Your Own First-Hand Experience. Harrisburg, PA: Stackpole Books, 1989. Out of print.

Forrest, Louise Richardson, and Denise Casey. *Field Guide to Tracking Animals in Snow*. Harrisburg, PA: Stackpole Books, 1988.

Kieran, John. *A Natural History of New York City: A Personal Report after Fifty Years of Study and Enjoyment of Wildlife within the Boundaries of Greater New York*. 2nd ed. New York: Fordham University Press, 1982.

Kiviat, Erik, and Karl Beard. *The Northern Shawangunks: An Ecological Survey*. New Paltz, NY: Mohonk Preserve, 1988. Out of print.

Krieger, Louis C. *The Mushroom Handbook*. New York: Dover Publications, 1967. Out of print.

Matthews, Anne. *Wild Nights: Nature Returns to the City*. New York: North Point Press, 2001.

Miller, Dorcas S. *Berry Finder: A Guide to Native Plants with Fleshy Fruits for Eastern North America*. Berkeley, CA: Nature Study Guild, 1986.

Mittelbach, Margaret, and Michael Crewdson. *Wild New York: A Guide to the Wildlife, Wild Places and Natural Phenomena of New York City*. New York: Three Rivers Press, 1998.

Murie, Olaus Johan. *A Field Guide to Animal Tracks*. 2nd ed. Boston: Houghton Mifflin, 1982.

Niering, William A. *Wetlands*. New York: Knopf, 1985. Out of print.

Peterson, Roger Tory. *A Field Guide to the Birds: A Completely New Guide to All the Birds of Eastern and Central North America*. 4th ed. Boston: Houghton Mifflin, 1998.

Petrides, George A., and Janet Wehr. *A Field Guide to Eastern Trees: Eastern United States and Canada, Including the Midwest*. 2nd ed. Boston: Houghton Mifflin, 1998.

Robbins, Chandler S., Bertel Bruun, Herbert Spencer Zim, and Arthur Singer. *Birds of North America: A Guide to Field Identification*. 2nd ed. New York: St. Martin's Press, 2001.

Stalter, Richard. *Barrier Island Botany for the United States*. Dubuque, IA: William C. Brown Publishers, 1991. Out of print.

Stanne, Stephen P., Roger G. Panetta, and Brian E. Forist. *The Hudson: An Illustrated Guide to the Living River*. New Brunswick, NJ: Rutgers University Press, 1996.

Stokes, Donald W., and Lillian Q. Stokes. *A Guide to Animal Tracking and Behavior*. Boston: Little, Brown, 1986.

Sutton, Ann, and Myron Sutton. *Eastern Forests*. New York: Knopf, 1985. Out of print.

Williams, Deborah. *Natural Wonders of New York: Exploring Wild and Scenic Places*. 2nd ed. Lincolnwood, IL: Country Roads Press, 1999.

Winn, Marie. *Red-Tails in Love: A Wildlife Drama in Central Park*. New York: Pantheon Books, 1998.

Food

Angier, Bradford. *Field Guide to Edible Wild Plants*. Harrisburg, PA: Stackpole Books, 1974.

Conners, Tim, and Christine Conners. *Lipsmackin' Backpackin': Lightweight, Trail-Tested Recipes for Backcountry Trips*. Helena, MT: Three Forks, 2000.

Fleming, June. *The Well-Fed Backpacker*. 3rd ed. New York: Vintage Books, 1986.

Gray, Melissa, and Buck Tilton. *Cooking the One-Burner Way: Gourmet Cuisine for the Backcountry Chef*. 2nd ed. Guilford, CT: Globe Pequot Press, 2000.

Jacobson, Cliff. *Basic Essentials: Cooking in the Outdoors*. 2nd ed. Old Saybrook, CT: Globe Pequot Press, 1999.

McHugh, Gretchen. *The Hungry Hiker's Book of Good Cooking*. New York, 1982.

Pearson, Claudia, ed. *NOLS Cookery*. 4th ed. Mechanicsburg, PA: Stackpole Books, 1997.

Prater, Yvonne, and Ruth Mendenhall. *Gorp, Glop and Glue Stew: Favorite Foods from 165 Outdoor Experts*. Seattle, WA: The Mountaineers, 1982.

Viehman, John, ed. *Trailside's Trail Food*. Emmaus, PA: Rodale Press, 1993.

Geology

Bates, Robert Latimer, and Julia A. Jackson, eds. *Dictionary of Geological Terms*. 3rd ed. Garden City, NY: Anchor Press/Doubleday, 1984.

Chew, V. Collins. *Underfoot: A Geologic Guide to the Appalachian Trail*. 2nd ed. Harpers Ferry, WV: Appalachian Trail Conference, 1993.

Isachsen, Yngvar W., et al. *Geology of New York: A Simplified Account*. 2nd ed. Albany, NY: New York State Museum/Geological Survey, State Education Dept., University of the State of New York, 2000.

Raymo, Chet, and Maureen E. Raymo. *Written in Stone: A Geological History of the Northeastern United States*. 2nd ed. Hensonville, NY: Black Dome Press, 2001.

Van Diver, Bradford B. *Roadside Geology of New York*. Missoula, MT: Mountain Press Publishing Co., 1985.

Wyckoff, Jerome. *Reading the Earth: Landforms in the Making*. Mahwah, NJ: Adastra West, 1999.

———. *Rock Scenery of the Hudson Highlands and Palisades: A Geological Guide*. Glens Falls, NY: Adirondack Mountain Club, 1971. Out of print.

Health and Safety

Allen, Dan H. *Don't Die on the Mountain*. 2nd ed. New London, NH: Diapensia Press, 1998.

Auerbach, Paul S. *Medicine for the Outdoors: The Essential Guide to Emergency Medical Procedures and First Aid*. 2nd ed. New York: Lyons Press, 1999.

Bane, Michael. *Trail Safe: Averting Threatening Human Behavior in the Outdoors*. Berkeley, CA: Wilderness Press, 2000.

Forgey, William W. *Basic Essentials: Wilderness First Aid*. 2nd ed. Old Saybrook, CT: Globe Pequot Press, 1999.

———. *Wilderness Medicine: Beyond First Aid*. 5th ed. Guilford, CT: Globe Pequot Press, 2000.

Rosen, Albert P. *Health Hints for Hikers*. New York: New York-New Jersey Trail Conference, 1994.

Wilkerson, James A. *Medicine for Mountaineering and Other Wilderness Activities*. 5th ed. Seattle, WA: The Mountaineers, 2001.

Hiking and Camping

The Ten Essentials for Travel in the Outdoors. Seattle, WA: The Mountaineers, 1993.

Angier, Bradford. *How to Stay Alive in the Woods: A Complete Guide to Food, Shelter, and Self-Preservation— Anywhere*. 2nd ed. New York: Black Dog & Leventhal, 2001.

Berger, Karen. *Everyday Wisdom: 1001 Expert Tips for Hikers*. Seattle, WA: The Mountaineers, 1997.

———. *Hiking and Backpacking: A Complete Guide*. New York: W.W. Norton, 1996.

Churchill, James E. *Basic Essentials: Survival*. 2nd ed. Old Saybrook, CT: Globe Pequot Press, 1999.

Fletcher, Colin. *The Complete Walker III: The Joys and Techniques of Hiking and Backpacking*. 3rd ed. New York: Knopf, 1984.

Frazine, Richard Keith. *The Barefoot Hiker: A Book About Bare Feet*. Berkeley, CA: Ten Speed Press, 1993.

Getchell, Annie, Dave Getchell, Jon Eaton, and Joanne Allen. *The Essential Outdoor Gear Manual: Equipment Care, Repair, and Selection*. 2nd ed. Camden, ME: Ragged Mountain Press, 2000.

Goll, John, and Harry Roberts. *The Camper's Pocket Handbook: A Backcountry Traveler's Companion*. 2nd ed. Old Saybrook, CT: Globe Pequot Press, 1998.

Hollomon, Kurt D., Greg Eiden, and Cat Arnes. *On Foot: A Journal for Walkers, Hikers and Trekkers*. San Francisco: Chronicle Books, 1999.

Howe, Steve. *Making Camp: The Complete Guide for Hikers, Mountain Bikers, Paddlers and Skiers*. Seattle, WA: The Mountaineers, 1997.

Jacobson, Cliff. *Basic Essentials: Camping*. 2nd ed. Guilford, CT: Globe Pequot Press, 1999.

Kuntzleman, Charles T. *The Complete Book of Walking*. New York: Pocket Books, 1978.

Logue, Victoria. *Backpacking: Essential Skills to Advanced Techniques*. Birmingham, AL: Menasha Ridge Press, 2000.

Meyer, Kathleen. *How to Shit in the Woods: An Environmentally Sound Approach to a Lost Art*. 2nd ed. Berkeley, CA: Ten Speed Press, 1994.

Moser, David S., and Jerry Schad, eds. *Wilderness Basics: The Complete Handbook for Hikers and Backpackers*. Seattle, WA: The Mountaineers, 1993.

Roberts, Harry, and Adrienne Hall. *Basic Essentials: Backpacking*. 2nd ed. Old Saybrook, CT: Globe Pequot Press, 1999.

Ross, Cindy, and Todd Gladfelter. *A Hiker's Companion: 12,000 Miles of Trail-Tested Wisdom*. Seattle, WA: The Mountaineers, 1993.

Seaborg, Eric, and Ellen Dudley. *Hiking and Backpacking*. Champaign, IL: Human Kinetics, 1994.

Sumner, Louise Lindgren. *Sew and Repair Your Outdoor Gear*. Seattle, WA: The Mountaineers, 1988.

Townsend, Chris. *The Backpacker's Handbook*. 2nd ed. Camden, ME: Ragged Mountain Press, 1997.

Viehman, John, ed. *Trailside's Hints and Tips for Outdoor Adventure*. Emmaus,

PA: Rodale Press, 1993.

Wood, Robert S. *Dayhiker: Walking for Fitness, Fun, and Adventure*. Berkeley, CA: Ten Speed Press, 1991.

Hiking and Camping – Children

Barile, Mary, and Joanne Michaels. *Let's Take the Kids!: Great Places to Go with Children in New York's Hudson Valley (Including the Catskills, the Adirondacks to Lake George, the Berkshires, and Cooperstown)*. 2nd ed. New York: St. Martin's Griffin, 1997.

Cary, Alice. *Parents' Guide to Hiking and Camping: A Trailside Guide*. New York: W.W. Norton, 1997.

Euser, Barbara J. *Take 'Em Along: Sharing the Wilderness with Your Children*. Evergreen, CO: Cordillera Press, 1987. Out of print.

Foster, Lynne, and Martha Weston. *Take a Hike!: The Sierra Club Kid's Guide to Hiking and Backpacking*. Boston: Little, Brown, 1991. Out of print.

Silverman, Goldie. *Backpacking with Babies and Small Children: A Guide to Taking the Kids Along on Day Hikes, Overnighters, and Long Trail Trips*. 3rd ed. Berkeley, CA: Wilderness Press, 1998.

Sisson, Edith A. *Nature with Children of All Ages: Activities and Adventures for Exploring, Learning and Enjoying the World around Us*. Englewood Cliffs, NJ: Prentice-Hall, 1982. Out of print.

Hiking and Camping – Map and Compass

Fleming, June. *Staying Found: The Complete Map and Compass Handbook*. 3rd ed. Seattle, WA: The Mountaineers, 2001.

Jacobson, Cliff. *Basic Essentials: Map and Compass*. Rev. 2nd ed. Old Saybrook, CT: Globe Pequot Press, 1999.

Kjellström, Björn. *Be Expert with Map and Compass: The Complete Orienteering Handbook*. 2nd ed. New York: Collier, 1994.

Randall, Glenn. *The Outward Bound Map and Compass Handbook*. 2nd ed. New York: Lyons Press, 1998.

Hiking and Camping – Winter

Conover, Garrett, and Alexandra Conover. *A Snow Walker's Companion: Winter Trail Skills from the Far North*. Camden, ME: Ragged Mountain Press, 1995. Out of print.

Dunn, John M. *Winterwise: A Backpacker's Guide.* 2nd ed. Lake George, NY: Adirondack Mountain Club, 1996.

Gorman, Stephen. *Winter Camping.* 2nd ed. Boston: Appalachian Mountain Club, 1999.

Prater, Gene, and Dave Felkley. *Snowshoeing.* 4th ed. Seattle, WA: The Mountaineers, 1997.

Randall, Glenn. *Cold Comfort: Keeping Warm in the Outdoors.* New York: Lyons Books, 1987.

Weiss, Hal. *Secrets of Warmth: For Comfort or Survival.* 2nd ed. Seattle, WA: The Mountaineers, 1998.

History

Adams, Arthur G. *The Catskills: An Illustrated Historical Guide with Gazetteer.* 2nd ed. New York: Fordham University Press, 1990.

Bedell, Cornelia F. *Now and Then and Long Ago in Rockland County, New York.* 3rd ed. New City, NY: Historical Society of Rockland County, 1968, reprinted 1992.

Burgess, Larry E. *Mohonk, Its People and Spirit: A History of One Hundred Years of Growth and Service.* Fleischmanns, NY: Purple Mountain Press, 1996.

Carmer, Carl Lamson. *The Hudson.* 50th anniversary ed. New York: Fordham University Press, 1992.

Clyne, Patricia Edwards. *Hudson Valley Tales and Trails.* Woodstock, NY: Overlook Press, 1989, reprinted 1997.

Cohen, David Steven. *The Ramapo Mountain People.* New Brunswick, NJ: Rutgers University Press, 1974, reprinted 1994.

De Lisser, Richard Lionel. *Picturesque Catskills: Greene County.* Cornwallville, NY: Hope Farm Press, 1894, reprinted 1967. Out of print.

Diamant, Lincoln. *Chaining the Hudson: The Fight for the River in the American Revolution.* New York: Carol Publishing Group, 1989.

Dunwell, Frances F. *The Hudson River Highlands.* New York: Columbia University Press, 1991.

Evers, Alf. *The Catskills, from Wilderness to Woodstock.* 2nd ed. Woodstock, NY: Overlook Press, 1982.

Fried, Marc B. *Tales from the Shawangunk Mountains: A Naturalist's Musings: A Bushwhacker's Guide.* Glens Falls, NY: Adirondack Mountain Club, 1981. Out of print.

Haagensen, Alice Munro. *Palisades and Snedens Landing from the Beginning of History to the Turn of the Twentieth Century*. Tarrytown, NY: Pilgrimage, 1986. Out of print.

Haring, Harry Albert. *Our Catskill Mountains*. New York: G.P. Putnam's, 1931.

Howat, John K. *The Hudson River and Its Painters*. New York: Viking Press, 1972. Out of print.

Howell, William Thompson. *The Hudson Highlands*. New York: Walking News, 1933, reprinted 1982.

Ketchum, Robert Glenn, and James Thomas Flexner. *The Hudson River and the Highlands: The Photographs of Robert Glenn Ketchum*. New York: Aperture, 1985.

Mack, Arthur C. *The Palisades of the Hudson: Their Formation, Tradition, Romance, Historical Associations, Natural Wonders and Preservation*. New York: Walking News, 1909, reprinted 1982.

Murphy, Robert Cushman. *Fish-Shape Paumanok*. Great Falls, VA: Waterline Books, 1964, reprinted 1991. Out of print.

O'Brien, Raymond J. *American Sublime: Landscape and Scenery of the Lower Hudson Valley*. New York: Columbia University Press, 1981. Out of print.

Ransom, James Maxwell. *Vanishing Ironworks of the Ramapos*. New Brunswick, NJ: Rutgers University Press, 1966. Out of print.

Schaefer, Vincent J. *Vroomans Nose: Sky Island of the Schoharie Valley*. Fleischmanns, NY: Purple Mountain Press, 1992.

Serrao, John. *The Wild Palisades of the Hudson*. Westwood, NJ: Lind Publications, 1986.

Smeltzer-Stevenot, Marjorie, and Jack Focht. *Old Burying Grounds within Harriman and Bear Mountain State Parks*. Ashland, OH: BookMasters, 1992. Out of print.

Smeltzer-Stevenot, Marjorie. *Footprints in the Ramapos: Life in the Mountains before the State Parks*. Ashland, OH: BookMasters, 1993. Out of print.

Smith, Philip Henry. *Legends of the Shawangunk (Shon-Gum) and Its Environs, Including Historical Sketches, Biographical Notices, and Thrilling Border Incidents and Adventures Relating to Those Portions of the Counties of Orange, Ulster, and Sullivan Lying in the Shawangunk Region*. 2nd ed. Syracuse, NY: Syracuse University Press, 1965. Out of print.

Snyder, Bradley, and Karl Beard. *The Shawangunk Mountains: A History of Nature and Man*. New Paltz, NY: Mohonk Preserve, 1981. Out of print.

Stalter, Elizabeth. *Doodletown: Hiking through History in a Vanished Hamlet on the Hudson.* Bear Mountain, NY: Palisades Interstate Park Commission Press, 1996.

Van Zandt, Roland. *The Catskill Mountain House.* 1st paperback ed. Hensonville, NY: Black Dome Press, 1966.

Waterman, Laura, and Guy Waterman. *Forest and Crag: A History of Hiking, Trail Blazing, and Adventure in the Northeast Mountains.* Boston: Appalachian Mountain Club, 1989.

Trail Guides

Albright, Rodney, Priscilla Albright, and Kenneth Kindler. *Short Nature Walks on Long Island.* 7th ed. Guilford, CT: Globe Pequot Press, 2001.

Anderson, Katherine S., and Peggy Turco. *Walks and Rambles in Westchester and Fairfield Counties: A Nature Lover's Guide to 36 Parks and Sanctuaries.* Woodstock, VT: Backcountry Publications, 1993.

Anderson, Scott Edward. *Walks in Nature's Empire: Exploring the Nature Conservancy's Preserves in New York State.* Woodstock, VT: Countryman Press, 1995.

Appalachian Long-Distance Hikers Association. *Appalachian Trail Thru-Hikers' Companion.* 8th ed. Harpers Ferry, WV: Appalachian Trail Conference, 2001. New edition published annually.

Barrett, Joyce, ed. *Day Walker: 32 Hikes in the New York Metropolitan Area.* 2nd ed. Mahwah, NJ: New York-New Jersey Trail Conference, 2001.

Bruce, Dan "Wingfoot". *The Thru-Hiker's Handbook.* 11th ed. Hot Springs, NC: Center for Appalachian Trail Studies, 2001. New edition published annually.

Buff, Sheila. *Nature Walks in and around New York City.* Boston: Appalachian Mountain Club, 1996.

Chazin, Daniel D. *Appalachian Trail Data Book, 2001.* 23rd ed. Harpers Ferry, WV: Appalachian Trail Conference, 2000. New edition published annually.

Della Penna, Craig, and Tom Sexton. *Rail-Trail New York.* Guilford, CT: Globe Pequot Press, 2002.

Fagan, Jack. *Scenes and Walks in the Northern Shawangunks.* 2nd ed. New York: New York-New Jersey Trail Conference, 1999.

Fallesen, Gary. *Peak Experiences: Hiking the Highest Summits in New York, County by County.* Fishers, NY: Footprint Press, 2000.

Geffen, Alice M, and Carole Berglie. *Walks and Rambles on Long Island.* Woodstock, VT: Backcountry Publications, 1996.

Gourse, Leslie. *The Best Guided Walking Tours of New York City for Residents and Visitors: Exploring the Neighborhoods of Manhattan and Other Boroughs.* Chester, CT: Globe Pequot Press, 1989. Out of print.

Henry, Edward G. *Catskill Trails: A Ranger's Guide to the High Peaks. Book One: The Northern Catskills.* Hensonville, NY: Black Dome Press, 2000.

——. *Catskill Trails: A Ranger's Guide to the High Peaks. Book Two: The Central Catskills.* Hensonville, NY: Black Dome Press, 2000.

Harrison, Marina, and Lucy D. Rosenfeld. *A Walker's Guidebook: Serendipitous Outings near New York City: Including a Section for Birders.* 3rd ed. New York: M. Kesend, 1995.

Kick, Peter, Barbara McMartin, and James M. Long. *50 Hikes in the Hudson Valley: From the Catskills to the Taconics, and from the Ramapos to the Helderbergs.* 2nd ed. Woodstock, VT: Backcountry Publications, 1994. Out of print.

Kiviat, Erik. *Mills and Minnows: A Walk Down the Saw Kill: Self-Guided Nature Trail.* Annandale-on-Hudson, NY: Hudsonia Ltd., 1986.

Lenik, Edward J. *Iron Mine Trails.* New York: New York-New Jersey Trail Conference, 1996.

McAllister, Lee. *Hiking Long Island: A Complete Guide to Parks and Trails.* Mahwah, NJ: New York-New Jersey Trail Conference, 2001.

McAllister, Lee, and Myron Steven Ochman. *Hiking the Catskills: A Guide for Exploring the Natural Beauty of America's Romantic and Magical Mountains on the Trail and "Off the Beaten Path."* New York: New York-New Jersey Trail Conference, 1989. Out of print.

Myles, William J. *Harriman Trails: A Guide and History.* 2nd ed. New York: New York-New Jersey Trail Conference, 1999.

New York-New Jersey Trail Conference. *Appalachian Trail Guide to New York-New Jersey.* 14th ed. Harpers Ferry, WV: Appalachian Trail Conference, 1998. New edition forthcoming in 2002.

——. *Guide to the Long Path.* 4th ed. New York, NY: New York-New Jersey Trail Conference, 1996. New edition forthcoming in 2002.

——. *New Jersey Walk Book.* New York: New York-New Jersey Trail Conference, 1998. New edition forthcoming in 2002.

Ostertag, Rhonda, and George Ostertag. *Hiking New York.* Helena, MT: Falcon Press, 1996.

Rajtar, Steve. *Hiking Trails, Eastern United States: Address, Phone Number, and Distances for 5,000 Trails, with Indexing of over 200 Guidebooks.* Jefferson, NC: McFarland & Co., 1995.

Scheller, William. *AMC Guide to Country Walks near New York.* 2nd ed. Boston: Appalachian Mountain Club, 1986. Out of print.

Scherer, Glenn, and Don Hopey. *Exploring the Appalachian Trail: Hikes in the Mid-Atlantic States: Maryland, Pennsylvania, New Jersey, New York.* Mechanicsburg, PA: Stackpole Books, 1998.

Todeschini, David, and William Maki. *The Mid-Atlantic Trailblazer: A G.P.S. Trail Guide.* Montvale, NJ: Telson Communications, 1996.

Turco, Peggy. *Walks and Rambles in Dutchess and Putnam Counties: A Guide to Ecology and History in Eastern Hudson Valley Parks.* Woodstock, VT: Backcountry Publications, 1990.

———. *Walks and Rambles in the Western Hudson Valley: Landscape, Ecology, and Folklore in Orange and Ulster Counties.* Woodstock, VT: Backcountry Publications, 1996.

Wadsworth, Bruce C. *Guide to Catskill Trails.* 2nd ed. Lake George, NY: Adirondack Mountain Club, 1994.

Weinman, Steve. *A Rock with a View: Trails of the Shawangunk Mountains.* New Paltz, NY: Steve Weinman, 1995. Out of print.

INDEX

Page numbers in **bold** refer to trail descriptions.
Page numbers in *italics* refer to illustrations.

NEW YORK-NEW JERSEY TRAIL CONFERENCE 1920

I f you enjoy this book, we invite you to join the organization of hikers and environmentalists that published it—the *New York-New Jersey Trail Conference*. Since our founding in 1920, Trail Conference volunteers have built and presently maintain 1,500 miles of publicly accessible hiking trails in New York and New Jersey, from the Delaware Water Gap to the Catskills and the Taconics.

As a Trail Conference member, you will receive the *Trail Walker*, a bi-monthly source of news, information, and events concerning trails and hiking. The *Trail Walker* lists hikes throughout the NY-NJ region by many of our 75 member hiking clubs.

Members are entitled to purchase our authoritative maps and guides at significant discounts *(see reverse)*. Our highly accurate trail maps printed on durable Tyvek® enable you to hike with assurance in northern New Jersey, the Catskills, Harriman State Park, the Shawangunks, the Kittatinnies, Sterling Forest, and the East and West Hudson Highlands.

Trail Conference members are also entitled to discounts of 10% (and sometimes more!) at most outdoor stores and many mountain inns and lodges.

Your membership helps to give us the clout to protect and maintain more trails. If you want to experience pristine nature in the broader metropolitan New York area, you will most likely use a Trail Conference trail. As a member of the New York-New Jersey Trail Conference, you will be ensuring that public access to nature will continue to expand. So please join by contacting us now.

For rates and contact information, see reverse.

MEMBERSHIP CATEGORIES
Rates valid through March 31, 2002

	Individual	*Joint*
Regular	❏ $21	❏ $26
Sponsor	❏ $45	❏ $50
Benefactor	❏ $95	❏ $100
Student/Senior	❏ $15	❏ $20
Life	❏ $400	❏ $600*

* two adults at same address

Check out these other publications available from the New York-New Jersey Trail Conference:

	Retail	Members
MAPS		
Sterling Forest Trails	$7.95	$5.95
Harriman-Bear Mountain Trails	$8.95	$6.75
East Hudson Trails	$8.95	$6.75
West Hudson Trails	$7.95	$5.95
Catskill Trails	$13.95	$10.45
Kittatinny Trails	$12.95	$9.75
Shawangunk Trails	$9.95	$7.75
South Taconic Trails	$4.95	$3.75
North Jersey Trails	$7.95	$5.95
Hudson Palisades	$5.95	$4.75
BOOKS		
Hiking Long Island	$19.95	$15.95
Day Walker	$16.95	$13.55
Circuit Hikes in Northern New Jersey	$14.95	$11.95
Scenes & Walks in the No. Shawangunks	$10.95	$8.75
New Jersey Walk Book	$15.95	$12.75
Iron Mine Trails: NY-NJ Highlands	$8.95	$7.15
Harriman Trails: A Guide and History	$16.95	$13.55
Long Path Guide	$9.95	$7.95
A.T. Guide for NY & NJ w/ 6 maps	$19.95	$15.95

NEW YORK-NEW JERSEY TRAIL CONFERENCE
156 Ramapo Valley Road ❖ Mahwah, NJ 07430 ❖ (201) 512-9348
www.nynjtc.org

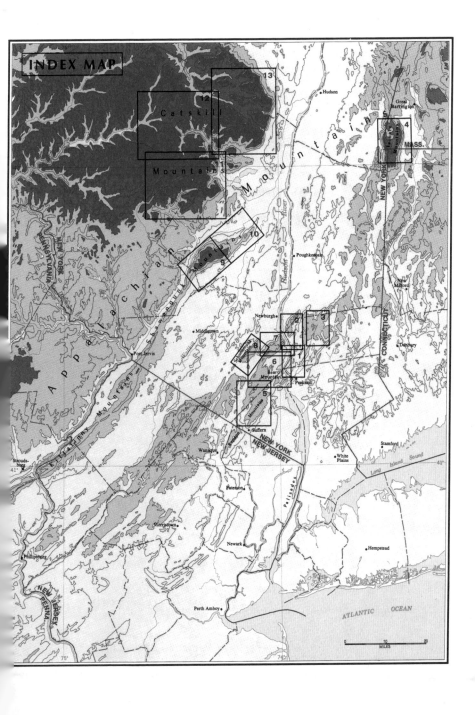

INDEX MAP

LEGEND

———————— Marked Trail

(B) Blue (BL) Black (BR) Brown (G) Green

(W) White (Y) Yellow (R) Red (O) Orange

— — — — — — Unmarked Trail or Woods Road

——— — — ——— State Boundary

——— — — ——— County Boundary

══════════ Highway

———————— Main Road

———————— Secondary Road

P   Parking

KO   Keep Out

★   Viewpoint

S   Shelter

◉   Tower

⚒   Mine

✕   Quarry or Pit

•   Spring or Well

Marsh

•*1423*   Spot Height in Feet
(contours every 100 feet, except in the Catskills)

+ + + + + Railroad

+ + + + Abandoned Railroad

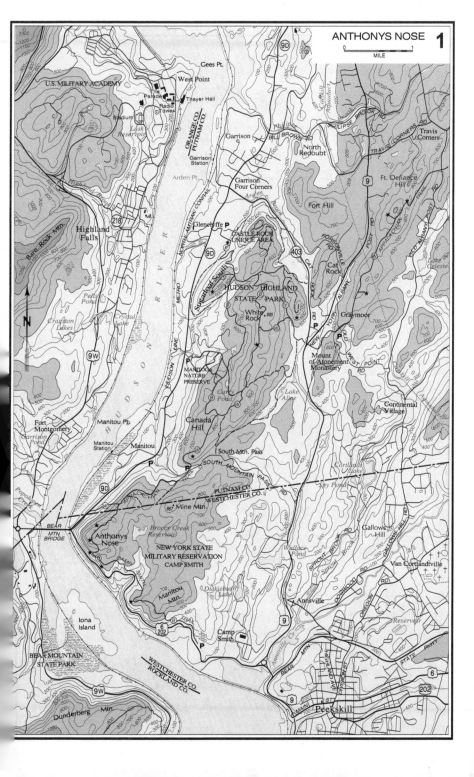

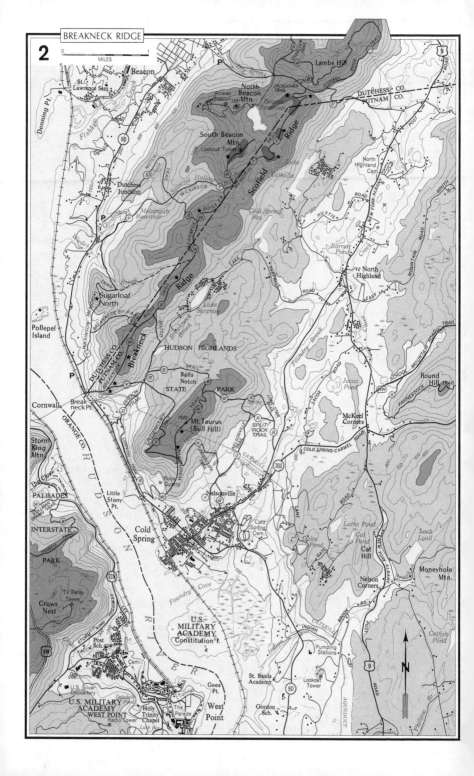

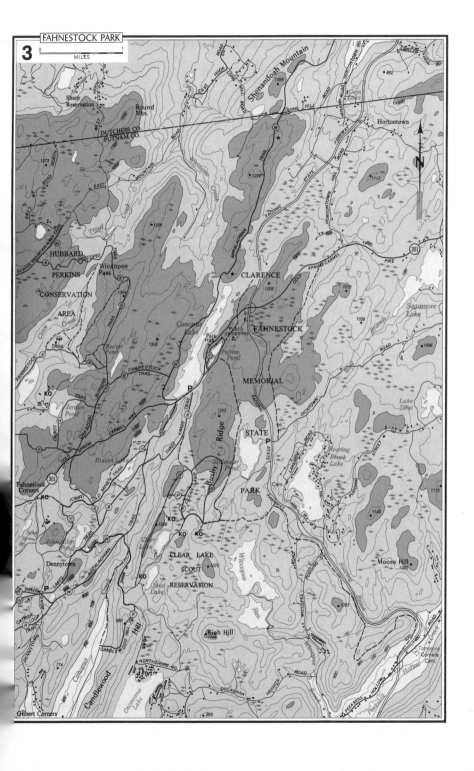

3

0 — 1
MILES

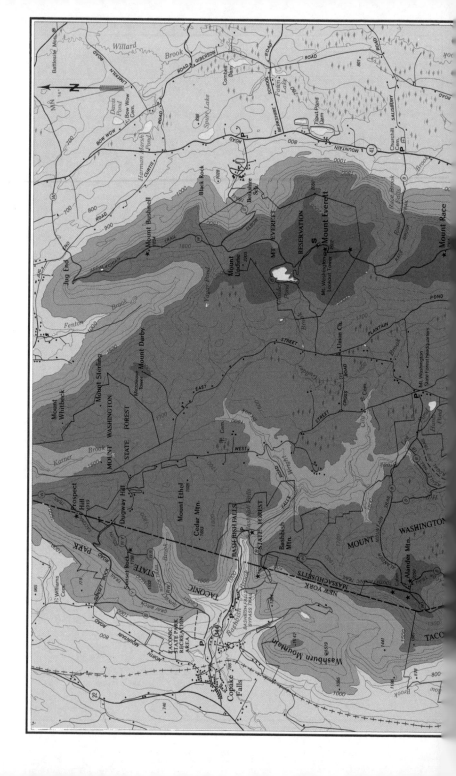

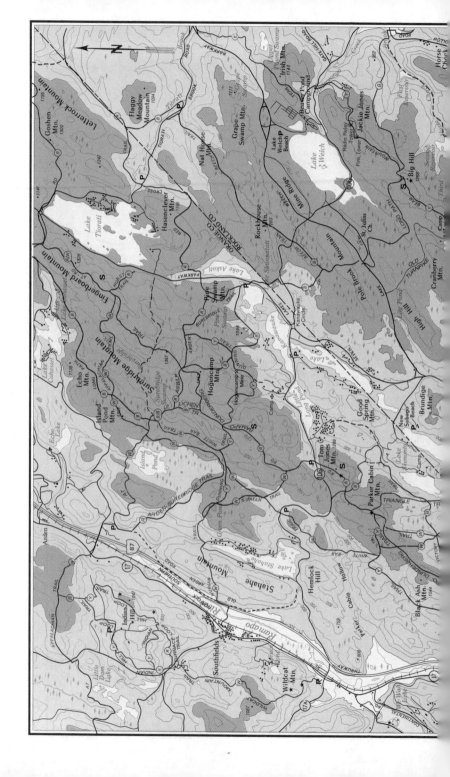

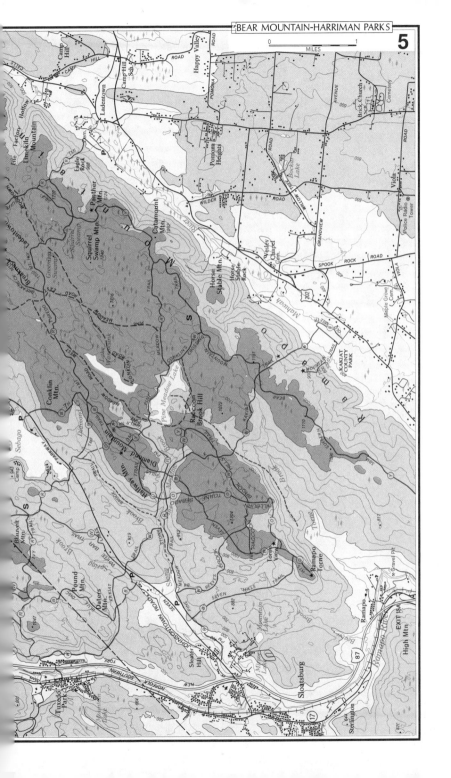

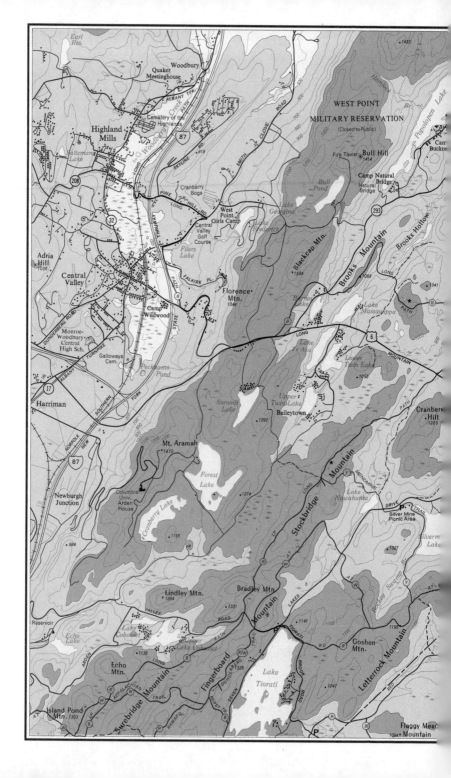

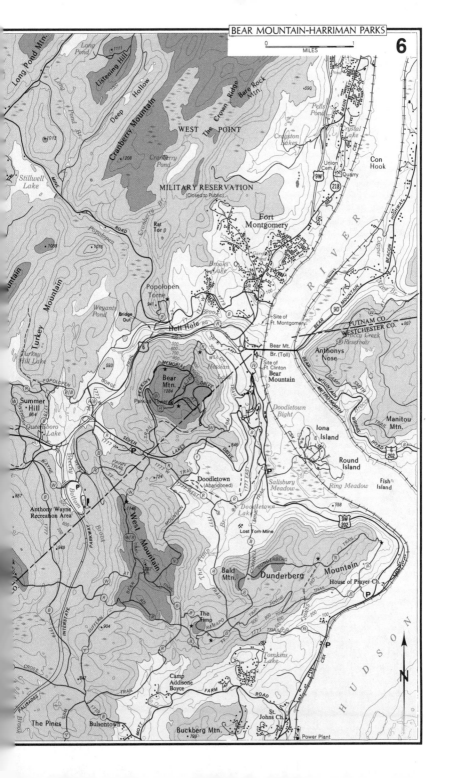

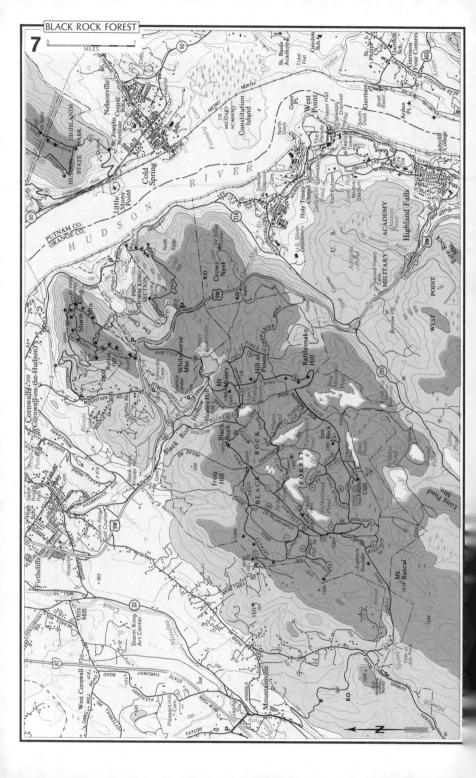

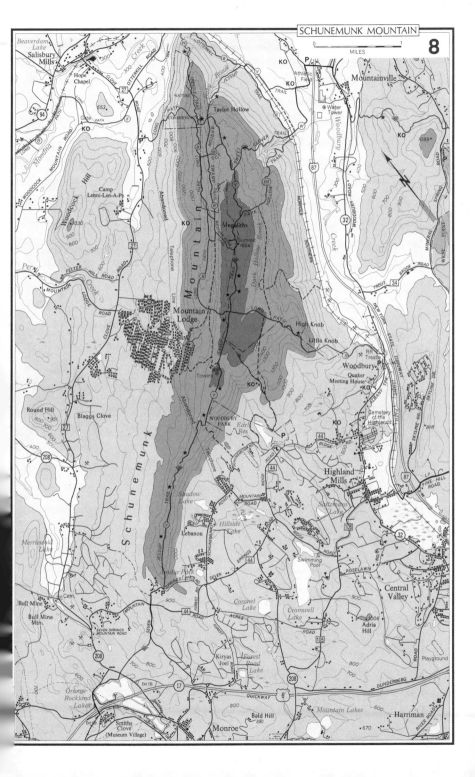

0   1
MILES

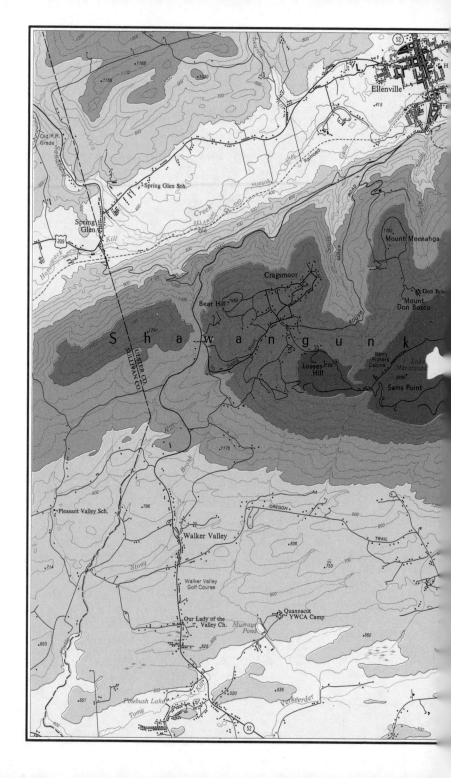

Danny Goldberg has been in the music business since the 1960s as a journalist, PR person, personal manager whose clients included Nirvana and Bonnie Raitt, and president of three major record companies: Atlantic Records, Warner Bros. Records, and Mercury Records. He currently runs Gold Village Entertainment and is the author of *How the Left Lost Teen Spirit*. He lives in New York City with his wife and two children.